Collins
dictionary of

The Bible

CW01426198

Ma___ _____an
and
Martin Manser

Collins

Other titles by Martin Manser available from Collins

Collins Dictionary of Saints
Best-Loved hymns and readings
Best-Loved Christmas carols, readings and poetry

Collins, part of HarperCollins*Publishers*
77–85 Fulham Palace Road, London w6 8jb
www.collins.co.uk

First published in Great Britain in 1998 by Macmillan

This expanded edition published 2005 by Collins

10 9 8 7 6 5 4 3 2 1

Introductory essays written by Andrew Stobart.
Consultant editor: Debra Reid

A catalogue record for this book is available from
the British Library.

978-0-00-732929-8

Typesetting by Rowland Phototypesetting Ltd,
Bury St Edmunds, Suffolk
Printed and bound in Great Britain by
Clays Ltd, St Ives plc

Contents

List of introductionary essays   see below
Lists of charts and maps   iv
Introduction   v
Dictionary of the Bible   1

Introductory essays on key subjects

The authority and inspiration of the Bible   21
An overview of the Bible   32
Bible translation   34
The Books of the Law   110
The Gospels and Acts   120
Prophetic Books   145
Historical Books   169
The relationship between the Old Testament and
     the New Testament   201
Poetry and Wisdom Books   245
Apocalyptic writings   257
New Testament Letters   263

Charts

Animals 10
Armour and weapons 16
Arts and crafts 17
Birds 37
Calendar, Jewish 44
Clothing 51
Colours 53
Diseases and illnesses 71
Feasts and festivals 96
Food and drink 99
God, names and titles of 116
Herbs and spices 132
Insects and arachnids 143
Jesus Christ, miracles of 157
Jesus Christ, names and titles of 158
Jesus Christ, parables of 160
Jesus Christ, prayers of 161
Jewels and precious stones 162
Kings and queens of Israel 178
Levi/Levites, family tree 186
Metals and stone 206
Musical instruments 213
Noah, family tree 219
Occupations 224
Plagues of Egypt 236
Plants 237
Rivers 261
Seas 273
Trees and bushes 299
Valleys 305
Weights and measures 312

Maps

World of the Bible vi
Old Testament Israel viii
New Testament Israel ix
Paul's journeys x

Introduction

This dictionary is for anyone who wants a quick-reference guide to the Bible. Entries consist of the main people, places, customs, religious and cultural aspects, events, and institutions of the Bible. Each book of the Bible is covered, showing its structure, background, and its famous passages. Our aim has been to answer such basic questions as: Who was *Cain*? Who was *Onesimus*? What is the book of *Isaiah* about? What is the significance of the *Assyrians*? What is the *Tabernacle*? What does the Bible mean by *hope*? When did *Jonah* live? We have included Bible references in most entries so that readers can use the book with the Bible.

Many charts are included to cover not only historical and religious subjects (e.g. Kings and queens of Israel, parables of Jesus Christ) but also cultural aspects, e.g. armour and weapons, occupations. A full list of charts is given on page iv. Maps complement the main text and follow hereafter. There are also Introductory Essays on key topics distributed through the book with relevant references.

This book will appeal not only to Christians who want to know more about the Bible but also to those from other religious backgrounds and those of no religious faith. Our approach has been non-denominational, with the aim of the book seeking to comment on and explain the content of the Bible in its own terms.

The work of Stephen Travis as Consulting Editor is much appreciated, and his helpful comments on the text were most valuable. The Introductory Essays were written by Andrew Stobart, with Debra Reid as Consulting Editor.

Thanks are due to many people who have offered advice, help, and encouragement: Chris Stewart of Macmillan, Stuart Olyott, Trevor Cooling, Peter Cantley, Rosalind Desmond, Lynn Elias, Lynda Drury.

Martin Selman died on 22 December 2004, while this edition was being prepared for publication. He is remembered not only for his hard work but also his humble and helpful spirit. 'Precious in the sight of the Lord is the death of his saints' (Psalm 116:15).

Martin H. Manser

World of the Bible

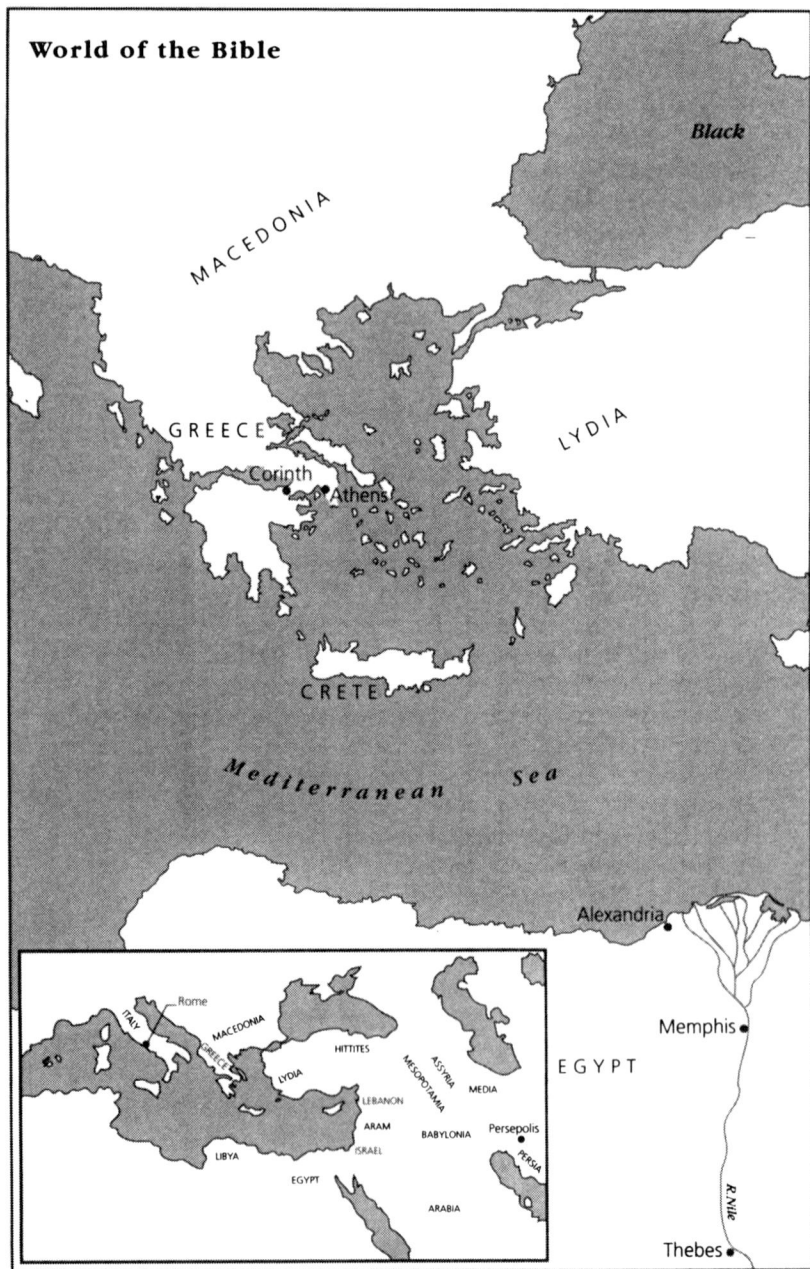

Black

MACEDONIA

LYDIA

GREECE

Corinth

Athens

CRETE

Mediterranean Sea

Alexandria

Memphis

EGYPT

R. Nile

Thebes

Rome

ITALY

MACEDONIA

GREECE

LYDIA

HITTITES

MESOPOTAMIA

ASSYRIA

MEDIA

LEBANON

ARAM

BABYLONIA

Persepolis

ISRAEL

PERSIA

LIBYA

EGYPT

ARABIA

Sea

Caspian sea

HITTITES

R.Halys

Ararat Mts.

MITANNI

MESOPOTAMIA

ASSYRIA

Taurus Mts.

Carchemish

Haran

Nineveh

MEDIA

Zagros Mts.

Aleppo

Nimrud

Ecbatana

Ugarit

R. Euphrates

Asshur

R. Tigris

CYPRUS

LEBANON

Mari

Hamath

Kadesh

Tadmor

Byblos

Sidon

Damascus

BABYLONIA

Tyre

ARAM

Babylon

Susa

Nippur

Jerusalem

Dead Sea

Ur

ISRAEL

SINAI

Persian Gulf

ARABIA

0	400 kilometres
0	250 miles

Red Sea

Old Testament Israel

New Testament Israel

Paul's Journeys

ITALY
Rome
Puteoli
Adriatic Sea
MACEDONIA
Philippi
Thessalonica
Berea
ACHAIA
Corinth
Cenchrae
Athens
Rhegium
SICILY
Syracuse
MALTA
Fair Havens
Phoenix
Mediterranean

| 0 | 400 kilometres |
| 0 | 250 miles |

Paul's first missionary journey
Paul's second missionary journey
Paul's third missionary journey
Paul's journey to Rome

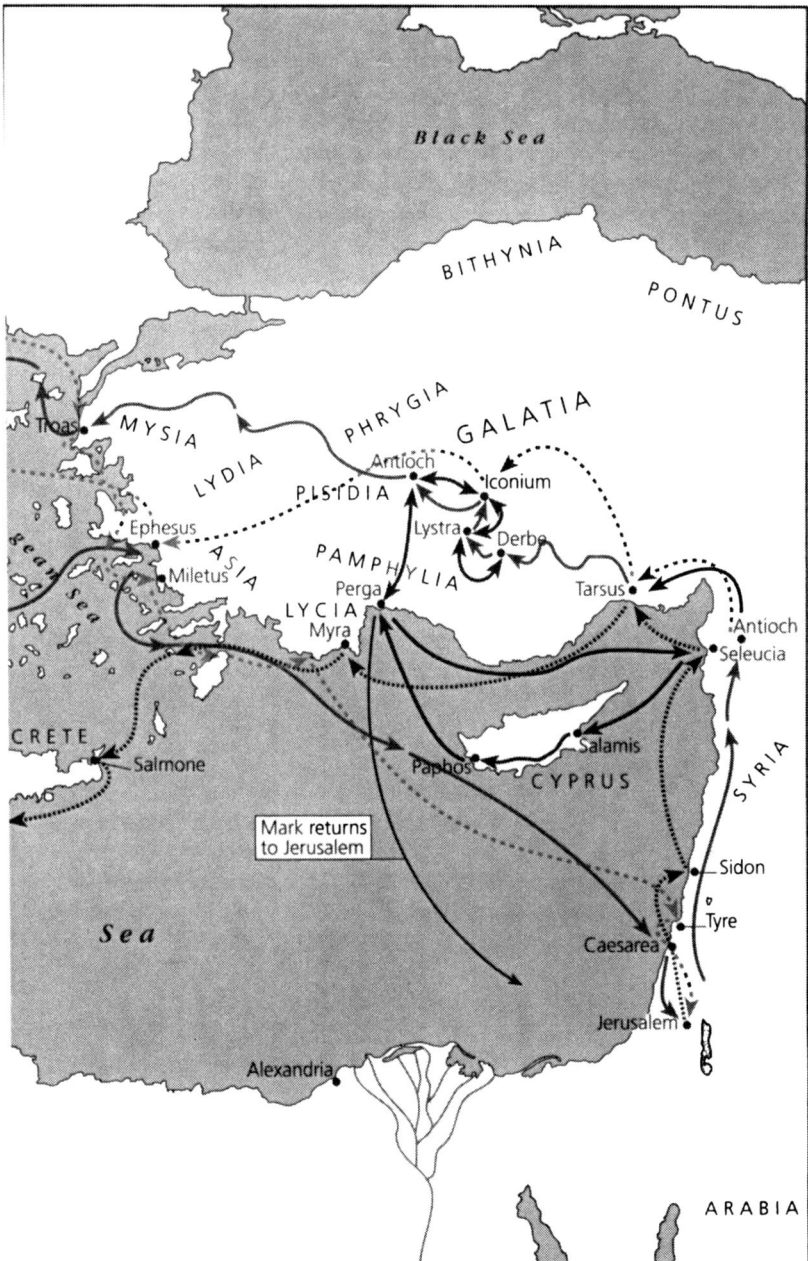

Black Sea

BITHYNIA

PONTUS

PHRYGIA

GALATIA

Troas

MYSIA

LYDIA

Antioch

PISIDIA

Iconium

Ephesus

ASIA

Lystra

Derbe

Miletus

PAMPHYLIA

Perga

Tarsus

LYCIA

Myra

Antioch

Seleucia

Aegean Sea

CRETE

Salmone

Paphos

Salamis

CYPRUS

SYRIA

Mark returns
to Jerusalem

Sidon

Sea

Tyre

Caesarea

Alexandria

Jerusalem

ARABIA

a

Aaron Moses' elder brother and Israel's first high priest. His main role was to assist Moses. He was involved in several controversies, especially in making and worshipping the golden calf (Exodus 32) and in publicly criticizing Moses (Numbers 12). Later Aaron was himself opposed by Moses, but God confirmed his leading role through the rod that budded (Numbers 17). See also MOSES.

Ab see CALENDAR, JEWISH.

abaddon see HELL.

abba An Aramaic word meaning 'father', used as a title for God in the New Testament. Both Jesus and the early church addressed God in this way, indicating the closeness of their relationship with him (Mark 14:36; Romans 8:15–16).

Abednego see SHADRACH, MESHACH AND ABEDNEGO.

Abel Adam and Eve's second son. He worshipped God through faith (Hebrews 11:4) but was murdered by his brother Cain.

Abiathar High priest in David's reign and one of David's trusted advisers, until he supported Adonijah to succeed David. He was expelled from office for this disloyalty and became the last priest of Eli's line, in fulfilment of prophecy (1 Kings 2:26–7).

Abib see CALENDAR, JEWISH.

Abigail A woman of beauty, wisdom and faith who saved her first husband Nabal from an act of revenge which David intended against him. She married David after Nabal died (1 Samuel 25).

Abihu see NADAB AND ABIHU.

Abijah, King of Judah (c. 915–913 BC) see KINGS AND QUEENS OF ISRAEL.

Abimelech 1. The name of two Philistine kings. Both were deliberately misled by Abraham and Isaac concerning the status of their wives Sarah and Rebekah (Genesis 20:1–18; 26:7–11). The elder Abimelech was more alert to God's attitude than Abraham.

2. A son of Gideon who became king over the city-state of Shechem. He murdered seventy of his brothers, but died three years later as a punishment from God (Judges 9).

Abishai A son of David's sister and, like his brothers Joab and Asahel, a commander in David's army. He was intensely loyal to the king, but had a tendency to be impetuous (1 Samuel 26:8–9).

Abner Commander-in-chief in Saul's army. He was murdered by David's commander Joab, who was suspicious when Abner tried to join David (2 Samuel 3:22–7).

abomination Something that is particularly offensive to God, especially an idol or other object of pagan worship. The 'abomination that causes desolation' refers to altars erected to pagan gods in the temple (Daniel 9:27; Matthew 24:15).

Abraham The chief recipient of God's promises in the Old Testament and regarded by Jews as the father of their people. Abraham probably lived in the early centuries of the second millennium BC during the Middle Bronze Age, and though his existence cannot be explicitly confirmed from outside the Bible, it is indirectly supported by several factors. Similar names to his original name Abram (= the father (God) is exalted) have been found from the nineteenth century BC (Abamram, Abiram). Several customs in Abraham's family life such as adopting a servant (Genesis 15:1–4) or having a child by a wife's slave (Genesis 16:1–4) are attested around the middle of the second millennium BC. The phrase 'Abram the Hebrew' (Genesis 14:13) may link him with the 'Apiru or Habiru, who were people of secondary status known in the ancient Near East from the fifteenth century BC.

The story of Abraham in Genesis 11:27–25:11 is organized around the theme of how God began to fulfil in his lifetime some of the promises he had made to him. When God called Abraham at Ur in Southern Iraq (Acts 7:2–3) and at Haran (Genesis 11:31–12:1), he promised him a land, many descendants, a great name, and said he would become a blessing to many peoples (Genesis 12:2–3). Abraham's continuing childlessness, however, was a serious threat to all these promises, and during the period of waiting, he attempted to find his own ways of producing an heir (Genesis 15:1–4; 16:1–4, 15–16), though he also grew in faith as God confirmed his intentions in a covenant (Genesis 15:1–6; 17:1–27). Isaac was eventually born when Abraham was 100 years old (Genesis 21:1–5), but God continued to test Abraham, commanding him to offer his son as a sacrifice. Abraham's obedience to God and his confidence that 'The LORD Will Provide' (Genesis 22:14) make him the supreme example of faith in the New Testament (Romans 4; Hebrews 11:8–19; James 2:20–6). Abraham's final actions in buying a family burial ground (Genesis 23) and obtaining a wife for Isaac (Genesis 24) point to a future fulfilment of the promises of land and descendants. See also FAITH; HEBREW.

Abram SEE ABRAHAM.

Absalom David's third son, who overthrew his father and exercised kingship for a brief time while David fled across the Jordan. David regained the throne as a result of Absalom receiving bad advice, but despite all this, David was grief-stricken at Absalom's tragic death in an accident (2 Samuel 15:1–19:8).

acceptance Usually refers to God's favourable reception of human beings and of their worship of him. God accepts people in the Old Testament on the basis of his covenant, and in the New Testament on the basis of the new covenant established by the death of Christ. People in their turn must accept the gospel which Jesus offers them (1 Timothy 1:15).

access The opportunity and privilege of entering into God's presence. In the Old Testament this was made possible by God's provision of Israel's sacrificial system. In the New Testament, Christ's death on the cross and the work of the Holy Spirit are the basis on which people may come to God (Romans 5:2; Ephesians 2:18).

Achaia The Roman province which covered the southern part of Greece (2 Corinthians 9:2). Its capital was at Corinth. See map of PAUL'S JOURNEYS.

Achan Was stoned to death with his family for stealing plunder from the city of Ai which should have been dedicated to God (Joshua 7).

Achish A king of the Philistine city of Gath who offered David asylum when Saul was pursuing him (1 Samuel 27).

Achor, valley of A phrase meaning 'valley of trouble' referring to the place near Ai where Achan was punished by death (Joshua 7:26).

Acts of the Apostles

The continuation of the story of Luke's Gospel. Whereas the Gospel is about 'all that Jesus began to do and to teach' (Acts 1:1), Acts is about what Jesus continued to do and teach in the early church through the work of the Holy Spirit. In fact, the Spirit's activity is so central it might be better called 'The Acts of the Holy Spirit'. Luke's involvement is mentioned in the prologue (1:1–2; cf. Luke 1:1–4) and indicated by the 'we' passages where the author joins Paul on his travels (e.g. 16:10–17). The date of Acts is linked with that of Luke's Gospel, and the whole work was probably written in the early 60s after Paul's arrival in Rome or possibly in the 80s.

Structure

Witnesses to Jerusalem (1:1–5:42)
Witnesses to Judea and Samaria (6:1–11:18)
Witnesses to the ends of the earth (11:19–28:31)

Famous passages

Jesus' ascension to heaven (1:4–11)
The Day of Pentecost (2:1–41)
Stephen, the first martyr (6:8–8:1)
Saul's conversion (9:1–19; 22:3–16; 26:9–18)
The start of the first missionary journey (13:1–3)
The Council in Jerusalem (15:1–35)
Paul shipwrecked (27:27–28:10)

The book describes how the gospel was taken from Jerusalem to Rome. It shows how Jesus' promise to the disciples was fulfilled, that 'you will be my witnesses in Jerusalem, and in all Judea and Samaria, and to the ends of the earth' (1:8). The effects of Pentecost on the church in Jerusalem (chapters 1–5) are followed by the spread of the gospel to Judea and Samaria through persecution (6:1–11:19). In the final stage, further persecution brought the gospel to Antioch, which became the base for expansion to Rome (11:20–28:31). Two leaders dominate the book. Peter's role in chapters 1–12 is as God's messenger to the Jews, though he comes to realize that the Gentiles are just as much part of God's plan. In chapters 13–28, the task of taking the gospel to the Gentiles falls to Paul, who travels to Cyprus, Asia Minor and Greece three times before making his final journey to Rome.

Acts is a book of speeches and action. The frequent speeches are either evangelistic, explaining the message about Jesus, or a defence of Christianity, often in the setting of a courtroom. They contain the essential elements of the Christian message, and centre on Jesus' identity as Messiah and Lord (2:36) and on the fact of his resurrection. The actions either show the effect of the message, such as the conversion of 3,000 people at once (2:41), or are signs confirming its power, as with Paul's extraordinary miracles (19:11). The result was that despite persecution, misunderstandings and disagreements, the early church quickly became established in many parts of the Roman Empire.

Adam The name of the first man as well as the Hebrew word for 'mankind', though the distinction between the individual and corporate meanings is not always clear in Genesis. In the New Testament, Adam usually represents the human race in its sinful rebellion against God (Romans 5:12–21), though he is also the first man and 'the son of God' (Luke 3:38). see also EVE.

Adonijah A son of David who was thwarted in his attempt to succeed David by his father's decision to appoint Solomon as king instead (1 Kings 1:1–2:25).

adoption Adoption of a child is rarely mentioned in the Bible, though Moses' adoption by an Egyptian princess is an important example of the practice. More often, adoption is a theological idea concerning the way in which sinners who are by nature God's enemies are made into children of God through faith in Christ (Galatians 4:4–7). God's adoption of Israel as his firstborn son is an important Old Testament background to this idea.

adultery A sexual relationship outside marriage by someone who is already married. It is consistently condemned in the Bible and is the one possible ground for divorce allowed by Jesus (Matthew 19:9). The Bible treats adultery as much more than a physical act. Jesus extended it to include adultery in the heart, i.e. lust (Matthew 5:27–30), and it is often used as an example of Israel's unfaithfulness to God (Hosea 2:2–23).

advice The benefit of seeking advice in decision-making is constantly underlined, and is especially important for those in leadership (Proverbs 11:14). A distinction is made, however, between human advice which can be unreliable and God's advice which provides sure guidance (Psalm 32:8).

agriculture Ancient Israelite society was based on agriculture, which explains why the work for which human beings were created is described as working and caring for the ground (Genesis 2:15). All agricultural activity is regarded as dependent on God's provision, for while human beings sow and nurture their crops, God alone gives the increase (1 Corinthians 3:7).

The agricultural year was entirely dependent on the weather, since the rains did not come for six months in the summer. Crops were sown with the early rains in the autumn, and matured with the spring rains in March and April. A second planting could also be included in a good year. The main crops were wheat and barley, vines and olives, though vegetables, fruit and nuts were also important. Crops were sown by hand, and the soil was ploughed with a single-handed plough drawn by oxen. Grain was harvested with a sickle and bound into sheaves, and then winnowed on a threshing-floor at the edge of the village. Harvest was a time for great rejoicing and thanksgiving to God, since the farmer was always at the mercy of drought, pests and war (Deuteronomy 16:13–15). See WEATHER.

Ahab, King of Israel (c. 869–850 BC) A notorious king of Israel, who actively promoted Baal worship and persecuted Yahweh's prophets, including Elijah. Politically, Ahab was successful and he made Samaria a wealthy city, but the Bible is more concerned about his moral and spiritual attitude (1 Kings 16:29–22:40). See ELIJAH; JEZEBEL.

Ahasuerus see XERXES.

Ahaz, King of Judah (c. 735–715 BC) A king who enthusiastically followed pagan practices, including sacrificing his son and building a pagan altar in the temple precincts. He refused to believe in God, and his reliance on Assyrian help instead made Judah dependent on them for a century (2 Kings 16).

Ahaziah, King of Israel (c. 850–849 BC) see KINGS AND QUEENS OF ISRAEL.

Ahaziah, King of Judah (c. 842 BC) see KINGS AND QUEENS OF ISRAEL.

Ahijah A prophet who predicted that Jeroboam would receive most of Solomon's kingdom, but that the northern kingdom would go into exile because of Jeroboam's idolatry (1 Kings 11:29–39).

Ahimelech A priest murdered by Saul for assisting David by giving him the shewbread and Goliath's sword (1 Samuel 21:1–9; 22:11–19). See also BREAD.

Ahithophel A highly respected counsellor of David, who committed suicide after giving bad advice to Absalom (2 Samuel 16:15–17:23).

Ai The site of Israel's first major failure in its effort to conquer the Promised Land. When Achan's sin was uncovered, Joshua captured it at the second attempt (Joshua 7:1–8:29). It is often identified with modern et-Tell, but this remains uncertain.

alcohol see WINE AND BEER.

alien A special term for foreigners who lived in Israel. They were free people, and in many ways lived the same way as ordinary Israelites, but they did not enjoy full legal rights. Israel's laws made special provision for their support on the basis that the Israelites themselves had been aliens in Egypt (Deuteronomy 10:19).

alleluia see HALLELUJAH.

alliances Israel made several alliances with its neighbours, though some, such as that with the Gibeonites (Joshua 9–10), were seen as a substitute for faith in God. The most productive was David's alliance with the Phoenicians who helped to build the temple.

almighty see GOD, NAMES AND TITLES OF.

almond see TREES AND BUSHES.

aloes see PLANTS.

Alpha and Omega see JESUS CHRIST, NAMES AND TITLES OF.

altar A place where sacrifice was offered. The Tabernacle and the Temple had two altars, a large bronze altar of burnt offering in the courtyard and a golden incense altar inside the building (Exodus 27:1–8; 30:1–10; 2 Chronicles 4:1, 19). Pagan altars were also built throughout Israel, including sometimes in the Temple itself. Archaeologists have discovered several Israelite altars, some with raised corners which the Bible calls the 'horns' of the altar. See also TABERNACLE.

Amalek, Amalekites A large nomadic group in southern Palestine. They became traditional enemies of Israel because they opposed the Israelites who came out of Egypt (Deuteronomy 25:17–19).

Amasa Joab's replacement as commander of David's army until he was murdered by Joab (2 Samuel 19:13; 20:8–12).

Amaziah, King of Judah (c. 800–783 BC) see KINGS AND QUEENS OF ISRAEL.

ambition Viewed positively and negatively in the Bible. While encouragement is given to people who want to do God's will and aim for what is good (Philippians 3:13–14), disapproval is shown towards those who are motivated by self-interest (Philippians 2:3).

amen A Hebrew word meaning 'surely', used most frequently to indicate acceptance of God's words, especially his promises (Galatians 1:3–5).

amethyst see JEWELS AND PRECIOUS STONES.

Ammon, Ammonites Ammon lay to the east of the Jordan, between Moab to the south and Gilead to the north. Its capital, Rabbath-Ammon, is modern Amman. The Ammonites were often in conflict with Israel, and David became their king for a time (2 Samuel 12:29–31). Archaeology reveals a high material culture during the Iron Age until the Babylonian campaigns of the sixth century BC.

Amnon A son of David who was killed by his brother Absalom for raping Tamar, Amnon's half-sister (2 Samuel 13:1–29).

Amon, King of Judah (c. 642–640 BC) see KINGS AND QUEENS OF ISRAEL.

Amorites A term used in ancient literature to refer to several different groups of people, and which really means 'westerners'. The Bible uses it mainly alongside the Canaanites to describe several groups among the pre-Israelite inhabitants of Palestine (Numbers 13:29). Elsewhere it refers to groups in various parts of the ancient Near East, especially those who established strong kingdoms in Mesopotamia in the early second millennium BC.

Amos A prophet who was active about 760 BC. Like his contemporary Hosea, he was unpopular for criticizing the kingdom of Israel, predicting its downfall unless the people repented. His warnings

were fulfilled when Israel fell to the Assyrians in 722 BC. see also
AMOS, BOOK OF.

Amos, book of

Structure
Prophecies against various nations (1:1–2:16)
Prophecies against Israel (3:1–6:14)
Five visions (7:1–9:10)
Israel's future restoration (9:11–15)

Famous passages
Selling righteous people for a pair of sandals (2:6)
The Day of the LORD (5:18–20)
Amos' call to be a prophet (7:14–15)

A prophetic book from the mid-eighth century BC, which like Hosea
is addressed to the northern kingdom of Israel. Its message of
judgement is similar to Hosea's, except that Amos' approach is more
stark. Amos concentrates on the contrast between God's goodness to
Israel when he set them free from slavery in Egypt and made them
his own family, and Israel's current preference for greedy and selfish
living. Amos particularly criticizes contemporary religion, which was
entirely concerned with right ritual rather than justice and right
behaviour (4:4–5; 5:21–6). Though he prophesied that Israel would go
into exile (5:27; 6:7), he also pleaded with God not to destroy his own
people (7:1–9). Even though God did not comply with Amos' request
because the people stubbornly stuck to their sinful ways, the final
promises of restoration (9:11–15) show that God's mercy had the last
word.

The book is notable for its majestic view of God, especially in
some of the hymn-like passages (4:13; 5:8–9; 9:5–6), and for its
challenge that faith must involve the whole of life. Its emphasis on
social justice continues to influence modern Christian thought and
action.

Anakites One of the pre-Israelite groups in Palestine who were noted
for being tall and strong (Deuteronomy 9:1–2).

Ananias 1. A believer who lived in Damascus. He healed Paul's
blindness and told him of God's plan for him to be a missionary
(Acts 9:10–19).

2. A high priest before whom Paul was tried (Acts 23:2).

Ananias and Sapphira A husband and wife in Jerusalem who died
suddenly because they lied to the church and to God (Acts 5:1–11).

anchor SEE BOATS AND SHIPS.

Ancient of Days see GOD, NAMES AND TITLES OF.

Andrew One of the twelve apostles and the brother of Simon Peter. A fisherman like his brother, he had an important role in introducing people to Jesus (John 1:35–42; 6:8; 12:22).

angel The word means 'messenger' and can refer to human beings, though it normally describes unseen spiritual beings. The latter may serve God or the devil, though the Bible is far more concerned with the former group. Angels play an increasingly important role in biblical thought. Whereas in the earlier part of the Old Testament they are simply unseen servants of God (Psalm 103:20–1), by the end of the Old Testament they are divided into archangels and others, and receive names such as Michael and Gabriel. The New Testament emphasizes their role in serving Jesus and individual believers, including the idea of guardian angels (Matthew 4:11; 18:10).

Angel of the LORD A special term which usually in the Old Testament, though never in the New Testament, refers to a revelation of God himself, often in human form. This angel is recognizable as divine by his speech and actions, though full realization about his identity often dawns only gradually (Exodus 3:1–6; Judges 13:2–23).

anger God shows his anger against all forms of sin and wickedness, including pride, injustice, idolatry and disobedience. When God is angry, it is always with good cause and under control, and is never an arbitrary show of pique. God is also often said to be 'slow to anger'. The display of God's anger can be terrifying and sudden (2 Samuel 6:7; Acts 5:1–11), but apart from God's final day of wrath (Rom 2:5), it is never as bad as it should be because God always mixes mercy with anger (Habakkuk 3:2). Also, the consequences of God's anger can be avoided through trusting in the work of Christ (Romans 5:9).

Human anger can be acceptable or unacceptable. It is justified as a reaction to sinful behaviour, but even then it must be strictly limited (Ephesians 4:31). More often, human anger is sinful, since it can easily get out of control and lead to taking revenge. Human anger is therefore to be avoided wherever possible, and people should follow God's model of being slow to anger (1 Corinthians 13:5). Any attempt at vengeance is to be left to God because only he acts with true justice (Romans 12:17–19).

animals A wide variety of animals are mentioned in the Bible, though some that are mentioned less frequently cannot be identified precisely. The problem of identification is made more difficult since some animals like the lion are no longer found in the area, though they were common in Palestine in biblical times. Land animals are best divided into domestic and wild animals. Of the domestic animals, the most common are flocks of sheep and goats and herds of cattle. These were often symbols of a person's wealth, and sometimes camels were also included. Pigs and dogs were also domesticated, but were treated as unclean. The common beast of burden was the donkey, and David was the first to introduce the horse into Israel. Wild animals roamed the deserts and forests, including the bear, lion, hyena, leopard, jackal and wolf as well as deer, gazelles, wild goats and various smaller creatures like badgers, weasels, snakes and lizards. Solomon imported exotic creatures such as apes and baboons, but Israel's ivory came from elephants in Africa and Asia. Water creatures occur less frequently, and it is uncertain whether whales are mentioned. Job's detailed descriptions of the behemoth and leviathan may refer to the hippopotamus and the crocodile, but certainty is impossible (Job 40–1). See also BIRDS; INSECTS AND ARACHNIDS.

Animals	
Domestic animals	
Camel	Genesis 24:10–11; Ezra 2:67
Cattle (cow, bull)	Job 18:3; Isaiah 30:23
Dog	Psalm 59:14–15; Matthew 15:26–7
Donkey/Ass	Numbers 22:21; Matthew 21:2
Goat	Genesis 27:9; Daniel 8:5–8
Horse	1 Kings 10:26; Zechariah 1:8
Pig	Leviticus 11:7; Luke 15:15–16
Sheep	1 Samuel 16:11; Ezekiel 34:11–22
Wild animals	
Bear	2 Samuel 17:8
Deer	Psalm 42:1
Fox	Judges 15:4–5
Gazelle	2 Samuel 2:18
Jackal	Micah 1:8
Leopard	Jeremiah 13:23
Lion	1 Peter 5:8
Snake	Ecclesiastes 10:11
Wild donkey	Job 39:5–8
Wild ox	Numbers 23:22
Wolf	John 10:12
Worm	Psalm 22:6

Sea creatures	
Crocodile (?)	Job 41:1–34
Fish	John 21:6–11
Great sea creatures	Genesis 1:21
Hippopotamus (?)	Job 40:15–24

Annas see CAIAPHAS.

Annunciation The angel Gabriel's announcement to Mary that she would give birth to the Messiah (Luke 1:26–38).

anointing, anointed The act of pouring oil over somebody or something to indicate that it was special in some way. When people were anointed, it was often a sign that God had chosen and equipped them to carry out a particular task. In such cases, the oil symbolized the outpouring of God's Spirit. Priests and kings were appointed in this way (Exodus 29:7; 1 Samuel 16:13), and the concept was also applied figuratively to prophets, judges and the Servant of God (Isaiah 42:1). It also included the gift of God's Spirit to Christians (1 John 2:20). The term 'the anointed one' or 'Messiah' was used of some of the early kings, but does not occur in its technical sense in the Old Testament. Greek *christos* also means anointed, and when not used as a title for Jesus refers to the expectation of a person specially chosen and equipped by God who would establish God's kingdom. see MESSIAH.

ant see INSECTS AND ARACHNIDS.

antichrist A term used in John's Letters of leaders who oppose Christ. Similar figures include 'the man of lawlessness' (2 Thessalonians 2:3–12) and 'the beast' (Revelation 11:7).

Antioch 1. A city in Syria which was the site of the first major Gentile church and from which Paul was sent on his missionary journeys (Acts 11:22–30; 13:1–3). See map of PAUL'S JOURNEYS.
2. A town in Pisidia in southern Asia Minor, visited by Paul on his first missionary journey (Acts 13:14–52). See map of PAUL'S JOURNEYS.

Antiochus The 'little horn', etc., of the Book of Daniel is an allusion to the Seleucid king Antiochus IV (Epiphanes) who desecrated the temple in 167 BC (Daniel 7:8–11, 20–6).

anxiety An attitude of worry and unease characterized by a failure to trust God. It arises from being preoccupied with oneself and with physical and material things. It can be remedied by reordering one's priorities towards God and by a commitment to trust him (Matthew 6:25–34).

apocalypse A type of mainly Jewish literature characterized by revelations of the supernatural world and of the end of the world, presented in symbolic language. It flourished in the context of oppression and persecution from the second century BC. Examples in the Bible include parts of Daniel and the prophets such as Isaiah 24–7, Ezekiel 38–9 and Zechariah 14, and the Book of Revelation.

apocalyptic An understanding of the supernatural world and of the end of the world found in apocalypses such as Revelation, parts of several Old Testament books and Jewish literature. Apocalyptic means 'revealed', and refers to the manner in which angelic beings convey the meaning of the last things.

Apocrypha A group of books whose status is disputed as to whether or not they should be included in the Bible. The term Apocrypha means 'hidden' or 'secret', and the books of the Apocrypha are sometimes also known as the Deuterocanonical books. These books were preserved in Greek but many of them were probably originally in Hebrew or Aramaic. They were part of the Greek translation of the Old Testament (known as the Septuagint), though even then their value was regarded as somewhat ambiguous, and for many centuries, they also circulated in the Latin (Vulgate) Bible. At the Reformation, the Roman Catholic Church confirmed their place in their editions of the Bible, but the Protestant denominations excluded them. The number of books varies in different traditions, as does the type of literature involved. The main books are the short stories of Tobit and Judith, the Additions to Esther and Daniel (the latter include Susanna, Bel and the Dragon, and the Song of the Three Children), the historical works of 1 and 2 Maccabees, the wisdom books of the Wisdom of Solomon and Ecclesiasticus (also known as Ben Sira), and the additions to Jeremiah known as Baruch and the Letter of Jeremiah. Those of less certain status include 1 and 2 Esdras, 3 and 4 Maccabees, the Prayer of Manasseh, and Psalm 151. They have been preserved in Greek but many were probably written originally in Hebrew or Aramaic.

Apollos A gifted teacher in the early church. He began at Ephesus, where his initial enthusiasm for christianity needed some correction, and then moved to Corinth where he became an effective debater with the Jews (Acts 18:24–8).

apostasy Based on a Greek word, the term means rebellion against God. The danger of falling away from God is often mentioned, and many examples are included in both the Old Testament and the New Testament (Psalm 95:7–11; Hebrews 10:26–31).

apostle Based on a Greek word meaning 'one who is sent', the term refers primarily to the twelve disciples whom Jesus sent out in the power of the Spirit to take the gospel to the world. Their basic qualification was that they had been with Jesus during his earthly ministry and had witnessed his resurrection, and Matthias replaced Judas on that basis. However, others were added to their number, among whom the most important was Paul (1 Corinthians 15:7–9; Acts 14:4; Galatians 1:19). The apostles were recognized as the founders of the church, comparable in status with the prophets of the Old Testament, because of their authoritative teaching of the gospel and establishing of new churches. Their authority was challenged by others who also called themselves apostles, but Paul based his defence of genuine apostles on their suffering for the gospel and the evidence of their ministry in the churches they had planted. The word *apostle* is also used more generally to refer to a representative or messenger of a particular church (2 Corinthians 8:23; Philippians 2:25).

apple see FRUITS.

Aquila and Priscilla A husband and wife who were close friends of Paul (Acts 18:1–3). They had an influential teaching ministry and travelled widely for the sake of the gospel.

Arabah The Jordan valley south from the Sea of Galilee to the Gulf of Aqabah, and also the associated wilderness areas. The Dead Sea is sometimes called the Sea of the Arabah (Joshua 3:16). See map of OLD TESTAMENT ISRAEL.

Arabia, Arabs Israel's contacts with the Arabs to the south and east of Palestine developed from the time of Solomon onwards, and were mainly with the North Arabian tribes. The links were mainly based on trading and military activities (2 Chronicles 21:16–17; Ezekiel 27:21). See map of WORLD OF THE BIBLE.

arachnids see INSECTS AND ARACHNIDS.

Aram, Arameans The earliest Arameans lived in northern Mesopotamia before 2000 BC, and may be connected with the first biblical Arameans (Genesis 25:20), who lived in the Haran area (called Aram Naharaim). The Old Testament also mentions several Aramean states in Syria c. 1000–700 BC, of which Damascus was the most important (2 Samuel 8:5–6). They were often in conflict with Israel and Judah. See map of OLD TESTAMENT ISRAEL; WORLD OF THE BIBLE.

Ararat The mountain range in modern Turkey where Noah's ark landed (Genesis 8:4), and the biblical name of the ancient kingdom of Urartu. See map of WORLD OF THE BIBLE.

Araunah The name of a Jebusite who sold what became the Temple site to David (2 Samuel 24:18–25). He is called 'Ornan' in Chronicles (1 Chronicles 21:18–22:1).

archaeology An important aspect of biblical study, since so much of the biblical story is part of ancient Near Eastern history, including Egypt, Syria, Assyria, Babylonia, Persia, Greece and Rome as well as Palestine. Biblical archaeology is part of the wider study of the ancient world rather than a separate science. The chief value of archaeology for biblical study is therefore to relate modern knowledge of the ancient world to the biblical text and vice versa. Most of the time, archaeological discovery has amplified our understanding of the Bible's incidental features rather than of major events, though because this involves the kind of information that would be difficult to invent with any accuracy, it provides good support for the authenticity of the biblical record. However, it is not generally the task of archaeology to prove whether the Bible is authentic or not, mainly because the archaeological record is so haphazard and because so much evidence from the ancient world has been lost for ever. The exact places where Jesus was born, died and resurrected, for example, will almost certainly never be known.

Excavation can uncover anything from whole cities to individual houses and their contents, but inscriptions are particularly important. Cuneiform texts like the fourteenth-century BC Amarna letters or the biblical and other manuscripts from the Dead Sea Scrolls inform us about contemporary ideas as well as about actual people and places. Important buildings that have been preserved include the theatre at Ephesus where Paul was judged (Acts 19:29) and Ahab's palace at Samaria with its splendid ivories. But it is the smaller finds that are often the most informative about what life was like, such as altars with their horned corners (cf. Exodus 27:2), brief letters from Lachish telling desperately of the advancing Babylonian armies (cf. 2 Kings 25:1) or the skeletal remains near Jerusalem of a crucified man with the nails still attached to his body (cf. John 20:25). Archaeology will never provide all the answers to questions about biblical history, and it often contributes further problems of its own, but as new discoveries are made it opens up further possibilities of illustrating life in Bible times.

archangel see ANGEL.

architecture Comparatively few monumental buildings have been preserved in Palestine, because of the perishable nature of most building materials used. Major buildings were constructed largely of timber and limestone, though ordinary houses were often made of mud-brick. Larger towns were usually fortified, and were constructed round a central area that included a palace or administrative centre and sometimes a sanctuary. The tripartite structure of Solomon's temple with its porch, outer and inner rooms (2 Chronicles 3:3–9) has parallels in Phoenician sanctuaries. The standard house had four rooms, of which the central 'room' was a courtyard which acted as an entrance to the others. This provided accommodation for animals and people, and wealthier families sometimes added an upper storey. See also HOME; TEMPLE.

Arimathea see JOSEPH OF ARIMATHEA.

ark of the covenant A golden box placed between two cherubim in the Most Holy Place in the Tabernacle and the Temple. It contained the Ten Commandments, a jar of manna and Aaron's rod that budded. The ark was sometimes regarded as no more than a lucky charm, and the reality of God's holy presence could make it dangerous for the unwary (1 Samuel 5:1–7:1; 2 Samuel 6:6–15), but primarily it symbolized the blessings of God's presence among his people and God's commitment to his covenant promises. The ark was probably destroyed by the Babylonian armies in 587 BC. See also TABERNACLE; TEMPLE.

ark, Noah's A large floating container measuring c. 150 × 25 × 15 metres in which Noah preserved his immediate family and representatives of different kinds of animals in the great flood (Genesis 6:14–22). Similar vessels are described in other ancient flood stories, but unlike Noah's boat, their cuboid shape made them quite impractical for their intended purpose. See also NOAH.

arm Often used symbolically, especially of physical strength (Genesis 49:24) or conversely of physical weakness in comparison with God's strength (Job 40:9). God's arm, however, is always strong, even when associated with the weakness of his servant (Isaiah 53:1).

armageddon see MEGIDDO.

armour and weapons The main weapons of attack were the sword, spear, javelin, war club and bow and arrow. The sword is the commonest weapon mentioned in the Bible, and was usually a long straight sword kept in a sheath, though a shorter dagger-type version was used from earliest times. The bow was also widely used, and arrows were usually held in a quiver. Bows might have either a single curve or be double-convex, but the composite bow in which wood or bronze were bonded with animal horn and sinews provided much greater effectiveness. The sling was used mainly by shepherds against wild animals. The main defensive weapons were the shield and helmet. Shields were normally either the small round type often carried by archers or the large rectangular version which protected most of the body. These and the helmets were sometimes made of metal (as with Goliath's helmet), though the Assyrians wore long pointed helmets with neck protectors. Body armour was also often worn. Most armies were equipped with larger weapons, including chariots, siege-machines and battering rams. Personal items of armour are given a spiritual significance in Isaiah 59:17; Ephesians 6:10–17.

Armour and weapons	
Armour	
Coat of armour	2 Chronicles 26:14
Greaves	1 Samuel 17:6
Helmet	Jeremiah 46:4
Shield	1 Kings 10:16–17
Weapons	
Bow and arrow	Psalm 11:2
Dagger	2 Samuel 2:16
Javelin	1 Samuel 17:6
Siege-machine	2 Chronicles 26:15
Sling	1 Samuel 17:40
Spear	Nehemiah 4:21
Sword	Exodus 32:27
War club	2 Samuel 23:21

army Israel's armies were originally based on tribal militias who were called out in times of crisis, and standing armies were not introduced until the time of Saul and especially David. Even then, Israel relied entirely on infantry. Solomon was the first to incorporate horses and chariots into the army, though the cavalry does not seem to have become permanent. Most conflicts were based on pitched battles, though representative duels as between David and Goliath were used in earlier times, and a wide variety of tactics could be employed. Israel's armies were organized under commanders or captains who were in charge of groups theoretically between 50 and 1,000. Actual numbers were usually smaller, as with Roman armies where centurions usually commanded fewer than 100 men and legions had less than the theoretical 6,000 men. The major empires of the ancient world depended on their armies, especially the Egyptians, Assyrians, Babylonians, Persians, Greeks and Romans, but the Bible emphasizes that even mighty armies are powerless against him (Exodus 14–15; Judges 4–5). The Bible anticipates God's final victory over the world's armies when they gather against his people. See also BATTLES.

Arnon, River A wadi flowing westwards into the Dead Sea, and the traditional boundary in Transjordan separating Israel from Moab (Judges 11:18). See map of OLD TESTAMENT ISRAEL.

aroma see SMELLING.

arrows see ARMOUR AND WEAPONS.

Artaxerxes The name of three Persian emperors. Artaxerxes I (465–424 BC) was associated with Nehemiah (Nehemiah 2:1) and probably Ezra (Ezra 7:7), though the latter might be linked with Artaxerxes II (404–359 BC).

Artemis A Greek goddess of the moon and hunting whose Latin name was Diana. She had a great temple in Ephesus, where her statue was thought to have fallen from heaven (Acts 19:27–8, 35).

artisans see OCCUPATIONS.

arts and crafts The Israelites were less advanced technologically than some of their neighbours, but seem to have practised and appreciated a wide variety of artistic skills. Ordinary life relied on basic skills in working with clay, metal, wood, stone and fibres, but high-quality work could also be produced by those with more expert abilities. In ancient times, the skills of Bezalel and Huram, who were master craftsmen on the Tabernacle and Temple respectively, were much admired, and ivory work discovered at Samaria and elsewhere provides evidence of great artistic ability. As a Phoenician, Huram illustrates Israel's willingness to import skills from outside, especially in connection with the decoration of the Temple. Though few examples of their creativity survive, the Israelites were involved like their neighbours in producing wallpaintings, wood-carving, metalwork and seal-engraving. Fine art depended on the patronage of kings and priests, and was most likely to be found in palaces and temples.

Arts and crafts

Artistic skills

Dance	Matthew 14:6
Embroidery	Exodus 38:23
Gem engraving	Exodus 28:11
Music	1 Chronicles 16:5–6
Textile work	Genesis 37:3
Weaving	Exodus 39:22

Building crafts

Carpentry	Isaiah 44:13
Metalwork	Isaiah 44:12
Pottery	Jeremiah 18:1–4
Silversmithing	Acts 19:24
Stonemasonry	2 Chronicles 24:12
Tanning	Acts 9:43

Asa, King of Judah (c. 913–873 BC) A king who led a religious reformation in his early years, but who later put his faith in human resources rather than God (1 Kings 15:9–24).

Asahel An enthusiastic soldier and fast runner in David's army. He was reluctantly killed by Abner but his death was avenged by Asahel's brother Joab (2 Samuel 2:18–23; 3:27).

Asaph, Heman and Jeduthun The three leading musicians among the Levites appointed by David to lead Israel's worship. Their names appear in headings to the Psalms in connection with different collections of psalms.

Ascension, the The moment when the resurrected Jesus was taken up to heaven in the clouds (Acts 1:9–11). He was returning to his Father and his heavenly throne, from where he poured his Spirit on the church at Pentecost ten days later. An angel told the watching disciples that Jesus' second coming would take place in the same manner as his ascension. Though the ascension is described in physical terms because Jesus had a physical body, its main purpose is to show that Jesus was exalted to ultimate authority in heaven because he had completed his work on earth.

Ashdod One of the five main Philistine cities, 6 kilometres south-east of the modern town (1 Samuel 5:1–7). In the New Testament it was known as Azotus. See map of NEW TESTAMENT ISRAEL; OLD TESTAMENT ISRAEL.

Asher 1. The eighth son of Jacob (Genesis 30:12–13).
2. A tribe descended from Asher that lived in the coastal area northwards from Mount Carmel (Joshua 19:24–31). See map of OLD TESTAMENT ISRAEL.

Asherah A Canaanite fertility goddess known in the Old Testament as Baal's consort (Judges 3:7), though she was the consort of El in the Ugaritic literature of ancient Syria. The Old Testament often refers to the Israelites worshipping images of Asherah, though it is unknown whether these were representations of the goddess or a decorated wooden pole (1 Kings 15:13). See also BAAL.

ashes see DUST AND ASHES.

Ashkelon One of the five main Philistine cities and part of the modern city of the same name (Zephaniah 2:4–7). It remained independent for much of the biblical period and was the birthplace of Herod the Great. See map of OLD TESTAMENT ISRAEL.

Ashtoreth A Canaanite fertility goddess, known elsewhere as Ishtar, Athtar or Astarte, and similar to but distinct from Asherah (Judges 2:13).

Asia Always in the New Testament the Roman province in western Asia Minor based on Ephesus (Acts 16:6). The seven churches of Revelation were situated in the province (Revelation 2–3). See map of PAUL'S JOURNEYS.

assembly A formal term for gatherings of God's people for both religious and political purposes, especially the tribal assemblies in the pre-monarchy period and the national assemblies in the post-exilic restoration. The Greek word for 'church' can also be translated 'assembly' (Acts 14:27).

assurance A firm conviction concerning a person's faith in Christ. The nature of assurance relates both to the truth of the gospel of Jesus Christ and to the security of the believer's relationship with Jesus in this life and for the life to come, and focuses particularly on the believer's unchanging status as a child of God (Romans 8:14–17). The basis of assurance involves the work of the Holy Spirit in the life of the believer, the objective nature of the work of Christ, and reliability of God's word (John 17:8; Acts 2:32–6; 1 John 4:13). Since personal assurance depends on what God has revealed and is given through the Spirit, it can be experienced by young as well as mature believers. Personal experience, however, must be confirmed by objective evidence of spiritual growth in the believer's life if self-deception is to be avoided.

Assyria, Assyrians A country in northern Mesopotamia (modern Iraq) which established the powerful New Assyrian empire in the eighth and seventh centuries BC. It was based on the might of the Assyrian army, which could be very cruel, but the Assyrians were also a very cultured people who produced important architecture, literature and art. They conquered the kingdom of Israel in 722 BC, deporting many of the people and annexing their land (2 Kings 17:3–6). They also controlled Judah for over a century, though the Assyrian king Sennacherib suffered a humiliating and miraculous defeat in 701 BC through Hezekiah's faith and Isaiah's prophesying (2 Kings 18:9–19:37). The Assyrians were finally defeated by the Babylonians when Nineveh fell in 612 BC. See map of WORLD OF THE BIBLE.

astrology see OCCULT.

Athaliah, Queen of Judah (c. 842–837 BC) A violent woman from Ahab's family who was Judah's only queen. She tried to murder Judah's royal family but was removed in a coup (2 Kings 11).

athletics A metaphor for the Christian life, especially in relation to the need for single-minded training, persevering when the going gets difficult, and the certainty of a final reward (1 Corinthians 9:24–7; 2 Timothy 4:7–8).

atonement A term which means 'a making at one' and refers to the way in which God through Christ brings sinners into a right relationship with himself. The concept is central to the New Testament, but it has important Old Testament roots. God made provision for Israel's sins to be forgiven and so maintain its covenant relationship with him. This was based on sacrifices for sin, which could be offered by individuals and by the nation on the annual Day of Atonement, though effective atonement also required the sinner's repentant attitude. Strictly speaking, because it was founded on God's gracious promises, atonement could be achieved independently of animal sacrifice (Psalm 51). However, the Old Testament pattern suffered from certain difficulties, such as the inability of Israel's sacrifices to provide permanent atonement or to deal with the internal aspects of forgiveness.

The work of Christ both fulfils the Old Testament pattern and makes up for its deficiencies. Because Jesus lived a perfect sinless life, he died as an acceptable sacrifice for sinners, 'the righteous for the unrighteous' (1 Peter 3:18). The Letter to the Hebrews particularly emphasizes that Christ was God's true High Priest and that his self-offering in death was the once for all sacrifice for sin. This means that Christ's work is of world-wide and eternal significance. He brought to an end the need for any other atoning sacrifice, and made the benefits of his death available to all human beings (1 John 2:2). He brings human beings into a new covenant relationship with God, removing the effects of sin and providing them with a completely secure relationship with God. It is impossible to convey the full meaning of atonement in a single word. Although reconciliation is perhaps the most comprehensive term, it also includes redemption, forgiveness, justification and victory over evil. See also ATONEMENT, DAY OF.

Atonement, Day of An annual ceremony centred on two complementary sacrifices indicating the complete removal of Israel's sins (Leviticus 16). The blood of one sacrificial animal was taken by the high priest into the Most Holy Place and sprinkled over the atonement cover, and a second sacrificial animal called the scapegoat was then led away into the wilderness, never to return.

Augustus see CAESAR.

authority The right to act and require some form of obedient response. All human authority, whether in the church or the world as a whole comes ultimately from God and must be exercised responsibly. God always permits and sometimes provides the exercise of political authority. He requires obedience to human authorities as a means for the proper ordering of society and the restraint of evil. The only clear exception to this in the Bible is when human authorities deny the freedom of the gospel (Acts 4:18–19). Those who suffer injustice are to bring their cause before God who 'sets up kings and deposes them' (Daniel 2:21).

God's authority is exercised by Jesus who rules in heaven following his resurrection and ascension (Matthew 28:18; Hebrews 1:3). God's authority is also expressed in his words. These were intrinsically recognized as having the power to require obedience whether in the form of promise, law or prophecy. As God's words were collected together in written form in both Old Testament and New Testament, they developed into an authoritative scripture which was recognized as coming from God. Within the church, God's authority is conveyed by the Holy Spirit, especially through its leaders and their teaching of the gospel. As the gospel was proclaimed in the power of the Spirit, its authority to bring unbelievers to faith was demonstrated. Although Christian leaders are given authority in the church, they are accountable to God for the exercise of their authority. They are to follow Christ's example not by lording it over people but by serving them in love, and the same pattern is to be applied within the family. In this way, Christian authority shows itself distinct from all other claims to authority.

The authority and inspiration of the Bible

The significance of the Bible in the Christian faith can be understood in terms of its authority and its inspiration.

What authority does the Bible have? The New Testament has authority as it comprises the foundation documents of the Christian faith. They were chosen by the church because they were considered to faithfully relate the events and significance of the life, death and resurrection of Jesus Christ. From the very beginning, though, Christians also took and used the Jewish scriptures, known in the Christian Bible as the Old Testament. For Christians, these had authority not least because they were the scriptures Jesus himself knew and quoted from. In the writings and prophecies of the Old Testament, Christians found helpful keys for interpreting what God had done in and through Jesus, and what they as the church were now supposed to be and do in the world. The Old and New Testament scriptures were thus the official documents of the church, compiled into a 'canon' (from the Latin and Greek for 'rule', referring to the church's decision).

Deciding which books to include in the canon of scripture was a long process. For the Old Testament, the five books of the Pentateuch were decided upon by the Jewish community by the fourth century BC, while the 'Prophets' and the 'Writings' were not settled on until the second century BC and the first century AD respectively. Even then, there were discussions over the positioning of some books within the canon (Song of Songs, Ecclesiastes, Esther). Some books which were not included in the Hebrew Old Testament were added to the Greek Septuagint; twelve of these can be found in the Apocrypha section of some Bibles.

In addition to taking over the canon of the Old Testament, the early church recognised 27 books that had been written after the events of Jesus' life, death and resurrection. There were a number of contenders for books and letters to be included. Thirteen letters of Paul were decided upon early in the second century, soon followed by the four Gospels and Acts. Recognition of the other letters and Revelation followed later, and the church councils in Laodicea (AD 363) and Carthage (AD 397) confirmed the canon that was already in use within the church.

However, the Bible is not authoritative because the church officially recognised it; rather, the canon was recognised because the books were already seen to be authoritative. God's people had identified them as carrying the message of God. This explains why the Bible is called 'the Word of God'. The Bible has authority because it is not merely a collection of human religious writings, but because through the different human authors, God's message is heard. This is known as the Bible's 'inspiration'.

To say that the books of the Bible were inspired by God does not mean that their human authors played no part in their composition, as if they merely wrote down the words of a dictation. On the other hand, neither does the concept of biblical inspiration mean that the authors had a good idea and wrote it down as a word from God. Inspiration is not so much a theory about how the Bible was written, as a statement of what the Bible is. It means that the words of the Bible are at one and the same time both human words – with cultural, stylistic and literary characteristics – and also the divine words God speaks in a situation. Inspiration is a way of affirming equally the human elements of the Bible, which require study and analysis, and the divine character of the Bible, which requires obedience and faith.

Two other terms often applied to the Bible in connection with inspiration are infallibility and inerrancy. Infallibility means that the Bible does not mislead its readers in any way, but is a trustworthy guide with regard to matters of God and faith. Inerrancy asserts more strongly that the Bible does not contain any error with regard to matters of fact, at least in the original manuscripts. Inerrancy was widely debated from the nineteenth century onwards, as theologians tried to protect the authority of the Bible from those who saw it as merely a human document apparently contradicted by some results from the scientific world. This term may no longer be considered the most helpful way to describe the Bible, but at the very least, it points to the Bible's authoritative role in revealing the true God and his intentions for the world.

In the final analysis, the Bible's authority is seen in the role it plays in the life of the Christian and the church. The affirmation of the Christian faith, testified to in scripture, is that salvation is only through faith in Jesus Christ, in complete dependence upon the grace of God. The Bible not only proclaims this experience as a possibility, but also reflects it as a reality in its various writings. The Bible is authoritative for the church and for individual Christians because it both resonates with their contemporary experience, and challenges them to new ways of living and thinking that enable them to grow in faith and live in God's kingdom.

autumn see SEASONS.
avenger of blood see VENGEANCE.
awe see FEAR.

axe see TOOLS.

Azariah, King of Judah (*c.* 783–742 BC) Also known as Uzziah. Judah prospered under his rule, which was marked by various innovations, but God punished him with a skin disease as he became proud (2 Kings 15:1–7).

Azotus see ASHDOD.

b

Baal The main god of the Canaanites in the Old Testament, though in Ugaritic literature of an earlier period he was subordinate to El, the head of the Canaanite pantheon. He was a nature god and a god of war, and was known by different names in different localities, such as Baal Melqart of Tyre or Baal-Berith (Judges 8:33). The contest at Mount Carmel showed he was powerless in comparison with Yahweh (1 Kings 18:16–39). When not used as a name, the term means 'lord' or 'husband'.

Baasha, King of Israel (c. 900–877 BC) see KINGS AND QUEENS OF ISRAEL.

Babel A name which means 'gate of God', which is also the meaning of Babylon, but it is not clear whether Babel in the Old Testament (Genesis 10–11) refers to the city of Babylon. The Old Testament story of the tower of Babel concerns the building of a ziggurat or temple-tower, but is really a story of human pride. The link with the idea of the confusion of languages is based on a word of similar sound (Hebrew *balal*).

Babylon The name of a city and its surrounding area (also called Babylonia) in southern Mesopotamia (modern Iraq), and the centre of one of the world's great empires. There were two main periods of Babylonian greatness. The first was the Old Babylonian empire of Hammurabi in the eighteenth century BC, which produced one of the ancient world's most important law collections, known as the Laws of Hammurabi. These laws have several similarities with the laws of the Old Testament. The second period was the New Babylonian empire from 626–539 BC, based on the ascendancy of the southern Babylonian Kaldu tribe from whom the name Chaldean comes. It reached its height under Nebuchadnezzar, who conquered Judah, razed Jerusalem to the ground and deported its population to Babylonia in 597 and 587 BC (2 Kings 25). Though Babylon was a centre of learning and culture and the home of Nebuchadnezzar's hanging gardens, one of the seven wonders of the ancient world, the Jews exiled there longed constantly for home (Psalm 137). In the New Testament, Babylon is a symbol for Rome and for a prosperous human society which has no time for God. Its fall is celebrated with much rejoicing in heaven and precedes the final establishment of God's kingdom (Revelation 18:1–19:3). See map of WORLD OF THE BIBLE.

backsliding see APOSTASY.

baker see OCCUPATIONS.

baking see COOKING.

Balaam An expert in divination from the north Euphrates area hired by a Moabite king to curse the Israelites on their way to the Promised land. God, however, prevented him carrying out his intentions, and gave him a prophecy about God's plans to bless Israel (Numbers 24:3–9). The story of Balaam's donkey merely confirms his slowness in understanding the true God, in contrast to his reputation for divination. Another story about him is known from an Aramaic text from c. 700 BC.

Balak A Moabite king whose plan to hire Balaam to curse the Israelites backfired when Balaam pronounced God's blessing (Numbers 22–4).

balm see HERBS AND SPICES.

ban In the Old Testament the word is used for a special custom when people or things were dedicated completely to God. The ban itself might be a declaration of God's judgement or an act by which something or someone was excluded from normal use. The expression 'to put to the ban' referred originally to God's decision that the Canaanites should be completely destroyed and that the Israelites were prohibited from making any use of their possessions (Deuteronomy 7:26; 20:16–18). Later, it incorporated the practices of exclusion from the community (Ezra 10:8) and excommunication from the church (1 Corinthians 5:1–5).

banner Usually a battle standard, but used of God and of a Messianic figure as the ultimate rallying points for God's people (Exodus 17:15; Isaiah 11:10).

banquet Used mainly in the New Testament for the Messianic banquet, symbolizing the rich blessings to be enjoyed in heaven (Revelation 19:9).

baptism The word is originally a Greek term meaning dipping or immersing in water. The practice originated in Jewish ceremonial washings, and was also part of the initiation ceremonies at Qumran, but it was through John the Baptist that it became a central feature of church life. Surprisingly, baptism does not seem to have been a major feature of Jesus' ministry, though his disciples did baptize on his behalf (John 4:2).

John the Baptist taught baptism as a sign of repentance, and Jesus submitted to John's baptism as an act of solidarity with sinners as well as a mark of his own commitment to God's will (Matthew 3:11–17). The early church adopted baptism on Jesus' own instruction as an expression of a person's initial commitment to Christ in faith and repentance. The phrase 'in/into the name of' indicated entry into a relationship of belonging to God (Matthew 28:19). Baptism was also closely associated with the gift of the Holy Spirit and with the idea of union with Christ. In the latter case, the picture of a believer's death and resurrection seems to be based on the practice of immersion (Romans 6:3–4). It is possible that children were baptized in New Testament churches as part of Christian households (Acts 16:33). See also SACRAMENT.

Barabbas A robber and murderer in whose place Jesus was crucified, in accordance with a custom of releasing one prisoner at Passover time (Matthew 27:15–26).

Barak An Israelite leader who commanded Israel's tribal mercenaries alongside Deborah against Canaanite forces. God gave Israel a famous victory by means of the weather, but the honour went to a woman, Jael, who killed the Canaanites' leader, Sisera (Judges 4–5).

barley see CEREALS.

Barnabas A Jewish-Cypriot leader in the early church who had an important ministry in encouraging others. He contributed generously to the Jerusalem church, but his most important action was in persuading the leaders there to accept Saul of Tarsus as a genuine convert (Acts 9:26–7). After leading the young church at Antioch, he was sent out from there with Saul (later Paul) on the church's first missionary journey (Acts 13:1–3). Barnabas was initially the leader, but soon graciously gave way to his younger colleague's greater gifts. Though he separated from Paul over whether Barnabas' cousin Mark should accompany them on a second journey and went his own way to Cyprus, Paul continued to express his admiration for him (Colossians 4:10; 2 Timothy 4:11).

barrenness Several examples are mentioned of barren women who were able to give birth, even in old age, as a result of God's promise or a prophecy (Genesis 21:1–7; Luke 1:36–7). Otherwise, barrenness was often a sign of God's disfavour, especially in relation to the Promised Land itself (Psalm 107:33–4).

Bartholomew One of the twelve apostles, but his name is only included in lists in the first three Gospels (Mark 3:18). Probably the same as Nathanael, who is mentioned only in John's Gospel (John 1:45–51).

Bartimaeus A blind beggar from Jericho who received his sight from Jesus as a result of his persistence (Mark 10:46–52).

Baruch Jeremiah's secretary who faithfully wrote down two editions of his master's prophecies (Jeremiah 36:4–32). His name is also associated with several apocryphal books. See also APOCRYPHA.

Barzillai A wealthy but generous man who helped David when he was fleeing from Absalom (2 Samuel 17:27–9). David never forgot Barzillai's kindness, and instructed Solomon to continue providing for his family (1 Kings 2:7).

Bashan A fertile plateau and a mountain area east of the Sea of Galilee and north of Gilead (Ezekiel 39:18). It was allocated to the half-tribe of Manasseh, but the Israelites were not always able to hold the area. In the New Testament, Jesus healed the Gadarene demoniacs in this region. See map of OLD TESTAMENT ISRAEL.

basin see TABERNACLE.

basket A common container for carrying all kinds of goods, including for presenting firstfruits of the harvest to God (Deuteronomy 26:2). Paul was lowered over the walls of Damascus in a hamper-style basket (Acts 9:25).

bathing see WASHING.

Bathsheba A beautiful woman with whom David committed adultery while her husband Uriah was fighting in Israel's army (2 Samuel 11:2–5). David's first child by her died at seven days old, but her second son, Solomon, became David's successor (1 Kings 1:11–40).

battles Warfare occurs frequently in the Bible, especially in Israel's attempt to occupy the Promised Land. Military conflict could be decided by representative combat (1 Samuel 17; 2 Samuel 2:12–17) as well as by pitched battles. Descriptions of Israel's battles are greatly influenced by the role played by God, who often gave Israel victory or handed them over to defeat in unusual circumstances. The Egyptians were defeated at the Red Sea (Exodus 14) and Jericho taken (Joshua 6), for example, without Israel's army coming into contact with the opposition, and Israel was sometimes victorious even when greatly outnumbered (Judges 7; 2 Chronicles 14:9–15). God might also punish Israel, however, through military defeat (Joshua 7; 2 Kings 17:1–23). Tactics of various kinds were employed, often based on detailed reconnaissance, and including the elements of surprise and speed. The struggle against sin involves individual believers in personal battles, for which God provides both assurance of success and the necessary spiritual weapons (Ephesians 6:10–17; 1 John 2:13–14). The Bible also speaks of a final battle when human and spiritual forces of wickedness take up the offensive against God and his people, but Christ will defeat his opponents and establish his kingdom for ever. See also ARMOUR AND WEAPONS; ARMY.

beans see FOOD AND DRINK.

bear see ANIMALS; STARS.

Beast, the A symbolic description of two opponents of God in the Book of Revelation. One is from the Abyss or bottomless pit, wages war against God and his people and is defeated by Christ in the last battle (Revelation 13:1–10; 19:19–20). The other acts on the authority of the first (Revelation 13:11–18). They represent earthly powers that persecute the church, and their defeat is assured.

Beatitudes see SERMON ON THE MOUNT.

beauty Whether it is spiritual or physical, beauty's true worth must be acknowledged by giving due credit to God as its creator: 'He has made everything beautiful in its time' (Ecclesiastes 3:11). God himself is also worthy of all admiration and enjoyment as the one who is supremely beautiful. When the true source of beauty is not recognized, beautiful things or people can become objects of idolatry or some other kind of snare. Beauty in people may be internal or external, with the former having the advantage over the latter since it does not necessarily fade away. God's choice of Jerusalem gives it an attractiveness irrespective of its physical qualities (Psalm 48:2).

bed see HOME.

bee see INSECTS AND ARACHNIDS.

Beelzebub A name for Satan, based on the name of the god of Ekron and meaning 'lord of flies' (2 Kings 1:6; Matthew 12:24).

beer see WINE AND BEER.

Beersheba An important fortified town in southern Judah, and the traditional southern boundary of Israel (modern Bir es-Seba'). Abraham and Isaac lived there in patriarchal times, but by the eighth century it had become a centre for pagan worship (Amos 8:14). See map of OLD TESTAMENT ISRAEL.

beggar, begging Though begging probably existed throughout most of Israel's history, the law encouraged people to show kindness to the poor. Some of the most notable New Testament healings are of people begging in the street (Mark 10:46; John 9:8; Acts 3:2–3).

behaviour A person's outward actions are a vital sign of their attitude towards God, since they are accountable to God for everything they do. While good behaviour is commended, it cannot earn a person favour with God. Perfection is the only acceptable standard, and only Jesus fulfils that requirement. Good behaviour is important for believers as an indicator of genuine faith (James 2:14–26). While failure can always be forgiven for those who repent, bad behaviour by so-called believers shows either the absence of real faith or renders them liable to a limited form of judgement (1 Corinthians 3:12–15).

Bel and the Dragon see APOCRYPHA.

belief see FAITH.

Belshazzar Co-regent with Nabonidus, the last king of Babylon and crown prince. He is mentioned in Daniel and in Babylonian sources, and is the ruler whose death was predicted by the 'writing on the wall' (Daniel 5). See also DANIEL.

belt see CLOTHING.

Benaiah The captain of David's bodyguard whom Solomon made commander-in-chief of Israel's army as a reward for his loyalty (1 Kings 2:35).

Benedictus The Latin name of the prophecy of Zechariah, father of John the Baptist, celebrating his son's birth (Luke 1:68–79). See also MAGNIFICAT; NUNC DIMITTIS.

Ben-Hadad The name of two or three rulers of the Aramean kingdom of Damascus in the ninth and eighth centuries BC. On the assumption that there were three such individuals, Ahab's opponent was Ben-Hadad II (1 Kings 20).

Benjamin Jacob's youngest son, whose mother, Rachel, died in childbirth. Though initially kept at home when his brothers went to Egypt to find food, he became the means by which Joseph was reconciled to his brothers (Genesis 42:20–45:15). See also BENJAMINITES.

Benjaminites The tribe descended from Benjamin. They occupied the smallest area of any of the tribes, though this included Jerusalem (Joshua 18:11–28). They were engaged in civil war with the rest of Israel before the monarchy (Judges 20–1), and were eventually incorporated into larger Judah. Famous members included King Saul and the apostle Paul. See map of OLD TESTAMENT ISRAEL.

bereavement see BURIAL AND MOURNING.

Bethany The name of two places in the Gospels. The better known is 3 kilometres east of Jerusalem, where Jesus was based during the last week of his earthly life and where Lazarus, Mary and Martha lived (Mark 14:3–9). The other is a place east of the Jordan where John baptized (John 1:28). See map of NEW TESTAMENT ISRAEL.

Bethel An important town throughout the biblical period, formerly called Luz and usually identified with modern Tell Beitin. It was one of the first places in the Promised Land where Abraham built an altar, and the site of Jacob's dream of a stairway from heaven (Genesis 12:8; 28:11–22). It is best known, however, as a major sanctuary on the northern kingdom's southern boundary and a rival to the Jerusalem temple, only 19 kilometres to the south (1 Kings 12:26–33). See map of OLD TESTAMENT ISRAEL.

Bethlehem A village 9 kilometres south-west of Jerusalem, made famous as the home of David and the birthplace of Jesus in fulfilment of prophecy (Micah 5:2; Matthew 2:4–8). The exact site of Jesus' birth remains unknown. See maps of NEW TESTAMENT ISRAEL; OLD TESTAMENT ISRAEL.

Bethuel A background figure in the negotiations between Bethuel's son Laban and Abraham's servant which resulted in Bethuel's daughter Rebekah becoming Isaac's wife (Genesis 24:50). See also REBEKAH.

betrayal Though Jesus' betrayal by his disciple Judas Iscariot is the most notorious example mentioned in the Bible (Matthew 26:14–16, 47–56), it is certainly not the only instance. Betrayal is regarded as something particularly bad which arouses very deep feelings, but Jesus told believers to expect it as part of being persecuted for the sake of the gospel (Matthew 10:21).

Bezalel A skilled craftsman who was in charge of the building of the Tabernacle (Exodus 31:2–5).

Bible Derived through Latin from a Greek word meaning 'books', the word refers to the Bible as a collection of sixty-six books. It is divided into the thirty-nine books of the Old Testament, which was originally written in Hebrew and Aramaic, and the twenty-seven books of the New Testament, first written in Greek. Most of the authors of the Old Testament books are unknown, though in the New Testament the writers of at least most of the letters are known. The text of the Bible is remarkably well preserved, with over 4,000 manuscripts of the Greek New Testament from the second century AD to the invention of printing. This compares very favourably with other ancient texts such as Caesar's *Gallic Wars*, for which only eight manuscripts are known. The oldest Old Testament manuscripts are those from the Dead Sea Scrolls of the second and first centuries BC.

The first Bible translation was that of the Old Testament into Greek in the second and first centuries BC. This was known as the Septuagint, and it rather than the Hebrew is often quoted in the New Testament. This was followed by other important ancient versions in

Aramaic, Syriac and Latin. The Latin translation of Jerome from the fourth century AD became Europe's standard Bible until the Reformation, when the practice of Bible translation really began to mushroom. The major English version for many years was the Authorized or King James Version of 1611, which has only recently been replaced as the most widely used translation. Currently, no single English translation commands universal acceptance, but major versions include the New International Version (NIV), Good News Bible (GNB), New Revised Standard Version (NRSV), New Jerusalem Bible (NJB) and the Revised English Bible (REB). Around the world, the Bible has been translated into well over 2,000 languages, and is easily the world's best-selling book. See also INTERPRETATION, BIBLICAL; SCRIPTURE.

An overview of the Bible

Genesis begins by identifying the God of the Bible as the creator of the entire universe. God placed humankind in a privileged position as sharers in his friendship and stewards of the rest of creation. However, Adam and Eve did not respond to God's trust with their own, and in disobeying him they lost both his friendship and the cooperation of his creation.

God's answer began to unfold when Abraham was singled out as the one through whose descendants God would restore the situation. Due to a severe famine, Abraham's grandson Jacob and his family settled in Egypt, where over 430 years they grew to the size of a small nation. The Egyptians, however, treated them harshly and made them slaves. After displaying his power in the plagues, God used Moses to lead the Israelites out of Egypt, an event known as the Exodus. The escaping Israelites first reached Mount Sinai where God made a covenant with them, showing by way of promises and laws how they were to live in his friendship and care for their people and land.

So far, they had no land of their own, but this was to change as Moses' leadership was passed to Joshua. Joshua led the Israelites into Canaan, which had been promised to Abraham, but which until now had been occupied by other peoples. At last, they were God's people living God's way in the land God had given them.

However, all was not well. The surrounding peoples began fighting with the Israelites for land, and the leaders of Israel had to be soldier-statesmen, called judges. On the whole, with the exception of people like Ruth and Boaz, Israel was failing to live the way God had intended, worshipping the gods of Canaan rather than the true God. Soon they wanted a king like the other nations, so God gave them first Saul and then David.

With David, Israel reached its high point. David brought peace and stability to the nation, while Solomon, his son, built the Temple in Jerusalem as the centrepiece of Israel's worship of God. It was a time of economic, political and religious prosperity, when many psalms and proverbs were written.

It was all too short-lived. With the death of Solomon, the nation divided into two: the northern kingdom of Israel, and the southern kingdom of Judah. Generally speaking, the kings of the northern kingdom led people away from the worship of God; Judah was slightly more successful, though it too had numerous bad kings.

Throughout this time, God repeatedly sent prophets to his people, pleading with them to turn away from idols and enjoy his friendship and rule. Elijah, Amos and others preached to the northern kingdom, but they were ignored and when it was captured by the Assyrians in 722 BC, the northern kingdom dropped out of the story. Isaiah, Jeremiah and the prophets in Judah were also ignored and in 587 BC Jerusalem fell to the Babylonians. While exiled in Babylon, however, some Jews like Daniel retained their faith in God, while prophets like Ezekiel anticipated a better future.

In 539 BC Babylon was conquered by the Persians, who allowed the Jews to return to their homeland. A time of rebuilding began, first of the Temple, and then of the walls of Jerusalem. As the Old Testament closes, God's prophets are challenging the people to rebuild their faith. A four-hundred-year interlude, known as the inter-testamental period, bridges the gap between the Old and New Testaments. During this time, first the Greek and then the Roman Empire exerted military, political and cultural influence over the returned Jews. By the beginning of the New Testament, the Romans had brought relative peace, but the Jews still looked for God to liberate them from Roman control and to re-establish Israel as a great kingdom through his chosen king, the Messiah.

The new era was heralded by John the Baptist when he identified Jesus, a young Jew who had been born in Bethlehem, as the Messiah – the One through whom God would fulfil all his promises to Israel. Through his life, Jesus showed that he had a special relationship with the God of Israel and that he could exercise authority over creation. Jesus announced that the time of God's rule and blessing, known as the kingdom of God, had arrived with him, demonstrating this by his acceptance of marginalised people, and his miracles. The kingdom Jesus brought, however, was not what many Jews were expecting. His claims brought him into conflict with the religious and political leaders, and he was executed by the Romans on a cross. Yet three days later, his body was missing from the tomb where it had been laid, and Jesus himself, alive, met with many of those who had followed him.

After forty days, Jesus ascended into heaven, and in a further ten days, his disciples were filled with the gift of the Holy Spirit. From Jerusalem, followers of Jesus spread out across the world, first locally, but then, particularly through Paul and his companions, even to the heart of the Roman Empire, establishing small communities, or churches. The pastoral and doctrinal issues encountered led to the writing and circulation of letters including those now in the New Testament. The message was simple yet profound: the God of creation and of Israel is the God and Father of Jesus Christ. Jesus' life, death and resurrection were not for himself but for us, and through them he has demonstrated God's love, saved us from the power and effect of sin and made it possible for all creation to enjoy God's friendship and rule. This message is to be shared with all people until Jesus returns to make God's blessing and rule an eternal reality.

Bible translation

As both Judaism and Christianity spread across the world and entered different cultures and ages, it was important for their scriptures to be translated for those who did not have knowledge of the original languages in which they were written.

The original language of the Old Testament was Hebrew, with the exception of a few portions of Ezra, Daniel and Jeremiah, which were written in Chaldee, or Biblical Aramaic. Sometime before the third century BC most of the Old Testament was translated into Aramaic, the local language of Jews in Palestine. These texts, known as the Targums, offer a paraphrase and interpretation of the Hebrew. By the mid-third century BC, many Jews were living in Greek-speaking cities, so a Greek version was

produced called the Septuagint (LXX), so named after the seventy
(or seventy-two) scribes who are thought to have translated it.

All of the New Testament manuscripts were written in Greek. As
the church spread throughout the ancient world, the New
Testament, or sometimes just parts of it, was translated into
numerous languages, including Latin, Syriac and Coptic. The most
influential translation of the whole Bible for the Western Church,
however, was Jerome's Latin translation at the end of the fourth
century. This version, known as the Vulgate, was the official Bible
of the church throughout the Middle Ages until the 16th century
Reformation.

Even before the Reformation, attempts were made to produce
an English translation. The Venerable Bede translated John's
Gospel into Anglo-Saxon in the 7th century, while the Lindisfarne
Gospels date from around AD 950. John Wycliffe was the first to
translate the entire Bible into English near the end of the
fourteenth century. Though he translated from the Latin Vulgate,
he was also critical of some of the practices of the Roman Church,
so his work was banned and his followers persecuted. Wycliffe's
own body was exhumed and burned because of his 'heretical'
views.

The next major event in Bible translation was the work of the
Dutchman Erasmus at the beginning of the 16th century. He
produced a new edition of the Greek New Testament, and a
correspondingly revised Latin version. In paying closer attention
to the original languages, Erasmus paved the way for the work of
the Reformation.

William Tyndale began his life work of translating the Bible into
English in 1525, having fled to the continent to escape hostile
church authorities in England. He used the original languages,
and was the first to publish a printed New Testament in English.
Tyndale was considered a heretic, however, and in 1536 he was
captured and publicly strangled and burned.

Tyndale's work, though, was not in vain, as his influence can be
seen in subsequent translations. In 1535, Miles Coverdale had
edited and published a complete English Bible, and in 1539 the
Matthew Bible was printed in England itself. Other versions
followed, including the Geneva Bible, which was the first Bible to
include verse numbers, and was popular among the common
people.

In 1611, the Authorised, or King James, Version was published,
and was intended to replace the confusing mass of versions. It had

been commissioned by King James I, and was produced by a committee of fifty-four scholars. For nearly three hundred years, this version was unequalled, and it had a significant influence on the development of the English langauge.

At the end of the nineteenth century, the Revised Version was prepared, which changed the text of the Authorised Version in the light of more accurate original manuscripts. Published in 1885, it marked a watershed, after which the number of English versions grew, suiting many different needs.

Versions following the style of the Revised Version, such as the New American Standard and the New Revised Standard, attempt to give a very literal rendition of the original manuscripts. Other versions, such as the Good News Bible and the Contemporary English Version, focus on dynamic equivalence; that is, translating not only words but also concepts from the original into contemporary equivalent English expressions. Other translations, such as *The Message*, offer a paraphrase, using easily-accessible contemporary language. Then there is the New International Version, which stands between the literal group and those attempting dynamic equivalence, and its various editions.

Constant changes in language and cultural idioms mean that the work of translation is never finished. However, while there are so many different English versions, there are still many languages that do not yet have their own translation of the Bible.

Bildad see ELIPHAZ, BILDAD AND ZOPHAR.

Bilhah Rachel's female servant whom she gave to her husband Jacob and by whom he had two sons, Dan and Naphtali (Genesis 30:3–8).

birds A wide variety of birds are mentioned in the Bible, though some species cannot now be identified with precision. They range from large birds of prey such as eagles and vultures, to desert birds like the owl and the ostrich, and to more domesticated varieties such as sparrows, doves and pigeons. A number of migrant birds like storks and swallows are also mentioned, as Palestine is on one of the main migratory routes between Europe and Africa. Birds occasionally played important roles, such as Noah's use of the raven and the dove after the great flood or Elijah being fed by ravens during a famine. More frequently, however, birds are referred to in the context of sacrifice and ritual, and doves and pigeons were regularly offered to God. Birds were also divided into those that could and those that could not be eaten as part of Israel's laws on uncleanness.

Birds	
Cock	Matthew 26:34
Eagle	Isaiah 40:31
Dove	Genesis 8:8–12
Hen	Matthew 23:37
Owl	Isaiah 34:11
Partridge	1 Samuel 26:20
Pigeon	Luke 2:24
Quail	Psalm 105:40
Raven	1 Kings 17:4–6
Sparrow	Luke 12:6–7
Stork	Psalm 104:17
Swallow	Psalm 84:3
Vulture	Matthew 24:28

birthright see FIRSTBORN.

bishop In the New Testament, the term means 'overseer' and is equivalent to 'elder'. A church might have several such bishops at once (Philippians 1:1). The New Testament is more concerned with a bishop's spiritual and personal qualifications than with his office or function (1 Timothy 3:1–7). See also ELDER.

bitterness Though such an attitude often arises as a result of difficult personal circumstances, it is a sin that is to be firmly resisted. Christians must forgive rather than foster bitter feelings (Ephesians 4:31–2).

black see COLOURS.

blacksmith see OCCUPATIONS.

blamelessness A necessary condition for being accepted by God, as demonstrated supremely in Jesus' sacrificial death (Hebrews 9:14). Through their faith in Jesus, believers are regarded as blameless, and even though their current lives are not perfect, God will ensure they are blameless at the last day (Jude 24).

blasphemy Speech or action which misuses and dishonours God's name, and which is condemned in the third commandment (Exodus 20:7). In the New Testament, the concept was extended to speaking against God's representatives and against the temple. The punishment was death by stoning, and both Jesus and Stephen were put to death after being accused of blasphemy. Blasphemy against the Holy Spirit involves determined, persistent rejection of God, which cannot be forgiven because of its extreme seriousness (Mark 3:28–30).

blemish A sign of physical weakness which disqualified animals from being offered to God (Leviticus 22:21). Often in the New Testament, it refers to any spiritual or moral failure which might prevent a person from being acceptable to God, but Jesus will make the church spotless through his own perfection (Ephesians 5:27).

blessing A physical or spiritual gift provided by God and the act by which such gifts are given. Because God's blessings are always good, they indicate God's basic benevolent attitude towards human beings. God's original intention was that everyone should live under his blessings, and some blessings such as the means for producing food are given to everyone. However, God also promised special blessings through Abraham which have now been fulfilled in Christ. These include 'every spiritual blessing in Christ' (Ephesians 1:3), that is, everything that God has provided to enable human beings to enjoy life to the full. These gifts are available through faith in Jesus and by obeying him, though in this life they will often be experienced through suffering.

Blessing also includes the idea of praise and thanksgiving, especially the act of returning thanks to God for his gifts of blessing. God can be blessed for himself even in cases of extreme deprivation or persecution (Job 1:21; Acts 16:19–25). Believers are to bless one another in the name of the Lord by praying for them to receive God's gifts, especially through the famous Aaronic blessing (Numbers 6:24–6).

blindness see DISEASES AND ILLNESSES.

blood An important biblical word which has three different associations. Firstly, it has great significance as a symbol of life (Leviticus 17:11). The spilling of blood, which refers to violent death, is particularly serious. The eating of blood is also forbidden in Old Testament law, and advised against in the church for the sake of good relationships between Jews and Gentiles (Acts 15:29). Secondly, blood refers to the atoning death of a sacrificial victim, and especially to the death of Jesus Christ on the cross. The shedding of Jesus' blood removes the effect of all sin in believers' lives and is the act which institutes the new covenant (Romans 3:25; 1 Corinthians 11:25; Hebrews 9:22). An alternative understanding is that sacrificial blood provides acceptance with God by virtue of the victim's life being released and surrendered to him. Thirdly, blood is a symbol of human guilt, both as a result of sin in general but especially of spilling innocent blood (Psalm 51:14).

blue see COLOURS.

boasting see PRIDE.

boats and ships Despite Palestine's long Mediterranean coastline, the Israelites were not generally enthusiastic sailors, and biblical references to boats and ships often relate to other nations (cf. Ezekiel 27:25–9). Syrians from Tyre and Sidon built and crewed Solomon's fleet (1 Kings 9:26–8), while Jehoshaphat's attempt to construct his own fleet ended in disaster (2 Chronicles 20:35–7). 'Ships of Tarshish' is probably a term for ocean-going trading vessels (Isaiah 60:9), and Tarshish may be connected with Tartessus in Spain. Early Phoenician ships relied on sail power, and were built with a keel and had a fence-like structure along the deck. Merchant galleys propelled by oars were also used in the Mediterranean. The New Testament refers to various sizes of craft, from small fishing-boats on the Sea of Galilee (Matthew 4:21–2) to large grain ships which sailed between Egypt and Italy. The latter was the kind of vessel in which Paul sailed to Rome (Acts 27:6–44), though his other voyages were probably undertaken in smaller coastal boats.

Boaz A wealthy and kind man who married his widowed relative Ruth according to the custom of levirate marriage (Ruth 3–4). Their son Obed was an ancestor of David. See also MARRIAGE; RUTH.

body of Christ see CHURCH.

body, human The body is viewed positively as something that has been created by God, and the Bible does not share the view of the Stoics and the Gnostics that matter was evil. Rather, the body puts people in awe of God and inspires them to praise him (Psalm 139:13–16). Its strength and beauty are to be admired, and it is to be appreciated and cared for. Though temptation and sin are at work through the body, for the Christian it becomes a temple for the Holy Spirit. Believers are also to offer their physical bodies to God as the supreme act of worship (Romans 12:1).

The body comprises physical, spiritual and psychological elements (1 Thessalonians 5:23). Internal features such as the spirit or heart can express a person's relationship with God through dependence of the human spirit on God's Spirit or the creation of a new heart that is sensitive to God. Various physical organs are also used symbolically to express attitudes and emotions. The liver, for example, is the seat of the emotions (Psalm 73:21), the stomach symbolizes the inner thoughts (Ezekiel 3:3) and the heart represents the mind and will (Proverbs 16:1). But biblical thought regards each person as a unity and not as a collection of several components, with the individual parts expressing some aspect of the whole rather than an isolated feature. The body is finally subject to death. It can, however, be renewed through regeneration, and the Bible speaks of the future life in terms of bodily resurrection and a spiritual body rather than a disembodied spirit (1 Corinthians 15:35–57). Jesus also bears the marks of his suffering in his heavenly body.

boldness Believers are encouraged to be bold in approaching God and in making the gospel known to others (Acts 4:29–31; Hebrews 10:22). This attitude comes from being confident about the truth of the gospel and secure in one's own relationship with God. See also CONFIDENCE.

bones In Hebrew thought, human bones can represent both life and death, and are a mark of one's state of health. The Hebrew phrase 'bone and flesh' represents a living body (Job 2:5), and healthy bones are a sign of a healthy person (Proverbs 15:30). The bones of dead people are to be treated with respect, and anyone who touches unburied bones becomes unclean (Numbers 19:16).

book see WRITING.

book of the covenant A term for the collection of laws in Exodus 20:22–23:33, and also for the scroll discovered by Josiah in the temple (2 Kings 23:2). The latter included part or all of Deuteronomy.

book of the law A term referring to various collections of Old Testament laws, and probably a way of referring to the written form of God's law. It was important in guiding God's people and for providing a foundation for national life (Joshua 1:7–8; Nehemiah 8:1–18).

book of life In the Old Testament, the term refers to a list of those who are physically alive (Psalm 69:28) but in the New Testament to those who will be part of the life to come (Revelation 3:5).

booths, feast of see TABERNACLES, FEAST OF.

born again see NEW BIRTH.

borrowing and lending Encouragements are given to be realistic as well as generous. God's people are to be willing to lend without charging interest or necessarily expecting repayment (Deuteronomy 23:19–20). They must also not be too proud to borrow, as Jesus' own example shows (Matthew 21:1–3), but must be equally aware of the responsibilities of repaying loans and providing restitution for loss.

boundary The Old Testament makes special provision for marking property boundaries to reduce exploitation of the poor (Deuteronomy 19:14).

bow and arrow see ARMOUR AND WEAPONS.

bowls see TABERNACLE; UTENSILS.

branch 1. Branches of various kinds were used in making temporary shelters for the Feast of Tabernacles. Palm branches were particularly popular as a way of welcoming Jesus on his final entry into Jerusalem (Matthew 21:8).

2. A special Old Testament term for the Messiah, indicating his descent from David's line (Jeremiah 23:5–6).

bread The staple food of people throughout the ancient Near East. Special loaves called the 'bread of the Presence' (or shewbread) were kept in the Tabernacle or Temple. The manna in the wilderness was called 'bread from heaven' (Exodus 16:4). See also TABERNACLE; TEMPLE.

breastpiece/breastplate A piece of clothing worn over the chest. The breastpiece was worn by the high priest (Leviticus 8:5–9). It was decorated with twelve stones representing Israel's twelve tribes, and contained the Urim and Thummim for decision-making. A breastplate was part of a soldier's armour, and is used as a symbol of the righteousness of the believer (Ephesians 6:14). See also PRIEST.

bribery Though the practice was forbidden in the Old Testament, examples do occur and are roundly condemned (Isaiah 5:22–3; Acts 24:26).

brick see ARCHITECTURE.

bride, bridegroom see MARRIAGE.

brimstone see SULPHUR.

bronze see METALS AND MINING.

bronze altar see ALTAR.

builder see OCCUPATIONS.

buildings see ARCHITECTURE.

Bul see CALENDAR, JEWISH.

bull see ANIMALS.

burial and mourning Where possible, corpses were buried in a rock-cut tomb. Several have been found around Jerusalem in the New Testament period, and Abraham's family were all buried in a cave near Hebron (Genesis 49:29–32). In the later examples, the body would be laid in a recess behind a ledge, and the entrance closed by a large boulder. Poorer people were laid in common graves, and the graves of criminals or enemies were sometimes marked with a pile of stones. Burial places of various kinds were usually located outside the city. To leave a body unburied was a mark of great disrespect, and cremation was not an Israelite practice.

Burial took place as soon as possible, sometimes on the same day as death, and was marked by extensive mourning customs. Professional, usually female, mourners played an important role, singing traditional laments (Mark 5:38–39). People would tear their clothes, wear sackcloth, let their hair hang loose, and scatter dust and ashes (2 Samuel 1:11–12), though the Israelites were forbidden to adopt the Canaanite practices of cutting themselves and shaving the front of the head. In the New Testament period, the corpse was anointed with perfumes and embalmed, and then wrapped in grave clothes. Mourning ceremonies might last for some time. Seven days was common around the time of Christ, while Jacob was mourned for seventy days in Egypt (Genesis 50:3).

burning bush A bush to which Moses was attracted in the wilderness because it appeared to be burning without being consumed. The Bible attributes this to the presence of the holy God, and attempts to explain the incident by identifying a particular species of bush or some natural phenomenon such as St Elmo's fire have not been successful (Exodus 3:1–6).

burnt offering A common type of Israelite sacrifice in which an animal was offered completely to God (Leviticus 1; 6:8–13). It was also known as a whole offering. The idea lying behind it is probably to represent a worshipper's giving of themselves entirely to God.

bush see TREES AND BUSHES.

bushel see WEIGHTS AND MEASURES.

butler see CUPBEARER.

butter see FOOD.

buying and selling Various kinds of transactions are mentioned, especially the sale of land and of slaves, and the importance of conducting business according to God's standards is underlined. Fairness and honesty should characterize the business dealings of God's people, who must avoid greed and exploitation. Special respect must be given to the Sabbath (Nehemiah 13:15–22) and to the Temple (Matthew 21:12–13).

C

Caesar The title of the Roman emperors from Augustus to Nero. Those mentioned in the New Testament are Augustus (27 BC–14 AD; Luke 2:1), Tiberius (14–37 AD; Luke 3:1), and Claudius (41–54 AD; Acts 11:28), though Nero (54–68 AD) with his persecution of Christians also casts his shadow over the early church.

Caesarea A city named after Caesar Augustus, which was the official residence of Herodian kings and Roman procurators. It was situated on the Mediterranean coast about 100 kilometres north-west of Jerusalem and based around its artificial harbour. It was the scene of the conversion of the Roman centurion Cornelius (Acts 10). Philip brought Christianity there, and Paul appeared before Felix and was imprisoned there for two years (Acts 23:23–26:32). See map of NEW TESTAMENT ISRAEL; PAUL'S JOURNEYS.

Caesarea Philippi A city at the foot of Mount Hermon in northern Transjordan. Earlier called Paneas, it was renamed by Philip the tetrarch in honour of Caesar Augustus, the epithet distinguishing it from Caesarea on the coast. It is the place where Peter first recognized Jesus as the Messiah (Matthew 16:13–20). See map of NEW TESTAMENT ISRAEL.

Caiaphas High priest of the Jews who supervised the trials of Jesus (John 18:24–8) and of Peter and John (Acts 4:6). He seems to have acted alongside his father-in-law, Annas.

Cain Adam and Eve's eldest son, who murdered his brother Abel. He became a wanderer, but God placed some kind of mark on him for his protection (Genesis 4).

calamus see PLANTS.

Caleb One of two Israelite spies who entered the Promised Land because of his wholehearted faith (Numbers 13–14).

Calendar, Jewish After the exile, the year began in the spring after the Babylonian pattern, though there is some evidence that in the pre-exilic period it began in the autumn. The Israelites followed a lunar calendar with months of twenty-nine or thirty days, a system which required an extra or intercalary month from time to time. The months were known by numbers as well as by names, so that Nisan or Abib was also known as the first month (in the spring). The names of the months were changed after the exile. Dates were often reckoned by seasons or by major festivals (John 7:2, 37), and sometimes by reference to the reigns of foreign emperors (Luke 2:1).

Calendar, Jewish			
First month	Nisan or Abib	Mar/Apr	Exodus 13:4
Second month	Iyyar or Ziv	Apr/May	1 Kings 6:1
Third month	Sivan	May/Jun	Esther 8:9
Fourth month	Tammuz	Jun/Jul	
Fifth month	Ab	Jul/Aug	
Sixth month	Elul	Aug/Sep	Nehemiah 6:15
Seventh month	Tishri or Ethanim	Sept/Oct	1 Kings 8:2
Eighth month	Marchesvan or Bul	Oct/Nov	1 Kings 6:38
Ninth month	Kislev	Nov/Dec	Nehemiah 1:1
Tenth month	Tebeth	Dec/Jan	Esther 2:16
Eleventh month	Shebat	Jan/Feb	Zechariah 1:7
Twelth month	Adar	Feb/Mar	Esther 3:7

calf, golden An object of worship made by the Israelites while Moses was with God on Mount Sinai (Exodus 32). Though Moses destroyed it, similar calves were worshipped in the northern kingdom at Dan and Bethel (1 Kings 12:28–33).

call An experience in which God calls individuals to serve him, though it usually involves some objection on their part. It was characteristic of the prophets, the servant of the Lord, and the apostles (Isaiah 6:1–8). Also used of God's invitation to all people to turn to him (Acts 17:30).

Calvary see GOLGOTHA.

camel Used mainly by the patriarchs and by Israel's neighbours, especially the Arabs, as a beast of burden (1 Kings 10:2).

Cana A small town in western Galilee which was the site of Jesus' first miracle (John 2:1–11). See map of NEW TESTAMENT ISRAEL.

Canaan, Canaanites In the Old Testament and other ancient texts, Canaan or Canaanite is used in three different senses: (i) the coastal plain of Syria-Palestine, especially the Phoenician cities to the north;

(ii) the whole of Syria-Palestine; and (iii) as a word for a 'trader'. The Bible uses it to refer rather loosely to the pre-Israelite inhabitants of the Promised Land. In this sense it overlaps with the Amorites, with whom the Canaanites had lived in Syria–Palestine from before 2000 BC. In some biblical passages, the Canaanites were found in the valleys and the coastal plain, while the Amorites lived in the hills (Numbers 13:29).

For most of the Old Testament period and earlier, the Canaanites were organized in small city-states. They were assimilated rather than conquered by David in the tenth century BC. Canaanite culture, however, especially its religious ideas and practices, was a constant threat to Israel's well-being, and in the end, the writer of Kings saw its influence as a major factor in Israel's downfall (2 Kings 17:7–23). Their commitment to idolatry and the lack of morality is repeatedly attacked in the Old Testament. A fuller picture of Canaanite life and literature occurs in fourteenth- and thirteenth-century BC texts found at Ugarit in northern Syria.

Capernaum An important town (modern Tell Hum) on the north-western shore of the Sea of Galilee. Though Jesus performed several miracles there, the people did not respond to his ministry (Matthew 11:23–4). Excavation there has revealed the best preserved synagogue in Galilee, dating from the third or fourth century AD. See map of NEW TESTAMENT ISRAEL.

capital punishment see DEATH PENALTY.

capstone see CORNERSTONE.

captain see ARMY.

captivity see EXILE.

caravan see TRADE; TRAVEL.

Carmel, Mount The name of a mountain range stretching south-east from the Mediterranean near Acre, and of its chief peak at the north-western end where Elijah defeated the prophets of Baal (1 Kings 18). See map of NEW TESTAMENT ISRAEL; OLD TESTAMENT ISRAEL.

casting of lots see LOTS, CASTING OF.

cattle An important sign of wealth and often used for sacrificial purposes (Genesis 12:16). Oxen were important working animals, though the fattened ox was a sign of luxury (Matthew 22:4).

caves see BURIAL AND MOURNING.

cedar see TREES AND BUSHES.

celebrations see FEASTS AND FESTIVALS.

celibacy see SINGLENESS.

Cenchrea see map of PAUL'S JOURNEYS.

censer see TABERNACLE.

census Conducted for either military or taxation purposes. Though David was criticized for conducting a census, he was probably motivated by pride rather than obedience to God (2 Samuel 24). The census which brought Joseph and Mary to Bethlehem (Luke 2:1–5) has parallels with other Roman examples.

centurion see ARMY.

Cephas see PETER.

cereals The main varieties of corn were barley and wheat. Barley was the population's main staple food, since it can grow on poorer soil than wheat. The main type of wheat was emmer, which was similar to the hard wheat widely grown in Hellenistic times. Wheat was a symbol of God's generous provision for his people (Psalm 147:14).

chaff Husks and stalks blown away during the winnowing process or subsequently burned, and a symbol of wicked people and their fate before God (Psalm 1:4).

chair see HOME.

Chaldea, Chaldeans see BABYLON.

character The qualities that make someone a particular kind of person. Good character is important as a complement to a believer's behaviour and faith in God. In the Sermon on the Mount, Jesus describes the kind of characteristics that he expects of his disciples and which he exhibited in his own life (Matthew 5:3–10). Paul highlights love as the supreme element in Christian character (1 Corinthians 13). The qualities God requires can only be achieved as the Holy Spirit produces his fruit in believers' lives (Galatians 5:16–26).

chariot see TRAVEL.

cheese see FOOD.

Chemosh The chief god of the Moabites (1 Kings 11:7), mentioned on the Moabite Stone as well as in the Old Testament. See also MOAB, MOABITES.

cherub, cherubim A type of heavenly being that served God in his holy presence. Winged figures representing cherubim were located above the ark of the covenant in the Most Holy Place (Exodus 25:18–22). Ezekiel also portrays them with hands and faces as well as wings, and having complete freedom of movement (Ezekiel 10). Cherubim is the Hebrew plural of cherub. See also TABERNACLE.

chief priest see PRIEST.

child, children see FAMILY.

child sacrifice This practice was occasionally observed in the ancient Near East, mainly in Phoenicia. A few examples are mentioned in Israel, even though it was expressly forbidden in Old Testament law as a foreign pagan custom. God's provision of a substitute instead of the sacrifice of Abraham's son Isaac (Genesis 22) may be an implied condemnation of the practice.

childbirth Pain in childbirth is explained as a consequence of the fall of Adam and Eve, but it does not take away either the parents' sense of joy or God's involvement. God is frequently said to be actively involved in the birth of a child, especially when a previously barren couple see their prayers answered. The births of Isaac and Jesus are special demonstrations of God doing the impossible (Genesis 18:14; Luke 1:36–7).

Chinnereth see GALILEE, SEA OF.

chisel see TOOLS.

Christ see JESUS CHRIST, LIFE OF.

Christian First used as a nickname in the mainly Gentile church at Antioch in Syria, with the sense of 'one who belongs to Christ' (Acts 11:26). Though it occurs only three times in the New Testament and is only one of several descriptions of believers, the term became established very quickly.

Chronicles, 1 and 2

Structure

    Genealogies of all Israel (1 Chronicles 1–9)
    Reigns of David and Solomon (1 Chronicles 10–2 Chronicles 9)
    Kingdom of Judah (2 Chronicles 10–36)

Famous passages

    God's covenant with David (1 Chronicles 17:1–15)
    David's prayer of thanks (1 Chronicles 29:10–20)
    God appears to Solomon (2 Chronicles 7:11–22)
    Jehoshaphat's victory (2 Chronicles 20:1–30)
    Manasseh's conversion (2 Chronicles 33:10–17)

The history of God's people in 1 and 2 Chronicles starts with Adam and ends with an invitation to return from the Babylonian exile. Since it covers some of the same ground as Samuel and Kings, Chronicles is sometimes regarded either as a supplement to these books or as an alternative version of Israel's history. But Chronicles is actually quite different from these earlier works. It was completed much later than Samuel or Kings, probably in the early fourth century BC, and was written for a different audience. While it is difficult to be absolutely sure about Chronicles' precise purpose, references to the restoration of Israel in the books' final paragraph and in God's promise to Solomon in 2 Chronicles 7:11–22 seem to provide a strong clue. The latter passage, which has no parallel in Kings, highlights God's promise to 'forgive their sin and [will] heal their land' (2 Chronicles 7:14). This emphasis on restoration, which is amplified by individual examples like the conversion of the notorious king Manasseh (2 Chronicles 33:1–20), suggests that Chronicles is about God's intention to restore the people and the land after the exile.

The work has been put together by an editor (often called the Chronicler) who has used a considerable number of sources from both inside and outside the Bible. The biblical sources are particularly important. The Chronicler has used the Old Testament's historical books as a framework and has also quoted extensively from the law, the prophets and the Psalms. The effect of this approach is to show how God's purposes have remained essentially unchanged throughout the Old Testament period.

The major themes of Chronicles are based on God's promises, especially those given to David and Solomon, about the Jerusalem temple and the Davidic monarchy. Examples are taken from Israel's past to provide a pattern for the present and hope for the future. The Chronicler is keen to see the old forms of worship established after the exile (cf. 2 Chronicles 8:12–15; 29:3–36), and by concentrating on the pre-exilic history of Judah rather than of Israel he implies that David's descendants remain central to God's purposes after the exile. However, the Chronicler is also concerned for all Israel. By mentioning occasions when northerners and southerners worshipped together (2 Chronicles 30:1–27), and by including the genealogies of 1 Chronicles 1–9, he shows that all the tribes are still part of Israel.

church The Bible refers to the church as a group of people committed to Jesus Christ rather than as an institution or a building. Church buildings did not develop until well after the New Testament, since Christians met initially in synagogues and then in houses. The few details of the church as an institution which are mentioned are far less significant than the idea of the church as a living organism.

Church is the New Testament term for the people of God. It continues the Old Testament concept of Israel as the people of God, and many of the same descriptions used of Israel such as God's bride or God's flock are also applied to the church (Acts 20:28–9; Ephesians

5:25–32). The church comprises those who follow Jesus as Messiah and Lord, whatever their background, and the New Testament emphasizes their unity in the faith much more than the emerging differences between churches. The idea of unity is also reflected in other metaphors for the church such as the body of Christ, God's household or family and God's building or temple.

The church is universal, regional and local. Its wider unity is sometimes expressed in practical terms, such as through Paul's collection in Greece and Asia Minor for the support of poor Christians in Jerusalem. The Bible is remarkably quiet about forms of church government, with local churches having some freedom to develop their own structures. Rather, emphasis is placed on the need for leaders to be gifted by God and of good character, and on church members' taking their responsibilities seriously. The basic features of church life were fellowship, teaching, prayer and breaking of bread or the Lord's Supper (Acts 2:42), and new converts were brought into the church through baptism.

The church exists to be God's people in the world (1 Peter 2:9–10), with a twofold responsibility towards God and towards unbelievers. In relation to God, the church is to praise him and to live in union with Christ through the power of the Spirit. In relation to the world, the church is to take the gospel to every nation in order to make further disciples of Christ. To this end, Jesus poured out his Spirit on the church at Pentecost so that they could be his witnesses to the ends of the earth (Acts 1:8).

Cilicia A Roman province in south-eastern Asia Minor, linking Syria and Asia Minor. Tarsus, the birthplace of Paul, was one of its major cities (Acts 21:39).

cinnamon SEE HERBS AND SPICES.

circumcision The practice of cutting off the foreskin of the penis. The custom was observed in many ancient societies at puberty or as a premarital rite, but it was performed in Israel on babies a week old. It goes back to Abraham's son Isaac, for whom it was a physical sign of God's covenant promise that many descendants would come from him (Genesis 17). Circumcision became increasingly important after the exile as a sign of belonging to Judaism, but in the New Testament, only the inward circumcision of the heart as a metaphor for obedience to Christ has any value before God (Romans 2:25–9).

cistern An underground reservoir for storing water collected from a spring or from rainfall. Joseph and Jeremiah were left to die in such places (Genesis 37:20–8; Jeremiah 38:6–13).

cities of refuge Six cities that were set apart as places of asylum for people who had killed accidentally (Numbers 35:6–34). The guilty person was to stay there until the current high priest died, and was then free. Three were situated on each side of the Jordan so that no one had too far to go. It is unknown whether these regulations were ever put into practice.

city Cities are referred to from the beginning of the Bible (Genesis 4:17) to its end (Revelation 21:1–22:6). Though cities are neutral in themselves, they have a tendency to bring out the best and the worst in human society. A good example is the contrast in Revelation between the cities of Babylon and of Jerusalem, representing opposite types of human communities. The former portrays the sins and destruction of Rome while the latter is the holy city where God lives with his people.

Regional life in Palestine centred on walled cities which were often the capital of small city-states. An administrative complex was located at the city's centre, while the city gate was an important area for commerce and law. The city or *polis* in New Testament times was a place of Greek culture with its own privileges, though this is only marginally reflected in the New Testament itself. Much more important is the role of Jerusalem as the place God chose as his earthly dwelling-place. Since, however, the earthly Jerusalem is the place where Jesus was killed, it will be destroyed like Sodom (Isaiah 1:10; Revelation 11:8) and be replaced by the heavenly Jerusalem as the city of the new covenant.

Claudius see CAESAR.

clay see ARTS AND CRAFTS.

clean and unclean A ritual concept according to which anything could be either clean or unclean. Various things such as food, animals and objects might be regarded as unclean, as well as people involved in experiences such as disease, sexual intercourse or touching a corpse. The concept is best explained as a way of symbolizing varying degrees of holiness. Clean things were associated with what was ordinary, but were less sacred than holy things. Unclean things represented the Gentiles, clean things the Israelites, and holy things the priests. Uncleanness could be removed by waiting certain periods of time, by washing and by sacrifice. Jesus abolished the ceremonial distinction between clean and unclean, and emphasized the moral aspects instead (Mark 7:17–23), but faithful Jews like Peter found it hard to change their old ways (cf. Acts 10:9–48).

climate see WEATHER.

cloak see CLOTHING.

clothing Men's clothing usually consisted of a loincloth from the waist to the knee, a shirt or tunic of linen or wool reaching to the knees or ankles, and the cloak, which was thrown over one or both shoulders with openings for the arms at the sides. The shirt was often worn with a belt, and the cloak was presumably worn only in colder weather. A folded square of cloth or turban was worn as protection against the sun, and sandals were the normal form of footwear. Women's clothing was similar to men's, but was probably distinguished by its colour, variety and style. The women wore a long cape covering their heads and reaching down to the ankles, and wealthy women also wore a veil. For special occasions, more costly material such as high-quality linen or purple cloth was worn, and white was often the preferred colour. Decorated hems and edges were also a means of showing off clothes to special effect. Joseph's 'coat of many colours' is usually now thought to be a long-sleeved garment, and since most cloaks were sleeveless it was clearly of special value. In New Testament times, the longflowing stole or robe was used for non-manual tasks. Jesus told his disciples not to be anxious about clothing, since God would provide whatever his people needed (Matthew 6:25–34).

Clothing

Men's clothing

Belt	1 Samuel 18:4
Cloak	2 Timothy 4:13
Decorated coat	Genesis 37:3
Hairy cloak	Matthew 3:4
Loincloth	Job 12:18
Robes	Mark 12:38
Sandals	Joshua 5:15
Tassels	Matthew 23:5
Tunic or shirt	Luke 3:11
Turban	Ezekiel 24:17

Women's clothing

Cape	Isaiah 3:22
Decorated coat	2 Samuel 13:18–19
Head-dress	Isaiah 3:20
Jewellery	Isaiah 3:18–23
Linen garments	Proverbs 31:24
Veil	Song of Songs 4:1

coal Associated with domestic cooking, with blacksmiths, and with
the fire on the altar. Burning coal sometimes symbolized God's
holiness (2 Samuel 22:8–9).

coat of armour see ARMOUR AND WEAPONS.

coins see MONEY.

Colossae A cosmopolitan city between Ephesus and Sardis, about
15 kilometres south-east of Laodicea (in modern Turkey). The city
was declining in the first century AD, but a church was founded there
by Epaphras (Colossians 1:7). Paul wrote one letter to the church and
another to Philemon, who was a member there. See also COLOSSIANS,
LETTER TO THE.

Colossians, letter to the

Structure
 Christ and his church at Colossae (1:1–2:5)
 Continuing the Christian life (2:6–4:6)
 Final greetings (4:7–18)

Famous passages
 A hymn to Christ (1:15–20)
 Raised with Christ (3:1–4)

Paul probably wrote Colossians from prison in Rome about 60 or
61 AD, though Ephesus in the mid–50s is another possibility. Paul's
authorship of Colossians has sometimes been questioned on the
basis that it contains ideas that are later than Paul's other writings,
but the close connection between 4:7–18 and Philemon makes it very
likely that Paul wrote both letters.

The letter was written against the background of the 'Colossian
heresy', a teaching which included both Jewish and Greek elements.
This teaching seems to have been promoted by a spiritual élite with
mystic tendencies who insisted on aspects of Greek philosophy and
on the observance of Jewish laws such as the sabbath and religious
festivals.

Paul's response was to emphasize the supremacy and sufficiency
of Christ for everything in the Christian life. A person who believes
in Christ does not need to add anything to what Christ is or what he
provides. Just as 'in Christ all the fulness of the Deity lives in bodily
form', so Christians 'have been given fulness in Christ' (2:9–10). As a
result, they are to live out their faith on the basis that they have
already died and been raised with him (2:6, 11–12; 3:1–4).

colours Though a wide range of colours is mentioned in the Bible,
they are not referred to frequently. This is partly because the

Israelites were less interested in colour for its own sake, and partly because the Bible does not contain a wide range of aesthetic literature. The Old Testament tends to associate colour with the material of which an article is made, so that purple meant reddish, usually woollen, cloth. New Testament Greek concentrates more on the contrast between light and shade than between different colours. Throughout the Bible, colours are often used symbolically, white often representing purity and red being linked with war and death.

Colours	
Black	Song of Songs 5:11
Blue	Exodus 26:1
Brown	Zechariah 1:8
Crimson	Isaiah 63:1
Green	Mark 6:39
Purple	Acts 16:14
Red	Isaiah 1:18
Scarlet	Joshua 2:21
White	Mark 9:3
Yellow	Revelation 9:17

colt see DONKEY.

comforter see COUNSELLOR.

coming of Christ see LAST THINGS.

commander see ARMY.

commandments see TEN COMMANDMENTS.

commemorate see REMEMBER, REMEMBRANCE.

commitment Dedication of oneself to God as a response to God's giving of himself to his people and the world. God expects people to be wholeheartedly committed to him and to his will for their lives, as in the 'first and greatest commandment' that people must love God with all their heart, soul, mind and strength (Matthew 22:37–8). The clearest example of this is Jesus' own commitment to his Father as summarized in his prayer: 'Not as I will, but as you will' (Matthew 26:39). Conversely, commitment to worldly values and especially half-hearted commitment to God are consistently criticized (Revelation 3:15–16). See also WHOLEHEARTEDNESS.

Communion see LORD'S SUPPER.

compassion An aspect of God's loving nature, especially his sympathy with and understanding of human weakness. Jesus' ministry was motivated by compassion, and is reflected in his concern for sinners, his seeking the lost, and many of his healing

miracles (Matthew 9:36; Mark 1:41). Also a central element in
Christian character, which should be practically demonstrated
through action (1 John 3:17). See also LOVE.

complaints Complaints are sometimes encouraged as well as
discouraged. The Israelites in the wilderness were punished for
complaining constantly against God because they did not believe in
his provision (Numbers 11:1–6). On the other hand, the Psalms and
Job often contain complaints which God approves as an expression
of a sufferer's faith (Psalm 64:1).

conceit see PRIDE.

concubine A husband's female partner, but without the status of a
wife. Such women were commonly found in more wealthy
households in the ancient world. Abraham and Jacob produced
children through their wives' slavegirls, and Solomon had hundreds
of concubines in addition to his wives (1 Kings 11:3).

confession Admitting sin is part of repentance. God promises
faithfully to forgive all who repent, but expects confession to be
accompanied by relevant actions. It is sometimes appropriate to
confess one's sins to another person (James 5:16). See also REPENTANCE.

confidence A firm trust or belief. Christian confidence is based on
God's promise rather than personal feeling or achievement,
especially concerning the complete forgiveness which Christ
achieved through his death. Because of this sure foundation,
believers can show boldness in the world and persistence in
suffering (Hebrews 10:35–6). See also BOLDNESS.

congregation see CHURCH.

conscience An inner ability which enables a person to distinguish
between right and wrong. Though it is a gift from God, by itself it is
not a completely reliable guide. The conscience can be cleansed
through confession of sin (Hebrews 10:22), though persistent sin can
reduce or even nullify its effectiveness (1 Timothy 4:2). Christians
may legitimately differ from one another over secondary matters on
grounds of conscience.

consecration see COMMITMENT; SANCTIFICATION.

contentment An attitude of quiet happiness towards life. It is
especially commended by Paul (Philippians 4:11–13), and is
characterized by a conviction that God is always with his people and
will always provide for them, whatever their circumstances. It is
based on faith, not on stoicism or fatalism.

conversion Though the actual word is rare in the Bible, the term
describes the common experience by which a person turns to Christ
in repentance and faith (Acts 20:21). Strictly speaking, conversion

refers to a human activity, but underlying it is the work of God's
grace (Ephesians 2:8–9). Conversion involves a complete change of
direction in life because through it a new relationship with God is
established. See also FAITH; REPENTANCE.

conviction of sin A strong sense of self-awareness that a person is
guilty before God because of the presence of sin in their life. This is
attributed to the work of the Holy Spirit, but is also stimulated by a
knowledge of the requirements of God's law (John 16:8–11).
Conviction often, but certainly not automatically, leads to repentance
and faith (Luke 15:17–21).

cooking Almost all food was prepared at home. Most meals were cooked
over an open wood fire, though bread and other food was baked in
rough pottery or in a mud-brick oven situated in the courtyard (Exodus
8:3). Most cooking pots were made of pottery, with a rounded base and
wide neck. Cooking methods included boiling, roasting and baking.
Meat, vegetables and corn are mentioned as cooked foods.

copper see METALS AND STONE.

cor see WEIGHTS AND MEASURES.

coriander see HERBS AND SPICES.

Corinth A major port in ancient Greece and the Roman Empire. It
was known for its wealth, its athletics, its immorality and its
religious pluralism. The church which Paul founded (Acts 18)
reflected this cosmopolitan, largely Gentile background, but though
this caused more problems than usual, Paul's letters suggest that the
worst was already past. See also CORINTHIANS, 1 AND 2. See map of
PAUL'S JOURNEYS.

Corinthians, 1 and 2

Structure

1 Corinthians
    Thanks for the church (1:1–9)
    Divisions in the church (1:10–4:21)
    Issues in the church (5:1–11:1)
    Worship in the church (11:2–14:40)
    The resurrection (15:1–58)
    Personal requests (16:1–24)

2 Corinthians
    Thanks for God's comfort (1:1–11)
    Paul defends his ministry (1:12–7:16)
    Collection for Christians at Jerusalem (8:1–9:15)
    Paul boasts in God's strength and grace (10:1–13:14)

> **Famous passages**
> 'We preach Christ crucified' (1 Corinthians 1:23)
> The greatest gift is love (1 Corinthians 13)
> The resurrection (1 Corinthians 15)
> The ministry of reconciliation (2 Corinthians 5:18–21)
> 'God loves a cheerful giver' (2 Corinthians 9:7)
> Paul's sufferings (2 Corinthians 11:16–12:10)

Paul had frequent and sometimes stormy contacts with the church at Corinth. It is likely that he wrote them at least four letters, of which 1 Corinthians is the second (cf. 1 Corinthians 5:9) and 2 Corinthians probably the fourth (cf. 2 Corinthians 2:3; 7:8). The former was written early in 55 AD while Paul was in Ephesus and the latter from Macedonia about a year later. In between these two letters Paul also wrote a letter 'with many tears' (2 Corinthians 2:4) following a 'painful visit' (2 Corinthians 2:1). It is possible that 2 Corinthians 10–13 is itself the tearful letter, since the style and content of these chapters shows a marked change from chapters 1–9, but other explanations are possible, including that chapters 10–13 may be a fifth letter.

Paul's correspondence with Corinth provides evidence of the depth of the difficulties. 1 Corinthians deals with a range of serious pastoral problems, including divisions in the church, sexual immorality and incest, lawsuits between fellow Christians, marriage and divorce, eating food previously sacrificed to idols, financial support for Christian ministers, disorderly behaviour at the Lord's Supper, misuse of spiritual gifts in worship and heretical views on the resurrection. 2 Corinthians is more concerned with a single issue, namely Paul's defence of his ministry against accusations by certain leaders at Corinth that he was acting on his own authority and not competent to be an apostle.

But it was not all bad news. Paul affirms that the Corinthians did not lack any spiritual gift, and he gives praise for what God has already done in their lives (1 Corinthians 1:4–9; 6:11). He is also delighted with a good report from Titus (2 Corinthians 7:5–16), and boasts to other churches about their generosity towards the Christians in Jerusalem (2 Corinthians 9:1–2).

Three themes seem to draw most of these issues together. First, the nature and life of the church as the 'body of Christ' and the 'temple of God' must be expressed in unity and love. Second, Christian ministry must often come to terms with suffering and weakness. These are not necessarily a disadvantage, since God's power is 'made perfect in weakness' (2 Corinthians 12:9). Third, the ups and downs of the present life belong in the context of God's final purposes. The Christian life must be lived between the twin poles of the power of the cross (1 Corinthians 1:10–4:21) and the sure and certain hope of the resurrection (1 Corinthians 15; 2 Corinthians 5:1–10).

corn see CEREALS.

Cornelius A Roman centurion who became Peter's first Gentile convert and on whom the Holy Spirit came as had happened at Pentecost. The whole experience confirmed that the gospel was just as much for Gentiles as for Jews (Acts 10–11).

cornerstone Either a foundation stone, or in Psalm 118:22 and its New Testament quotations, the capstone which completes an arch or is laid at the top corner of a building. The concept is applied to Christ and the apostles in the New Testament (Ephesians 2:20).

corruption see BRIBERY.

cosmetics and perfumery Cosmetics and perfumes were widely used in the ancient world. Their basic purpose was hygienic and to protect the body with oil against the effects of the sun. More expensive varieties, however, were also used, especially by women, to enhance beauty. Black mineral pastes for the eyes and eyebrows were particularly popular (Jeremiah 4:30). Religious uses included the holy anointing oil and incense (Exodus 30:25).

couch see HOME.

council of Jerusalem A special meeting of the early church which confirmed God's intention to treat Gentiles and Jews on an equal basis. A circular letter was sent to Gentile churches acknowledging this, but also asking them to recognize certain Jewish sensibilities and keep the Old Testament's basic moral standards (Acts 15).

counsellor A term for Jesus and the Holy Spirit meaning one who helps, strengthens and speaks for another (John 14:16–17; 1 John 2:1).

courage see BOLDNESS.

courtyard see TABERNACLE.

covenant The Bible's main word for describing the relationship between God and his people, but also frequently used of inter-human relationships. In ordinary usage, it is a legal word for a contract or treaty between two or more individuals or groups. These kinds of covenants can include marriage contracts, friendship pacts and international treaties, and may be between equals or between a superior and an inferior party. When the word is applied to God's relationship with his people, however, it has a different emphasis, being primarily associated with God's free commitment rather than a contract, though God still formally binds himself to his people.

God entered into a series of covenants which emphasize both God's promises and his laws. The main Old Testament covenant was at Mount Sinai, when Israel agreed to obey God's laws after he had redeemed them from slavery in Egypt. The covenants with Abraham and his family (Genesis 12:1–3) and with David (2 Samuel 7:1–17), however, provide a wider context for the Sinai covenant and focus on God's promises, for Israel's existence was a sign that God had kept his promise to Abraham. The universal covenant with Noah (Genesis 9:8–17) is a little different, though it too centres on a promise that God would not again destroy the world by a flood.

The Old Testament speaks of a 'new covenant', also called a 'covenant of peace' and an 'everlasting covenant'. The New Testament mentions this covenant explicitly, especially in Jesus' reference at the Last Supper to 'the new covenant in my blood'. Jesus meant that he would bring the new covenant into effect by his death, and alluded to the institution of a covenant by a ceremony involving a sacrifice or a special meal. The new covenant is also called a better covenant, because it provides permanent forgiveness of sins and is open to anyone, not just the Jews. It brought the church into being as the people of the new covenant. Christians have debated whether the Bible speaks of one type of covenant characterized by law and another by promise or of only one covenant that developed in different stages. But the New Testament's stress on the new covenant's Old Testament roots suggests there is a greater continuity than discontinuity throughout the Bible.

covenant box see ARK OF THE COVENANT.

covetousness see GREED.

cows see ANIMALS.

crafts see ARTS AND CRAFTS.

creation A term for the activity by which God is thought to have brought the universe into being and also for that which God created. The concept of creation depends on the idea of a Creator God. This aspect of God's activity is assumed throughout the Old Testament, but in the New Testament is attributed specifically to Jesus. The New Testament also makes explicit that the whole concept of creation is received by faith (Hebrew 11:3). This is not an alternative to a scientific approach to the origins of the universe, since the Bible itself supports the idea of creation on the basis of observing the world. But the Bible is less concerned with how the world came into being than with human beings' responsibility towards the one who made them and with God's absolute sovereignty over all things.

The work of creation is expressed within a six-day framework. Whatever the equivalent of this in scientific terms, the speed of God's creating highlights his ability to bring into being things which did not previously exist. The Bible also speaks of the perfection of God's original creation, which was later spoiled by human disobedience. Since human beings alone were made in God's image, they are regarded as God's crowning achievement, and this view is maintained despite the subsequent breakdown of their relationship with God. God even shares with human beings the work of sustaining and maintaining the created world by giving them the responsibility of looking after it. However, God will replace the present world with a new creation since the former continues to be contaminated by human sin. This task, which Christ has already begun by making every believer part of a 'new creation', will be completed at Christ's return.

Crete Probably referred to in the Old Testament as Caphtor. In the New Testament, Titus led a church there which Paul had probably planted (Titus 1:5). See map of PAUL'S JOURNEYS; WORLD OF THE BIBLE.

crime and punishment The concept of crime is as much a religious as a legal matter since it is closely linked with the justice of God. Since God is the only one who is absolutely just and he is the Judge of all the earth (Genesis 18:25), all crimes are ultimately committed against him. He gave Israel its laws (Exodus 24:3), though these also reflect the customs and practices of the ancient Near East. Within Israelite society, crimes were regarded as offences against individuals or communities. The victims made accusations before the judges, who acted on behalf of the local or national community by imposing an appropriate punishment if an accusation was substantiated. A close link exists between the concepts of a criminal act, and the subsequent guilt and punishment, since the same Hebrew word can refer to all three aspects. A principle of equivalence existed between crime and the punishment (Exodus 21:23–5; Obadiah 15), which led to a wide variety of punishments. The death penalty was available for a range of crimes including adultery and witchcraft, though imprisonment was not widely practised. Punishment generally involved retribution, correction and vindication, and sometimes included compensation for the victim. Jesus and the apostles were flogged (Matthew 27:26; Acts 5:40). See also DEATH PENALTY; LEGAL SYSTEM.

crimson see COLOURS.

crops see AGRICULTURE.

cross, crucifixion The practice of punishing criminals by nailing them to a cross was a mainly Roman custom used only for the lowest types of offenders. Archaeologists have uncovered the bones of a young crucified man from the first century AD in Jerusalem. His ankles were pierced by a single nail, and it is clear that his bones had been broken (see John 19:31–3). The cross is central to the New Testament (1 Corinthians 1:17–18), and has subsequently become the chief symbol of Christian faith. It represents not only the means by which Jesus died, but also that he 'died for our sins' (1 Corinthians 15:3), bringing forgiveness and peace with God as the benefits of his death (Colossians 1:20).

cubit see WEIGHTS AND MEASURES.

cumin see HERBS AND SPICES.

cup see UTENSILS.

cupbearer An important official in the ancient world who often had great influence as a friend of a king. This is illustrated by Nehemiah's role before Artaxerxes I of Persia (Nehemiah 1:11). The 'butler' (Authorized (King James) Version) in the story of Joseph was actually a cupbearer (Genesis 40:1).

curse Words spoken against someone threatening some form of trouble or misfortune. Curses in the Bible were pronounced by God and by human beings, but though magic curses were well known in ancient times and are mentioned in the Bible, they have no power in comparison with God's word (Numbers 22–4). God's curse is both condemnation of sin and a pronouncement of punishment. Jesus' death brings release from the curse of the law, that is, from the punishment that is due to every human being because they have disobeyed God's law (Galatians 3:10–14).

curtain see TABERNACLE.

Cush, Cushites see ETHIOPIA.

cymbal see MUSIC AND MUSICAL INSTRUMENTS.

cypress see TREES.

Cyprus An important centre of Minoan and Mycenean civilization in ancient times. It was mainly associated in the Bible with the missionary enterprises of Paul and Barnabas, who was a native of the island (Acts 13:4–12; 15:39). See map of PAUL'S JOURNEYS.

Cyrene A port in Libya in North Africa. The Simon who caried Jesus' cross came from this city (Mark 15:21) as did some Jewish Christians who began taking the gospel to the Gentiles (Acts 11:20).

Cyrus A Persian emperor (549–530 BC) who is best known in the Bible for conquering Babylon and allowing the Jewish exiles to return home (Ezra 1:1–4). This latter policy is confirmed by the 'Cyrus cylinder', which indicates it was applied to many subject peoples. See map of WORLD OF THE BIBLE.

d

dagger see ARMOUR AND WEAPONS.

Dagon A deity worshipped widely in the ancient Near East. Outside the Old Testament, he was generally known as Dagan, and was probably a corn god, but in the Old Testament he was the chief god of the Philistines. His statue fell and broke in the presence of the ark of the covenant, symbolizing his impotence before the Lord (1 Samuel 5). See also PHILISTINES.

daily life Life was hard for ordinary Israelites. They lived in what was basically an agricultural society, and life was not made any easier for the majority by an increasing move to the towns, though in certain periods a privileged few enjoyed a higher standard of living. People generally lived in extended families, and the standard four-roomed house also included a courtyard for the animals. Furniture was extremely simple, comprising one or two chairs and tables and some wooden beds with a wicker covering (2 Kings 4:10). Pottery jars were used for storage. Cooking was done in an oven or on an open fire, and light came from simple oil-lamps (Acts 20:8). Clothes were usually made of wool or linen, and consisted of a loincloth and a long tunic, sometimes with an outer cloak. Women wore jewellery and ornaments as they had opportunity, but few could have afforded very much. Life was very dependent on the weather and the harvests, and a bad year could be disastrous, since despite the humaneness of Israel's laws there was no welfare state as such. People sometimes even had to sell land and property and themselves into slavery, simply in order to try to feed and clothe their families (2 Kings 4:1).

Damascus The most important of several city-states in Syria in Old Testament times, and situated at the crossroads of important trade routes. David brought it under Israelite control, but for much of the tenth to eighth centuries BC it was in conflict with the northern kingdom of Israel. Paul was converted as he travelled there to persecute Christians, but had to escape over the city wall from his own Jewish persecutors (Acts 9). See map of WORLD OF THE BIBLE.

Dan 1. The fifth son of Jacob (Genesis 30:3–6). See also DANITES.

2. A city on Israel's northern border. One of the northern kingdom's two national sanctuaries was there, centred on the worship of a golden calf (1 Kings 12:28–30). See map of OLD TESTAMENT ISRAEL.

dance Occasionally mentioned as a form of entertainment but more often as part of Israelite worship. Examples of the latter are usually spontaneous responses to a special mark of God's activity rather than a regular element of worship (Exodus 15:20; 2 Samuel 6:14–15; Jeremiah 31:13).

Daniel Exiled to Babylon as a young man and given the Babylonian name Belteshazzar (Daniel 1:1–7). He was appointed to high authority in the Babylonian and Persian kingdoms, but suffered for his faith, being dramatically rescued by God in the lions' den (Daniel 6). Through a gift for interpreting dreams and visions, he told kings of God's plans for them and warned about future persecution of the Jews. See also DANIEL, BOOK OF.

Daniel, book of

Structure

Stories about Daniel in Babylon (1:1–6:28)
Daniel's dreams and visions (7:1–12:13)

Famous passages

The burning fiery furnace (3:1–30)
Belshazzar's feast (5:1–31)
Daniel in the lions' den (6:1–28)
A son of man in the clouds (7:13–14)

This book falls into two distinct parts. The first contains stories about Daniel while he was in exile in Babylon for over sixty years (chapters 1–6), while the second contains a series of dreams and visions given to him there (chapters 7–12). Because of the presence of so much visionary material, the book is often compared with a kind of Jewish literature known as apocalyptic, but the inclusion of historical material in chapters 1–6 sets Daniel apart from true apocalyptic literature. Since some of the visions refer to the time of the Maccabean revolt in the second century BC, the book is often thought to have been written at that time, but the favourable treatment of Daniel by Babylonian and Persian kings in chapters 1–6 makes this view difficult. An earlier date of writing in or soon after the sixth century BC is equally possible, though much depends on whether the book is thought to predict or be involved in the events it describes. A further difficulty is that it is written in two languages, Hebrew and Aramaic, but the reason for this remains unclear.

This is an important book about how God's people can survive under unsympathetic, sometimes explicitly hostile, foreign rule. It shows God at work in human empires and politics, establishing his own kingdom. The message of the book is that all human kingdoms are temporary but that God's kingdom will last for ever (e.g. chapter 7) and, if necessary, God will resurrect his people from death (12:1–3). The theme of God's protection is repeatedly illustrated in Daniel's own life. See also APOCALYPSE.

Danites An Israelite tribe, descended from Dan. They originally settled in the south, but migrated north in the judges period. Its most famous member was Samson (Judges 13–16). See map of OLD TESTAMENT ISRAEL.

Darius 1. Darius the Mede is mentioned in Daniel as successor to the Babylonian empire. He cannot be positively identified from other sources, but may be the Persian general Gobryas or the Persian king Cyrus.

2. Darius I of Persia (521–486 BC) enabled the Jews to rebuild their temple.

darkness Though often used symbolically, darkness is an aspect of nature created by God. It is viewed quite neutrally, with God equally at home in darkness and light (Psalm 139:11–12). As a metaphor, it stands for both sin and judgement (1 John 1:6). Those who reject the light of God's truth will be sentenced by God's judgement to outer darkness (Matthew 22:13).

dates see FOOD.

daughter see FAMILY.

David, King (c. 1000–961 BC) Israel's greatest king and a direct ancestor of Jesus. His greatness is based on two features, his military conquests which resulted in Israel's only empire and God's covenant promise of an eternal dynasty and kingdom.

The first phase of David's life (1 Samuel 16–31) describes Samuel anointing David privately as Saul's successor, and Saul's repeated attempts to kill David after he had become a national hero by defeating Goliath and attacking the Philistines. After Saul died, David became king, first over Judah and then over all Israel, making Jerusalem his capital after capturing it from the Jebusites. This action united the tribes under his kingship, and he cemented Israel's new-found unity by restoring the ark to the centre of national life in Jerusalem (2 Samuel 1–8). The final phase of the biblical account which is often called the Succession History (2 Samuel 9–20; 1 Kings 1–2) contains several stories about personal conflict within David's family, which was only resolved when Solomon was established as his successor.

David's achievements were considerable. He transformed Israel from a disjointed and defeated group of tribes into an empire which included nations such as the Philistines, Moabites and several Aramean kingdoms (in modern Syria). For the first time, Israel had a central structure under a king, though David's organization was modest compared with that set up by Solomon. As a gifted musician he contributed to the Book of Psalms, though the Bible does not specify how many psalms he actually wrote (the psalm titles probably do not speak about authorship). But David had very real weaknesses, as shown by his adultery with Bathsheba and his engineering of her husband Uriah's death. His indulgence of his sons was less dramatic, but its consequences were equally devastating. Because David repented, however, the Bible portrays him as a forgiven man.

David is chiefly known for the covenant God made with him (2 Samuel 7). Through him, God promised to build two houses, one in the form of a dynasty and the other in the form of the temple built by Solomon. The second biblical account of David in 1 Chronicles 10–29 shows how this promise continued throughout the monarchy and beyond. Several parts of the Old Testament in fact refer to the idea that a future son of David would establish God's kingdom on earth, and the New Testament repeatedly shows how this hope was fulfilled in Jesus (Romans 1:3).

dawn Often symbolizes the coming of God's activity and of fresh hope (Psalm 37:6; Isaiah 9:2), though also a time when wickedness is exposed (Ephesians 5:11–14).

day see TIME.

Day of Atonement see ATONEMENT, DAY OF.

Day of Judgement see JUDGEMENT.

Day of the LORD A Hebrew expression referring to a time when God acts or makes himself known in a particularly significant way. In origin it is associated with God's help for Israel in their battles to occupy the Promised Land, and because of this it became a symbol of Israel's hope that God would finally intervene on their behalf (Amos 5:18–20). But the prophets warned that God would act to fulfil his purposes rather than his people's expectations and that the Day would be one of judgement for Israel as well as salvation. Their threats were fulfilled as the kingdoms of both Israel and Judah fell. In the New Testament, the term describes the time when Christ will be fully revealed at his return to remove all forms of evil and finally establish his eternal kingdom.

This event will be accompanied by signs throughout the natural world, and people are warned to be ready at any time.

deacon A New Testament term for a church leader, though the New Testament emphasizes the personal qualities required rather than their precise status and function. Deacons seem to have been gifted in the areas of administration and social care. The two passages which mention women in this connection (Romans 16:1; 1 Timothy 3:11) are more likely to describe female deacons than a separate group of deaconesses or deacons' wives.

Dead Sea Palestine's largest inland area of water, into which the River Jordan flows. At an average 427 metres below sea level, it is the lowest place on the surface of the earth and the saltiest area of water in the world because of the chemical deposits it contains. Known in the Bible as the Salt Sea or the Sea of the Arabah (Deuteronomy 3:17), it formed a barrier between Judah on the west and Moab and Edom on the east. See map of WORLD OF THE BIBLE; OLD TESTAMENT ISRAEL; NEW TESTAMENT ISRAEL.

Dead Sea Scrolls A collection of about 500 manuscripts discovered after the Second World War at Qumran, north-west of the Dead Sea. They comprised the library of a Jewish religious community in the first century BC and the first century AD. The community were almost certainly Essenes, who agreed by covenant to seek to obey God's laws and refused to accept the leadership of the high priests in Jerusalem. The Scrolls, which include parts of every Old Testament book except Esther, contain the oldest Hebrew Old Testament manuscripts and witness to the reliability, though also to the variety, of the Old Testament text.

deafness see DISEASES AND ILLNESSES.

death Though the Bible acknowledges death as the common experience of every living thing, Genesis indicates that it was not part of God's original plan for human beings but became part of their experience as a punishment for disobedience. This situation was redeemed by the death of Jesus, who took God's punishment for sin on himself in order to set others free through the gift of eternal life (Romans 6:23). For those who do not accept this gift, there is the prospect of God's final judgement which is called the second death (Revelation 20:6). But for those who do accept it, the cross represents the destruction of death (2 Timothy 1:10) because its sting, that is its penalty, has been removed for ever.

death penalty Part of the legal systems of the ancient world, including Israel where the common method of capital punishment was stoning. In the Old Testament, it was considered particularly appropriate for murder, but was also sanctioned for a range of other crimes such as adultery, blasphemy or witchcraft. Sometimes God himself imposed the punishment directly (Exodus 12:29), though on other occasions he allowed a lesser penalty (Genesis 4:15). See also CRIME AND PUNISHMENT; STONING.

Deborah An outstanding woman who was a prophet and led Israel as a judge. She enabled Barak to defeat occupying Canaanite forces under Sisera at the battle of Megiddo (Judges 4–5). The Song of Deborah (Judges 5) is thought to be one of the oldest pieces of Hebrew poetry.

debt Loans in the Old Testament period were made to help fellow Israelites through times of difficulty, though the law prohibited one Israelite charging interest to another (Exodus 22:25). Poor harvests were a common cause of debt in Israel's agricultural society, though exploitation was not unknown, and unpaid debts sometimes led to slavery. Foreigners could be charged interest for commercial purposes, and in the New Testament the practice of commercial loans is assumed (Luke 19:23).

Decalogue see TEN COMMANDMENTS.

Decapolis An area south and east of the Sea of Galilee containing ten independent Gentile cities which Jesus visited twice during his ministry (Mark 7:31). See map of NEW TESTAMENT ISRAEL.

deceit God takes a particularly serious view of deceit, since it is this aspect of human nature that gives rise to sin: 'the heart is deceitful above all things and beyond cure' (Jeremiah 17:9). The commandment not to bear false testimony prohibits deceit (Exodus 20:16), and it is also forbidden to Christians, especially leaders (2 Corinthians 4:2).

Dedication, Feast of The Jewish festival of Hanukkah, commemorating the rededication of the temple by Judas Maccabeus in December 164 BC (John 10:22).

deer Deer and gazelles were common in biblical times, and were known for their agility and grace (Proverbs 5:19; Isaiah 35:6).

defilement see CLEAN AND UNCLEAN.

Delilah A Philistine woman who betrayed Samson to the Philistines by persuading him to tell her the secret of his strength (Judges 16:4–21). See also SAMSON.

deliverance see REDEMPTION; SALVATION.

demons Though people in the ancient world were often in fear of demons and evil spirits, the Old Testament rarely mentions them except to warn people against contact with them. They are more evident in the New Testament, especially in connection with Jesus, who exposed their existence and delivered people from the moral, spiritual and physical harm they caused. Jesus' power over the spirits was a sign that God was with him, though those who opposed Jesus also illogically accused him of acting by the power of Satan (Luke 11:15). Jesus gave similar authority to his followers to release people from the influence of demons and evil spirits (Luke 10:17; Acts 5:16).

denarius see MONEY.

depression Symptoms of both severe spiritual discouragement and clinical depression occur in the Bible, sometimes overlapping with each other. As well as the example of Elijah (1 Kings 19:1–9), several psalmists seem to be afflicted in this way through despair, anxiety, and even a desire for death. The Bible emphasizes that God hears the prayers of depressed people and encourages them to put their trust in him (Psalm 42:5, 11). See also DISCOURAGEMENT.

desert see WILDERNESS.

despair see DEPRESSION.

Deuteronomic History A term often used for the Old Testament books Deuteronomy – 2 Kings. They form a continuous story from Israel's arrival at the edge of the Promised Land to the fall of Jerusalem. They also have a common theological outlook based on God's covenant with Israel in Deuteronomy by which events and people in Israel's history are evaluated. Each individual book has its own style, however, and the compilers of the Deuteronomic History, often called the Deuteronomists, are best thought of as editors rather than authors. Their contribution is found mainly in the structure of each book and in speeches and prayers (e.g. 2 Samuel 7; 1 Kings 8). See also DEUTERONOMY; JOSHUA; JUDGES; KINGS; SAMUEL.

Deuteronomy, book of

Structure

Historical review (1:1–4:43)
The meaning of the law (4:44–11:32)
Detailed laws (12:1–26:19)
Confirming the covenant (27:1–30:20)
Preparing for the future (31:1–34:12)

Famous passages

The Ten Commandments (5:6–21)
The Shema and the greatest commandment (6:4–5)
God's love for Israel (7:7–8)
Living by the words of God's mouth (8:3)
Moses dies overlooking the Promised Land (34:1–12)

As the last of the five books of the Law, Deuteronomy is really a summary of the whole Law. It is set at an important moment in biblical history, when Israel stood on the east bank of the Jordan ready to enter the Promised Land. The book's climax is a covenant renewal ceremony, when the children of the generation who left Egypt committed themselves to obey God in the Promised Land. The book begins with two surveys. The first (1:1–4:43) demonstrates from history that God alone has brought Israel to the edge of the Promised Land in spite of themselves. The second (4:44–11:32) explains the inner meaning of Israel's covenant laws as a dynamic of mutual love. Israel is commanded to love God totally (6:5; cf. Matthew 22:34–40) in response to God's greater love for Israel (7:7–8; 10:15). The middle section of the book (chapters 12–26) is a collection of specific laws. Worship and right behaviour are to be Israel's chief priorities, characterized by a genuine humanitarian concern, especially for widows, orphans and resident foreigners. This is followed by instructions about renewing the covenant (chapters 27–30) and future blessing under Joshua's leadership (chapters 31–4). Because the book is arranged on the pattern of ancient treaties and covenants, Deuteronomy is sometimes called a covenant document, but it is best regarded as a theological adaptation of the treaty form.

Deuteronomy is important, partly because of its developed theology of law and partly because it presents law as 'preached law'. It has an 'almost evangelical fervour' (F.F. Bruce), and makes regular appeals about responding to God's word. It is also one of the Old Testament books most frequently quoted in the New Testament (e.g. Matthew 4:7, 10). The origin of Deuteronomy is much debated. Although composed almost entirely of speeches by Moses, it is sometimes thought to come from a much later time. Its style is noticeably different from the rest of the Pentateuch, and because it shares several features with a lawbook discovered in Josiah's reign (2 Kings 22–3), some scholars believe it belongs to a reform movement for centralization and purity of worship in the eighth and seventh centuries BC. However, Deuteronomy's idealism suggests it may have been completed before Israel fully occupied the land, perhaps in the time of the judges or the early monarchy.

devil, the see SATAN.

Diana see ARTEMIS.

Diaspora see DISPERSION.

Didymus see THOMAS.

diligence Hard work and perseverance are often commended (Proverbs 21:5), whether in the tasks of daily life or in spreading the gospel. Without faith, however, a diligent attitude achieves nothing, since it is God who makes people's work effective (Psalm 127:2).

dill see HERBS AND SPICES.

Dinah Jacob's only daughter. Her brothers attacked the people of Shechem after she was raped by the local ruler's son (Genesis 34).

dinner see MEALS.

disappointment A sense of sadness or frustration. It is often a consequence of life's uncertainties and of human unreliability, but may also occur when God does not act as people expect. A proper response involves obeying God's will as well as patient faith. Since God's promises are trustworthy, those who trust him are never ultimately disappointed (Romans 5:5).

discernment 1. A special gift from the Holy Spirit that enables people to see what God is doing in the hidden circumstances of people's lives (2 Kings 6:8–17; John 4:16–18).
2. The ability to make right decisions based on the wisdom and knowledge found in God's word (Proverbs 8:8–9).

disciple A New Testament term meaning a learner or pupil, and used both for the twelve apostles and for believers in general (Matthew 10:1; Luke 6:13). It is also applied to the followers of others, especially of John the Baptist and the Pharisees.

discipleship The word does not occur in the Bible, but is frequently used for the way of life expected of those who follow Jesus. The theme is especially common in the Gospels, where Jesus explains that discipleship involves committing one's whole life to God. Jesus is the model for discipleship, with the cross as its symbol (Mark 8:34–5) and his servanthood its pattern (Mark 10:42–5). However, discipleship also results in receiving the blessings of the kingdom of God, both in this life and in the life to come (Mark 10:28–30).

discipline 1. According to the model of parental correction, God is portrayed as a loving father who moulds his people's lives so that they become more like his children (Hebrews 12:5–13).
2. A self-imposed commitment to avoid sin and keep the will of God.
3. The maintaining of standards in church life, sometimes resulting in the expulsion of individual members (1 Corinthians 5:9–13).

discouragement A sense of unhappiness commonly experienced by believers. It usually arises from fresh evidence of their own tendency to sin and from the pressures of an unbelieving world (2 Corinthians 1:8–9). It can be resisted by prayer and persistence, and by acknowledging that believers can never be separated from God's sustaining love. See also DEPRESSION.

diseases and illnesses Any attempt to compare ancient diseases with modern knowledge must accept that descriptions of disease in the

Bible are based on observation rather than on precise technical language. Some terms have also changed their meaning over the centuries, especially in the case of leprosy. Leprosy is a very broad term in the Bible, often being associated with ritual uncleanness. Its symptoms involved discoloration of cloth and buildings as well as human skin, which is very different from modern leprosy, known technically as Hansen's disease. Common diseases mentioned in the Bible include blindness, boils and sores, deafness, fever, haemorrhages, mental disorders, paralysis, plagues of various kinds and speech impediments. The pain of childbirth also occurs frequently. All human pain and suffering ultimately goes back to God's punishment at the fall, but although God occasionally afflicted individuals with illness as a result of disobedience, Jesus and the Book of Job make a point of denying any simple equation between sin and suffering. God's people often suffer disease, both as a consequence of their humanness and as part of God's intention to mature and refine their faith in him (Psalm 38:2–3; Philippians 2:26–7). Physical disease is sometimes used as a picture for sin, which is incurable apart from God's healing work. See also HEALTH AND HEALING.

Diseases and illnesses	
Blindness	Mark 10:46
Boils	Job 2:7
Deafness	Mark 7:32
Epilepsy	Matthew 17:15
Fever	Luke 4:38
Haemorrhaging	Matthew 9:20
Lameness	Matthew 11:5
Mental illness	Daniel 4:28–37
Muteness	Matthew 9:32
Paralysis	Acts 8:7
Skin disease ('leprosy')	Leviticus 13–14
Tumours	1 Samuel 5:6
Wasting disease	Leviticus 26:16

dish see UTENSILS.

dishonesty see DECEIT; LIE.

disobedience see OBEDIENCE AND DISOBEDIENCE.

dispersion A term for the scattering of the Jews across the ancient world as a result of the exile in the sixth century BC. The term is also applied to the church, either because Christians were geographically widely spread or more likely because they were separated from their ultimate home in heaven (1 Peter 1:1).

divination see OCCULT.

divorce and remarriage Though not part of God's original intention for marriage, divorce was occasionally permitted in the Old Testament (Deuteronomy 24:1). Only men were allowed to divorce their wives, and the grounds, which were not specific, were interpreted both narrowly and liberally. Jesus emphasized the sanctity of marriage, but acknowledged the possibility of divorce because of human weakness, though he allowed only the single ground of adultery (Matthew 19:8–9). He also at least strongly discouraged remarriage and may have prohibited it (Luke 16:18). A higher standard was expected in the church than outside it, though grounds for divorce and remarriage for Christians may occur in 1 Corinthians 7:15–16, 27–8.

doctor see HEALTH AND HEALING; OCCUPATIONS.

dog Mainly a semi-wild scavenger in ancient times, and viewed as an unclean carrier of disease. The negative associations are applied to people (2 Samuel 16:9; Philippians 3:2), but the use of shepherd dogs and a possible reference to pets (Matthew 15:26) suggests a more positive view.

donkey Widely used throughout the ancient Near East as the basic means of transport and for agricultural purposes. It was also considered a suitable mount for royalty in peacetime (cf. Zechariah 9:9).

doorkeeper see GATEKEEPER.

doubt A distinction must be made as to whether doubt occurs within or outside the broader context of active faith in God. Those who do not believe in God's power or desire to act in particular situations are regarded simply as unbelievers. However, those who are perplexed by God's dealings but who ask God to help them resolve their difficulties are commended for their questioning (Job 42:7–9). The appearance of Jesus to 'doubting Thomas' is recorded in John 20:24–9.

dove see BIRDS.

dowry see MARRIAGE.

doxology A formal expression of praise, often found at the end of documents or of sections of documents (Jude 24–5).

drachma see MONEY.

dreams Mainly associated with divine communication, though ordinary dreams are also mentioned. The dream was not widely used as a way of receiving messages from God, and was often viewed negatively. It is interesting that Joseph (Genesis 40–1) and Daniel (Daniel 2, 4), the two main dream interpreters of the Bible, lived in non-Israelite societies. Direct communication and the need for interpretation both occur. See also VISIONS.

dress see CLOTHING.

drink see FOOD AND DRINK.

drunkenness Since wine, and to a lesser extent beer, were common in ancient Israel, it is the abuse of strong drink rather than its use that is criticized. Drunkenness is a shameful thing that undermines people's judgement and tends towards violence (Proverbs 20:1; Isaiah 28:7), and is particularly to be avoided by Christian leaders (1 Timothy 3:2–3).

dust and ashes Used mainly as a symbol, especially of the temporary nature of human life, since human beings were made of dust and will return to dust (Genesis 3:19). Dust sprinkled on the head was a common sign of mourning.

e

eagerness An attitude which should characterize the way believers serve God and their desire for spiritual maturity (2 Peter 1:10), but also a description of the manner in which people often pursue their own selfish ambitions (Zephaniah 3:7).

eagle see BIRDS.

ears Often represent the seat of hearing, and can therefore symbolize obedience to or rejection of God's words. In the same way, even God is said to have ears which are always open to his people's prayers (2 Chronicles 7:15). The custom of piercing the ear indicated a slave's intention to be bound permanently to his master (Exodus 21:6), and the high priest's ears were smeared with blood at his ordination (Leviticus 8:23–4).

earth Used of the world in general and also the land as distinct from sea and sky. In the first sense, it was created entirely by God, and it remains permanently subject to him. Human beings were made out of the dust of the earth, as is illustrated by the association between Adam and the Hebrew word for 'ground' (*'adama*) (Genesis 2:7). However, the earth has become affected by disease and death as a result of human sin, and is portrayed as groaning while it waits for the renewal of all things, including the creation of a new earth (Romans 8:19–22).

earthquake Though recognized as natural phenomena (Amos 1:1), earthquakes are usually regarded as a sign of God's power (Exodus 19:18; Acts 16:26), especially that which took place at Jesus' resurrection (Matthew 28:2). They are also particularly associated with the time of the end.

Ebal, Mount A mountain just outside Shechem (modern Nablus), where the Israelites confirmed their covenant with God after entering the Promised Land (Joshua 8:30–5).

Ebenezer An expression meaning 'stone of help', referring to a public memorial about God's support for Israel (1 Samuel 7:12). It was also

the name of a place where the Philistines defeated Israel
(1 Samuel 4:1–11).

Eber The person from whom the Hebrews were apparently
descended, though the Bible does not make any explicit connection
between Eber and the Hebrews (Genesis 11:15–17).

Ecclesiastes, book of

Structure

Introduction (1:1–11)
Various sayings on wisdom and meaninglessness (1:12–11:6)
Poem on youth and old age (11:7–12:8)
Conclusion (12:9–14)

Famous passages

A time for everything (3:1–8)
Poem on youth and old age (11:7–12:8)
'Of making many books there is no end' (12:12)
The whole duty of man (12:13–14)

One of the most enigmatic books in the Bible. Neither the English
title, which is actually a Greek word meaning 'someone who takes
part in an assembly', nor the Hebrew title *qoheleth* meaning
'teacher/preacher', provide any real clue to what it is about. It is also
difficult to find any overall structure apart from a distinctive
introduction and conclusion. Even the repeated words and phrases,
such as 'vanity' or 'meaninglessness', do not provide a key to unlock
the book's mysteries.

The compiler often gives the impression of creating paradoxes or
even contradictions, as in 4:5–6 where he shows that laziness achieves
nothing but then discourages hard work. The aim is apparently to
consider a subject from several possible angles, without necessarily
drawing any clear conclusion. This has resulted in very different views
of the book, some seeing the compiler as a pessimist and cynic while
others see the compiler as someone who encourages the enjoyment of
life. A probable view is that it shows life without God as empty, and
concludes with an appeal (chapter 12) to remember and to fear, i.e.
worship, God. The book is post-exilic despite the allusion to Solomon
(chapters 1–2), though whether it shows evidence of Greek philosophy
or is as late as the third century BC is increasingly questioned.

Ecclesiasticus SEE APOCRYPHA.

Eden, Garden of The place where Adam and Eve lived, and from
which they were driven as a punishment for disobeying God
(Genesis 2:8; 3:24). Reference to the Tigris and Euphrates flowing

from it indicates that it was a real place, though things like the trees of life and of the knowledge of good and evil suggest that it possessed more than just physical qualities. It has been located in southern Iraq, or in an area of eastern Syria known in ancient times as Beth-Eden.

Edom, Edomites A rugged, mountainous area to the south of the Dead Sea and of Judah. There was frequent hostility between the Edomites and the Israelites. The problem is traced back both to the Edomites' refusal to allow the Israelites to travel through their land on their way to the Promised Land (Numbers 20:14–21) and to Esau's hostility with Jacob, since the Edomites were Esau's descendants (Genesis 36:1–19). Little is known about the Edomites, though it is known that they worshipped a god named Qaus and that the main north-south trade route east of the Jordan passed through their land. That route was known as the King's Highway. See also ESAU. See map of OLD TESTAMENT ISRAEL.

education Teaching took place in the home rather than in schools, though synagogues played an increasingly important role in the late Old Testament and New Testament periods. In the same period, Hellenistic schools would also have had some influence on Jewish communities. Parents had the responsibility for teaching their children the law of God, which included spiritual, moral, social as well as intellectual instruction. According to the Old Testament, the basis of all knowledge and wisdom was 'the fear of the Lord', i.e. an attitude of faith and respect for God and his word (Proverbs 1:7). Festivals such as the Passover were an important opportunity for teaching children the ways of God (Exodus 12:26–7).

A system of education outside the home may well have developed under Solomon to meet the needs of training his many officials. Later on, the wise and the scribes were teachers in Israel, and by New Testament times some received the honorific title of Rabbi. The Bible gives some clues about educational methods, which included approaches such as parables, acrostics, numerical patterns and various memory techniques. Teaching was also an important part of life in the church's worship, though the home remained the main place where children were educated.

Eglon 1. A city in southern Judah captured by Joshua (Joshua 10:34–5). 2. A Moabite king assassinated by Ehud the judge (Judges 3:12–25).

Egypt, Egyptians The most important African country in the Bible. The land is dominated by the region of the Nile where most of the people lived. Its history goes back to around 3000 BC, but the first significant mention in the Bible is of Joseph as prime minister of

Egypt, perhaps under one of the Hyksos (= 'chiefs of foreign lands')
Pharaohs in the seventeenth or sixteenth centuries BC. Joseph's
family stayed in Egypt until perhaps the thirteenth century when
they fled persecution there at the exodus, though this was probably a
minor incident as far as the Egyptians were concerned. The New
Kingdom from the mid-sixteenth to the mid-eleventh centuries BC
was Egypt's greatest period of influence, and included the brief but
spectacular reign of Tutankhamun in the fourteenth century BC.
After this, Egypt began to decline, though it exercised power in
Palestine under Shishak (or Sheshonq I) in the tenth century. The
Israelites sometimes turned to Egypt for help, especially against
Assyrian threats in the eighth century and at the end of the seventh
century, but Egypt's final attempt at international dominance came
to grief at the hands of the Babylonian army at Carchemish in
605 BC. For the rest of the biblical period, Egypt was largely subject
to foreign empires.

Egypt enjoyed one of the most advanced cultures in the ancient
world. It produced an extensive literature, which had an occasional
influence on the Old Testament as in the close resemblance between
the Wisdom of Amenemope and the 'Sayings of the Wise' in Proverbs
22:17–24:22. Egyptian religion involved a complex set of polytheistic
beliefs, particularly concerning the afterlife when the Egyptians
attempted to take the good things of this world into the next.
However, the Old Testament looks forward to a time when Egyptians
will worship the Lord (Isaiah 19:19–25). See also PHARAOH. See map
of WORLD OF THE BIBLE.

Ehud The second of the judges, who defeated Moabite occupation
forces in central Palestine after killing their king, Eglon (Judges
3:12–30).

Ekron One of the five main Philistine cities, modern Khirbet
el-Muqanna'. It was on the Philistines' northern border with
Judah (1 Samuel 7:14). See map of OLD TESTAMENT ISRAEL.

El Elyon see GOD, NAMES AND TITLES OF.

El Olam see GOD, NAMES AND TITLES OF.

El Shaddai see GOD, NAMES AND TITLES OF.

Elah, King of Israel (c. 877–876 BC) see KINGS AND QUEENS OF ISRAEL.

Elam, Elamites Though rarely mentioned in the Bible, Elam was one
of the most important nations of the ancient world. It was centred
on the plain of Khuzistan between the Tigris and the eastern
mountains, and its main city was Susa (Daniel 8:2).

elder A local leader in Israel, recognized on the basis of his age and
experience. A body of elders took charge of local affairs, while

nationally they could request and appoint a king (2 Samuel 5:3). Their role continued throughout most of the biblical period, and though it was somewhat reduced while the monarchy was in existence, they again took a significant role under Ezra. The title was also important in the New Testament church, where it seems that the tradition continued of recognizing senior members among their communities (Acts 20:17). Their role was similar to if not identical with that of bishops. See also BISHOP.

Eleazar A son of Aaron and his successor as high priest alongside both Moses and Joshua (Numbers 20:26).

election An important Christian teaching about God's sovereign choosing of his people. The word has a special theological sense in the Bible which is quite different from the modern sense of the exercise of democratic choice. The idea is found throughout the Bible, but each Testament has a distinctive emphasis. Its origins go back at least to God's call of Abraham, though in the Old Testament it is mainly concerned with God choosing Israel as his own people. The New Testament develops this idea and concentrates on God's choice of the church as his people and individual believers within it (Romans 9–10).

The idea is frequently criticized on the grounds that it leaves no room for human response to God, but this is based on a misunderstanding of the Bible's perspective. The main concern is to show that God's sovereign purpose for his people is guaranteed, especially through the work of Christ, and it points to God's love and grace as the unshakeable basis of his people's relationship with him (Deuteronomy 7:7–8; Ephesians 2:8–10). Election gives the believer a sense of security before God. The appropriate response is a sense of privilege rather than pride and a life characterized by gratitude and loving service.

Eli A high priest whose family was removed from office because of their lack of concern for the ways of God (1 Samuel 3:11–14). The fact that this message was conveyed by his young assistant Samuel only underlines Eli's failure to hear God and his unfitness to lead Israel.

Eliakim The best-known individual of this name was one of King Hezekiah's most trusted and senior officials (Isaiah 22:20–4).

Eliashib A high priest in the time of Nehemiah. Though he helped to rebuild Jerusalem, he made marriage alliances with Israel's enemies (Nehemiah 13:4–9).

Eliezer Abraham's most important servant. Having been adopted by his master while Abraham had no son of his own (Genesis 15:2–3), he effectively ruled himself out of the family's inheritance by graciously arranging Isaac's marriage (Genesis 24).

Elihu The fourth and youngest of Job's friends, who advised Job to look to God for an explanation of his suffering rather than to the unhelpful arguments of the three other friends (Job 32–7). See also ELIPHAZ, BILDAD AND ZOPHAR.

Elijah An important prophet who was active in the northern kingdom of Israel in the ninth century BC. His background is unknown except that he came from Tishbe in Gilead. His ministry was largely spent in opposing the kings of the ruling Omride dynasty, namely Ahab and his sons Ahaziah and Jehoram (1 Kings 17–19, 21; 2 Kings 1–2). Their promotion of Baal worship was a direct threat to Yahweh's supremacy as the God of Israel. Elijah therefore challenged 400 priests of Baal to a contest at Mount Carmel to show the people that Yahweh was the only true God. Elijah was persecuted by Ahab's wife Jezebel, but God protected him and his predictions of the deaths of Ahab and Jezebel were both fulfilled. The result of his ministry was the preservation of a faithful remnant of people who worshipped God. His work was characterized by several miracles, and he was eventually taken up to heaven in a whirlwind rather than actually dying. Later, his name was associated with the expectation of a forerunner of the Messiah, which Jesus explained was fulfilled in John the Baptist (Malachi 4:5–6; Matthew 11:12–14). See also AHAB; ELISHA; JEZEBEL.

Eliphaz, Bildad and Zophar Job's three friends who tried to comfort him in his extreme suffering. Though initially they sat quietly with Job, they tried at length to convince him of a traditional doctrine that great suffering must imply some great sin. To Job they were 'miserable comforters' (Job 16:2), and God rejected their views on the basis that their theology took no account of God's personal concern for Job. See also ELIHU.

Elisha Elijah's successor as the leading prophet of the northern kingdom in the latter half of the ninth century BC. His ministry was different from Elijah's, being more concerned with leading prophetic guilds and with demonstrations of God's miraculous power (1 Kings 19:19–21; 2 Kings 2:1–8, 15; 13:14–21). He was also more of a seer, communicating his message in pictures as well as words. He emphasized the contrast between true faith and the unbelief of Israel's kings, and spoke about God's sovereignty over the nations, as illustrated by his healing of the Syrian general Naaman and his predictions concerning the kings of Damascus. See also ELIJAH.

Elizabeth John the Baptist's mother and a close relative of Jesus' mother Mary, who encouraged Mary with a prophecy about her unborn son (Luke 1:42–5).

Elohim see GOD, NAMES AND TITLES OF.

Eloi, Eloi, lama sabachthani An Aramaic phrase used by Jesus at the cross (Matthew 27:46; Mark 15:34). It is a quotation from Psalm 22:1 and means, 'My God, my God, why have you forsaken me?'

Elul see CALENDAR, JEWISH.

embalming see BURIAL AND MOURNING.

embroidery see ARTS AND CRAFTS.

emerald see JEWELS AND PRECIOUS STONES.

Emmanuel see IMMANUEL.

Emmaus A village 11 kilometres from Jerusalem to which two of Jesus' disciples were walking when Jesus met them after his resurrection (Luke 24:13). It cannot now be identified.

En Gedi An important oasis on the west side of the Dead Sea, famous for its fertility and its perfumes (Song of Songs 1:14).

encouragement An important activity for believers based on the concept of the church as a body united in love. Fellow Christians are strongly urged to strengthen one another, both by stimulating them to greater confidence in God and through practical support. The chief sources of encouragement are God and the Scriptures (Joshua 1:6–9; Romans 15:4). The circumstances in which people need encouragement are extremely varied, but they particularly include times when people are tempted to sin or to give up the faith because of persecution (Hebrews 10:19–39).

end of the world see LAST THINGS.

endurance The ability to persist in the Christian faith, which is frequently necessary because of the persecution of Christians in New Testament times. Christians are encouraged to look to Jesus as their chief example of one who was faithful to his Father even to death, since like him they will receive their full reward (Hebrews 12:1–3).

enemies God's people were frequently under attack throughout the Bible. Israel suffered from various invaders in the Promised Land as well as from some of its previous inhabitants such as the Philistines. The church was similarly persecuted by various groups, sometimes as a result of Roman imperial policy. But the chief enemies of God's people are the human heart with its tendency towards sin and the unseen forces of wickedness headed by the devil and his angels. God, however, has provided his people with all the necessary defence (Ephesians 6:10–17). See also PERSECUTION.

Enoch An ancestor of Noah who did not die but was taken up to heaven (Genesis 5:24). This incident led to his becoming famous in the intertestamental period.

envy Though traditionally known as one of the seven deadly sins, this description does not appear in the Bible. Envy is, however, the subject of the tenth commandment, 'You shall not covet' (Exodus 20:17), and it is consistently condemned throughout the Bible. It can be extremely destructive, leading to family divisions (Genesis 27:41) and even murder (Genesis 4:3–8).

Epaphras A colleague of Paul who calls him 'fellow-prisoner' (Philemon 23). He founded churches in Asia Minor, including Colossae and Laodicea.

ephah see WEIGHTS AND MEASURES.

Ephesians, letter to the

Structure

God's purposes in Christ (1:1–3:21)

Christian life in the world (4:1–6:24)

Famous passages

'It is by grace you have been saved, through faith' (2:8)

'Keep the unity of the Spirit' (4:3)

Apostles, prophets, evangelists, pastors and teachers (4:11)

The mystery of marriage (5:21–33)

Putting on God's armour (6:10–17)

One of Paul's most majestic letters, in both subject-matter and style. The first part (chapters 1–3) emphasizes the grandness of God's plan, the exaltation of Christ, and the church as the fullness of the body of Christ. These themes are presented as aspects of God's ultimate purpose to show that God will 'bring all things in heaven and on earth together under one head, even Christ' (1:10). The second part (chapters 4–6) draws out the implications of what it means to be 'in Christ', a distinctive phrase in the letter. In relation to the world, the church should be a society united by the love of Christ. In work and family relationships, Christians should respect every person in Christ. In relation to the unseen world, God has provided spiritual armour by which Christians may stand their ground.

The letter is not tied to any particular situation, and may well have been a circular letter to churches in the Ephesus area. Its general character has sometimes led to the conclusion that it is a later summary of Paul's teachings, but its autobiographical content makes this view difficult. Assuming that it is by Paul, it was probably written from prison in Rome in the early 60s AD.

Ephesus The most important city and commercial hub of the Roman province of Asia. Its famous buildings included the theatre and the temple of Diana (Artemis), both mentioned in Acts 19. It was also an important Christian centre in New Testament times, probably based on a network of house churches, and received two New Testament letters (Ephesians; Revelation 2:1–7). See also EPHESIANS, LETTER TO THE. See map of PAUL'S JOURNEYS.

ephod see PRIEST.

Ephraim Originally the name of Joseph's second son who was adopted by his grandfather Jacob and given the blessing of the firstborn (Genesis 48:8–20). Later, Ephraim became the most important tribe in the northern kingdom of Israel, and its name was even used occasionally as an alternative for Israel. It occupied the central highlands west of the Jordan. See map of OLD TESTAMENT ISRAEL.

Epicureans A school of Greek philosophers named after their founder, Epicurus. They sought to achieve happiness by avoiding pain, and rejected Paul's teaching about the resurrection (Acts 17:16–34).

epilepsy see DISEASES AND ILLNESSES.

Esau Esau and Jacob were twin brothers, but they were very different from each other. Esau hated his younger brother because Jacob took the firstborn's birthright and his blessing (Genesis 25:29–34; 27:1–40), and would have killed Jacob had the latter not run away. They were eventually reconciled as a result of God's intervention and Esau became the ancestor of the Edomites. See also EDOM; JACOB.

eschatology see LAST THINGS.

1 Esdras see APOCRYPHA.

2 Esdras see APOCRYPHA.

Eshcol, valley of An area near Hebron from which Israelite spies brought back a large cluster of grapes, symbolizing the fertility of the Promised Land (Numbers 13:23–4).

Essenes see DEAD SEA SCROLLS.

Esther A Jewish woman of outstanding beauty who became queen of the Persian king Xerxes. Her name is probably Persian, though she also had a Jewish name, Hadassah, meaning 'myrtle'. Though initially dependent on her uncle Mordecai, her faith, wisdom and courage were crucial in enabling Jews in Persia to escape a plan to kill them (Esther 4:11–17; 7:1–8:8). See also ESTHER, BOOK OF.

Esther, additions to see APOCRYPHA.

Esther, book of

Structure
Esther becomes queen (1:1–2:18)
Esther and Mordecai defeat Haman's plot (2:19–7:10)
The Jews preserved (8:1–10:3)

Famous passage
'For such a time as this' (4:14)

A story about Esther, a Jewish queen of Persia, and her uncle Mordecai who managed to thwart a plot to destroy the Jews. The book is traditionally regarded as a record of events in the reign of the Persian king Xerxes I (486–465 BC), though because most of the information cannot be verified one way or the other it is sometimes called a historical novel. However, the accurate references to Persian life and culture suggest that the book can be taken seriously as an historical work. A longer version of Esther is preserved in the Greek translation of the Old Testament, and these Additions are preserved in the Apocrypha.

The book shows a generally favourable attitude towards the Persians and was probably written during the period of the Persian empire, though a date in the third century BC when the Jews were ruled by the Greeks is also possible. The book does not mention God explicitly, but shows how God's providence is effective in human affairs, even reversing the plans of powerful political leaders. Other important themes include the origins of the Jewish festival of Purim which celebrates the Jews' deliverance from destruction (9:18–32), and the important role believers can play in the highest affairs of state.

eternal life The most important gift given to those who put their faith in Jesus (John 3:16). It refers to a quality of life by which a person can know God for ever through Jesus (John 17:3). The experience of eternal life always begins in this life, but its benefits will only be fully appreciated in the life to come. These benefits are guaranteed for ever, however, since death is accompanied by the promise of resurrection and the enjoyment of God's presence. See also SALVATION.

eternity Phrases such as 'for ever and ever' or 'all ages' refer not to an abstract timelessness but to a different quality of lasting time in which God lives (Galatians 1:5). Whereas human beings are temporary creatures bound by created time, human language can only speak of God as one who is enduring and changeless in unending time.

By also revealing himself in human time, God enables human beings to live with him eternally through faith in Christ.

Ethanim see CALENDAR, JEWISH.

Ethiopia, Ethiopians Often called Cush in the Bible and referring to an area stretching south from Aswan to the junction of the Nile near modern Khartoum. Its greatest period was c. 720–660 BC when Ethiopia controlled the Nile valley, and during this period it assisted Hezekiah unsuccessfully against Assyria. The Ethiopian eunuch's knowledge of the Old Testament (Acts 8:27–35) may reveal his contacts with Jewish settlements in the area. See map of WORLD OF THE BIBLE.

Eucharist see LORD'S SUPPER.

eunuch The Hebrew *saris* means 'a court official' as well as someone who is 'castrate' whether by nature or by human action. The case of Potiphar who is called a *saris* and yet was married shows that the Hebrew term did not necessarily refer to a man's physical condition (Genesis 39:1, 7). Jesus also referred to spiritual eunuchs as those who had denied themselves normal human desires in order to serve God better (Matthew 19:12). The conversion of the Ethiopian eunuch is recorded in Acts 8:26–40.

Euphrates, River The more western of the two great rivers of ancient Mesopotamia (the other is the Tigris), which rises in eastern Turkey and flows through Syria and Iraq into the Persian Gulf. The western bend of the river in Syria formed Israel's ideal northern boundary, but only under David did Israel's influence extend so far north (2 Samuel 8:3). See map of WORLD OF THE BIBLE.

evangelism The principles and practice of making the gospel about Jesus Christ known to those outside the community of believers. Recognition of the necessity of this task developed only gradually, since Israel had little understanding about telling others about the will of God. Jesus, however, brought about a decisive change, though even his message about the coming of the kingdom of God was largely confined to 'the lost sheep of Israel' (Matthew 15:24). Only after the Spirit was poured out was the church really equipped to take the good news to the ends of the earth (Acts 1:8).

The evangelism of both Jesus and the early church involved proclaiming the word of God in various ways. The task was to bring people to accept Jesus as Messiah and Lord by repenting of their sins and putting their faith in God, and despite much opposition and persecution, their teaching and preaching was effective. It was also accompanied by various signs, especially of healing. By the end of the New Testament period, the gospel had been taken from

Jerusalem to Rome and churches had been planted in many parts of the Roman Empire.

evangelist 1. Used in the New Testament for someone with a special gift for spreading the gospel, whether in one locality (2 Timothy 4:5) or in several (Acts 21:8). This gift was often exercised alongside other gifts.

2. Later, used for the writers of the four Gospels.

Eve The wife of Adam, specially created from one of his ribs (Genesis 2:21–3). She was the mother of Cain, Abel and Seth. See also ADAM.

everyday life see DAILY LIFE.

evil Physical and moral evils are an inevitable part of life in this world. The general human experience of evil is a consequence of the fall when God punished human beings for their disobedience (Genesis 3), and the Bible regularly affirms that God remains sovereign over all evil practices while maintaining that he himself is incapable of moral evil. Though experiencing God's punishment is unpleasant, it does not necessarily mean either that God is evil or that he is the author of evil. The Bible does not provide specific answers to questions about the relationship between the goodness of God and the origin of evil or about the nature of evil, though it does indicate that human experience of evil is closely related to the freedom to choose between right and wrong. The Bible also indicates that evil arises from the activity of an unseen person called the devil or Satan.

God responds to evil in several ways. First, he holds everyone responsible for their evil actions, and employs a mixture of justice and mercy to maintain a sense of order in human society, even though his use of human beings to do so sometimes results in lawlessness. Second, he is able to make use of evil actions by reversing their intended effects and making them conform to his purposes, as demonstrated supremely by the cross (Acts 2:23–4). Third, he has already defeated evil's ultimate power by fully confronting its agony and injustice at the cross (1 John 3:8), and he will finally destroy it completely at Christ's second coming.

evil spirits see DEMONS.

ewe see SHEEP.

excommunication The removal of a church member because of serious and persistent sin. Since it is rarely mentioned in the New Testament, it was probably rarely necessary. It was only to be employed after other avenues of private and public correction had been exhausted (Matthew 18:15–17) and was intended to prevent the further spread of sin (1 Corinthians 5:4–13).

exile, the The consequences of the collapse of the kingdoms of Israel and Judah in 722 and 587 BC when their inhabitants were taken to Assyria and Babylonia respectively. The whole experience is understood as God punishing his people for their persistent rejection of his will and as the fulfilment of his covenant threats (2 Kings 17:7–23; 2 Chronicles 36:15–20). The Babylonian exile formally ended with Cyrus' edict in 539/8 BC permitting the Jews to return home, but many families either took several decades to make up their minds to do so or never returned at all. The whole experience had a deep psychological effect on the Jews, many of whom remained scattered across the nations, either because of their deep discouragement or because living in the Promised Land no longer had the same significance for them. However, the exile was also a very formative period, when prophets such as Jeremiah and Ezekiel were active and the editing of the so-called Deuteronomic History was finally completed. The emergence of these Old Testament books helped the Jews to understand God's ways in the exile and provided them with fresh hope, both for the immediate and more long-term future (Jeremiah 30–3). See also RETURN FROM EXILE.

Exodus, book of

Structure

Israel enslaved in Egypt (1:1–2:25)
God calls Moses to deliver Israel (3:1–7:7)
God brings Israel out of Egypt (7:8–15:21)
Israel in the wilderness (15:22–18:27)
God's covenant with Israel at Sinai (19:1–24:18)
Israel worships God at the Tent (25:1–40:38)

Famous passages

Moses at the burning bush (3:1–10)
The ten plagues (7:14–12:30)
Crossing the Red Sea (13:17–14:31)
God at Mount Sinai (19:9–25)
The Ten Commandments (20:1–17)
The covenant at Mount Sinai (24:1–11)
The golden calf (32:1–35)
Moses sees God (33:12–34:7)

The book of Exodus describes the central moment in Old Testament history when the Israelites left Egypt as slaves, crossed the Red Sea and entered into a covenant with God at Mount Sinai.

Through this series of events, Israel became a nation in its own right for the first time. Exodus is not primarily a historical account, however, but a theological interpretation of Israel's national origins, based upon what it meant to be the Lord's people. God's nature is revealed through his name (3:13–14; 6:2–3) pronounced in Hebrew something like 'Yahweh' (*yah*way), and explained as 'I am who I am' or 'I will be what I will be' (3:14). This means that he will always be with Israel, working on their behalf and making himself known to them. Different aspects of God emerge through the book. Yahweh is a redeemer and liberator (chapters 1–18), a covenant-making God (chapters 19–24), and a God of holiness and glory (chapters 25–40). The climax occurs when God proclaims his name (34:6–7), which shows that God is essentially merciful.

A phrase frequently found in Exodus is 'that you will know that I am the LORD'. The fact that it is addressed to Egypt (7:17) as well as Israel (29:46) suggests that God wants everyone to know who he really is, whether they believe in him or not. Egypt and the Pharaohs learn about Yahweh through extended conflict ending in death and defeat. Israel's encounter with God results in a special relationship known as a covenant, formalized at Mount Sinai. The covenant binds God and Israel together, identifying Israel as Yahweh's people, and giving them laws to help them live with God and with one another. Worship is the central focus of the covenant, expressed particularly through the Passover festival (12:1–13:16) and the ceremonies recognizing God's holy presence at the Tent (chapters 25–40). The purpose of Israel's freedom from slavery at the start of the book is to lead them to worship God.

Exodus is widely agreed to have been compiled from a variety of sources, sometimes called J, E and P, though no agreement exists as to when and how the hypothetical sources were combined. The book includes various literary types such as narrative (chapters 1–19, 24), law (chapters 20–3), and liturgy (chapters 25–40), but the most productive approaches to its interpretation are based on the careful overall arrangement. See also EXODUS, THE.

exodus, the The word is a Latin form of a Greek word meaning 'going out', and refers to the event when the Israelite slaves left Egypt and spent forty years travelling towards the Promised Land. The Book of Exodus provides several historical and geographical details, and though no clear reference to the exodus has yet been found outside the Bible, several incidental features suggest its basic historicity. These include the presence of Semitic peoples like the Israelites in ancient Egypt, the authentic Egyptian names of the store cities Pithom and Rameses (Exodus 1:11), and the archaeological record in Palestine. The exodus is often placed in the first half of the thirteenth century BC, though a few date it to the fifteenth century BC. Much historical detail remains unclear, however, including the location of the Red Sea crossing, of Mount Sinai and the route through the wilderness, And modern reconstructions of the event should only be attempted with caution.

The biblical record understands the exodus as the supreme moment when God delivered his people from slavery and created Israel as a nation. God alone subdued Egypt, with Israel as no more than spectators and Moses as a rather reluctant leader, despite his great faith and courage. God's mighty victory becomes a model for further acts of divine deliverance elsewhere in the Bible (e.g. Isaiah 11:10–16; 43:16–21). The exodus account contains several examples of God's direct intervention such as the burning bush, the plagues, and crossing the Red Sea on dry ground, which have caused problems for some readers. Though in the case of some of the plagues, a sequence of natural phenomena may be involved, the account takes it for granted that God exercises great freedom in being active in human events.

eye Often used symbolically to indicate a person's attitude (Proverbs 21:4) and especially their sense of spiritual awareness. Human eyes are to be lifted towards God (the Bible never mentions closing one's eyes for prayer!), and will ultimately see God (Psalm 123:1–2; 1 John 3:2). Reference to God's eyes is a way of saying that he sees everything, including people's motives as well as their actions (Zechariah 4:10).

Ezekiel A priest who prophesied to the Babylonian exiles. Little is known of his personal life except that he was struck dumb for a while and was not allowed to mourn for his wife (Ezekiel 3:26–7; 24:15–27). His prophecies sometimes involved him in strange behaviour and colourful visions, but this does not detract from his important contribution to biblical thought at a critical time in Israel's history. See also EZEKIEL, BOOK OF.

Ezekiel, book of

An important but unusual book of Old Testament prophecy. It is set in Babylonia, where Ezekiel was exiled in 597 BC, and contains prophecies he received between 593 and 571 BC. His messages are sometimes conveyed through bizarre dramas like eating a scroll (3:1–3) or lying on his side for 430 days (4:1–17), and through imaginative visions like the magnificent description of

Structure
Prophecies against Judah (1:1–24:27)
Prophecies about other nations (25:1–32:32)
Restoration of God's people (33:1–48:35)

Famous passages
A vision of God (1:1–28)
Ezekiel as a watchman (33:1–20)
The valley of dry bones (37:1–14)
The river streaming from the temple (47:1–12)

God (chapter 1) or of the glorious new temple (chapters 40–8). The frequent symbolic language is explained by Ezekiel's background in temple ceremonial, for he was a priest as well as a prophet.

The main issue in the book is whether God would remain with his people in exile. His presence is expressed through the images of a cloud of God's glory and a divine throne supported by angelic figures, and when the cloud leaves the temple for Babylonia (chapter 10), it seems as if God has abandoned the Israelites completely. However, the book not only reassures the exiles that God's glory is still with them in Babylonia (chapter 1), but promises that he will return to a new temple in Jerusalem (43:1–7).

The early years of Ezekiel's ministry take place before Jerusalem is finally destroyed, and the first part of the book is mainly a call to repentance in the hope that the ultimate catastrophe could still be avoided. This teaching on repentance is an important development over earlier parts of the Old Testament. Ezekiel shows that since each generation inherits neither its predecessors' sins nor their faith, everyone is individually responsible to God for their own actions. However, God will always deal favourably with those who repent, because, as Ezekiel repeatedly makes clear, God does not wish anyone to die (chapter 18). Ezekiel's hope for the future is characteristically vivid. It centres on the promise of a new heart and a new spirit (chapter 36) and on an idealistic vision of a new land and a new temple (chapters 40–8). The vision of the valley of dry bones (chapter 37) makes it plain that this future is dependent entirely on God's initiative. The bones which represent the nation of Israel can only be resurrected as God breathes life into them, which he does through the words of Ezekiel.

Ezra An important reformer in post-exilic Judaism, whose main achievement was to establish the law of God as the basis of the Jewish community. He was appointed by the Persian king Artaxerxes, probably Artaxerxes I in the mid-fifth century BC, as something like a 'Minister for Jewish Affairs' to teach the Jewish law and ensure that the Jews kept the Persian law (Ezra 7:11–26). See also EZRA, BOOK OF.

Ezra, book of

Structure
> First return from exile (1:1–2:70)
> Rebuilding the temple (3:1–6:22)
> Ezra's reforms (7:1–10:44)

Famous passages
> Cyrus' edict (1:2–4; 6:3–5)
> Dedicating the temple (6:13–18)
> Ezra's commission (7:11–28)
> Ezra's prayer (9:5–15)

The book falls into two distinct sections. The first (chapters 1–6) is a brief account of the restoration period, from Cyrus' edict in 539/8 BC permitting the Jews to return home from exile to the dedication of the rebuilt temple in March 515 BC. The second section (chapters 7–10) deals with some of Ezra's work as spiritual leader of the Jewish community. Since the date of Ezra's arrival is the 'seventh year of the king' (7:8), i.e. 458 BC assuming the reference is to Artaxerxes I, at least fifty-seven years exists between chapters 6 and 7. If this 'seventh year' refers to Artaxerxes II, i.e. 398 BC, then the gap is of course even larger.

The books of Ezra and Nehemiah were originally a single work. Together they form the most important historical source available for the restoration of the Jewish people in Palestine in the sixth and fifth centuries BC. Several important sources lie behind the book of Ezra, including what is generally called the 'Ezra memoir' (which also includes parts of Nehemiah 8–10) and some Aramaic documents (4:6–6:15; 7:12–26). The book shows how God worked through human politics to re-establish his people in Judah, and emphasizes the central role of the temple and of the law in the process of reformation.

f

face To see a person's face is both to recognize them and to be accepted by them. The contrasting expression about hiding one's face implies rejection. Both ideas are applicable to human beings and to God. To see God's face means to be blessed (Numbers 6:25–6) but when he turns his face away the consequences are serious (Micah 3:4).

failure Even the great people of the Bible are described as being guilty of various forms of failure. King David committed adultery and murder, for example, and Peter denied three times knowing Jesus. But forgiveness and restoration are always possible, and the Bible repeatedly underlines that no failure is beyond redemption for those who repent of their sin (Luke 5:29–32).

faith Several types of faith are mentioned in the Bible, but it is essentially an attitude of mind and heart by which a person entrusts themselves to God. The Bible's own definition is that 'faith is being sure of what we hope for and certain of what we do not see' (Hebrews 11:1). This verse refers to the object of faith as the unseen God and his promises, especially concerning Jesus Christ (John 14:1), and the effect of faith as a deep assurance about God and his ability to keep his promises. This sense of assurance does not mean the believer has no doubts, but rather that an awareness of God's unfailing love and provision can sustain a person in all the circumstances of life.

The experience of faith begins with saving faith, that is, a complete trust in Jesus Christ that he can make a person right with God through his death on the cross. Faith of this kind is the only means of salvation and is often contrasted with an attempt to gain acceptance with God through human pride and achievement (Romans 3:21–8). This quality of faith is demonstrated throughout Old Testament history (Hebrews 11), and is available to anyone irrespective of their background. Faith is then expected to develop in the life of each believer, so that it becomes a way of life (Galatians 2:20). Growth in faith usually involves some form of testing, if not persecution, as illustrated supremely by Abraham and by Paul's various trials on his missionary journeys. The genuineness of a person's faith is also shown by the extent to which they obey God. Verbal claims to faith are worthless unless they are supported by appropriate actions (James 2:14–26). In addition to the life of faith, the New Testament mentions a special gift of faith (1 Corinthians 12:9), which can be exercised on occasions of particular need such as severe illness (Acts 3:1–10) or famine (1 Kings 17:2–6).

Though faith is a human activity, the ability to believe is ultimately God's gift (Ephesians 2:8–9). God provides faith to those who ask him, but it is also stimulated by hearing and reading God's word (Romans 10:14–17). Finally, faith is sometimes understood as the basic objective core of Christian belief, especially in the phrase 'the faith' (Jude 3).

faithfulness In addition to commitment shown in ordinary human relationships, faithfulness is a distinctive aspect of God's love and the love that he expects to see in those with whom he enters into a covenant relationship (Deuteronomy 7:9). Faithfulness is part of the character of God, which he shows by fulfilling his promises. The idea is reflected in the Hebrew word *hesed*, often translated 'steadfast love', which is particularly characteristic of God. God's faithful love was always available to his people, even when they turned away from him (Psalm 51:1; 2 Timothy 2:13). In return, God expected his people to be faithful to him by obeying his words (1 Kings 2:3–4) and by being committed to each other (1 Peter 4:10). Covenants between human beings were particularly intended to be marked by the faithfulness of the parties involved towards one another (1 Samuel 20:8), though the Bible commends faithfulness wherever it occurs (Luke 16:10). Faithfulness is especially appropriate towards other members of one's family, notably within marriage (Hebrews 13:4). It was also to be shown by those in authority (1 Corinthians 4:1–2) and towards those in authority (2 Samuel 15:21).

faithlessness Turning away from God after having previously followed him is viewed as a particularly serious matter (Hebrews 6:4–8). The parable of the sower mentions various causes of faithlessness such as superficial faith, the attraction of other things, or anxiety over worldly matters. The example of Old Testament Israel, who often abandoned the Lord for other gods, is not to be imitated (Hebrews 3:7–12).

fall, the The term as such does not appear in the Bible, but is used by theologians to describe the first sin and its consequences (Genesis 3). First, the idea of a fall assumes that God created a perfect world before Adam and Eve disobeyed God's command about not eating the fruit of the tree of the knowledge of good and evil. Second, it recognizes that as a result of that one sin, human life has changed irrevocably and that the world continues under the pain and suffering of God's curse. Paul explains that all human beings have become sinners and are subject to death (Romans 5:12–14). Under the influence particularly of Augustine, this led to the development of the doctrine of original sin, according to which every person is born with an inevitable tendency towards sin. Third, the fall of the human race is associated with the fall of the devil and his angels from heaven, but whereas the latter's punishment is certain, Christ is able to set human beings free from all the effects of the fall. See also SIN.

falling away see APOSTASY.

false prophets/teachers These were a constant problem in both the Old Testament and the New Testament, though false prophets were a greater threat to Israel and false teachers to the church. The description 'false' applies essentially to what was said, and could refer either to something misleading that was spoken in the name of the Lord or to words that made no claim to come from God. However, such people could also be false in the sense that they did not always act from the best of motives, and might be influenced by a desire for personal advancement, greed, divination or a lack of concern for the truth.

God's people are repeatedly warned to be on their guard against such people, especially those who claim to speak for God. All teaching was to be checked against God's written word, and prophecy was always to be tested to see whether it was authenticated by events or not (Deuteronomy 18:21–2; 1 Thessalonians 5:19–22). Since false prophets and teachers effectively relied on their own ideas, their claims to authority must be investigated, and their lives must be tested to see whether they are consistent with God's moral standards. False teachings mentioned include legalism, various combinations of Christian truth and contemporary ideas, and denying that Jesus was the Messiah. Those who promoted such teachings were to be resisted and refuted, and were liable to God's severe judgement.

false witness see LIE, LYING.

family The Israelite concept of the extended family is much broader than the modern Western nuclear family of two parents and their children. In biblical times, the family or household incorporated not only the grandparents but also dependent workers such as slaves and servants and even temporary residents. The family idea was also reflected in Israel's social structures, with each tribe being regarded as a family of clans and each clan a family of families. Even the nation was thought of as one large family in which everyone was descended from a common ancestor. The family ideal was maintained spiritually through the idea that God was Israel's spiritual Father, though the church made greater use of this concept than Israel did. Christians referred to God as their heavenly Father and to fellow believers as brothers and sisters, and called the church 'the family of God' (1 Peter 4:17).

Israel's sense of family solidarity within a tribal structure remained strong, though it suffered from various demographic changes, especially the urbanization process during the monarchy and the dispersion during and after the exile. The continuity of the Israelite family was maintained by several important customs. Family unity was strengthened by encouragement to marry within the tribe. Family property was inherited by the eldest son, who also had the responsibility of continuing the family name, though it is not known at what stage younger sons might move out and set up their own household. Parents without a son might occasionally adopt a trusted servant as a son (Genesis 15:2–3), though daughters could also inherit property in the absence of sons (Numbers 27:1–11). Ultimate authority within the family rested with the father, though women also played a significant role. Mothers were to be given equal respect with fathers (Exodus 20:12), and were as much involved with their children's education as fathers (Proverbs 1:8). See also HOME.

famine Famines can be described both as natural events and as phenomena under the sovereign control of God. As a sanction for disobedience, famine is often associated with God's judgement (Deuteronomy 28:15–18; Jeremiah 14:11–18), but God always warned his people in advance in such circumstances, and provided for them in unexpected ways (Genesis 42:1–47:12; 1 Kings 17:2–16).

farming see AGRICULTURE.

fasting The practice of going without food and sometimes drink. The only regular requirement to fast was on the annual Day of Atonement (Leviticus 16:29; Acts 27:9), but people also fasted voluntarily or through custom. Four fast days, for example, were observed after the exile (Zechariah 8:19) and the Pharisees fasted twice a week (Luke 18:12). Jesus fasted for a forty-day period at the beginning of his ministry, and the early church also fasted on certain special occasions. The purpose of the practice is not explained specifically, but it is clear that it gave people an opportunity to make time for God a greater priority than their own bodily needs. Fasting is often associated with prayer. This might include confession and repentance or asking God for help in times of special need such as military invasion or when particular guidance was required (2 Chronicles 20:1–4; Acts 13:2–3). The true nature of fasting is presented in Isaiah 58. See also PRAYER.

fatherhood see FAMILY.

favour see GRACE.

favouritism In contrast to repeated assertions that God is totally impartial in all his dealings, both Israel and the church sometimes gave special preference to individuals and groups, but always with disastrous consequences. The principle of equal treatment before God and people was enshrined in the law and the gospel (Leviticus 19:15; James 2:8–9).

fear A distinction is made between ordinary human fear and the fear of God. A wide range of human fears are mentioned, including fear of the future, persecution, death, God's judgement, and enemies. Fear of people is particularly common, such as Jacob's fear of Esau's revenge (Genesis 32:11) or the disciples' fear about the news of Paul's conversion (Acts 9:26). Fear brought about by supernatural events is also frequent, especially when God was at work in unexpected ways (Daniel 5:9; Acts 10:4). Though such fears are often justified, the Bible regularly encourages people to turn their fear into trust in God, since God is always far greater than the thing of which they are afraid (Psalm 23:4; John 14:27).

The fear of God is a typical biblical way of expressing both reverence and love for God. In this sense, fear is a positive thing which God desires in his people (Deuteronomy 6:2; 1 Peter 2:17). This fear really describes the faith that should characterize a person's basic approach to life, and is regarded as the basis of true wisdom (Proverbs 1:7). The term 'God-fearer' was a traditional way of referring to someone, usually a non-Jew, who had become a worshipper of the Lord (Acts 10:2).

feasts and festivals According to Old Testament law, the life of every Israelite was supposed to be organized around the three great annual festivals of Passover and Unleavened Bread, Pentecost or Weeks, and Tabernacles or Booths. These festivals provided opportunities for them to celebrate together thanking God for all he had done, in relation to each year's harvest and to his great actions on Israel's behalf, especially the exodus. They were based on God's deeds in creation and covenant, and were quite different from the festivals of Israel's neighbours which were related to the agricultural cycle. Israel's great festivals were still observed in New Testament times, and Jesus used them to illustrate his teaching (John 7:37–9) or in the case of Passover to explain the meaning of his death (Matthew 26:26–9;1 Corinthians 5:7). Pentecost was the occasion when the Holy Spirit was given to the early church (Acts 2).

The Old Testament also lists several other festivals of greater and lesser importance. The most significant was the Day of Atonement preceding the Feast of Tabernacles, when Israel's sins were annually forgiven (Leviticus 16). Other festivals included Hanukkah or Dedication, celebrating the rededication of the temple in 164 BC (1 Maccabees 4:52–9), and Purim, which recalled a great deliverance for the Jews in Persia (Esther 9:18–32).

Feasts and festivals		
Sabbath		Exodus 20:8–11
New moon		Numbers 28:11–15
Passover	Month 1, Day 14	Leviticus 23:5
Unleavened Bread	Month 1, Days 15–21	Leviticus 23:6–8
First fruits/Weeks/ Pentecost	50 days after harvest starts	Deuteronomy 16:9–12
Trumpets	Month 7, Day 1	Leviticus 23:23–5
Day of Atonement	Month 7, Day 10	Leviticus 23:26–32
Tabernacles/Booths	Month 7, Day 15	Leviticus 23:33–43; John 7:2
Purim	Month 12, Days 14–15	Esther 9:18–19

feet Can represent the whole person, often in relation to either the direction of their life (Psalm 17:5) or their status in relation to God (Psalm 40:2). To be at the feet of Jesus or God normally indicates worship in the presence of his majesty (Revelation 1:17). To be beneath someone's feet is to be subject to them (Ephesians 1:22–3).

Felix, Marcus Antonius Procurator of Judea from c. 52–9 AD, before whom Paul was tried, but who preferred receiving bribes to providing justice (Acts 23:23–24:27).

fellowship The sharing of a common life on the basis of a mutually acceptable relationship between the parties involved. The purpose of the gospel is that believers may have fellowship with God and with other believers. Fellowship between God and his people means the existence of a completely open relationship between them. This is made possible by the death of Jesus, experienced through the Holy Spirit, and established with the Father (1 John 1:3, 7; 2 Corinthians 13:14). Fellowship between believers is reflected in the concept of the church as a body in which every member belongs to everyone else and works alongside others for the sake of the gospel. It is illustrated in the sharing of possessions and in making provision for the poor. It is celebrated in the Lord's Supper or Communion through a common sharing of the benefits of Christ's death.

fellowship offering Also known as the peace offering or shared offering. This was a common type of Old Testament sacrifice in which a small portion of a sacrificial animal was offered to God and the rest was eaten by priests and worshippers in a communal meal. The fellowship offering included freewill offerings, thanksgiving offerings, and offerings resulting from a vow (Leviticus 3:1–17; 7:11–34).

festivals see FEASTS AND FESTIVALS.

Festus, Porcius Felix's successor as procurator of Judaea, who twice heard Paul's testimony before sending him to Caesar (Acts 24:27–26:32).

fever see DISEASES AND ILLNESSES.

fig, sycomore-fig tree One of the commonest trees in Palestine, which can grow to 11 metres high, and whose shade was highly valued (Micah 4:4). Important references include the fig-leaves which provided coverings for Adam and Eve's nakedness (Genesis 3:7) and the immediate withering of a fig-tree which Jesus cursed (Matthew 21:18–22).

finger see HAND.

fir see TREES AND BUSHES.

fire In addition to its ordinary domestic uses, fire is often associated with punishment, both literally and as eternal fire (Leviticus 20:14; Revelation 20:10). However, it is also frequently used as a symbol of God's presence, especially in relation to his holiness and purity (Hebrews 12:29). Prayers answered by fire are special signs of the power of God (Leviticus 9:23–4).

firstborn Every firstborn son enjoyed the privilege of a larger share of the inheritance. This was known as his birthright, and although its exact nature may originally have been at the father's disposal, it developed into the fixed form of a double portion (Deuteronomy 21:15–17). The double portion also symbolized direct succession even where family descent was not involved (2 Kings 2:9).

Jesus' description as God's firstborn emphasizes that he receives as of right all the privileges due from his heavenly Father (Colossians 1:15). Firstborn sons also had a special place in ceremonial law, since each family had to redeem them at the exodus by killing a Passover lamb (Exodus 12:1–30).

firstfruits The first part of any crop was to be offered to God as a special sign of thanks, since he was the one who had provided the means for it to grow. This was marked especially by the Feast of Firstfruits or Weeks, later known as Pentecost, when the firstfruits of the wheat harvest were brought to God (Leviticus 23:9–14).

fish, fishing Fishing in the Sea of Galilee was probably a common occupation throughout biblical times, but it became important only in the New Testament because four of Jesus' disciples were fishermen. Fish were caught by spears, hooks or nets, and were an important part of the Israelite's diet. Reference to a Fish Gate in Jerusalem suggests the existence of a fish market in the city. Fishing is also used symbolically, of God's judgement (Jeremiah 16:16) and of evangelism (Matthew 4:19). The fish became an important Christian symbol in the early church, where the letters of the Greek word for fish, *ichthus*, represented Jesus (i) Christ (ch) of God (th) the Son (u) Saviour (s).

flea see INSECTS AND ARACHNIDS.

fleece see SHEEP AND GOATS.

flesh In the Old Testament, usually refers to the physical aspects of human beings and sometimes animals, and is often associated with what is weak and temporary. In the New Testament, especially Paul, it often includes sinful attitudes and actions (Romans 8:1–13; Galatians 5:19–21). This is not because the body is regarded as sinful in itself, but because *flesh* means humanity in contrast to God.

flies see INSECTS AND ARACHNIDS; PLAGUES OF EGYPT.

flint see METALS AND STONE.

flock see SHEEP AND GOATS.

flogging see CRIME AND PUNISHMENT.

flood, the Genesis 6–8 describes an apparently universal flood. Apart from Noah's family who survived in the ark, the whole human race was wiped out, though the practice in Hebrew narrative of concentrating entirely on the immediate context suggests that a more localized flood might be meant. Mention of the ark landing on the mountains of Ararat in modern Turkey merely confirms the general Middle Eastern setting. Support for the basic concept of an extensive catastrophic flood comes from the existence of similar flood stories around the world, especially in ancient Mesopotamian literature which has a number of particularly close parallels to the biblical story. The biblical account, however, is distinct in explaining that the flood was the result of God's anger against human sin, and in mentioning God's covenant promise that despite human nature remaining unchanged, he would never again destroy the earth in the same way. See also ARK, NOAH'S.

flour see CEREALS; FOOD AND DRINK.

flowers see PLANTS.

flute see MUSIC AND MUSICAL INSTRUMENTS.

food and drink The main food-producing plants were corn, the vine and the olive tree. The staple food was bread, which was made from either wheat or barley. Meat came from cattle and sheep but was rarely eaten, and the fattened calf was eaten only on special occasions (Luke 15:23). Fish was an important source of food, though poultry was probably less common. Honey and milk products such as butter and cheese were popular, and fruit and vegetables were widely available. Vegetables included lentils, beans, cucumbers, leeks, onions and garlic, and nuts were also popular. The fig was the commonest fruit, but grapes, dates, melons, pomegranates and probably apples were well known. Salt was used as a preservative, and herbs such as mint, dill and cummin were used for seasoning. Olive oil provided the main cooking oil and was also used as food. Apart from water, wine seems to have been the commonest drink, though milk was quite often drunk, and beer was certainly available.

Food and drink

Corn

Barley	Deuteronomy 8:8
Millet	Ezekiel 4:9
Spelt	Exodus 9:32
Wheat	Psalm 81:16

Meat and fish

Calf	Luke 15:23
Fish	John 21:12–13
Goat	Judges 6:19
Lamb	2 Samuel 12:4
Ox	Nehemiah 5:18
Partridge	1 Samuel 26:20
Poultry	Nehemiah 5:18
Quail	Numbers 11:31–4
Venison	Deuteronomy 14:5

Fruit

Almonds	Genesis 43:11
Apple	Song of Songs 2:3
Dates	2 Samuel 6:19
Fig	Matthew 7:16
Grapes	Isaiah 5:2
Melon	Isaiah 1:8
Nuts	Song of Songs 6:11
Pomegranate	Joel 1:12
Raisins	1 Samuel 25:18

Vegetables

Beans	Exekiel 4:9
Carob	Luke 15:16
Cucumbers	Numbers 11:5
Garlic	Numbers 11:5
Lentils	Genesis 25:34
Leeks	Numbers 11:5
Onions	Numbers 11:5

Other foods

Butter	Proverbs 30:33
Cheese	1 Samuel 17:18
Egg	Luke 11:12
Honey	Ezekiel 3:3
Mustard	Matthew 13:31
Salt	Matthew 5:13

Drinks

Beer	Proverbs 20:1
Milk	Judges 4:19
New wine	Proverbs 3:10
Sweet drinks	Nehemiah 8:10
Sweet wine	Amos 9:13
Water	John 4:13–14
Wine	Proverbs 23:31
Wine vinegar	John 19:29

food laws Animals were divided into those that were clean and unclean. Detailed lists of animals in Leviticus 11 and Deuteronomy 14 show that a range of animals such as pigs, rabbits, fish without fins and scales and most insects were prohibited as food, though the reasons for making such distinctions are primarily ceremonial rather than hygienic or dietary. See also CLEAN AND UNCLEAN.

fool, folly A fool is not someone who has no intelligence, but a person who behaves without wisdom. Foolishness and wisdom are always understood in practical rather than intellectual terms. The foolish person is therefore one who rejects advice, is lazy, who makes no provision for the future, or who is all talk and no action (Proverbs 1:20–33). Folly particularly involves rejecting God's ways, like the rich fool who gathered material but not spiritual wealth (Luke 12:16–21) or the person who did not build their life on the foundation of God's word (Matthew 7:26–7).

footstool Usually refers to the ark, the temple, the earth or God's enemies as God's footstool, emphasizing God's complete supremacy over them (Psalm 110:1; Isaiah 66:1).

foreigner Israelite law encouraged a hospitable and caring attitude towards foreigners, but prohibited acceptance of foreign religious ideas and practices where these detracted from the standards of Yahwism (Leviticus 19:33–4; Deuteronomy 7:1–6). Idolatry and sexual prostitution were particularly strongly discouraged. On the other hand, non-Israelite believers like the Moabite Ruth or Rahab the prostitute from Jericho were welcomed into Israelite communities. The temple was intended especially to encourage foreigners to worship Yahweh (1 Kings 8:41–3; Isaiah 56:3–8) See also ALIEN.

foreknowledge The idea that God knows all things before they happen and acts to bring them into being, even the tragedy of the cross (Acts 2:23). It particularly emphasizes that God's relationship with his people is secure and that their salvation is no accident (Romans 8:29; 1 Peter 1:2). It is not an alternative to human responsibility and is quite different from determinism, since God is always responsive to human repentance and faith (Isaiah 55:6–7). See also PREDESTINATION.

forgiveness The action by which a person is set free from guilt, whether by God or a human being. Forgiveness is concerned with the more personal aspects of redemption and atonement, which deal more generally with the removal of sin and evil. The Bible emphasizes God's absolute and undeserved gift of forgiveness to those who put their trust in Jesus as the heart of the Christian gospel. God offers forgiveness to all through the sacrificial death of Christ, since all human beings are guilty before God (Ephesians 1:7; Colossians 1:14). It is the task of those who proclaim the gospel to make this offer known (2 Corinthians 5:18–19), but the offer is not effective unless the guilty person receives it. When it is received, however, that person is completely forgiven. Forgiveness is primarily a description of a person's standing before God rather than a matter of feeling.

Those who have received God's forgiveness show it is genuine in two ways. First, a person who claims to have been forgiven forgives other people their sins (Matthew 6:14–15; 18:21–35). Second, they recognize the need for ongoing confession of sin and receipt of forgiveness because they still live imperfectly in this life (1 John 1:9).

forks see TABERNACLE.

fortification Cities in the ancient Near East were usually fortified by walls. These could be up to 9 metres high, and were sometimes casemate walls of double thickness. The walls were strengthened by towers, and entrance to the city was through large gates (2 Chronicles 8:5).

foundation In relation to actual buildings, the foundations of the temple were of special significance (1 Kings 6:37; Ezra 5:16). It is also important that firm foundations are laid in people's lives (Matthew 7:24–5) and in the church (1 Corinthians 3:11).

fox see ANIMALS.

fragrance Used mainly of the smell of incense offered in sacrifice, and by extension of worship that was acceptable to God. In the New Testament, used also of the sacrifice of Christ and of the attractiveness of the gospel (Ephesians 5:2; 2 Corinthians 2:14–16). See also SMELLING.

frankincense A yellow resin used in perfumes, as a medicine, and as incense offered to God (Exodus 30:34; Matthew 2:11).

free will The ability for people to make decisions for themselves is an essential part of the biblical view of human beings, even though their actions often offend God and result in his judgement. This freedom is constrained by two factors, however. First, the free operation of the human will never takes place outside God's overall control. When the things people do displease God, they remain accountable to him, and God is able to use even their wicked actions for his own purposes (Acts 2:23). Second, people are actually enslaved by their own sinful nature, from which only Christ can set them truly free (Romans 7:14–25).

freedom According to the Bible, only Christ can make people genuinely free (John 8:31–6). All other forms of freedom are either licence to please oneself or an illusion brought about by bondage to sin. The paradox of genuine freedom is that it can only be experienced through acknowledging the lordship of Christ and living by his laws and teaching. God's intention throughout the Bible is to set people free from whatever enslaves them. This basic theme which was established at the exodus from Egypt has been developed in a particular way by liberation theologians around the world. It was also the theme of Christ's ministry, whose proclamation of freedom developed the Old Testament idea of jubilee (Luke 4:18–19; cf. Isaiah 61:1–2), which involved cancelling all debts and restoring what had been lost. The freedom that Jesus provides should be understood on a broad scale. Though his primary task is to set people free for ever from the guilt, power and consequences of sin and from the influence of Satan, he also liberates them from other forms of bondage such as poverty, blindness and oppression (Luke 4:18). This work will be completed at his second coming.

friendship The benefits of friendship are widely recognized, especially mutual support in difficult times (Proverbs 18:24; Ecclesiastes 4:9–10). Notable examples of a deep commitment between friends include David and Jonathan (1 Samuel 18:1–3) and Paul's many friends who worked with him in the gospel. 'Friend' was a special term for a trusted royal adviser (2 Samuel 15:37).

frogs see PLAGUES OF EGYPT.

fruit of the spirit A term used to describe Christian character produced by the Holy Spirit (Galatians 5:22–3). Though people may naturally possess some of the qualities mentioned, as an integrated whole they are the work of God rather than the product of human nature.

fruitfulness God's original instruction to 'be fruitful and increase in number' (Genesis 1:28) reflects his intention for human beings to prosper, and God promises throughout the Bible that he will make his people fruitful (Psalm 1:1–3; John 15:1–17). However, the balance between material and spiritual prosperity varies, and the benefits of faith in God are often experienced through suffering (Mark 10:29–30).

fruits The most popular fruit was the fig, which was often made into fig-cakes, as well as being used for medicinal purposes. Grapes were widely available, though they were used more for wine-making than for eating. Other common fruits were the pomegranate, melon and probably the apple, though oranges and lemons developed in Palestine only after the biblical period.

fuel Most people used sticks from trees and shrubs for fires, though dung was used by the poor and charcoal by the rich (1 Kings 17:12; John 21:9).

furnace These were used for various purposes, including refining metals such as silver or smelting copper, firing pottery, or making bricks. The 'fiery furnace' into which Daniel's friends were thrown may well have been a brick-kiln (Daniel 3).

furniture and furnishings see HOME.

future see LAST THINGS.

g

Gabriel One of the two archangels mentioned in the Bible (the other is Michael), who also frequently occurs in intertestamental literature. His name means 'man of God'. He acted as an intermediary for Daniel and for Mary, and his most important task was to announce the Messiah's birth (Luke 1:26–38).

Gad 1. The seventh son of Jacob. See also GADITES.
2. A prophet of David's time who was particularly involved in the matter of David's census (2 Samuel 24).

Gadara, Gadarenes Gadara was one of the ten cities of the Decapolis, 10 kilometres south-east of the Sea of Galilee (modern Umm Qeis). Matthew 8:28 locates Jesus' healing of two demon-possessed men in this area. See map of NEW TESTAMENT ISRAEL.

Gadites A tribe descended from Gad who occupied southern Gilead in Transjordan. They are also mentioned in the ninth-century BC Moabite Stone. See map of OLD TESTAMENT ISRAEL.

Galatia An area in Asia Minor (modern Turkey). The churches to whom Paul wrote the Letter to the Galatians were either those mentioned in Acts as Pisidian Antioch, Iconium, Lystra and Derbe in the Roman province of Galatia or others in the traditional area of Galatia in the north around Ancyra (modern Ankara), Tavium and Pessinus. See also GALATIANS, LETTER TO THE. See map of PAUL'S JOURNEYS.

Galatians, letter to the

A short but important letter by Paul which deals with the true nature of the Christian gospel. The Galatian Christians were being tempted away from the gospel by people who insisted that Gentile Christians should follow certain Jewish practices such as circumcision and observing special days. Paul, however, saw this teaching as a perversion of Christianity. He called it 'a different gospel' (1:6) and described the Galatians as bewitched and foolish

> **Structure**
>> Turning away from the gospel (1:1–10)
>> The gospel of faith in Christ (1:11–4:11)
>> Freedom in Christ and the Spirit (4:12–6:10)
>> The gospel of the cross (6:11–18)
>
> **Famous passages**
>> 'I have been crucified with Christ' (2:20)
>> Christian adoption (3:26–4:7)
>> 'All one in Christ Jesus' (3:28)
>> The fruit of the Spirit (5:22–3)

(3:1). The main proposition of the letter (2:15–21) is that faith in Christ is sufficient for everything in the Christian life, in contrast to the teaching that God also requires Gentiles to observe the law of Moses. This leads on to Paul's plea that Christians should live in true freedom, based on what Christ has done and characterized by the qualities produced in their lives by the Holy Spirit ('the fruit of the Spirit', 5:22–3). This is consistent with the new law of Christ that Christians must love one another (5:13–15; 6:2).

The Galatian Christians lived in Asia Minor, though the precise area is not agreed. The date of the letter is linked with the question about where the churches were, and probably belongs in the period 50–7 AD, though it could be before the Council of Jerusalem c. 48/9 AD.

Galilee An upland area of northern Israel, bordered on three sides by plains, the Jordan valley to the east, Esdraelon to the south and the coastal plain to the west. It comprises the high plateau of Upper Galilee and the limestone hills of Lower Galilee. The area was of little importance in Old Testament times, but came into prominence in the second century BC and was made famous as the area where Jesus grew up. Lower Galilee where Jesus actually lived was a fertile area crossed by important trade routes, but most of the towns mentioned in the Gospels have now disappeared. See map of NEW TESTAMENT ISRAEL; OLD TESTAMENT ISRAEL.

Galilee, Sea of The second largest inland area of water in Palestine, lying 211 metres below sea level, and also known as the 'Sea of Kinnereth' (Chinnereth), the 'Lake of Gennesaret' and the 'Sea of Tiberias' (Luke 5:1–2). Important towns such as Capernaum and Tiberias lay on its shores, and the Gospels describe it as having a busy fishing industry. See map of NEW TESTAMENT ISRAEL; OLD TESTAMENT ISRAEL.

gall see HERBS AND SPICES.

Gallows see CROSS.

Gamaliel Paul's Jewish teacher who advised the Sanhedrin to adopt a cautious attitude to the first Christians (Acts 5:33–40).

games and sport Little is known about the way the ancient Israelites relaxed, though music and dancing were certainly popular. The main references to sport are to athletics, which the Jews learnt from the Greeks, though the references mainly illustrate aspects of the Christian life rather than describe real activities (1 Corinthians 9:24–7; 2 Timothy 2:5). However, other kinds of games were well known. Wrestling and archery are mentioned several times, while gaming boards for something like draughts have been discovered in various parts of the ancient Near East. Evidence of children's games includes whistles, rattles and model animals and chariots.

gardens see EDEN; GETHSEMANE.

garment see CLOTHING.

gate An important meeting-place in ancient cities where activities such as trade and the operation of justice took place (Ruth 4:1–12).

gatekeeper A Levitical official whose job involved guarding the temple gates and looking after temple finances (1 Chronicles 26).

Gath One of the five major Philistine cities, probably located at modern Tell es-Safi. It was the home of David's enemy Goliath, but its king, Achish, supported David when the latter was being pursued by the Philistines (1 Samuel 17; 27). See map of OLD TESTAMENT ISRAEL.

Gaza One of the five major Philistine cities, located at the southern edge of Canaan. It occupied an important position on the coast, and is often mentioned in ancient texts. The Israelites rarely controlled it, though Samson killed many of its inhabitants when he died (Judges 16:21–30). See map of NEW TESTAMENT ISRAEL; OLD TESTAMENT ISRAEL.

gazelle see DEER.

Geba A town whose name means 'hill'. It was 11 kilometres north of Jerusalem, at the kingdom of Judah's northern boundary.

Gedaliah Appointed by the Babylonians as governor of Judah after Nebuchadnezzar had captured it, but was assassinated within a few months (2 Kings 25:22–6).

Gehazi Servant of the prophet Elisha, who assisted in a miraculous resurrection but later succumbed to the temptation of greed (2 Kings 4:11–37; 5:19–27).

Gehenna The Hebrew name of a valley south-west of Jerusalem. Through its reputation as a place for the passing of children through the fire (2 Kings 21:6) it became a symbol of God's rejection and hence of hell.

genealogy A list of names indicating some kind of family connection. Genealogies are common in some parts of the Bible, since ancient societies viewed them as an important way of conveying certain kinds of information. They were arranged in either linear or segmented form. The former is a descending or ascending list of names, and the latter includes people from the same generation. Their purpose was not to list every generation, but to establish a person's legitimacy to perform certain tasks or to demonstrate continuity, especially as part of God's purposes through history (Matthew 1:1–17).

generation A distinctive biblical term used in a variety of senses. In the formula 'these are the generations of' it means family history, but more often it may refer either to certain characteristics of a particular group of people (Psalm 24:6; Luke 9:41) or simply to a long period of time (Genesis 15:16).

generosity A characteristic of God which he expects to see reflected in all his people. God is generous in providing everyone with the necessities of life and the means to enjoy them, whether they believe in him or not, but he is particularly generous to his people. He showers them with all kinds of gifts (Psalm 23:6; Ephesians 1:3), and they are expected to give freely to others in return (2 Corinthians 8:1–15). Their generosity is a sign of God's undeserved kindness and a contrast with the grasping attitude of people around them. See also GIVING.

Genesis, book of

The book of Genesis is in two distinct parts. The first (chapters 1–11) records Israel's version of the origins of the world and the human race, while the second (chapters 12–50) traces the way in which God's promises worked out in Abraham's family from Abraham to the time of Joseph. The two parts are closely connected, since God's promises are his response to the avalanche of human sin in chapters 3–11 that threatened to destroy God's good creation. The book's turning point is God's call to Abraham (12:1–3), which is a second new beginning parallel to the creation of the world. In both cases, God's word creates something new out of chaos, and God blesses what he has created (cf. 12:2–3 and 1:28). The contrast between the two parts of the book, however, is that whereas Adam and Eve refused to obey God's word (3:1–7), Abraham believed it (15:6). In contrast to Adam and Eve being banished from God's presence (3:22–4), Abraham was accepted by God and made right with him (15:6).

Structure
  Creation and fall (1:1–3:24)
  Spread of sin (4:1–11:26)
  Abraham (11:27–25:11)
  Ishmael and Isaac (25:12–26:34)
  Jacob and Esau (27:1–36:43)
  Joseph and his brothers (37:1–50:26)

Famous passages
  Creation of the world (1:1–2:3)
  Adam and Eve (2:4–3:24)
  Noah's flood (6:1–9:17)
  Tower of Babel (11:1–9)
  God's promises to Abraham (12:1–3)
  The sacrifice of Isaac (22:1–14)
  Jacob takes Esau's birthright (25:27–34)
  Jacob wrestles with God (32:22–32)
  Joseph goes to Egypt (37:1–50:14)

No one knows who wrote Genesis, since no firm evidence exists to support the traditional view of Moses' authorship. For a long time, many scholars believed Genesis was an amalgam of three sources, called J (= the Yahwistic source), E (= the Elohistic source), and P (= the Priestly source), from between the tenth and fifth centuries BC. Some also believe a long period of oral tradition lies behind these sources. In recent years, however, the book has increasingly been interpreted on the basis of its final shape and overall themes, for while its origins remain unknown, it can still be richly appreciated as a work of literature and theology.

Genesis has often been contrasted unfavourably with the discoveries of modern science and modern historical study. It is important to remember, however, that Genesis concentrates on God's role in creating the world, the human race and the Israelite people, and is not just a record of what took place. It is a mistake to oppose Genesis and science, and many scientists and theologians have seen them as complementing each other. Historically, many indirect points of contact exist between Genesis and the ancient world. Chapters 1–11 show repeated evidence of a Mesopotamian background, while the names, family customs and movements of the patriarchs' families provide many incidental, and therefore authentic, links with ancient Near Eastern history. The 'Patriarchal Age' is often placed in the first half of the second millennium BC, though some date it to the fourteenth century BC.

The Books of the Law

The first five books of the Old Testament are known collectively as the Law or the Pentateuch (from the Greek for 'five scrolls'). The former is misleading if 'law' is understood in the narrow sense of rules and regulations because, apart from Leviticus, the Books of the Law contain substantial sections of narrative recounting the early history of Israel. The Hebrew word translated as 'law' is *Torah*, which was understood as God's gift of love in teaching and instruction for life that was intended to kindle a loving response. As *Torah*, these books are the foundation documents of the Old Testament, and of the whole Bible, without which not much else would make sense.

Traditionally the books are attributed to Moses, though at least some sections, such as those dealing with events after his death, could not have been written by him, and Moses' authorship is only claimed at specific points (Exodus 24:4; Numbers 33:2; Deuteronomy 31:24). The books contain legal and narrative material, as well as occasional poetic sections. In the nineteenth and twentieth centuries, the interpretation of the Pentateuch was dominated by the Documentary Hypothesis theory developed most fully by Graf and Wellhausen, which assumed the existence of four sources, known as J, E, D and P, written at different stages in Israel's history. These were thought to have been edited together later, possibly around the time of the exile.

This source theory is no longer as attractive to scholars, who now focus more on the completed text and how it functions as a literary work. There was certainly a point at which the stories of Israel's beginnings were collected and recorded, but whenever and however that was, it resulted in the five Books of the Law, which read as one story with five different though overlapping sections. Their placement at the beginning of the Old Testament confirms their importance for the faith and life of Israel.

Genesis begins with eleven chapters of prologue, which trace various themes essential to the rest of the story. It records the creative intentions and activity of God and the conditions he established for human life. However, as humans failed to live within those conditions and in the light of God's intentions, God's good creation was disfigured. Chapters 12–50 begin the story of Israel, which, in the light of the prologue, is seen as God's creative answer to the situation. The main focus is on the four generations of the patriarchs: Abraham, Isaac, Jacob and Joseph. Jacob, after an encounter with God, was renamed Israel (Genesis 32:24–32), and Genesis ends with Israel's twelve sons in Egypt.

The narrative is picked up by Exodus, which recounts how the Israelites grew into a multitude of people, and then were brutally enslaved by the Egyptians. God does not forget about them, and he dramatically rescues them through the leadership of Moses with the night of the Passover (Exodus 12) and the miraculous crossing of the Red Sea (Exodus 14), two events which remain integral to Israel's life and faith. The rest of Exodus deals with the difficult journey through the wilderness towards the land of Canaan which God had promised to them. On the way God meets with his people at Mount Sinai and gives them the Ten Commandments and the rest of the law to show them how they should live in relationship with him and each other. Though not all the law is recorded here, some time is spent detailing the building of the Tabernacle as the place to respond to God's law in worship.

It is within the context of the Tabernacle that the book of Leviticus is set (1:1). The whole book is undergirded by a profound sense of the presence and holiness of God, which are to be carefully but joyfully reflected in Israel's worship and in the day-to-day life of the people. Leviticus is central to the Israelites' understanding of how they were to approach God – indeed, it was often the first book taught to their children. In addition, many of the concepts in Leviticus, such as atonement, or love for one's neighbour, form the background to the New Testament.

The book of Numbers, so called because of the censuses it contains, focuses on the period of forty years Israel spent in the wilderness before they entered the land of Canaan. It is a mixture of instructions about how to organise the nation and stories about the Israelites' repeated grumblings and failures to trust God. With the exception of Joshua and Caleb, all those who had come out from Egypt died before entering the promised land, because of their lack of faith.

The final book of the Law is Deuteronomy, which records the speeches Moses gave to the people of Israel on the eve of their entry into the land. It roughly follows the form of an ancient treaty document, in which Moses restates the law (*Deuteronomy* means 'second law') and challenges the people to renew their commitment to God. The book, and hence the Pentateuch, ends with the Israelites reaffirming their faith, and with Moses' death and Joshua's sucession as the one who will lead the people into the promised land.

Gennesaret, Lake of see GALILEE, SEA OF.

Gentiles The term comes from a Latin word for 'nations', but through common usage came to refer to those who were not Jews. Since, for the most part, the nations were not included in God's dealings with Old Testament Israel, by the first century AD some Jews had a negative view of the Gentiles. Though Jesus used the language of the time about 'Gentile sinners', he caused surprise by speaking about many Gentiles entering the kingdom of God. In contrast to the trickle of non-Jews who had joined themselves to God's people in the Old Testament, many Gentiles were attracted to Jesus. As Jewish people increasingly rejected the gospel, the apostles took the good news of Jesus to the Gentiles, and the New Testament teaches that the Gentiles are just as much part of God's people as the Jews. All barriers can be broken down by the gospel of Jesus (Ephesians 2:11–22).

gentleness A quality which God shows towards the wayward and the weak (Isaiah 40:11; Matthew 11:29). Christians are also expected to be gentle in all their dealings (Philippians 4:5).

gerah see WEIGHTS AND MEASURES.

Gerar A city south of Gaza in Philistine territory (modern Tell Abu Hurerah). It was associated especially with Abraham and Isaac (Genesis 20–1; 26).

Gerizim, Mount The more southerly of two mountains near Shechem (modern Nablus). It was here that the tribes stood to bless the people as they entered the Promised Land (Deuteronomy 27:12; Joshua 8:33). Later, it became the mountain where the Samaritans worshipped God (John 4:20).

Gershon, Gershonites The Gershonites were a group of Levites who were descended from one of Levi's sons called Gershon. Their various tasks included looking after the fabric of the tabernacle, providing musicians and acting as treasurers.

Geshem see SANBALLAT, TOBIAH AND GESHEM.

Geshur A city in Syria associated with David, and to which his son Absalom fled after murdering his brother Amnon (2 Samuel 13:37–8).

gestures This important aspect of human communication is not always easy to interpret, since the meaning of each action depends very much on the cultural presuppositions shared by those involved. Some memorable moments in the Bible are expressed through gestures, such as Jesus washing his disciples' feet (John 13:4–15) or the practice of anointing someone's head with oil (Psalms 23:5; 133:1–3). Gestures can be broadly divided into customary and symbolic actions. Customary gestures include the kiss of greeting, shaking the head as a sign of contempt, shaking the dust off one's feet as a mark of rejection, tearing one's clothes and putting dust on one's head in mourning, and standing or kneeling for prayer. Jesus and the prophets frequently used symbolic actions to convey their message, such as Jeremiah's teaching about pottery (Jeremiah 18–19) or Jesus breathing on the disciples as they received the Holy Spirit (John 20:21–3).

Gethsemane A garden near the Mount of Olives. It was a favourite place for Jesus and his disciples, but was also where Jesus experienced great agony in prayer (Matthew 26:36). Its name means 'oil press', and its exact site remains uncertain.

Gezer An important Canaanite city between Jerusalem and Joppa, which came under Israelite control only when one of the Pharaohs gave it to Solomon (1 Kings 9:16). See map of OLD TESTAMENT ISRAEL.

Gibeah A place-name meaning 'hill' and referring to two places in the Old Testament. The best known is Saul's birthplace (modern Tell el-Ful, about 5 kilometres north of Jerusalem), which served as his capital during his reign (1 Samuel 11:4–5).

Gibeon, Gibeonites An important city 9 kilometres north of Jerusalem, whose inhabitants tricked Joshua into making a treaty with them (Joshua 9). It was also the place where the sun stood still (Joshua 10:12–14). Excavations at the site (modern el-Jib) have revealed a large water-pit and water-tunnel (cf. 2 Samuel 2:12–13). See map of OLD TESTAMENT ISRAEL.

Gideon One of the judges who led Israel for forty years (Judges 6–8). Also called Jerub-Baal, he rose to prominence as a young man by challenging Israel's humiliating position under the Midianites. His leadership is demonstrated by his initial reluctance to take command, his hatred of idolatry and his courageous faith. Later, he turned down an offer of kingship, though he compromised with pagan worship.

gifts, spiritual Special gifts provided by the Holy Spirit to every believer. The various New Testament lists (Romans 12:6–8; 1 Corinthians 12:4–11, 28–30; Ephesians 4:11–13; 1 Peter 4:10–11) cover a range of activities including gifts of Christian leadership such as apostles and prophets, special gifts of speaking, discernment, healing, and practical gifts such as hospitality and service. Though the Spirit was at work in similar ways in the Old Testament, these gifts have been freely distributed since the outpouring of the Spirit at Pentecost. They may be given for special occasions or as permanent ministries. They are distinguished from natural gifts or other similar phenomena by God's special activity in the life of the individual concerned. Their purpose is to demonstrate God's power and presence in the world, especially in spreading the gospel and building up the church (Acts 1:8; 1 Corinthians 14:12) and they are to be exercised in love rather than for personal ends. See also HOLY SPIRIT.

Gihon 1. A river in Eden (Genesis 2:13).

2. A spring east of Jerusalem from which Hezekiah built a conduit to bring water into the city (2 Chronicles 32:30).

Gilboa, mount A range of hills on the south side of the Plain of Esdraelon where the Philistines killed Saul (1 Samuel 31).

Gilead 1. A son of Manasseh and the ancestor of a major part of Manasseh's tribe.

2. An area in Transjordan between the Dead Sea and the Wadi Yarmuk which also sometimes gave its name to the whole area of Israel east of the Jordan. It is a hilly area whose southern half provides fertile land for crops and animals, and whose northern section was richly forested in biblical times. It was populated by the tribe of Gad and the half-tribe of Manasseh, and was closely associated with the Reubenites to the south. See map of OLD TESTAMENT ISRAEL.

Gilgal The name of several places in Palestine, but usually an important town between the Jordan and Jericho. As the first place reached by the Israelites under Joshua, it was the site of the first Passover in the Promised Land and of a special commemoration of the crossing of the Jordan (Joshua 4:19–5:12). Later it became a centre for pagan worship (Amos 4:4). See map of OLD TESTAMENT ISRAEL.

Gittites The inhabitants of Gath. Some served in David's personal forces, and others were his personal friends (2 Samuel 15:18–22).

giving An important feature of Christianity, based on the Father's gift of the Son and the Son's giving of himself for sinful human beings (John 3:16; 1 John 3:16). God's nature as a giving God and his regular activity in giving gifts to all (Psalm 145:15–16) sets a pattern for his people to be generous in all their relationships. The principle of giving established in the New Testament is for Christians to give themselves first to God and then to others (2 Corinthians 8:5). God also promises that he will more than provide for those who give freely (Philippians 4:18–19). See also GENEROSITY.

glory An idea usually associated with God and referring to the majestic brilliance of all his qualities. God makes his glory known to people in various ways. It is revealed in the world he has made, and aspects of it are visible to everyone (Romans 1:20). It is also made known through his actions and through the church. In the Old Testament period, specific experiences of God's glory were given to individuals and to Israel (Exodus 33:18–23; 1 Kings 8:10–11), but the supreme revelation of the glory of God is in the person of Jesus (John 1:14).

An experience of God's glory had distinct physical as well as spiritual characteristics. It sometimes literally made a person's face shine (Exodus 34:29–35), or it might be accompanied by a cloud or by thunder and lightning, physically preventing people coming too close (Exodus 19:9–25; 40:34–5). An encounter with God's glory was potentially extremely dangerous and could be fatal, even when contact was made with an object representing God's presence, such as the ark, rather than with God himself (Exodus 33:20; 2 Samuel 6:6–7). Despite these difficulties, God wanted his people to be close to him in his glory. Jesus made this possible by revealing God's grace with his glory, but even Jesus' earthly ministry did not entirely remove the element of danger (Matthew 17:1–8; John 18:5–6). The Holy Spirit, however, enables Christians to have a continuing and transforming experience of God's glory (2 Corinthians 3:7–18).

Though God has given human beings a genuine glory of their own (Psalm 8:4–5), anything other than God is temporary and tarnished in comparison with him. However, human beings can be glorified through Christ. For the time being their glorification is a continuing process, but when he returns, they will enjoy his unmediated glory without any fear of ill-effects (Revelation 22:4–5).

gnats see INSECTS AND ARACHNIDS; PLAGUES OF EGYPT.

gnosticism A religious philosophy which affected the church in the early Christian centuries and whose ideas are often thought to be reflected in some of the New Testament letters. The name comes from the Greek word *gnosis*, 'knowledge'. It refers to the idea that a special form of spiritual knowledge was needed for salvation, which may be refuted in 1 Timothy 6:20 and in Colossians. The main Gnostic belief, however, was a cosmological dualism that matter was evil and was totally separate from the world of the spirit, which alone was good. This led to a view of Jesus as a spiritual redeemer but not a physical human being, and the attacks on this view in 1 John (e.g. 4:2–3) may reflect Gnostic influence. It remains unclear, however, whether Gnosticism was a Christian heresy or a pre-Christian belief, and also whether in either form it affected the church as early as New Testament times.

goal see AMBITION.

goat see SHEEP AND GOATS.

God, names and titles of Though God has many names in the Bible, he has one name that is particularly his own. It is written in Hebrew with the four consonants YHWH and was pronounced something like 'Yahweh' in early Christian times. By the late intertestamental period, the Jews generally regarded God's name as too holy to be spoken, and substituted the title 'the Lord', which is also the common term for God in the New Testament. The form 'Jehovah' is a hybrid of YHWH and the Hebrew word for Lord, and is certainly not God's actual name in Old Testament times. Yahweh is explained (but not translated) as 'I am who I am' (Exodus 3:13–14), conveying the idea of God as a dynamic being who is always with his people and always working on their behalf. It also indicates that his name cannot be fully explained through any single event, but that its meaning is revealed continually. Yahweh occurs with epithets attached, including Yahweh-yireh ('the LORD provides'), Yahweh-shalom ('the LORD is peace'), and Yahweh-shamma ('the LORD is there').

God is also known by the Hebrew words Elohim and El. These are general words for God but they are also used as names. Several epithets are also associated with El, such as El Shaddai ('God Almighty'), El Olam ('God Everlasting'), and El Elyon ('God Most High').

Individual names for God are often associated with particular aspects of his character. Some deal with his relationship with Israel, such as Holy One of Israel or Yahweh God of Israel. Some emphasize God's power and majesty, such as the Mighty One, the Ancient of Days, or the LORD of hosts, while others like God the Rock or God as a fortress highlight God as a source of security. Other important titles such as the Living God and God as Shepherd refer to various divine qualities.

God, names and titles of

Names based on Yahweh (Hebrew YHWH) ('The LORD')

Yahweh-elohim	Yahweh God	Genesis 2:4
Yahweh-nissi	Yahweh is my banner	Exodus 17:15
Yahweh-sabaoth	Yahweh of Hosts	2 Samuel 7:28
Yahweh-shalom	Yahweh is peace	Judges 6:24
Yahweh-shamma	Yahweh is there	Ezekiel 48:35
Yahweh-tsidkenu	Yahweh is our righteousness	Jeremiah 23:6
Yahweh-yireh	Yahweh provides	Genesis 22:8, 14

Names with El ('God')

El Bethel	God of Bethel	Genesis 31:13
El Elohe Yisrael	God the God of Israel	Genesis 33:20
El Elyon	God Most High	Genesis 14:18–20
El Olam	God Everlasting	Genesis 21:33
El Shaddai	God Almighty	Genesis 17:1

Other common names	
Ancient of Days	Daniel 7:9
The First and the Last	Isaiah 44:6
Fortress	Psalm 18:2
God of peace	Romans 15:33
God of your Fathers	Exodus 3:13
Holy One of Israel	Isaiah 12:6
King	Isaiah 6:5
Living God	Jeremiah 10:10
Maker	Jeremiah 10:16
The Mighty One	Luke 1:49
Redeemer	Isaiah 43:14
Refuge	Psalm 91:2
Rock	Psalm 78:35
Saviour	Titus 1:3
Shepherd	Psalm 80:1
Shield	Deuteronomy 33:29
True God	2 Chronicles 15:3

God, nature of The Bible takes the existence of God for granted. He can be known only in his relation to the world he has made, especially by human beings. The Bible affirms that God is known through his own revelation of himself rather than by what human beings discover about him. This revelation finds its most complete form in Jesus, in whom 'all the fulness of the Deity lives in bodily form' (Colossians 2:9). God's intention is to establish permanent relationships with people through Jesus, and he looks to them to respond to him in faith and love.

God is always described in personal terms. He is neither an idea nor a remote figure, but one who is able to enter into relationships with people because he himself is fully personal. In the New Testament, God's personhood is clearly expressed in terms of a unity of three persons in one, as Father, Son and Holy Spirit (Matthew 28:19), though this trinitarian concept is already present in the Old Testament. God's relationship with himself is a mystery, but is an essential element in understanding the biblical picture of God's nature and his work. As a person, God is a rational and purposeful being who ensures that his will is carried out. He is able to do this because he knows everything and controls everything, including things that are unseen as well as those that are seen (Colossians 1:15–18). Though he allows human beings the freedom to choose evil as well as good, he retains ultimate control even when they choose evil, since everyone is accountable to him.

Though God makes people in his image, he is different from them. He is self-existing and self-sufficient and is also infinite and eternal. He is a fully spiritual being who has life in and of himself and who is able to be everywhere. This means that he is not dependent on any outside agency, nor is he limited in any way by time or space (Isaiah 45:9–12). His perfection and changelessness are dynamic rather than static. He is therefore always consistent with himself, both at different periods of time and in his moral dealings with different people. He can always be relied on to be loving and gracious, since though he is holy, righteous and just, his will and nature is always to save sinners to turn to him in faith (Micah 7:18).

godliness An attitude of devotion to God in all areas of life. It is a characteristic that God expects in all his people. It is based on the pattern established by Jesus (1 Timothy 3:16), and is made possible through God's gift of power (2 Peter 1:3). God's people are sometimes called 'the godly' in the Old Testament (Psalm 32:6).

gods Though the Bible affirms that there is only one God, it also takes a practical approach to the beliefs of those who worship other deities. From the point of view of strict monotheism, this can sometimes lead to some rather surprising statements, for example that Yahweh is 'the great King above all gods' (Psalm 95:3). However, in every passage involving conflict between Yahweh and other gods, it is made plain that Yahweh alone has the right to be called God (1 Kings 18:39; 1 Corinthians 8:4–6). The Bible refers to gods of various nations, some of which were worshipped by the Israelites. The best known of those mentioned by name are the Canaanite deity Baal and his consort Asherah, but also included are the Babylonian gods Bel and Nebo (Isaiah 46:1) and the Greek gods Zeus and Hermes (Acts 14:12). See also IDOLATRY.

Gog and Magog Ezekiel 38–9 describes God's defeat of forces attacking Israel led by Gog of the land of Magog. Gog's name may be based on Gyges, King of Lydia (c. 660 BC), but it is probably symbolic of one who opposes God at the final battle (cf. Revelation 20:8).

gold The most valuable metal in ancient times and a symbol of Israel's prosperity under Solomon, who acquired it through widespread trading activities. In the tabernacle and the temple, especially the Most Holy Place, it symbolized God's kingship. Elsewhere, it was used for jewellery but also for divine images such as golden calves (Exodus 32:2–4; 1 Kings 12:28). See also SILVER.

golden calf see CALF, GOLDEN.

Golgotha The place outside Jerusalem where Jesus was crucified. It means 'place of the skull' (Matthew 27:33). It was called Calvary in the Latin translation of the Bible.

Goliath A Philistine giant who threatened Israel's army but whom David killed with a slingstone in a duel (1 Samuel 17).

Gomorrah see SODOM AND GOMORRAH.

Good Samaritan A man in one of Jesus' parables. He provides a striking illustration of the principle of loving one's neighbour by his care of an injured man from Judea, since Jews and Samaritans were traditional enemies (Luke 10:25–37).

goodness Goodness in the Bible is not an abstract idea but a quality defined by God, who alone can be called truly good (Matthew 19:16–17). As a moral and spiritual concept, goodness is what God approves, though the general non-moral sense of what is approved and appreciated by human society also occurs in the Bible. Though God created everything absolutely good (Genesis 1:31), his creation was spoiled by human sin. Since that time, human beings can experience goodness only in relation to God, in two ways. First, they should receive with thanksgiving the good gifts with which God has blessed them (James 1:17). These gifts are given to everyone (Acts 14:17), though God specializes in giving good gifts to his own children (Matthew 7:11). Second, people should obey God's commands. The commands themselves are good (Romans 7:12) and obedience involves doing good works (Ephesians 2:10). Works or actions may be regarded as good not because of their innate qualities but because they are carried out in a spirit of love. A good person is therefore someone whose life is characterized by doing the good things that God approves (Acts 10:38; 11:24).

Goshen An area in the East Nile Delta area of Egypt where Jacob's family were provided for during a famine (Genesis 47:27).

gospel The good news about Jesus Christ. It can be described from several perspectives, though all of them centre on the person and work of Jesus. On the widest level, the gospel is about the ultimate fulfilment of God's purposes and the establishing of God's kingdom through Christ's death and resurrection by which he destroyed sin, death, evil and Satan (1 John 3:8). On the personal level, it enables a person who is by nature a sinner to become a child of God and receive eternal life by repenting and believing in God, on the basis that Christ's death and resurrection puts them in a right relationship with God (Mark 1:15; Romans 10:9–10).

gospels The name given by the early church to the first four books of
the New Testament.

The Gospels and Acts

The word 'gospel' (Greek *euangelion*) originally had no specifically
Christian meaning. It was used in the Graeco-Roman world for an
announcement, for example, the proclamation concerning the
birth of the Roman emperor Augustus. When it was first used by
the early Christians, it referred to the oral message about what God
had done in and through the life, death, and resurrection of Jesus.
This was how Paul and the other New Testament letter-writers
usually used the word.

The four Gospels that stand at the beginning of the New
Testament were not written until at least thirty years after the
events of Jesus' life. Until then, the gospel message was handed
down by word of mouth and probably also in written records that
no longer survive. The authors of the Gospels, known as the
'evangelists', spent time remembering and collecting information
about Jesus' life to draw together into their written accounts. At
first, the four books had no titles, but soon they were ascribed to
Matthew, Mark, Luke and John. Finally, in the mid-second century
AD, Justin Martyr termed them 'Gospels'.

The Gospels form a distinct genre of literature. They do share
some similarities with other ancient writings, such as books of
'acts', which retell famous incidents from a person's life, or
'memoirs', which collect sayings and teachings. Perhaps they are
most like ancient 'lives' – biographies focusing on the character of
the person rather than exhaustively recounting details as in more
modern biographies. But there are also differences, which is not
surprising since the Gospels recount in narrative form the belief,
teaching and proclamation of the early church concerning Jesus,
who was not merely a person to be remembered, but was alive and
lived among them by his Spirit. The Gospels were written to
preserve the message about Jesus as well as his own words and
teaching, and to enable these to be taken to and taught in other
places. Each Gospel thus has distinctive characteristics due both to
its author and the readers for whom the author wrote.

Matthew, Mark and Luke are known collectively as the Synoptic
Gospels, because as well as their similar framework for Jesus' life,
they also retell many of the same stories about him, sometimes

almost word for word. Different explanations for this have been put forward, but the one most commonly held is known as the 'two source hypothesis'. In this view, Mark was the earliest Gospel to be written, perhaps only thirty years after Jesus' death and resurrection. Both Matthew and Luke used Mark as a source for their own gospels, alongside a second source, known as 'Q'. Q (from German *Quelle* meaning 'source') remains a hypothetical document in the minds of scholars, but is thought to have contained a written version of some of Jesus' teaching. Matthew and Luke drew from both these sources, as well as adding material of their own. In this way, each of the Synoptic Gospels, though similar, is also unique and reflects the characteristic style and concerns of its author.

Matthew's Gospel highlights the relationship of Jesus to the Old Testament, presenting Jesus as the Messiah the Jews had been longing for, as well as drawing attention to Jesus' teaching ministry by arranging the narrative around five main blocks of teaching material, mirroring the five books of the Pentateuch.

Mark does not focus as much on Jesus the teacher, but presents instead a fast-moving account of Jesus' life. Recurring themes in Mark include misunderstandings about Jesus, the necessity of his suffering and death, and the challenge of discipleship.

Luke's Gospel is the first part of a two-volume work which shows how the events of Jesus' life in the seemingly insignificant land of the Jews spread outwards until they reached even the heart of the Roman Empire. The Gospel portrays Jesus as the bringer of salvation, particularly to those who were considered to be on the margins of society: women, the poor, Samaritans, tax collectors, and sinners. The kingdom of God into which Jesus invited these social outcasts did not end with his death, resurrection and ascension; Luke's second volume, the Acts of the Apostles, continues to show how Jesus was at work, by his Spirit and through his disciples. Acts focuses on the growth of the church from Jerusalem, through Samaria, into the Gentile world, at first in the ministries of Stephen, Philip, Peter and others, but from chapter 13, almost entirely through the journeys of Paul and his companions.

The fourth Gospel, John, more obviously draws out the significance of Jesus' person and actions, and therefore has a different feel than the Synoptics. John makes use of literary imagery and language, such as the recurring theme of light and darkness. This Gospel is often seen as having a more developed understanding of Jesus' identity than the other three, though the difference is more a matter of emphasis than content. John's work is also carefully structured, with a series of 'signs' or miracles accompanied by discourses. As with the other Gospels, John's main concern was to show in his own way how Jesus brought the salvation God had promised.

The four Gospels and the book of Acts constitute the best existing records of the life and ministry of Jesus and the spread of Christianity through the witness of the early church.

gossiping Engaging in idle talk and spreading rumours is forbidden because of its destructive tendencies (Proverbs 16:28; 3 John 1:9–10).

government Final authority on earth as well as in heaven rests with God. It is God who ultimately appoints and deposes all human leaders (Daniel 2:21; John 19:11), for the purpose of the good ordering of society (1 Peter 2:13–14). He allows bad rulers to govern as well as good ones, since all are responsible to him for their actions. The New Testament encourages Christians to submit to human authorities, and only makes an exception when the proclamation of gospel is banned (Acts 4:18–20). Since all human government is imperfect, God will finally establish his own kingdom through his Messiah (Isaiah 9:6–7).

It is difficult to argue for the existence of a single preferred system of government in Israel since every arrangement proved fallible, but it is possible that the pattern first established in the Promised Land of a tribal fellowship with no regular human leader and God as Israel's only recognized permanent ruler contains the germ of an ideal. But in reality this pattern proved no better than the monarchy which followed, and both brought Israel to the brink of disaster. Certainly, no single approved system of church government is found in the New Testament, since as in the Old Testament, the key to successful human government is the acknowledgement of divinely appointed leaders who carry out their tasks in obedience to God.

governor see OCCUPATIONS.

grace God's undeserved favour to all. It is partly demonstrated by his reluctance to judge people for their sins, as reflected in the description of God as 'slow to anger' (Exodus 34:6). However, the primary mark of God's grace is the sending of his Son as a Saviour. Though human beings are by nature opposed to the gospel (Romans 5:8), God provides further grace so that people can accept Christ's love for them (Ephesians 2:8–9).

Grace is sometimes contrasted with law (Romans 6:14), but in fact the relationship between the two involves a delicate balance. Paul makes a double contrast between God's grace and legalism, and between Old Testament law and the gospel as a basis for acceptance with God. But neither of these mean that grace and law are opposed to each other. God's gift of the law to Israel was an act of grace, and God gives grace to his people to carry out his laws. This means that the grace God gives Christians enables them to do what he requires and does not absolve them from obeying his will (2 Peter 3:18).

grain see CEREALS.

grain offering A form of Old Testament sacrifice in which the produce of the field was offered to God, usually alongside another type of offering (Leviticus 2:1–16; 6:14–23).

grapes, grapevine see VINE.

grass Green grass was a temporary feature of the landscape because of the effect of the long dry summers, and was therefore a highly suitable picture of the brevity and uncertainty of human life (Isaiah 40:6–8). Its main function was as fodder for cattle, and the hay was sometimes mixed with more solid foodstuffs.

grasshopper see INSECTS AND ARACHNIDS.

Greece, Greek In the Old Testament, Greece is usually called by the Hebrew name Javan (= Greek *Ionia*) and is a distant country whose main contact with Israel was through trade and warfare (Isaiah 66:19). After Alexander the Great conquered Palestine in 331 BC, Greek culture increasingly influenced the Jewish way of life. Though some things such as the Greek language proved to be of great benefit for Judaism, Greek culture also came into severe conflict with traditional Judaism, especially in the background to the Maccabean revolt in the second century BC. In the New Testament, 'Greek or Hellenist' is either a general term for non-Jews (Acts 11:20) or describes Jews who adopted the Greek way of life (Acts 6:1). See also LANGUAGES. See map of WORLD OF THE BIBLE.

greed Covetousness or greed is particularly condemned in the Bible, as in the tenth commandment (Exodus 20:17). It is the opposite of contentment and trust in God's provision, and has no place in the lives of believers (Luke 12:15). Greedy people are encouraged to repent, since they are liable to God's judgement (Ephesians 5:5–6).

green see COLOURS.

grief see SUFFERING.

growth God's intention is for all creation to 'be fruitful and increase in number' (Genesis 1:28). This began to be fulfilled as human beings increased across the generations (Genesis 5) and geographically

(Genesis 11). It was particularly evident in Israel's spectacular growth (Exodus 1), though God's plan for their continuing growth was frustrated through Israel's failure to obey him (Deuteronomy 28:11–14). Promises of spiritual growth through Abraham's descendants (Genesis 12:2–3) found their main fulfilment in the church, especially the early church's rapid increase in numbers (Acts 6:7; 11:21; Galatians 3:6–9). Jesus' prediction of the spread of the gospel to every nation (Matthew 24:14) will be finally fulfilled in heaven (Revelation 7:9–10). All the increase experienced by God's people is ultimately attributable to God's blessing, though individual believers have a vital part to play in the process (1 Corinthians 3:6–7).

grumbling see COMPLAINTS.

guards Used for both military and religious purposes. The Levites were responsible for guarding the tabernacle and temple to ensure that its holiness was preserved (1 Chronicles 9:17–32).

guests Referred to in relation to private hospitality and to special occasions such as birthdays and weddings. Jesus often spoke about inviting unexpected guests to the Messianic banquet, which was a symbol of the pleasures to be enjoyed in heaven (Matthew 22:1–14; Luke 14:15–24).

guidance The practice by which God directs believers in their lives. It is related to a view of faith as an ongoing personal relationship with God and is based on the belief that God knows what is best for each individual because he loves them. Guidance is a fundamental feature of biblical faith, and its importance is highlighted by the contrasting fates of those who seek God's guidance and those who rely on their own resources for direction. Whereas the former are often led into fresh and more fruitful areas for serving God (Acts 13:1–3; 16:6–10), the latter will ultimately experience frustration and disaster (Psalm 146:3–4).

God guides in various ways, but the Bible emphasizes that personal trust in God and confidence in his willingness to communicate his will are more important than any particular method. However, certain sources of guidance are regularly used, such as God's written word, the word of a prophet, a personal communication from the Holy Spirit, or advice from fellow believers. In the Old Testament, special forms of guidance included the pillars of cloud and of fire and the priest's Urim and Thummim. Warnings are also given about avoiding unreliable sources of guidance, including the occult, idols, and false prophets or teachers. See also FAITH.

guilt The state of being in the wrong, often including the emotion which comes from being aware of being in a state of guilt. The Bible is primarily concerned with guilt before God, though it also refers to guilt before human beings. Guilt before God may arise from sin committed either deliberately or unintentionally (James 2:10; Leviticus 4:13), but awareness of it varied considerably, from those who felt it deeply (Psalm 51:3–5) to others apparently without a conscience (1 Timothy 4:2). However, God is angry with everyone who is guilty, and all are liable to his punishment (Exodus 20:5). A person who is guilty under human law is required to be dealt with according to those laws, but God sometimes deals with people directly because he is aware of human motives as well as actions. God's preference, however, is to remove guilt rather than punish the guilty. To this end, Israel's sacrifices were intended, alongside personal confession, to remove guilt and sin, though only the sacrifice of Jesus on the cross could remove guilt on a permanent basis. As a result of Jesus' death, a guilty conscience can be made clean and access into God's presence assured (Ephesians 2:18; Hebrews 9:14).

guilt offering An atoning sacrifice also known as the trespass offering. It was similar to the sin or purification offering, and was distinguished from it mainly by the fact that it was usually accompanied by a compensation payment to the injured party (Leviticus 5:14–6:7; 7:1–6). Like the sin offering, it was intended only for instances where a sin had been committed unintentionally.

h

Habakkuk, book of

> **Structure**
> Habakkuk questions God (1:1–2:20)
> Habakkuk's psalm to God (3:1–19)
>
> **Famous passages**
> God is too pure to look on evil (1:12–13)
> 'The righteous will live by their faith' (2:4)

An Old Testament prophetic book organized round two complaints which Habakkuk addresses to God (1:2–4; 1:12–2:1). God's intention to punish Judah by using the Babylonians (1:5–11) caused Habakkuk a moral problem, since the Babylonians were just as wicked as the people of Judah. God's reply emphasizes the need to live by faith in difficult times (2:2–5; cf. Romans 1:17), and that the Babylonians as well as the Jews were responsible to him for their behaviour (2:6–20). In a final psalm (chapter 3) the prophet expresses his own faith in God as he anticipates the coming disaster. Though nothing is known about Habakkuk himself, the book is a powerful contribution to biblical teaching on living through suffering.

Hadadezer A Syrian king whom David defeated and so extended Israel's influence as far as the River Euphrates (2 Samuel 8:3–11).

Hades A Greek word for the world of the dead, similar to the Hebrew concept of Sheol. It is a temporary resting-place for the dead from which they are released for final judgement. As a result of Christ's resurrection, he has complete control over Hades and Hades has no power over believers (Matthew 16:18–19; Revelation 1:18). See also SHEOL.

Hagar Sarah's female servant whom Sarah gave to her husband Abraham to produce a child. Ishmael's subsequent birth led to

Sarah's jealousy and Hagar's expulsion from the household, but God granted Hagar a special revelation of himself (Genesis 21:8–19).

Haggai, book of

Structure
Call to rebuild the temple (1:1–15)
Promises and blessings (2:1–23)

Famous passages
Earning wages to put into a purse with holes (1:6)
God will shake the heavens and the earth (2:7, 21)

All four prophecies in this short prophetic book are dated between August and December 520 BC. Haggai's main concern was that the temple in Jerusalem should be rebuilt. For nearly twenty years after the Jews started returning from exile, the temple ruins had been neglected because of the people's self-interest (1:3–6). However, Haggai promised that God's Spirit would help them build (2:4–5) and that the restored temple would bring them blessing in the present and the future. With this encouragement, the building work started again (1:14–15).

hail see PLAGUES OF EGYPT.

hallelujah A Hebrew expression often used in biblical worship meaning 'praise *(hallelu)* the Lord *(yah)*'. *Yah* is a short form of God's name Yahweh (Psalms 103–6).

Ham see SHEM, HAM AND JAPHETH.

Haman A high-ranking Persian official whose attempt to destroy the Jews was thwarted by the faith of Esther and Mordecai (Esther 3–9).

Hamath An important Syrian city (modern Hama) on the River Orontes which occasionally came under Israel's influence (2 Kings 14:28). See map of WORLD OF THE BIBLE.

hammer see TOOLS.

Hamor A Canaanite ruler whose family was killed by two of Jacob's sons after Hamor's son had raped their sister Dinah (Genesis 34).

hand Several symbolic actions are associated with hands, including taking oaths, giving blessing, making pledges and joining in fellowship. It was common to lift up or spread out one's hands to God in prayer and worship (Exodus 9:29; 1 Timothy 2:8). The right hand was the place of authority and honour (Matthew 25:33–4; Hebrews 1:3), and the ease with which God exercised authority is represented by his finger (Luke 11:20). Hands and fingers were also important as units of measurement.

handbreadth see WEIGHTS AND MEASURES.

hanging see CRIME AND PUNISHMENT; CROSS.

Hannah Mother of the prophet Samuel. She gave birth to him after God heard her desperate prayer because she was barren, and then dedicated him to the service of God (1 Samuel 1).

happiness Since genuine and lasting happiness is regarded as God's gift, it is often equated with blessedness. People can find happiness in God himself, especially through experiencing his presence with them (Psalm 16:11), as well as through human relationships and experiences (Ecclesiastes 9:7–10). Happiness is not to be treated as an end in itself, however, but as a product of obeying and trusting God (John 15:10–11). See also BLESSING; JOY.

Haran 1. A strategically located city on the Balih river in modern Turkey, whose name means 'crossroads'. Abraham lived there before travelling to the Promised Land (Genesis 11:31–12:4). See map of WORLD OF THE BIBLE

2. The brother of Abraham and father of Lot (Genesis 11:27).

Harlot see PROSTITUTION.

harp see MUSIC AND MUSICAL INSTRUMENTS.

harvest A joyful and important time in Israel's agricultural calendar, often indicating the health of the people's relationship with God. Though harvest was supposed to be a time for giving thanks for Yahweh's blessings (Psalm 65:9–13), the Israelites sometimes attributed their prosperity to other gods (Hosea 2:1–13). A poor harvest, however, was often regarded as a sign of God's displeasure (Jeremiah 12:13).

hatred An attitude as well as an emotion which is the opposite of love and a clear sign of human sinfulness. The only thing Christians should hate is evil, and they are instructed even to love their enemies (Matthew 5:43–8). Jesus' teaching about hating members of one's family is a striking way of saying that following Jesus must be a higher priority even than family loyalty (Luke 14:26–7).

haughtiness see PRIDE.

hay see GRASS.

Hazael A powerful king of Syria in the ninth century BC whom God appointed through Elijah and Elisha to punish Israel for the sins of Ahab's dynasty (1 Kings 19:15; 2 Kings 8:7–15).

Hazor The major city of Palestine (Joshua 11:10) north of the Sea of Galilee (modern Tell el-Qedah). Archaeology testifies to its importance, especially before the time of Joshua, and provides evidence of Solomon's fortifications there (1 Kings 9:15).

head Often associated with the idea of being first, whether in relation to leaders in general (Isaiah 9:14–15) or to Christ as head of the church (Ephesians 4:15). To lift up or bow the head indicated acceptance and submission respectively, while shaking the head was usually a sign of scorn (Matthew 27:39).

health and healing Illness and disease are understood both as a normal part of human existence in a world of suffering and pain and as a consequence of sinful behaviour. Though God's ultimate intention to remove all forms of suffering will enable people to live in perfect health (Revelation 21:4), this does not happen in this life, even for Christians. Believers are no more exempt than anyone else from disease, though they are encouraged to pray for God's healing and God provides them with healing gifts (1 Corinthians 12:9, 28; James 5:14–15). Answered prayer for healing involves both direct divine activity and the use of medicine (Acts 8:5–7; 1 Timothy 5:23).

Healing is one of God's major activities. This is especially evident in the ministry of Jesus, whose miracles of healing and exorcism were often seen as a sign that God was with him. The language of healing also describes God's work of salvation, since sin was a disease that only God could cure (Isaiah 53:5; Jeremiah 17:9). In contrast, God sometimes punished his people by inflicting them with various illnesses (Deuteronomy 28:27–9; 1 Corinthians 11:29–30).

heart Used most frequently for the inner being of God or of human beings, though reference to God's heart is comparatively rare. The heart was viewed as the seat of the intellect and the will as well as the emotions, reflecting the Israelite understanding of human beings as integrated persons. Even God's heart reveals emotion as well as a sense of purpose (Genesis 6:6; Psalm 33:11; Hosea 11:8). The human heart is the source of sin, and human beings cannot please God until he gives them a new heart which is sensitive towards him (Jeremiah 17:9; Ezekiel 36:26; Romans 2:29).

heaven The place where God lives. Though heaven is described in physical terms, the Bible uses figurative language to convey what is always understood as a spiritual reality. The nature of heaven is determined by the nature of God, who is the 'Father in heaven' (Matthew 6:9). Jesus went up to his Father in heaven therefore, not because heaven was thought to be geographically higher than the earth, but because God is greater than everything else. 'Heaven' may even be used as a synonym for God, as in the phrase 'I have sinned against heaven' (Luke 15:18).

Heaven is also the home of God's angels and of believers who have died or who will be taken there when Jesus returns. As the 'heavenly Jerusalem' (Hebrews 12:22), it is a perfect community untroubled by sin or suffering, where nothing can destroy its pleasures. Everything is centred on Jesus, who provides everything that is required. Even the sun is superfluous, since Jesus is heaven's light (Revelation 22:1–5). Activity in heaven is focused on worshipping God, because he has defeated and destroyed every form of evil.

heavenly host An expression for the angels who serve God in his presence. They came to earth to sing praise when Jesus was born (Luke 2:13).

Hebrew 1. An older synonym for Israelite. Its exact origin is unknown, and may go back to Eber, one of Abraham's ancestors (Genesis 11:14–17). More probably, it derives from a group of people in the ancient Near East known as Apiru or Habiru, who included various kinds of slaves and second-class citizens. The fact that the term was used in a derogatory sense by foreigners speaking about the Israelites suggests that the Israelites were sometimes viewed as belonging to this wider group (Genesis 39:17; Exodus 1:15–16). See also JEW.

2. see LANGUAGES.

Hebrews, letter to the

Structure
Jesus is superior over all rivals (1:1–4:13)
Jesus is God's ultimate high priest (4:14–6:20)
Jesus is the high priest of the new covenant (7:1–10:18)
Christians must keep faithful to Jesus (10:19–13:25)

Famous passages
Jesus compared with Melchizedek (7:1–28)
'Without the shedding of blood there is no forgiveness' (9:22)
The faith of Old Testament believers (11:1–40)
'Jesus, the author and perfecter of our faith' (12:2)
'Jesus Christ is the same yesterday and today and for ever' (13:8)

An unusual New Testament letter which lacks opening greetings and whose author and recipients remain uncertain. Though it has the form of a letter, in view of its frequent encouragements it is best viewed as a sermon. It was written to Jewish Christians, most likely in the 60s AD before the fall of Jerusalem, but it is unwise even to guess who wrote it.

The letter is about the relationship between Christ and the Old Testament. It describes that relationship in two ways, that Jesus is superior to the Old Testament and that he fulfils the Old Testament. He is God's Son in God's image (1:1–4) and God's High Priest, but it is his suffering that shows his supremacy, as a Son who was obedient to his Father (3:5–6; 5:7–8) and as a Priest who offered himself as a sacrifice. Jesus' priesthood is dealt with in some detail, showing that his saving work is final and complete since he carried out God's will perfectly. The letter also makes considerable use of an idea found in contemporary philosophy that earthly things are a reflection of an unseen heavenly world. The Old Testament system of worship is understood as a copy of the heavenly reality, but Hebrews also emphasizes that Jesus' humanity brought that reality to earth and that his death and exaltation provided believers with direct access to heaven. The letter ends with an appeal for Christians not to give up under persecution, but to exercise faith like the heroes of the Old Testament (chapter 11).

Hebron An important city in southern Judah, also known as Kiriath-Arba. Abraham lived there and several of his family were buried in a special plot of land he purchased (Genesis 13:18; 23:1–20). It was also David's capital before he moved to Jerusalem. See map of NEW TESTAMENT ISRAEL; OLD TESTAMENT ISRAEL.

Heel Jacob's name sounds like the Hebrew word for heel, as a reminder that he grasped his twin brother's heel as he was being born (Genesis 25:26).

Heifer A young cow sometimes offered in sacrifice, especially in the ceremony for purification from sin involving a red heifer (Numbers 19).

height see WEIGHTS AND MEASURES.

heir see INHERITANCE.

hell The place of final punishment in Jewish thought and in the New Testament, often mentioned by Jesus. It is a place for Satan and his angels and also for human beings who have rejected God in this life. Punishment in hell essentially involves separation from God, though the experience is described in various ways including unquenchable fire, outer darkness and weeping and gnashing of teeth (Matthew 3:12; 8:12). Interpreters continue to disagree whether the concept of eternal punishment involves never-ending suffering or destruction with permanent effects. Though the idea of a temporary purgatory residence in hell is present in some Jewish and Christian teachings, it does not occur in the New Testament. The word 'hell' comes from Greek 'Gehenna'. It is also known as Abaddon ('destruction') or the Abyss, though ought to be distinguished from more general terms for the realm of the dead such as Hebrew Sheol or Greek Hades. See also GEHENNA.

helmet see ARMOUR AND WEAPONS.

Heman see ASAPH, HEMAN AND JEDUTHUN.

hen see BIRDS.

herbs and spices Used for a variety of purposes. Cummin, dill, cinnamon and mint were used in preparing food and for flavouring wines. Various spices acted as the ingredients for the holy anointing oil for the priests, while others such as aloes and myrrh were employed more specifically in embalming. Other major uses included application as cosmetics and for medicinal purposes.

Herbs and spices	
Aloes	John 19:39
Balm	Jeremiah 8:22
Bitter herbs	Exodus 12:8
Calamus	Isaiah 43:24
Caraway	Isaiah 28:27
Cassia	Psalm 45:8
Cinnamon	Revelation 18:13
Coriander	Exodus 16:31
Cummin	Matthew 23:23
Dill	Matthew 23:23
Frankincense	Matthew 2:11
Galbanum	Exodus 30:34
Gall	Matthew 27:34
Garlic	Numbers 11:5
Gum resin	Exodus 30:34
Henna	Song of Songs 4:13
Mint	Luke 11:42
Mustard	Matthew 13:31
Myrrh	Matthew 2:11
Nard	Mark 14:3
Onycha	Exodus 30:34
Rue	Luke 11:42
Saffron	Song of Songs 4:14
Stacte	Exodus 30:34

heresy The Greek word *hairesis* really means 'party', and usually refers to Jewish groups such as the Pharisees or Sadducees or to divisions in the church (1 Corinthians 11:18). However, the idea of false teaching is also important in the New Testament. Believers must be especially wary of those who deny that Jesus was the Messiah or that he would return (2 Thessalonians 2:1–2; 1 John 2:22), and of the idea that something more than faith was necessary for salvation, such as observing Jewish laws or special religious experiences (Acts 15:1; Colossians 2:18).

Hermon, Mount Palestine's highest mountain at 2814 metres above sea level. It is located on Israel's northern boundary at the end of the Anti-Lebanon range (Deuteronomy 3:8). It is sometimes regarded as the place of Jesus' transfiguration (Matthew 17:1–8). See map of NEW TESTAMENT ISRAEL; OLD TESTAMENT ISRAEL.

Herod Agrippa I A grandson of Herod the Great who was known as 'Herod the King' (Acts 12:1), and ruled most of Palestine under the Romans, 41–4 AD. His sudden death was seen as God's judgement (Acts 12:19–23).

Herod Agrippa II The last of the Herods. He was son of Herod Agrippa I and ruled northern Palestine under the Romans, 48–100 AD. Paul was tried before him and found innocent (Acts 25:13–26:32).

Herod Antipas Son of Herod the Great and known as 'Herod the tetrarch' (Luke 3:19), ruling Galilee and Perea. He had John the Baptist beheaded (Mark 6:14–29) and mocked Jesus at his trial (Luke 23:6–12).

Herod the Great Ruled Palestine from 40–4 BC, and remembered for his great achievements, especially the restoration of the temple, and his great cruelty. His suspicion of a child born to be King of the Jews and subsequent murder of innocent babies is consistent with what is known of him elsewhere (Matthew 2:1–18).

Herodias Criticized by John the Baptist for marrying her husband's brother Herod Antipas, she arranged for John to be beheaded (Mark 6:17–29).

Heshbon A city in Transjordan (modern Tell Hesban) which changed hands regularly between Judah and Moab (Numbers 32:37; Jeremiah 48:2). See map of OLD TESTAMENT ISRAEL.

Hezekiah, King of Judah (c. 715–687 BC) A king whose faith saved Judah from being incorporated into the Assyrian empire. His anti-Assyrian policy resulted in Sennacherib besieging Jerusalem in 701 BC, but the latter unexpectedly withdrew after Hezekiah's prayer and Isaiah's prophecy (2 Kings 18:5–19:36; Isaiah 36:1–37:37). Later, however, Isaiah criticized him for over-confidence towards the Babylonians. Hezekiah was an enthusiastic builder, constructing the Siloam tunnel to safeguard Jerusalem's water supplies during the siege (2 Chronicles 32:27–30).

high place A place of worship outside Jerusalem. Examples have been uncovered at, for instance, Arad and Dan. Though high places were often located on higher ground, they were also built in other locations, especially at city gates. Though some were used for the genuine worship of Yahweh, the majority were centres of idolatry and cultic prostitution (2 Kings 17:11; 23:13–15).

high priest see PRIEST.

Hilkiah The high priest whose discovery of a law scroll in the temple archives led to a major religious reformation under Josiah (2 Kings 22:8–14).

hin see WEIGHTS AND MEASURES.

Hinnom, valley of see GEHENNA.

Hiram A king of Tyre who was friendly towards David and Solomon and provided materials and workmen for building the temple (1 Kings 5:1–12).

History of Susanna, the see APOCRYPHA.

Hittites 1. The rulers of Asia Minor between c. 1800–1200 BC, and the name of their smaller successor kingdoms in Syria (1 Kings 10:29). 2. Usually in the Bible, a pre-Israelite group in Canaan to whom Ephron and Uriah belonged (Genesis 23:10; 2 Samuel 11:2–27). See map of WORLD OF THE BIBLE.

Hivite A pre-Israelite group in Canaan who lived in the centre and north of the country (Joshua 11:19; Judges 3:3).

holiness In contrast to other religions where holiness refers to something or someone set apart for religious purposes, holiness in the Bible is first and foremost the distinctive quality of God himself. It represents the combination of all God's other attributes and is the quality which distinguishes him from everything else. God's holiness is radiated to others through the brilliance of his glory. It is also dangerous, and God set clear limits to protect his people from the possibility of death (Exodus 19:10–23). Even contact with holy objects associated with God's presence was sometimes fatal (Leviticus 10:1–3; 1 Samuel 6:19–20).

God's holiness had two contrasting effects. Though it instinctively emphasized the separation that exists between God and human beings and could lead to a deep awareness of personal sinfulness (Isaiah 6:1–5), it could also bring God into a close and permanent relationship with his people. This was possible because God's power to save was part of his holiness, enabling him to transform the lives of those who approached him in faith. God was therefore called 'the Holy One of Israel among you' (Isaiah 12:6), and the church was regarded as 'God's temple' because the Holy Spirit lived among them (1 Corinthians 3:16).

Holiness is closely associated with ethical purity. This characteristic of God which he required in his people (Leviticus 11:45; 1 Peter 1:15–16) involves setting one's life apart for God instead of conforming to the standards of the world (1 Peter 2:9–12). It can be achieved only by being committed to a Christian lifestyle and relying on the sanctifying activity of the Holy Spirit. In this way, believers' lives are gradually transformed, though the process will only be completed in heaven (Jude 24). See also SANCTIFICATION.

Holy of Holies see TABERNACLE; TEMPLE.

Holy Place see TABERNACLE.

Holy Spirit One of the three persons of the divine Trinity who is the unseen presence of God in the world. Though much more is said about him in the New Testament than the Old Testament, the Holy Spirit is part of the eternal Godhead who is equal with the Father and the Son (Matthew 28:19). His divinity and personality are consistently assumed (John 15:26). Though active in the world from the very beginning (Genesis 1:2), he came into prominence at Pentecost when he was given to the church by Jesus in fulfilment of various Old Testament promises (Acts 2). The particular qualities associated with the Holy Spirit include his power, his sovereignty, his creativity and his generosity.

His work in the church is concentrated on individual believers, to whom he provides gifts and in whom he produces fruit. The gifts of the Holy Spirit enable believers to serve God and build up the church (1 Corinthians 12–14) while the fruit of the Spirit is a sign of developing Christian character (Galatians 5:22–23). The Holy Spirit's overall purpose is to strengthen believers' relationship with God, assuring them that they are children loved by their heavenly Father (Romans 8:14–17). More generally, his task is to empower the church for mission to the world and to convict unbelievers of their need for God (Acts 1:8; John 16:7–11). The Holy Spirit can be resisted consciously or unconsciously (1 Thessalonians 5:19), but this incurs God's displeasure and, in its extreme form of blaspheming against the Spirit, is an unforgivable sin (Mark 3:29).

home The traditional Israelite home included an extended family as well as the animals. Though the early Israelite generations lived in tents, once they had settled in the Promised Land the majority lived in houses. The standard Israelite house was of the four-roomed type with a courtyard, though there was much variety between those belonging to the rich and the poor. Some houses had two storeys, like that in Jerusalem with an upper room where Jesus ate the Passover meal (Mark 14:15), and the roof (Luke 5:19) was sometimes used for various domestic activities. Furniture was usually simple, including a wooden table and chairs, and either wooden beds or straw mats (2 Kings 4:10). Wealthier homes had couches, which the Romans used to eat at the table, but little is known about decorations and fabrics. Oil-lamps provided lighting and pottery jars were used for storage. See also FAMILY.

homer see WEIGHTS AND MEASURES.

homicide see KILLING.

homosexuality The practice of sexual relations between two people of the same sex is forbidden. It is regarded as something unnatural and is sometimes associated with pagan moral and religious beliefs (Genesis 19:4–8; Romans 1:26–8).

honesty Telling the truth in love is an important requirement of Christian behaviour (Ephesians 4:15, 25), even when it is costly to do so (John 18:23). Its importance is particularly emphasized in worship, evangelism and in relationships in the church, since God is concerned with people's motives as well as their behaviour and the gospel is concerned with truth.

honey, honeycomb Was widely available in Israel, and often used in the Bible as a symbol for sweetness and attractiveness (Psalm 19:9–10; Ezekiel 3:3). This is well illustrated in the common description of Canaan as 'a land flowing with milk and honey' (Exodus 3:8).

hook see FISH.

hope A confidence based on God's promises about the future and also the content of those promises. The promises are based on the return of Jesus Christ in glory and the replacement of the present world with the perfect kingdom of God, but they also include the idea of personal resurrection and of an eternal inheritance in heaven (1 Peter 1:3–5). Confidence in God's promises is based partly on the reliability of God and his word and partly on Jesus' resurrection as evidence of God's ability to overcome death (1 Corinthians 15:20–58). This hope results in believers having a greater sense of assurance about God's purposes in their lives and gives them the ability to face persecution and even death in the knowledge that there is nothing to be lost and everything to be gained (Philippians 1:21–3).

Hophni and Phinehas Eli the priest's two sons, whom God punished because of their complete disregard for the responsibilities of the priesthood (1 Samuel 2:12–17).

Hormah A city in southern Palestine whose name 'destruction' refers to its complete dedication to God by the victorious Israelites (Numbers 21:1–3). The site is probably either Arad or Tell Masos.

horn 1. The ram's horn was used as an instrument for signalling and as a container for anointing oil (Joshua 6:4; 1 Samuel 16:13).
2. Horns often symbolized power and strength (Deuteronomy 33:17).
3. The horns of the altar were raised corners, as illustrated by a fine example discovered at Megiddo (Exodus 29:12).

hornet see INSECTS AND ARACHNIDS.

horse Though introduced into Israel only by David, horses quickly became an important part of Israel's army under Solomon (1 Kings 10:26). They were used more for military than for domestic purposes, and often represented military superiority. The horsemen in apocalyptic visions symbolize those who have great authority, including Christ himself as the great conqueror (Zechariah 6:1–8; Revelation 19:11–16).

hosanna The Greek form of a Hebrew word meaning '(Lord) save', and used as an expression of religious enthusiasm (Matthew 21:9, 15).

Hosea A prophet who was active in the northern kingdom of Israel in the eighth century BC a few years before it fell to the Assyrians. All that is known about his life concerns his marriage, separation and reconciliation with the prostitute Gomer, which was all part of his message of God's forgiving love. His children's names symbolized Israel's broken covenant with God. See also HOSEA, BOOK OF.

Hosea, book of

Structure
Hosea's marriage and God's forgiveness (1:1–3:5)
Israel is unfaithful to God (4:1–13:16)
God's love will restore Israel (14:1–9)

Famous passages
Hosea marries a prostitute (1:2–3)
'I desire mercy, not sacrifice' (6:6)
God's heart of love (11:8–9)

The first part of the book (chapters 1–3) contains an extreme example of dramatic prophecy which was apparently part of Hosea's real life experience. God instructs Hosea to marry a prostitute, and when inevitably she is unfaithful to him, tells him to take her back. Hosea's message through this is that God is willing to renew his covenant with Israel, even though they have been unfaithful to him by worshipping other gods.

Much of the rest of the book is a series of prophecies about Israel's deliberate rejection of God and his ways. It describes their idolatry, religious prostitution, greed, drunkenness, cheating in business and political machinations. Religious and political leaders are singled out for criticism, summarized in Israel's rejection of the Ten Commandments (4:1–2).

Despite the harsh words of God's judgement, which were fulfilled when Assyria defeated Israel and exiled its people in 722 BC, only a few years after Hosea's prophecies, God reaffirms his intention to

restore his undeserving people (chapter 14). The book contains some
of the most amazing statements about God's love found anywhere in
the Bible (11:1–4, 8–9; 14:4).

Hoshea, King of Israel (c. 732–722 BC) see KINGS AND QUEENS OF
ISRAEL.

hospitality The New Testament's command to provide hospitality is a
good example of how a well-established custom could be
transformed by practical Christian love (Romans 12:13). Itinerant
preachers were particularly dependent, as Jesus was, on the
hospitality of fellow believers. The risks involved were far
outweighed by the potential benefits of receiving blessing from one's
guests (Acts 28:7–9; Hebrews 13:1–2).

hour see TIME.

house see HOME.

household gods Images of personal or family gods which were either
kept in the home or used for protection while travelling (Genesis
31:19; Judges 18:14–15).

Huldah A female prophet who confirmed to King Josiah that the
coming destruction of Judah would be postponed because of King
Josiah's repentance (2 Kings 22:14–20). See also JOSIAH, KING OF
JUDAH.

humanity Human beings are the most important feature of God's
creation. They alone are God's children who are made in his image
(Genesis 1:27) and given overall responsibility for the created world.
However, their prosperity depended on maintaining an obedient
and trusting relationship with God, and after Adam and Eve's
disobedience, the reality of their sinful nature is shown by the way
each individual chooses their own way rather than God's (Isaiah 53:6).
Human beings are rescued from their sin by Jesus who is called the
'last Adam' (1 Corinthians 15:45). He redeems those who trust in him
by faith and restores their full rights as God's children (Galatians
4:4–7), but those who reject Christ remain subject to final judgement.
See also ADAM; EVE; MAN AND WOMAN.

humility This much misunderstood aspect of Christian character is
concerned with a proper recognition of a person's relationship with
God and other human beings. Though it involves a willingness to
take a lowly position, it can be combined with the exercise of
authority (Numbers 12:3). The example of Jesus shows the
importance of a humble attitude in obeying God's will (Micah 6:8;
Philippians 2:5–8). See also MEEKNESS.

humour The Bible contains a large number of examples of humour,
but because it is usually based on irony, it does not often come across

to Western readers as funny. Several instances occur in Jesus' parables, such as a camel attempting to pass through the eye of a needle or someone having a plank sticking out of their eye (Matthew 19:24; Luke 6:42).

hunting Not mentioned frequently, though Nimrod of Mesopotamia had a reputation as an outstanding hunter (Genesis 10:9). The use of several metaphors, especially in connection with persecution and judgement, indicates the use of nets, snares and hooks (Job 18:8–10; Psalm 10:2).

husband see MARRIAGE.

Hushai One of David's advisers whose courage and counsel enabled David to overcome Absalom's attempt to usurp his throne (2 Samuel 16:16–17:16).

hyena see ANIMALS.

hymn A song of praise to God. Many examples occur in the Old Testament, especially the Psalms, and focus on God's being and his activity as creator and deliverer of his people. The hymns of the New Testament centre on the person and work of Jesus (Colossians 1:15–18; Revelation 5:9–10). The use of hymns was strongly encouraged in the early church (Ephesians 5:19). See also PRAISE.

hypocrisy The practice of saying one thing and doing another in the context of people's relationship with God is consistently condemned. Jesus particularly criticized the Pharisees for this, describing them as whitewashed tombs (Matthew 23:27–8). Leaders must take special care to match actions and words and to be consistent in speaking to different groups (1 Corinthians 4:1–5; Galatians 2:12–13).

hyssop Probably to be identified with marjoram rather than the modern 'hyssop'. It was used in purification rituals and in drinking wine vinegar (Psalm 51:7; John 19:29).

i

I am A version of God's Old Testament name Yahweh or Jehovah
(Exodus 3:14). Jesus' use of this name was a clear indication of
his claim to be God, and led to accusations of blasphemy
(John 8:58–9).

Ichabod The name of Eli's grandson. It probably meant 'the glory
has departed' and symbolized the disastrous capture of the ark of
the covenant (1 Samuel 4:21–2).

Iconium An important city in Asia Minor (modern Turkey) where
Paul's preaching produced sharply divided reactions to the gospel
(Acts 14:1–7). See map of PAUL'S JOURNEYS.

idleness see LAZINESS.

idolatry The worship of images of gods and goddesses made of
wood, metal or stone. Though idols were common in the cultures
surrounding Israel, they were forbidden to the Israelites for two
reasons. The true God could not be reduced to anything made by
human hands, and other gods were a constant temptation for the
Israelites to abandon their allegiance to the Lord. Many Israelites
did actually worship idols, but many Gentiles in contrast became
Christians by turning away from idolatry. Despite the attractions
of idol worship, the Bible regularly treats idols as completely
worthless and ineffective (Isaiah 44:9–20; 1 Corinthians 8:4).
See also GODS.

illness see DISEASE AND ILLNESSES.

image of God A description of human beings, referring to that which
sets them apart from the rest of God's creation (Genesis 1:26–7). The
image probably refers to the special relationship that exists between
human beings and God rather than to any individual human quality,
and indicates that human beings are God's earthly representatives
who share a family likeness with him.

images see IDOLATRY.

imagination The ability which enables human beings to be creative, but which in God's sight has an inevitable tendency towards evil (Genesis 6:5).

Immanuel A Hebrew name meaning 'God with us'. The use of this name for Jesus indicates that he brought God's presence to earth when he was born (Matthew 1:22–3).

immigrants SEE ALIEN; FOREIGNER.

immorality Since morality in the Bible is understood as what God approves rather than conforming to accepted norms, immorality is about behaviour that displeases God. It includes all forms of wrong activity, as summarized in various lists in the New Testament letters (e.g., 1 Corinthians 6:9–10; Galatians 5:19–21) as well as in the laws of the Old Testament. The Sermon on the Mount makes clear that it also involves wrong motives as well as acting in unacceptable ways (Matthew 5:17–48). see also SIN.

immortality SEE ETERNAL LIFE.

imprisonment SEE CRIME AND PUNISHMENT.

incarnation The belief that the eternal God took on human bodily form in the person of Jesus Christ. The term is an attempt to do justice to the biblical teaching that Jesus was both fully divine and fully human, despite the difficulty of such a view from the perspective of either logic or traditional monotheism. It comes from a Latin expression meaning 'in flesh', and is based on statements that Jesus had come in the flesh, that is, that he had a physical human body (John 1:14; 1 Timothy 3:16). The idea also has roots in the Old Testament, where God appeared more than once in human form (Genesis 18:1–33; Ezekiel 1:26–8). See also THEOPHANY.

incense A substance which was burnt on a special altar in Israel's tabernacle and temple and which created a sweet-smelling odour. The ascending smoke of burning incense was a symbol of prayer rising up to God's presence (Psalm 141:2; Revelation 8:3–4). Incense was widely used in ancient religions, and in Israel was either frankincense resin or a mixture of spices. See also TABERNACLE.

incense, altar of SEE TABERNACLE.

incest Sexual relationships with members of one's close family, including some relatives by marriage, were explicitly forbidden (Leviticus 18:6–18; 20:11–21), though examples of the practice are known (Genesis 35:22; 2 Samuel 16:21–2).

increase SEE GROWTH.

Ingathering, Feast of SEE TABERNACLES, FEAST OF.

inheritance The basic principle in Israel was that land rather than personal possessions passed from one generation to the next.

Property was normally the responsibility of sons, with the eldest receiving a double share, though daughters inherited if there were no sons (Numbers 27:8–11). In cases where a man died childless, it was the responsibility of his brother or another close relative to marry his widow and produce an heir for the deceased person. The surviving brother or relative was known as the 'kinsman-redeemer' (Ruth 3:9–4:12). The Bible also frequently refers to God providing an inheritance for his people, based on the idea that God's people were his children. That inheritance could be the Promised Land, the blessings of heaven or even a relationship with God himself.

iniquity see SIN.

injustice see JUSTICE.

ink see WRITING.

inn see TRAVEL.

innocence Can refer either to the state of human beings before any sin was committed or to the legal position of individuals. It is also a description of Jesus (1 Peter 2:22) and a quality which believers are encouraged to aim for (Matthew 10:16).

inscriptions Knowledge of Biblical Hebrew and Aramaic has been considerably advanced by the discovery of inscriptions in those languages and an enormous number of documents in the related languages of Mesopotamia and Syria–Palestine. Few inscriptions have been preserved in Hebrew because they were largely written on perishable materials, but important texts include the Siloam tunnel inscription of the late eighth century BC and a tenth century BC agricultural calendar from Gezer. Study of the *koine* or vernacular Greek of the New Testament has also been stimulated by the discovery of thousands of Greek papyri describing aspects of ordinary life in New Testament times. All this material not only illustrates and informs our understanding of the Bible but enables it to be set firmly in the context of the history of the ancient world. See also LANGUAGES; WRITING.

insects and arachnids The locust is the insect most frequently mentioned in the Bible. Locusts are actually a type of grasshopper, but while the locust was famed for its destructive capabilities, the grasshopper was known for its smallness (Isaiah 40:22). Frequent references to honey indicates that bees were well known, though much of the honey was probably produced by wild bees. The related hornet was a large wasp with a painful sting. Of the other kinds of winged insects, flies and gnats were responsible for two of the plagues in Egypt (Exodus 8:16–32) and moths were associated with the damage they can cause to fabric. Ants and spiders were also

common, with the ant being famous in proverbial usage. The
nocturnal scorpion is also usually referred to in proverbs.

Insects and arachnids	
Ant	Proverbs 6:6–8
Bee	Judges 14:8
Flea	1 Samuel 24:14
Flies	Exodus 8:21–31
Gnat	Matthew 23:24
Grasshopper	Isaiah 40:22
Hornet	Exodus 23:28
Locust	Joel 1:4
Moth	Matthew 6:19–20
Scorpion	Luke 11:12
Spider	Job 8:14

inspiration The idea that the books of the Bible were written as a
result of God working directly through its human authors. The
concept of inspiration is usually implicit in the Bible, but explicit
statements are occasionally found (2 Timothy 3:16; 2 Peter 1:21). It
does not imply a dictation theory of authorship, but that God was
speaking by his Spirit through the different personalities and
circumstances of individual writers. God's involvement in the
writing process means that the inspiration of the Bible is of a
different kind from the literary inspiration of other writers. Biblical
inspiration is often closely associated with the idea that the Bible is
the result of God's revelation and that it speaks with the absolute
authority of God. It is also sometimes developed into the doctrines
of infallibility, which means that the Bible cannot mislead, and of
inerrancy, which means that it contains no mistakes. See also
AUTHORITY; REVELATION; SCRIPTURE.

instruction See EDUCATION.

instruments See MUSIC AND MUSICAL INSTRUMENTS.

intelligence See WISDOM.

intercession See PRAYER.

interest Israelites were not to charge one another interest because
they were all members of God's family (Exodus 22:25). This was
because loans were made in Israel to help needy people through a
difficult period, though it also doubtless reflected the high interest
rates in the ancient Near East, where annual percentages of 33.3 per
cent were common and 50 per cent not unusual.

intermarriage See MARRIAGE.

intermediate state A description of the condition of human beings between death and their final destiny which is decided at Christ's second coming. Since the Bible makes it clear that God's final decision is based on what a person has done in this life (Romans 2:6; 2 Corinthians 5:10), the intermediate state has no effect on one's ultimate destination. The doctrine of purgatory by which believers may achieve perfection through purifying and atoning suffering was developed long after the Bible was written. For unbelievers, the intermediate state involves waiting for resurrection and judgement. The believer, however, enjoys God's presence (Philippians 1:23). This probably means waiting as a bodiless spirit for the resurrection of the body, though some think that believers receive their spiritual body at death and then wait for the final coming of God's kingdom.

interpretation, biblical Every reader of the Bible invariably interprets what they read. One important reason for this is that every communication involves a process of interpretation between the words of a speaker or writer and a listener or reader. In the case of the Bible, this also involves appreciating the different languages and cultures of the Bible and the context in which each book was written. A further problem is that the Bible makes it clear that its message cannot be properly understood by human reason alone (1 Corinthians 1:18–2:16). It must be understood in the light of Jesus, who is its supreme interpreter (Luke 24:27), and with the help of God's Spirit (John 16:12–13). God has also provided teachers in order to assist in interpreting the Bible, especially in the task of relating its message to the circumstances of the reader (Ephesians 4:11–13). Because these circumstances differ so much from one locality and generation to another, Christians have often disagreed about the Bible's precise significance. On the other hand, anyone who wishes to read the Bible for themselves and who is willing to hear the Bible speak on its own terms receives great benefit (Psalm 119:98–100, 130).

iron see METALS AND MINING.

irony see HUMOUR.

Isaac Abraham and Sarah's promised son. His name, meaning 'he laughs', reflects his parents' incredulity at God's announcement of his birth (Genesis 17:17; 18:10–15). He is a rather shadowy figure between Abraham and Jacob. Though Isaac sometimes responded positively to God (Genesis 26:23–5; 28:1–5), God was often at work through his passivity, as when he was offered as a sacrifice (Genesis 22) and a wife was found for him (Genesis 24).

Isaiah An important prophet who prophesied in Judah for about fifty years from c. 740 BC. He was king Hezekiah's consultant, and according to Jewish tradition died by being sawn in half in Manasseh's reign (cf. Hebrews 11:37). See also ISAIAH, BOOK OF.

Prophetic Books

Prophets played a key role in the life of Israel by speaking on behalf of God, often at times of national significance. They appear throughout the historical books, bringing God's message to individuals and nations, presenting God's desire for how his people should live. Between the eighth and fifth centuries BC, however, there were sixteen prophets whose visions and prophecies were recorded as being of particular importance. In the Old Testament, they are arranged into two groups according to their length: four 'major' prophets (Isaiah, Jeremiah, Ezekiel, Daniel) and twelve 'minor' prophets (Hosea to Malachi). It is more helpful, though, to see them as they relate to events in Israel's history.

Amos and Hosea brought God's message to the northern kingdom of Israel. The mid-eighth century was a time of affluence for the nation under Jeroboam II, but Amos spoke out against hidden social injustice and warned of coming judgment if there was no return to God and his ways. Hosea's ministry covered the declining years of the northern kingdom before judgment finally came with Israel's defeat by Assyria in 722 BC. The message of God's unfailing love for his people, despite their unfaithfulness, and his desire that they might return to him, was illustrated by Hosea's marriage to the prostitute Gomer. 2 Kings 14:25 appears to locate Jonah within this period also, though Jonah's message was not to Israel but to the city of Nineveh, the capital of Assyria, which turned to God as a result.

Contemporary with Amos and Hosea but in the southern kingdom of Judah were Micah and Isaiah. Micah saw that Judah had been infected with the same sins of dishonest religion and injustice as Israel, and had a similar message of impending judgment. However, he also prophesied about a glorious future beyond the judgment with new leaders ruling in Jerusalem. The book of Isaiah forms a link between the next few stages in Judah's story, with the first main section (chapters 1–39) echoing Micah's message of judgment and distant hope.

The theme of the inevitability of judgment continued in the seventh century prophets. Zephaniah preached in the late seventh century, around the time of King Josiah's reforms in Judah (see 2 Kings 22–23). He, along with his contemporaries, also focused on the judgment of other nations. Habakkuk wrestled with the evil of the Assyrians and the Babylonians, whom God was using to judge his people. He was assured that God would bring them to account for their wicked and unjust behaviour, a message picked up by Nahum, who, unlike Jonah, declared the destruction of the Assyrians without any hope of salvation. This happened in 612 BC, when Nineveh fell to the Babylonians and Medes.

The prophet Jeremiah's life spanned the last decades of the nation of Judah and the first years of the exile in Babylon. His message of impending judgment was repeatedly ignored, and he himself was considered a traitor to the nation. He was not deported to Babylon, but remained first in Judah and then in Egypt, from where he wrote to the exiles, telling them not to expect to return to their homes in Judah soon. Lamentations, a book of poems about the destruction of Jerusalem, is traditionally attributed to him. It is uncertain where Joel should be placed chronologically, but his message of the imminent invasion of a foreign army fits this period leading up to the exile.

While in exile, the people still needed to hear God's word. Obadiah spoke a message of judgment to Edom, Judah's close neighbour, who had failed to help at the time of the Babylonian invasion. Daniel quickly rose to prominence in the court of Nebuchadnezzar after his deportation to Babylon. Parts of his work are considered to be apocalyptic, but Daniel also spoke a prophetic message of encouragement about God's future blessing if his people remained faithful. Ezekiel, too, found himself among the exiles. He began prophesying before Jerusalem itself had actually fallen, and spoke about the inevitable destruction of the city, the judgment of Judah and other nations, and a coming time of hope. Even if Isaiah was written earlier, it was to the exiles that the message of hope in the second section (chapters 40–55) was directed, while the final chapters envisage the picture of God's salvation coming to Jerusalem and the world after the end of the exile.

Though Cyrus issued his edict allowing the exiles to return to their homeland in 538 BC, initial enthusiasm about rebuilding the nation soon disappeared. Haggai brought his message in 520 BC, gently challenging the people to rebuild the temple of God.

Zechariah's ministry also supported the building project, while the latter part of his book looks to a future glorious reign of God. Writing about eighty years later, Malachi deals with the disillusionment and half-hearted worship of the returned exiles. His message, that God would personally return to the temple in judgment, is a fitting end to the Old Testament prophetic story, pointing forward to the events of the New Testament.

The prophets of the Old Testament spoke from within the context of the covenant that God had made with his people Israel. Their prophecy was recognised as the word of God, revealing the reality of the implications of that covenant for the nation's life. Though each prophecy was directed towards a particular situation and so was expressed in language from that context, a recurring theme throughout the prophecies is the twin messages of judgment for sin and the offer of salvation if people turn back to God. Many of the prophecies were written in poetic form and use an array of colourful language and imagery to stir the people of God to respond to his message.

Isaiah, book of

Structure

Judgement pronounced and forgiveness offered (1:1–6:13)
A new king to replace the present king (7:1–12:6)
Prophecies about foreign nations (13:1–23:18)
The vision of the end (24:1–27:13)
Judgement and hope (28:1–35:10)
Hezekiah's faith and failure (36:1–39:8)
God promises to redeem his people (40:1–55:13)
Restoring God's people (56:1–66:24)

Famous passages

Isaiah meets God in the temple (6:1–13)
'For to us a child is born' (9:6–7)
Comfort for God's people (40:1–11)
The death of God's Servant (52:13–53:12)
'The Spirit of the Sovereign LORD is on me' (61:1–3)

The best known and probably the greatest of the prophetic books, many of whose prophecies are fulfilled in the ministry of Jesus. It contains many famous sayings, such as the promise 'To us a child is born' (9:6) or the prediction of Jesus' death, 'he was pierced for our transgressions' (53:5). It has also inspired many artists and writers, as for example in Handel's *Messiah*.

The book as a whole, however, is more concerned with ancient Israel than with the future Messiah. Its prophecies belong to at least two periods in Israel's history. Much of chapters 1–39 is set in Judah in the eighth century BC and chapters 40–55 in the Babylonian exile in the later sixth century BC. The final section (chapters 56–66) is more difficult to place, and could belong to the eighth, sixth or fifth centuries BC. Because of these different backgrounds, it has often been thought that the book is the work of more than one prophet. On the other hand, if the book is understood as a whole, it could be either the work of the eighth-century Isaiah or a later literary collection based on his prophecies.

The book contains a remarkable mixture of God's judgement and promises. Chapters 1–39 speak of God's punishment of Judah through the Assyrians (chapter 10) and Babylonians (chapter 39) because it is rotten from the sole of the foot to the top of the head (1:6). Its people are guilty of pride, violence and social injustice, though similar criticisms are also applied to the nations generally (24:1–6). At the same time, Isaiah promises the coming of a new kingdom of God in a world completely at peace, beautifully symbolized by a wolf lying down with a lamb (11:1–9).

The theme of hope is developed more fully in chapters 40–66, which speak of release from exile for the Jews in Babylon (44:24–45:7) and salvation for people of all nations (45:22–3). This is made possible by God's Suffering Servant, who will die not just for Israel's sins but for those of all people (52:13–53:12). Consistent with this universal vision is the affirmation that there is only one God (45:5–6,18,21) who will create a new people comprising Jews and Gentiles and ultimately new heavens and a new earth (65:17; 66:22).

Iscariot see JUDAS ISCARIOT.

Ish-Bosheth Saul's successor as king who reigned briefly over the northern tribes while David ruled Judah (2 Samuel 2:8–4:12). The second part of his actual name Eshbaal was changed as a negative comment on Baal worship (*bosheth* means 'shame').

Ishmael, Ishmaelites Isaac's half-brother and Abraham's son by his wife's slave Hagar. Though not the main heir of God's promises, God promised Ishmael his descendants would become a great nation (Genesis 17:20; 21:17–18). His descendants the Ishmaelites were a tribal people who lived in Edom (Psalm 83:6), but God's promise has traditionally been thought to be fulfilled through the Arab peoples.

Israel 1. A name, meaning 'he struggles with God', which was given to Jacob as he wrestled with God (Genesis 32:28).
2. From the time of the exodus, the usual term for the twelve tribes. The name underlines their descent from Jacob, though it is used with several different senses. First, it was the name of the nation of Israel, often called literally 'the descendants of Israel'. Second, it had a special religious sense which drew attention to Israel's status as God's covenant people. Third, it became the name of the land which was previously known as Canaan and which the Romans later called Palestine. The different uses of the word Israel do not often cause confusion, but they do illustrate an ongoing tension over the nature of the people's true identity. An overlap between the political and religious senses is often present, but in some periods, there was a clear tendency to play down the significance of Israel's special relationship with God. On the other hand, the prophets of the Old Testament and Jesus and Paul in the New Testament continued to emphasize the importance of Israel's spiritual relationship with God, especially through the new covenant (Jeremiah 31:31–4; Romans 9:6–9). It was because Israel was God's people as well as a political nation that they continued to survive under various political formations. When Israel first settled in the Promised Land, they were organized as a tribal league, and were then led by judges and by kings. Exile followed the collapse of the monarchy, before Israel was reduced to the status of a province within successive world empires, despite briefly gaining independence in the second and first centuries BC. See map of NEW TESTAMENT ISRAEL; OLD TESTAMENT ISRAEL; WORLD OF THE BIBLE.
3. When the monarchy divided after Solomon's reign, the northern kingdom was known as Israel for 200 years (c. 922–722 BC) while the southern kingdom was known as Judah. Israel in its religious sense was applied to both kingdoms during this period (2 Chronicles 20:29; Amos 3:1). See map of OLD TESTAMENT ISRAEL.
4. In the New Testament, Israel is almost a synonym for the Jews. It is used particularly by Jews of themselves, and underlines the continuity of God's purposes in election and covenant for his people (Luke 24:21).
5. Occasionally in the New Testament, a term for the church (Galatians 6:16; Revelation 21:12).
Issachar 1. The ninth son of Jacob (Genesis 30:18). 2. A tribe south-west of the Sea of Galilee who may have been incorporated into the area of Zebulun, which was north-west of Issachar. See map of OLD TESTAMENT ISRAEL.

Ithamar A priest who was the youngest of Aaron's four sons. He was in charge of building the tabernacle (Exodus 38:21).

Ittai A Philistine soldier who was loyal to David in Absalom's rebellion (2 Samuel 15:19–22) and became a general in his army (2 Samuel 18:2).

ivory A sign of luxury in the ancient Near East (1 Kings 10:18; Amos 6:4). Several fine ivory carvings have been discovered at Samaria and Hazor.

j

Jabbok, River A river flowing westwards into the Jordan on the boundary between Ammonite and Gileadite territory, where Jacob wrestled with an angel (Genesis 32:22). See map of NEW TESTAMENT ISRAEL; OLD TESTAMENT ISRAEL.

Jabesh Gilead A town in Transjordan which honoured Saul because he had delivered it from attack (1 Samuel 31:11–13). Probably modern Tell Abu-kharaz on the Wadi Yabis near the Jordan. See map of OLD TESTAMENT ISRAEL.

jacinth see JEWELS AND PRECIOUS STONES.

jackal see ANIMALS.

Jacob The ancestor of the twelve tribes of Israel through his twelve sons. Family problems plagued much of his life. He stole his elder brother Esau's birthright and deceived his father into giving him the eldest son's blessing. When he fled to his mother's relatives and married the two sisters Leah and Rachel, his father-in-law continually made life difficult, though God blessed Jacob through these experiences. In old age, favouritism towards his two youngest sons Joseph and Benjamin caused further friction. He died in Egypt but was buried in the Promised Land as a final sign of his faith in God.

God used Jacob to begin to fulfil the promise that Abraham would become the father of a nation (Genesis 25:19–50:26). Particularly through major experiences of God at Bethel (Genesis 28) and Peniel (Genesis 32:22–32), Jacob was transformed from a scheming, arrogant materialist into a person who learned to trust God for his family as well as for himself (Genesis 47:28–49:28).

Jakin and Boaz see TEMPLE.

James, brother of Jesus One of Jesus' brothers who led the church in Jerusalem, presiding over the Council of Jerusalem (Acts 15). He was martyred in 62 AD. See also JAMES, LETTER OF.

James, letter of

Structure
Trials and temptations (1:1–18)
Evidence of true faith (1:19–2:26)
Dangers of the tongue (3:1–4:12)
Living for today and tomorrow (4:13–5:12)
Praying in faith (5:13–20)

Famous passages
True religion (1:27)
Faith and action (2:14–26)
Prayer and the ministry of healing (5:14–16)

A general letter not addressed to any particular church and one of two New Testament letters written by Jesus' brothers. It may be one of the earliest New Testament writings since it is often dated to the mid-40s AD. Its practical teaching draws on Old Testament wisdom and on the Sermon on the Mount, and deals with down-to-earth matters such as wealth, favouritism and the tongue. Evidence of genuine faith (2:14–26) includes concern for the poor (1:27) and prayer for those who are ill (5:14–16).

James, son of Alphaeus An apostle, probably also known as 'James the younger' to distinguish him from James, son of Zebedee (Mark 15:40).

James, son of Zebedee An apostle who was the lesser-known brother of John and one of Jesus' inner circle. Jesus predicted that James would suffer for his faith, and he is the first apostle known to have been martyred, c. 44 AD (Mark 10:35–9; Acts 12:2).

Japheth see SHEM, HAM AND JAPHETH.

jars see UTENSILS.

jasper see JEWELS AND PRECIOUS STONES.

javelin see ARMOUR AND WEAPONS.

jealousy Occurs in the Bible in two very different senses. God's jealousy (Exodus 20:5; 34:14) refers to his passionate commitment to his purposes and his people, and results in condemnation of idolatry and unfaithfulness. The same quality is occasionally applied to human beings (2 Corinthians 11:2). Alternatively, jealousy is a human emotion which can destroy other people (Genesis 4:3–8). See also ZEAL.

Jebus, Jebusites The former name of Jerusalem (2 Samuel 5:6–9). The Jebusites, who lived in the area, were an Amorite group.

Jeduthun see ASAPH, HEMAN AND JEDUTHUN.

Jehoahaz, King of Israel (*c.* 815–801 BC) see KINGS AND QUEENS OF ISRAEL.

Jehoahaz, King of Judah (609 BC) see KINGS AND QUEENS OF ISRAEL.

Jehoash, King of Israel (*c.* 801–786 BC) see KINGS AND QUEENS OF ISRAEL.

Jehoash, King of Judah see JOASH, KING OF JUDAH.

Jehoiachin, King of Judah (*c.* 598–597 BC) He reigned for three months before the Babylonians captured Jerusalem in 597 BC. He was released from prison in Babylon in 561 BC (2 Kings 24:8–17; 25:27–30).

Jehoiada High priest in the ninth century BC who installed the young prince Joash as king. He encouraged Joash in a religious reformation (2 Chronicles 23:1–24:16).

Jehoiakim, King of Judah (c. 609–598 BC) An unreliable and ostentatious king who also opposed the prophets. He died just before the Babylonians captured Jerusalem in 597 BC (2 Kings 23:34–24:7).

Jehoram/Joram, King of Israel (*c.* 849–842 BC) see KINGS AND QUEENS OF ISRAEL.

Jehoram/Joram, King of Judah (*c.* 849–842 BC) see KINGS AND QUEENS OF ISRAEL.

Jehoshaphat, King of Judah (*c.* 873–849 BC) An important king, whom the Bible presents in mixed terms. He showed great faith (2 Chronicles 20:1–30), and Judah prospered under him, but he acted unwisely in allying himself with Ahab's immoral regime in Israel (1 Kings 22:1–50).

Jehovah see GOD, NAMES AND TITLES OF.

Jehovah-Jireh see GOD, NAMES AND TITLES OF.

Jehovah-Nissi see GOD, NAMES AND TITLES OF.

Jehovah-Shalom see GOD, NAMES AND TITLES OF.

Jehovah-Shammah see GOD, NAMES AND TITLES OF.

Jehu, King of Israel (*c.* 842–815 BC) He came to power by killing the kings of Israel and Judah, but despite his initial excessive zeal, Israel declined under his leadership (2 Kings 9:14–10:36). His probable representation on the Black Obelisk of Shalmaneser III of Assyria is the earliest known portrait of any Israelite ruler.

Jephthah One of the judges, who defeated Ammonite forces on both sides of the Jordan and led Israel for six years. He sacrificed his daughter as a result of a careless vow to God (Judges 10:6–12:7).

Jeremiah A prophet who was active from 626 BC until after the fall of Jerusalem in 587 BC. Sometimes known as the 'weeping prophet', he was a deeply sensitive man (Jeremiah 8:21–9:1). He faced repeated rejection from his family as well as the people, and was finally taken against his will by some Jewish exiles to Egypt where he presumably died. See also JEREMIAH, BOOK OF.

Jeremiah, book of

Structure
Prophecies against Judah (1:1–25:38)
Biographical material about Jeremiah (26:1–45:5)
Prophecies about foreign nations (46:1–51:64)
The fall of Jerusalem (52:1–34)

Famous passages
The call of Jeremiah (1:4–19)
At the potter's house (18:1–19:15)
The new covenant (31:31–4)
A king burns Jeremiah's scroll (36:1–32)

An important prophetic book covering the period leading up to the Babylonian exile and the first part of the exile, though it is not arranged in any particular chronological order. It contains three basic types of prophetic material, prophetic messages by Jeremiah, extensive material about the prophet, and some editorial material similar in style to Deuteronomy. The arrangement of the book demonstrates the fulfilment of God's threats against Jerusalem, and that God still had good plans for Israel's future.

Jeremiah was fully involved in the events which led up to the fall of Jerusalem in 587 BC. He repeatedly called for obedience and repentance towards God, and emphasized the need for faith from the heart. The people's repentance was only superficial, however (3:10), and they continued to rely on external aspects of religion such as the temple and rituals (chapter 7). Jeremiah therefore announced that they had broken their covenant with God and would be taken into exile (11:1–12), but this only brought him into greater conflict. He told the people to surrender to the Babylonian armies, predicting a long exile of seventy years, but was thrown into prison and left to die in a waterless cistern. He remained a captive until Jerusalem fell (chapters 37–8).

In spite of this, Jeremiah also spoke about a fresh hope. He promised a new and lasting covenant which God would write on his people's hearts, characterized by the inwardness of genuine faith (31:31–4). He also spoke of the restoration of Jerusalem, which Jeremiah symbolized by buying a plot of land as the Babylonians besieged the city (32:1–33:16), and of a new king in David's line to replace the corrupt monarchy of his own day (23:5–6).

Jeremiah, letter of see APOCRYPHA.

Jericho An ancient city just north of the Dead Sea whose origins go back to *c*. 8000 BC. It is most famous for Joshua's attack when the walls collapsed (Joshua 5:13–6:27). Little trace exists of the city (modern Tell es-Sultan) at that time or for most of the Old Testament period. It was rebuilt by Herod the Great (37–4 BC) See map of NEW TESTAMENT ISRAEL; OLD TESTAMENT ISRAEL.

Jeroboam I, King of Israel (*c*. 922–901 BC) An official in charge of Solomon's forced labour policy who became the first ruler of the northern kingdom of Israel. He set up golden calves at Dan and Bethel and appointed his own priests rather than worship at Jerusalem (1 Kings 12:25–14:20).

Jeroboam II, King of Israel (*c*. 786–746 BC) Israel's most successful ruler, who increased its boundaries and its prosperity. His reign, however, saw an increasing gulf between rich and poor, and was sharply criticized by Amos and Hosea (2 Kings 14:23–9).

Jerusalem Though the name Jerusalem is known from long before the time of David, it was also known as Salem and as Jebus in pre-Israelite times. It was also called 'city of David' since David was the first to capture it for Israel (2 Samuel 5:6–9). The city was destroyed by Nebuchadnezzar, and though Nehemiah rebuilt it after the exile, it was destroyed again by the Romans in 70 AD. The site is built on two hills, and David's earliest city was built on the Ophel or south-eastern hill, where the original Zion was probably located. It is easily defended on all but the north side, though its water supply was vulnerable until Hezekiah dug a tunnel connecting a spring outside the walls with the Pool of Siloam. In the Bible, Jerusalem is the place of God's earthly residence (2 Chronicles 6:6), and of the heavenly city of God (Hebrews 12:22). See also ZION. See map of NEW TESTAMENT ISRAEL; OLD TESTAMENT ISRAEL; PAUL'S JOURNEYS; WORLD OF THE BIBLE.

Jesse David's father, to whose house in Bethlehem Samuel came to anoint Saul's successor as king (1 Samuel 16:1–13).

Jesus Christ, life of Jesus was born in or before 4 BC, but little is known of his life before the age of thirty except that he was a carpenter and grew up in a poor family in Nazareth (Matthew 13:55; Luke 2:51–2). His public ministry began with his baptism and his temptations for forty days in the wilderness (Matthew 3:13–4:11). For the next three years he travelled around Palestine, preaching and teaching and carrying out various miracles, healing people of various diseases. He concentrated on the Jewish people, leaving Palestine only rarely to visit Phoenicia and the Decapolis.

He lived as one of the poor, with no home of his own, and supported by his disciples. Opposition was common, especially from Jewish religious leaders, though his miracles made him popular with ordinary people. Highlights included the Transfiguration, possibly on Mount Hermon, and Peter's first recognition that he was the expected Messiah (Matthew 16:15–20).

The Gospels give special attention to the events of the last week of his life, especially the Last Supper, the garden of Gethsemane, his trial, crucifixion and resurrection. He ascended to heaven forty days later, but an angel promised he would return again, confirming what Jesus himself had taught.

Jesus Christ, teaching of Since Jesus' teaching is not recorded under particular topics, it is best described through its key themes. The central theme is the kingdom of God, which was about God's powerful activity in the world and his rule over people's lives. Obedience to God's will was therefore a sign of belonging to God's kingdom. Jesus amazed his hearers by saying that God's kingdom had already arrived in him as well as coming in the future, and that people could enter it there and then through faith in him.

Jesus frequently taught about his identity and his mission. He talked about God as his Father, and by carrying out his Father's will made an implicit claim to be God's Son. But he also spoke about establishing God's kingdom through being a servant, preferring the title 'Son of Man' for himself. Even his disciples could not understand this at first, because they like most Jews expected their Messiah to exercise a political and military triumph. Jesus, however, showed from his Bible, especially Isaiah 53, that God would fulfil his purposes through the suffering and death of his servant.

Jesus' teaching had a recognizable authority not evident with other religious teachers of the day, and he received the honorific title 'Rabbi'. Jesus expected a response to his teaching. He had come to call people to faith in God, and emphasized to the general consternation of the religious leaders that God wanted sinners to turn to him rather than those who boasted of their outward show and traditions. In the Sermon on the Mount especially (Matthew 5–7), he stressed the need for people to be obedient to God from their hearts. Parables such as the Prodigal Son (Luke 15) repeatedly underlined that he 'came to seek and to save what was lost' (Luke 19:10). At the same time, he did not minimize the possibility of judgement, warning that those who rejected his teaching were liable to God's punishment.

Jesus Christ, miracles of

Healing miracles

Groups of those who were ill	Matthew 12:15; 15:29–31; Mark 7:31–7
Man with a skin disease	Matthew 8:2–4; Mark 1:40–4; Luke 5:12–14
Roman centurion's servant	Matthew 8:5–13; Luke 7:1–10
Peter's mother-in-law	Matthew 8:14–15; Mark 1:29–31; Luke 4:38–9
Paralysed man	Matthew 9:2–8; Mark 2:3–12; Luke 5:18–26
Woman with bleeding	Matthew 9:20–2; Mark 5:25–34; Luke 8:43–8
Two blind men	Matthew 9:27–31
Man with a shrivelled hand	Matthew 12:10–13; Mark 3:1–5; Luke 6:6–10
Two blind men at Jericho	Matthew 20:29–34; Mark 10:46–52; Luke 18:35–43
Deaf and mute man	Mark 7:31–7
Blind man at Bethsaida	Mark 8:22–6
Man with dropsy	Luke 14:1–4
Ten lepers	Luke 17:11–19
Malchus' ear	Luke 22:50–1
Official's son at Capernaum	John 4:46–54
Invalid man beside pool	John 5:1–9
Man born blind	John 9:1–41

Exorcisms

Two men living among the tombs	Matthew 8:28–34; Mark 5:1–17; Luke 8:26–37
A mute man	Matthew 9:32–4
A blind and mute man	Matthew 12:22; Luke 11:14
Canaanite woman's daughter	Matthew 15:21–8; Mark 7:24–30
Boy with seizures	Matthew 17:14–19; Mark 9:14–28; Luke 9:37–42
Man in a synagogue	Mark 1:21–8; Luke 4:31–7
A crippled woman	Luke 13:11–13

Nature miracles

Calming the storm	Matthew 8:23–7; Mark 4:36–41; Luke 8:22–5
Feeding 5,000 men	Matthew 14:13–21; Mark 6:32–44; Luke 9:10–17; John 6:1–13
Walking on the water	Matthew 14:22–33; Mark 6:45–51; John 6:15–21
Feeding 4,000 men	Matthew 15:32–9; Mark 8:1–10
Coin in a fish's mouth	Matthew 17:24–7
Withering of fig-tree	Matthew 21:18–22; Mark 11:12–14, 20–4
Catching fish	Luke 5:1–11
Water turned into wine	John 2:1–11
Catching fish for breakfast	John 21:1–14

Resurrection miracles

Jairus' daughter	Matthew 9:18–19, 23–5; Mark 5:22–4, 35–43; Luke 8:41–2, 49–56
Widow's son at Nain	Luke 7:11–15
Lazarus	John 11:1–44

Jesus Christ, names and titles of

Titles concerning Jesus' divine nature

First and the Last (Alpha and Omega)	Revelation 22:13
Head	Ephesians 1:22
I am	John 8:58
Living One	Revelation 1:18
Lord	Acts 2:36
Righteous One	Acts 3:14
Son of God	Romans 1:4
Son of the Most High	Luke 1:32
True Light	John 1:9
Rock	1 Corinthians 10:4
Word of God	John 1:1

Titles concerning Jesus' Messiahship

Bright Morning Star	Revelation 22:16
Chief Shepherd	1 Peter 5:4
Christ/Messiah	Matthew 16:16
Faithful witness	Revelation 1:5
Head of the church	Colossians 1:18
High Priest	Hebrews 3:1
Immanuel	Matthew 1:23
King of the Jews	Matthew 27:37
Lamb of God	John 1:29
Last Adam	1 Corinthians 15:45
Lion of Judah	Revelation 5:5
Mediator	1 Timothy 2:5
Prince	Acts 5:31
Rabbi	John 1:38
Root and Offspring of David	Revelation 22:16
Saviour	Titus 1:4
Son of Man	Luke 19:10
Son of David	Matthew 20:30

The 'I am' sayings

The Bread of Life	John 6:35
The Gate	John 10:7
The Good Shepherd	John 10:11, 14
The Light of the World	John 8:12
The Resurrection and the Life	John 11:25
The True Vine	John 15:1
The Way, the Truth and the Life	John 14:6

Modern scholars have sometimes questioned whether the sayings of Jesus are an authentic reflection of his teaching, especially as the Gospel writers each present their own portrait of Jesus. However, the importance of teaching and learning within contemporary Judaism and Jesus' use of familiar Jewish methods of instruction suggests that the Gospels do indeed contain a reliable account of Jesus' own teaching.

Jesus Christ, parables of

Lamp under a bowl	Matthew 5:14–16; Mark 4:21–2; Luke 8:16–17; 11:33
Wise and foolish builders	Matthew 7:24–7; Luke 6:47–9
New cloth on an old garment	Matthew 9:16; Mark 2:21; Luke 5:36
New wine in old wineskins	Matthew 9:17; Mark 2:22; Luke 5:37–8
Sower and the seed	Matthew 13:3–8, 18–23; Mark 4:2–8, 13–20; Luke 8:5–8, 11–15
Weeds among the wheat	Matthew 13:24–30, 36–43
Mustard seed	Matthew 13:31–2; Mark 4:30–2; Luke 13:18–19
Yeast	Matthew 13:33; Luke 13:20–1
Hidden treasure	Matthew 13:44
Pearl of great value	Matthew 13:45–6
The fishing net	Matthew 13:47–50
Lost sheep	Matthew 18:12–14; Luke 15:4–7
Unmerciful servant	Matthew 18:23–35
Vineyard workers	Matthew 20:1–16
Two sons	Matthew 21:28–32
Vineyard tenants	Matthew 21:33–46; Mark 12:1–12; Luke 20:9–19
Wedding banquet	Matthew 22:1–14
The fig-tree and its leaves	Matthew 24:32–3; Mark 13:28–9; Luke 21:29–31
Wise servant	Matthew 24:45–51; Luke 12:42–6
Ten virgins	Matthew 25:1–13
Talents	Matthew 25:14–30
Sheep and goats	Matthew 25:31–46
Growing seed	Mark 4:26–9
Money-lender	Luke 7:41–3
Good Samaritan	Luke 10:30–7
Friend at midnight	Luke 11:5–8
Rich fool	Luke 12:16–21
Watchful servants	Luke 12:35–40
Unfruitful fig-tree	Luke 13:6–9
Seats at the wedding feast	Luke 14:7–14
Great banquet	Luke 14:16–24
The cost of discipleship	Luke 14:28–33
Lost coin	Luke 15:8–10
Lost (prodigal) son	Luke 15:11–32
Shrewd manager	Luke 16:1–8

Rich man and Lazarus	Luke 16:19–31
The master and servant	Luke 17:7–10
Unjust judge	Luke 18:1–8
Pharisee and tax collector	Luke 18:9–14
Ten minas	Luke 19:12–27

Jesus Christ, prayers of

Jesus' practice

The Lord's prayer	Matthew 6:9–13
Praying to his Father	John 12:27–8
Praying alone	Mark 1:35
Praying for others	John 17:1–26
Continuing in prayer for others	Hebrews 7:25
Praying for children	Matthew 19:13
Praying for his persecutors	Luke 23:34
Prayers of thanksgiving	Matthew 11:25–6; 26:26–7

Praying at or before major events

Praying at his baptism	Luke 3:21–2
Praying before choosing the apostles	Luke 6:12–13
Praying before he was transfigured	Luke 9:28–9
Praying in Gethsemane	Matthew 26:36–46
Praying on the cross	Matthew 27:46

Jethro Moses' father-in-law, also known as Reuel and Hobab. He advised Moses of the need to delegate his responsibilities (Exodus 18).

Jew Originally a term for an inhabitant of Judah or Judea. After the Babylonian exile, it gradually replaced the earlier term 'Israelite' as the usual term for a member of God's people. In the New Testament, it is used especially for those who belonged to the Jewish faith. The privilege of being a Jew is often mentioned, in relation both to Jesus' own Jewishness and because Jesus and the apostles preached the gospel first to Jews. In the Gospels, the term 'the Jews' refers particularly but by no means exclusively to Jews who opposed Jesus (John 7:1; 8:31), but the New Testament also emphasizes that the gospel is for Jews and Gentiles equally (Galatians 3:28). See also HEBREW; ISRAEL.

jewels and precious stones These are often mentioned in the Bible, though details of individual stones are not always certain. They were a form of wealth, and were used as a standard of value. As a symbol of great beauty and of great value, twelve jewels were worn as part of the high priest's breastpiece. The new Jerusalem was also made out of jewels. Jewellery could be worn by men as well as women, though is more frequently associated with the latter. Despite their attractiveness, the Bible values wisdom more highly (Proverbs 8:10–11).

Jewels and precious stones	
Agate	Exodus 28:19
Amethyst	Exodus 28:19
Beryl	Exodus 28:17
Carnelian	Revelation 4:3
Chalcedony	Revelation 21:19
Chrysolite	Exodus 28:20
Chrysoprase	Revelation 21:20
Coral	Ezekiel 27:16
Emerald	Exodus 28:18
Jacinth	Exodus 28:19
Jasper	Exodus 28:20
Onyx	Exodus 28:20
Pearls	Matthew 7:6
Ruby	Exodus 28:17
Sapphire	Exodus 28:18
Sardonyx	Revelation 21:20
Topaz	Exodus 28:17
Turquoise	Exodus 28:18

Jewish calendar SEE CALENDAR, JEWISH.

Jezebel A Phoenician woman from Tyre who married Ahab, King of Israel. She actively pursued a policy of promoting the worship of Melqart, the Baal revered in Tyre, and of opposing the worshippers of the Lord, especially the prophet Elijah (1 Kings 18:13–14; 19:1–2). See also AHAB; ELIJAH.

Jezreel A town (modern Zer'in) and a valley in north-eastern Israel. The town was Israel's second city under Ahab's dynasty (1 Kings 18:45–6). See map of OLD TESTAMENT ISRAEL.

Joab Commander-in-chief of David's armies, and a faithful supporter of David until he favoured Adonijah over Solomon as David's successor. He had a tendency to take a hard line, killing potential

rivals Abner and Amasa and being involved in Absalom's death
(2 Samuel 3:27; 18:14; 20:10).

Joash, King of Israel see JEHOASH, KING OF ISRAEL.

Joash, King of Judah (c. 837–800 BC) He became king at seven years
old after he was miraculously spared as a baby. Jehoiada the high
priest was a positive influence on him, but Joash later encouraged
idolatry and was implicated in the murder of Jehoiada's son
(2 Kings 12).

Job The main character of the Book of Job. He came from the land of
Uz (Job 1:1), which was associated either with Edom or north-west
Palestine. Though known among his contemporaries as 'the greatest
man among all the people of the East' (1:3), his subsequent
experiences of suffering and anguish brought a deeper
understanding of God. See also JOB, BOOK OF.

Job, book of

Structure

  Job's suffering (1:1–2:13)
  Dialogue between Job and his three friends (3:1–27:23)
  The source of true wisdom (28:1–28)
  Job sums up his plight (29:1–31:40)
  Elihu's speeches (32:1–37:24)
  God speaks to Job (38:1–42:6)
  Job is restored (42:7–17)

Famous passages

  Satan accuses Job (1:6–12; 2:1–7)
  Job's faith (1:20–21)
  I know that my Redeemer lives (19:25–7)
  Job repents (42:5–6)

The book of Job is rightly recognized as one of the classics of
ancient literature, though it is unknown who wrote it or when. It has
been dated as far apart as the patriarchal period of Genesis and the
post-exilic era. The book is written largely in dialogue form as Job
tries to make sense of the most extreme experiences of suffering,
including financial collapse, loss of health and the death of his
children. The greatest problem of all, however, is that this happened
to someone totally devoted to God – he was 'blameless and upright;
he feared God and shunned evil' (1:1, 8). His innocent suffering is
therefore a serious theological problem.

  Job's response takes him to the depths and heights of his faith. He
can accuse God of being his enemy (16:7–14), yet also be convinced

that God will fully vindicate him (19:25–7). His friends only increase his suffering, by repeating the traditional belief that such great suffering must imply some previous sin. Job, however, knows he is innocent of any such sin, but instead of rejecting his faith, he continues to lay his case before God. In the end (38:1–41:34), God does answer Job, but rather than answer Job's intellectual questions, he speaks about Job's relationship with him. Finally Job repents (42:1–6), not of any sin that caused his suffering but of speaking about things that he did not understand. He comes to realize that far from abandoning him, God has been deeply involved in his suffering. God even commends Job for doing 'what is right' (42:7–8). This view of innocent suffering as part of God's purposes in people's lives is an important preparation for the New Testament understanding of suffering.

Joel, book of

Structure
   Judgement on the Day of the LORD (1:1–2:17)
   Salvation on the Day of the LORD (2:18–3:21)

Famous passages
   'Rend your heart and not your garments' (2:13)
   The promise of the Spirit for all people (2:28–32)

The book of Joel is a collection of prophecies about the Day of the LORD. The first part (1:1–2:17) contains a vivid description of a locust swarm with which God is about to punish his people, but which could be avoided if the people repent of their sin. The locusts were probably real, though could refer to an invading nation. In the second part (2:18–3:21) God promises to restore his people, including the promise of God's Spirit for all believers fulfilled at Pentecost (2:28–32; Acts 2:17–21). The book can be placed anywhere between the ninth and fifth centuries BC. See also DAY OF THE LORD.

Johanan 1. Leader of a coup whose group took Jeremiah to Egypt (Jeremiah 43:4–7).

2. A high priest just after Nehemiah's time (Nehemiah 12:22–3).

1, 2 and 3 John

These three letters, all written in the same style and with similarities to John's Gospel, are often thought to have been written by the apostle John c. 90–95 AD. 1 John contains warnings against people with misleading teachings about Christ and Christian living. It emphasizes that because Jesus was a real human being as well as Messiah and Son of God, his death was completely effective in

---

Structure of 1 John
The truth about Jesus (1 John 1:1–4)
Living in the truth of Jesus (1 John 1:5–2:29)
God's love and Christian love (1 John 3:1–5:13)
Having confidence in God (1 John 5:14–21)

Famous passages
Walk in the light (1 John 1:7)
Jesus is faithful and just to forgive all sin (1 John 1:9)
God is love (1 John 4:8, 16)

---

dealing with sin and the devil. Christians must also struggle against sin and be committed to love their fellow believers. 2 and 3 John are also concerned with church life. 2 John underlines the importance of living by the teaching of Jesus, and 3 John is about Christian leadership.

John, Gospel of

Structure
Prologue (1:1–18)
Book of Signs (1:19–12:50)
Book of Glory (13:1–20:31)
Epilogue (21:1–25)

Famous passages
The word made flesh (1:14)
New birth (3:1–8)
The Bread of Life (6:25–59)
The Good Shepherd (10:11)
The raising of Lazarus (11:1–44)
Jesus promises the Holy Spirit (14:15–27; 15:26–7; 16:5–15)
Jesus prays for his disciples (17:1–26)

Even a quick reading shows that John's Gospel is distinctive. Unlike the other Gospels, it contains an introduction about Jesus as the eternal Word of God in human form (1:1–18), several long discourses by Jesus, like that on Jesus as the Bread of Life (6:25–59), and an explicit statement of its purpose, that readers should believe in Jesus as Messiah and Son of God (20:31).

Above all, it has a much higher proportion than the other Gospels of teaching by and about Jesus. The central issue is who Jesus is, or more accurately, how and why Jesus is the Messiah. Instead of gradually revealing Jesus' Messiahship, Jesus is given a variety of

Messianic titles from the beginning, including six times in the first chapter. In answer to the question about Jesus' identity, John emphasizes that he is the Son of his heavenly Father. He is the Son who has been sent to reveal the Father (1:18; 8:38) and who is united with the Father (17:22). The clear implication is that Jesus' words and actions are those of God himself. This view of Jesus is confirmed by other distinctive features in John, that Jesus is the Word (Greek *logos*) of God (1:1–14), that he is 'I am' (10:11; 15:1, etc.), and that the Holy Spirit was given to the disciples by Jesus (14:25–27).

The first half of the book contains several 'signs' or miracles (1:19–12:50), showing various ways in which God is working through Jesus. The second half contains John's account of Jesus' suffering and death (13:1–20:31). This is the critical 'hour' or 'time' (12:27) when Jesus provides salvation. This idea of Jesus' death as a decisive moment is supported by John's preference for 'eternal life' as a way of summarizing the benefits of believing in Jesus (17:3). The person who believes in Jesus is changed for ever.

This Gospel is traditionally associated with the apostle John, who is probably 'the disciple whom Jesus loved' (13:23; 19:26–7), and though the evidence falls short of proof, this remains the most probable view. If this is accepted, John probably wrote it c.90 AD, though a minority argue for the period 50–60 AD.

John Mark see MARK, JOHN.

John, the apostle An apostle who was part of Jesus' inner circle. The nickname 'son of thunder' suggests a lively, possibly aggressive personality, but one who was transformed by his association with Jesus into 'the disciple whom Jesus loved'. He was the only apostle to see the crucifixion and the first to see the empty tomb (John 19:26–7; 20:4–5). Later he became a leader in the Jerusalem and Ephesian churches. See also 1, 2, AND 3 JOHN; JOHN, GOSPEL OF; REVELATION, BOOK OF.

John the Baptist A relative of Jesus who is known chiefly in the New Testament as Jesus' forerunner. His ministry was characterized by the practice of water baptism and by the message of repentance (Matthew 3:1–17). Jesus regarded him as the last and greatest prophet, fulfilling the promise of a second Elijah (Matthew 11:11–14). Despite a successful ministry, he was killed by Herod Antipas for criticizing his marriage to his sister-in-law (Matthew 14:1–12).

Jonah An eighth-century prophet (2 Kings 14:25) who disobeyed God. Having tried unsuccessfully to avoid God's call to preach to Nineveh, he spoke about judgement when God wanted him to talk about his love. His escape after being swallowed by a large fish (the Bible does not call it a whale) finds some support from documented examples of similar cases. See also JONAH, BOOK OF.

Jonah, book of

Structure
Jonah runs away from God (1:1–2:10)
Jonah goes to Nineveh (3:1–4:11)

Famous passages
Jonah and a large fish (1:17–2:10)
God's concern for the city of Nineveh (4:11)

An unusual book about a prophet who tried to avoid God's call to go to Nineveh and who was angry with God when he was merciful to the Ninevites. It may be either an historical account about an actual prophet or a post-exilic parable about Jewish attitudes towards the Gentiles. The book's purpose has been widely debated, but the final chapter suggests it is about making the prophet (and the Jewish people) aware that God forgives all who repent (e.g. 4:2, 11). As such, it constitutes a powerful challenge to any narrow view of the nature of God.

Jonathan King Saul's eldest son, who was a more able soldier and exercised greater faith than his father. He made a covenant of friendship with David, to whom he showed outstanding loyalty at considerable cost to himself (1 Samuel 18:1–4).

Joppa A seaport on Palestine's Mediterranean coast where Peter learned in a vision that the gospel was for Gentiles as well as Jews (Acts 10). See map of NEW TESTAMENT ISRAEL; OLD TESTAMENT ISRAEL.

Joram see JEHORAM, KING OF ISRAEL; JEHORAM, KING OF JUDAH.

Jordan, River Israel's major river, flowing southwards from near Mount Hermon through a rift valley into the Dead Sea. It is nearly 200 kilometres long and flows through Lake Huleh and the Sea of Galilee, dividing the main part of Israel in the west from Transjordan in the east. It is associated with many important events, such as Israel's entry to the Promised Land on dry ground (Joshua 3–4) and Jesus' baptism (Matthew 3:13–17). See map of NEW TESTAMENT ISRAEL; OLD TESTAMENT ISRAEL; WORLD OF THE BIBLE.

Joseph of Arimathea A secret disciple and member of the Sanhedrin who provided his tomb for Jesus' body to be buried (Matthew 27:57–60). The location of Arimathea is uncertain, but is thought to be Rathamein in Samaria.

Joseph, husband of Mary Mary's husband, who cared for Jesus as though he were his earthly father (Matthew 1:18–2:23). A descendant of David, the silence of the Gospels about him during Jesus' ministry indicates that he died before Jesus reached thirty.

Joseph, son of Jacob Jacob's favourite son and his first son by Rachel, his favourite wife. He was the owner of the famous coat of many colours, which was actually more likely to have been a long-sleeved coat. His story (Genesis 37–50) contrasts the working of God's purpose in his life with his own immaturity, his father's over-indulgence and his brothers' jealousy. Joseph's faith, courage and wisdom eventually preserved his whole family in Egypt (Genesis 45:7–8), but only after much suffering. As a sign of his faith in God, he made his descendants promise to take his bones with them when they returned to Canaan. Joseph was made second only to Pharaoh in Egypt, and though he is not mentioned in existing records, several incidental details about him are confirmed in Egyptian sources, suggesting that the brilliant literary story of Joseph is historically reliable.

Joshua, book of

Structure
Preparing to enter the Promised Land (1:1–5:12)
The bridgehead in central Palestine (5:13–8:35)
Campaign in southern Palestine (9:1–10:43)
Campaign in northern Palestine (11:1–23)
Summary of defeated kings (12:1–24)
Tribal allocations of the Promised Land (13:1–21:45)
Joshua's farewell (22:1–24:33)

Famous passages
Rahab the prostitute (2:1–24)
The battle of Jericho (6:1–27)
Achan's sin (7:1–26)
The sun stands still (10:12–15)
Choose this day whom you will serve (24:1–27)

The first book in what is traditionally known as the Former Prophets (Joshua – 2 Kings) and the second in the so-called Deuteronomic History (Deuteronomy – 2 Kings). The first draft may have been written in the early monarchy. The first section (chapters 1–12) describes Israel entering the Promised Land through campaigns in the centre, south and north of Canaan. The second (chapters 13–21) allocates land to each tribe. The book ends (chapters 22–4) with Israel renewing the covenant.

The description of Israel's victories in chapters 1–12 is sometimes thought to be too idealistic, but this section probably refers to initial military successes rather than permanent settlements. It is supported by evidence of destruction in the thirteenth century BC at several Canaanite cities. The book also acknowledges that much of the land was not in Israel's possession (13:1; 15:63; 17:12–13).

The book's main theme is that Israel entered the Promised Land because God kept his promises (cf. 1:2–3; 23:14) and played a decisive role in Israel's battles (5:13–15; 11:20). Though the land was not fully occupied, future success would depend on obeying God's laws and keeping his covenant.

Historical Books

Twelve books from Joshua to Esther make up the historical writings of the Old Testament. In the Hebrew scriptures, six of these (Joshua, Judges, 1 and 2 Samuel, 1 and 2 Kings) are found within the 'Prophets' section and are known as the 'Former Prophets'. The designation of these as prophecy corresponded with their role in the life of Israel, showing how God's intentions were worked out in the nation's history. They are sometimes called the 'Deuteronomic History' because they seem to narrate the events of the nation in the light of the theological framework of Deuteronomy, perhaps for those struggling to come to terms with the exile.

The book of Joshua continues from the end of Deuteronomy with the death of Moses and the beginning of Joshua's leadership. He leads the tribes of Israel across the Jordan and into the land of Canaan. The land, however, was already occupied by various peoples, and the Israelites needed to fight to gain control. Joshua eventually gathered the whole of Israel together at Shechem, where the covenant with God was renewed. Much of the book is devoted to detailing the allocation of the land to the tribes of Israel, noting the areas successfully conquered, as well as those where the inhabitants of the land had not been driven out.

In the book of Judges these remaining inhabitants became a problem. The Israelites began to worship the local gods rather than the God who had brought them out of Egypt, and as a result, God let the surrounding tribes defeat and plunder them. When things got bad, the people would cry out to God, who would raise up a 'judge' to liberate them. Each judge was different, meeting the particular need of the nation at a particular time, but after each judge's death, the nation would again fall into sin.

The two books of Samuel, which were originally undivided, chart the beginnings of the nation's journey out of the time of the judges and takes kingship as its main theme. The first seven chapters introduce Samuel, a judge and prophet, who in chapters 8–10 was given the task of anointing Saul as the first king of Israel. Saul, however, did not rule wisely, and soon David comes onto the scene as the anointed heir to the throne, though for the rest of the first book he is on the run from Saul as a fugitive. After Saul was killed in battle, David became king and soon made Jerusalem his capital. In 2 Samuel 7, God made a covenant with David that his throne would be established for ever, a promise that led to Israel's hopes for a messianic leader. The rest of David's life gets a mixed review, as it becomes clear that his leadership abilities do not extend to his own family.

The books of Kings continue the account, starting with the death of David and the succession of his son, Solomon. With the building of the Temple in Jerusalem and the consolidation of the nation's riches, Solomon's reign is seen as the high point in Israel's history. After his death, though, the kingdom divides into two: the northern kingdom of Israel, and the southern kingdom of Judah. The rest of Kings records the fate of both kingdoms, giving summaries of varying lengths to the reign of each of the kings, assessing them according to their success or failure to follow God's ways. Israel falls to the Assyrians in 722 BC (2 Kings 17), while Judah survives for over a century, before falling to the Babylonians (2 Kings 25).

The remaining historical books fall within the 'Writings' section of the Hebrew scriptures. The two books of Chronicles cover roughly the same period as Kings. The concern of the Chronicler, however, is with the family line of David and the purity of worship in the temple. Consequently, the books contain many genealogies and assess only the kings of Judah, where the temple was located. A characteristic of the Chronicler's writing is his use of other sources and records.

Ezra and Nehemiah, also by the Chronicler, form one book in the Hebrew scriptures, and deal with the return of the exiles and the subsequent rebuilding of the temple and the nation. About eighty years after the return of the exiles, Ezra arrived in Jerusalem to teach the law of God and restore the worship of the temple. In 445 BC, Nehemiah returned to oversee the rebuilding of the walls of the city, and to implement a renewal of the covenant.

The final historical books fit into this framework. Ruth is set in the time of the judges, and forms a direct link to the books of Samuel by narrating how Ruth, a Moabite, became David's great-grandmother. The events of Esther probably occured between the time of the rebuilding of the temple in Jerusalem and the return of Ezra. Though the book does not mention God, its story fits in well with the other historical works by showing how God's people survived opposition by remaining faithful.

The historical writings show how Israel understood God to be at work within the history of the nation. Both God's judgments and God's blessings came to the nation in ways which often seemed very ordinary, as political, economic and cultural events. Even so, they were to be recognised as coming from God himself, giving Israel the opportunity to learn more about his character and how to live in his presence.

Joshua, high priest Also known as Jeshua, a high priest who was involved in rebuilding the temple after the exile (Zechariah 3:1–10).

Joshua, son of Nun Moses' assistant and successor, originally named Hoshea. He was one of only two adults who left Egypt who also entered the Promised Land, reflecting his outstanding faith in God (Numbers 13–14). He led Israel's military campaigns during their first five years in Canaan. Near the end of his 110-year life, he challenged Israel to renew their covenant with God (Joshua 23–4). See also JOSHUA, BOOK OF.

Josiah, King of Judah (c. 640–609 BC) A king who in his teenage years began a religious reformation which led to the discovery of an old 'Scroll of the law' and resulted in a national covenant renewal ceremony. He was tragically killed by Egyptian forces who were not at war with Judah (2 Kings 22:1–23:30).

Jotham, King of Judah (c. 742–735 BC) See KINGS AND QUEENS OF ISRAEL.

joy A deep sense of happiness associated with special events such as the birth of a child or military victory, and which often results from a personal experience of God. It is a quality of happiness which should characterize every Christian (Philippians 4:4), and was frequently seen in the early church. What particularly distinguishes Christian joy is that it can be experienced even in times of great difficulty (1 Peter 4:13). Throughout the Bible, it is often experienced in worship and in response to signs of God's work in people's lives.

Jubilee The fiftieth year in Israel when all debts were cancelled, slaves were released and property restored to its original owner, though it is unknown whether this idealistic practice was ever observed (Leviticus 25:8–55). Jesus used it as a picture of his own ministry of redemption (Luke 4:18–19). The name probably comes from the ram's horn blown at the start of the year.

Judah, kingdom and province of The kingdom of Judah in southern Canaan lasted from *c.*922 BC until the fall of Jerusalem in 587 BC (1 Kings 12:17–19; 2 Kings 25:21). It was ruled by David's descendants, apart from the brief reign of Queen Athaliah. Judah's greatest periods were under Uzziah and Hezekiah in the eighth century BC. After the exile, Judah was reduced to the status of a province under the Babylonians and Persians, though for some time it had its own governor of whom the best known are Zerubbabel and Nehemiah (Nehemiah 5:14). It became the Roman province of Judea in the first century AD. See map of OLD TESTAMENT ISRAEL.

Judah, son of Jacob Jacob's fourth son, and a leader among his brothers, though it seems he did not have high moral or spiritual standards (Genesis 38). See also JUDAH, TRIBE OF.

Judah, tribe of The most important of the tribes of Israel, occupying the southern part of Canaan and gradually absorbing several smaller tribal groups including Simeon and Benjamin. This larger Judah developed a separate identity by the time of the judges. The New Testament refers to Jesus' descent from Judah (Hebrews 7:14; Revelation 5:5). See map of OLD TESTAMENT ISRAEL.

judaizers A group who tried but failed to persuade the early church to continue to keep the Jewish law (Galatians 2:11–12).

Judas Iscariot The apostles' treasurer, who sometimes helped himself to their funds. He betrayed Jesus for thirty pieces of silver, but committed suicide because of remorse over Jesus' death (Matthew 26:14–16). The name Iscariot probably indicates his place of origin.

Judas, son of James One of the twelve apostles, probably also called Thaddaeus. His only claim to fame is a question asked at the Last Supper (John 14:22).

Jude, letter of

Structure
Warning against false teachers (1–16)
Encouragement to faith and love (17–25)

Famous passage
'To him who is able to keep you from falling ...' (24–5)

Like the Letter of James, a general letter written by one of Jesus' brothers. It is an urgent appeal to beware of false teachers who do not respect God's law and whose fate is illustrated in the Old Testament and other Jewish writings. It also assures believers that God will protect and preserve them from every effect of evil.

Judea A Greek and Roman name for the land of Judah. Though it could include the whole area of Palestine, in the New Testament it usually refers to the southern region alone, excluding Samaria and Galilee (John 4:3–4). See map of NEW TESTAMENT ISRAEL.

judgement The Bible speaks mainly about the judgement of God, who makes decisions about all human beings because all are accountable to him. These decisions may be made during and at the end of a person's life, but they are particularly associated with the final judgement when Jesus will judge the living and the dead and act against all forms of wickedness (Acts 17:31). The basis of God's judgement is always absolute fairness, and is concerned with people's motives as well as their actions. God also judges in a personal way, rather than acting automatically according to a fixed moral code of right and wrong. Far from resulting in arbitrary decision-making, this works to everyone's advantage because God is slow to anger and is aware of human limitations (Psalm 103:8–10). In fact, God often judges leniently during people's lives in the hope that they might heed his warnings and turn to him for salvation. Without faith in Christ, all are condemned, and God's mercy in delaying judgement should not be confused with the inevitability of final judgement (2 Peter 3:3–10). Believers, however, need not fear judgement, and will receive their own reward. See also MERCY.

judges 1. Leaders of Israel in the period between Joshua and the rise of the monarchy, c.1200–1000 BC. Initially raised up by God to deliver Israel from foreign invaders, they also led the nation. The word means 'rulers, governors'. See also DEBORAH; GIDEON; SAMSON; ELI; SAMUEL.

2. Important Israelite officials whose numbers were increased by Moses and Jehoshaphat (Exodus 18:21–6; 2 Chronicles 19:5–11). The Old Testament emphasizes the importance of their personal qualities.

3. The New Testament envisages Christians as judges over the church, the world and angels (Matthew 19:28; 1 Corinthians 6:1–6).

Judges, book of

The book covers the period of the judges, which lasted for approximately 200 years from Joshua's death until the rise of Israel's first kings. The period has sometimes been presented as a formative one, but the overriding impression is of a 'dark age' with the tribes separating from each other and from God. A prologue (1:1–3:6) and

Structure
Success and failure in occupying the land (1:1–2:5)
Cycle of idolatry, invasion and deliverance (2:6–3:6)
The judges (3:7–16:31)
Religious and moral decline (17:1–21:25)

Famous passages
Deborah and Barak defeat Sisera (4:1–5:31)
Gideon's fleece (6:36–40)
Gideon defeats the Midianites (7:1–25)
Jephthah's daughter (11:29–40)
Samson's riddles (14:8–20)
Samson and Delilah (16:4–22)

an epilogue (chapters 17–21) surround the stories of individual judges (3:7–16:31). Two groups of judges are mentioned. The six main judges such as Deborah, Gideon and Samson delivered Israel from various foreign enemies. A second group of minor judges, also six in number, are included only in lists (10:1–5; 12:8–15). The book shows that the chief threat to God's promise about Israel's occupation of the Promised Land came from within Israel, but that God was always ready to respond with compassion. Though he punished Israel by sending invaders, he sent deliverers (i.e. the judges) when they called on him for help (e.g. 3:9,15). Though Judges belongs to what is generally called the Deuteronomic History, its own distinctive style suggests it had been only loosely edited when it was incorporated in the larger work.

justice A quality of God which is reflected in his laws and which he expects to see maintained in all forms of human relationships (Micah 6:8). God's justice is always impartial and takes no account of privilege or status. For that reason, people who have suffered from injustice often appeal to God to act on their behalf (Psalm 7:6–11). In human affairs, God is committed to both personal and social justice. Though God's standards are the same for everyone, for the sake of the gospel believers should avoid taking one another to public courts and be willing to accept personal injustice (1 Corinthians 6:1–8).

justification An action by which God makes and declares people 'just' or 'righteous'. This action is at the heart of the Christian gospel, since without Christ no one can be justified before God. Justification is basically a legal concept, and refers to a person's status in a court of law rather than to their moral character. It was achieved by Jesus' dying as a representative of the unrighteous: 'Christ died for sins once for all, the righteous for the unrighteous, to bring you to God' (1 Peter 3:18). The resurrection is a vindication of all that Christ achieved by his death. Justification is therefore a gift of God which a person receives by putting their faith in Christ rather than in their own achievements (Romans 3:21–31), and its reality in a person's life is evident by their keeping God's requirements. The consequences of the New Testament understanding of justification were quite revolutionary, though as Paul shows, the idea was hardly new since it went right back to Abraham (Romans 4). Because faith was available to anyone, whether Jew or Gentile, justification by faith became the basis of belonging to the people of God. See also GOSPEL.

k

Kadesh-Barnea A place in north-eastern Sinai (probably modern Ain Qudeirat) where the Israelites spent most of their forty years in the wilderness (Deuteronomy 1:46).

Kenites A tribe from southern Canaan to which Moses' wife belonged and who were eventually incorporated into Judah (Judges 1:16).

Kerethites and Pelethites Two groups who were probably Philistines and who formed David's bodyguard (2 Samuel 15:18).

kidneys SEE LIVER AND KIDNEYS.

Kidron An intermittent river flowing southwards on the east side of Jerusalem. The Kidron Valley separated the city from the Mount of Olives (John 18:1).

killing The unjust taking of another person's life was one of the most serious crimes in the Bible, and on the principle that the punishment should be equivalent to the crime, the perpetrator was liable to the death penalty (Genesis 9:6). A clear distinction is made between murder and unintentional killing or manslaughter. In the latter case, six cities of refuge were provided to protect the killer against revenge by the dead person's family. Killing was permitted in war and the killing of animals was required in sacrifice, but even in these circumstances excess violence was always sharply criticized. See also SACRIFICE.

kindness A quality which is part of God's character and which he show to everyone in providing the necessities of life (Acts 14:17). In believers' lives, it is part of the fruit which the Holy Spirit works in them (Galatians 5:22–3).

king, kingship Though kingship was widespread in the ancient world, it arrived late in Israel, probably because God was regarded as Israel's only king (Judges 8:22–3). The introduction of human kings in Israel led to two contrasting tendencies. While the monarchy in both Judah and Israel ended in disaster, God established his own kingship on earth through his promises to David, eventually resulting in Jesus' kingship. Though God had a special interest in Israel's monarchy, all kings are subject to God's will and authority (Daniel 2:21).

kingdom of God, kingdom of heaven The central idea in the teaching of Jesus, especially in the Synoptic Gospels, for which Matthew generally uses the expression 'kingdom of heaven'. God's kingdom is concerned with his rule on earth and in heaven. The idea goes right back to the exodus (Exodus 19:6), though the main Old Testament references occur in the Psalms and the prophets (Psalm 103:19; Obadiah 21). This background encouraged many Jewish people to look forward to God's decisive intervention for Israel, but Jesus demonstrated, especially through his parables and his miracles, that the benefits of God's kingdom were available to all who believed in Jesus whatever their ethnic or social origins. The main new feature in Jesus' teaching on this issue was that he made God's kingdom inseparable from himself. The powerful presence of God's rule was demonstrated by his miracles and his bringing good news to the poor (Matthew 11:2–6, echoing the promise of Isaiah 35:5–6; 61:1). Since his death, resurrection and ascension Jesus has reigned from God's throne in heaven. The early church proclaimed the good news that Jesus had been exalted to kingly rule after his suffering and death, and they looked forward to the full revelation of God's kingdom at Jesus' second coming (Acts 28:31; 1 Corinthians 15:24–5; Revelation 11:15). See also LAST THINGS.

Kings, 1 and 2

Structure

Solomon succeeds David (1 Kings 1:1–2:46)
Solomon's reign (1 Kings 3:1–11:43)
The divided kingdoms of Israel and Judah (1 Kings 12:1–2 Kings 17:41)
The last years of the kingdom of Judah (2 Kings 18:1–25:30)

Famous passages

Solomon's wisdom (1 Kings 3:4–28)
Dedicating the temple (1 Kings 8:1–66)
Solomon and the Queen of Sheba (1 Kings 10:1–13)
Elijah and the prophets of Baal (1 Kings 18:1–40)
The fall of Israel (2 Kings 17:3–41)
Hezekiah and Sennacherib (2 Kings 18:13–19:37)
Josiah discovers the Book of the Law (2 Kings 22:3–23:25)
Nebuchadnezzar destroys Jerusalem (2 Kings 25:1–26)

These two books describe almost the whole of Israel's monarchy, covering about 350 years from Solomon to the exile. They are primarily a theological interpretation of events, especially from the perspective of prophets such as Elijah, Elisha and Isaiah. They were compiled during the exile by editors often called the Deuteronomists, a group whose viewpoint was based on God's covenant with Israel, particularly as described in Deuteronomy. A king's religious activities were more important than their political or military achievements. Believing kings like Hezekiah and Josiah are commended, while Omri, who founded a dynasty well known in the ancient world, is dismissed briefly. Individual kings are assessed as to whether they were committed to the worship of Yahweh or to idol worship, or whether they did what was right or evil before Yahweh.

Though it has been suggested that Kings was written to justify the exile, it is notable that Israel's history is set against various aspects of God's covenant. The attention given to the temple as God's earthly residence, and to God's purposes for David's dynasty, indicates an equal if not greater concern with the faithfulness of God's promises.

Kings and queens of Israel

Kings of United Israel

Saul	1042–1000 BC	1 Samuel 8–31; 1 Chronicles 10
David	1000–961 BC	1 Samuel 16:1–1 Kings 2:12; 1 Chronicles 11–29
Solomon	961–922 BC	1 Kings 1–11; 2 Chronicles 1–9

Kings and queens of Judah (southern kingdom)

Rehoboam	922–915 BC	1 Kings 12:1–24; 14:21–31; 2 Chronicles 10–12
Abijah	915–913 BC	1 Kings 15:1–8; 2 Chronicles 13:1–14:1
Asa	913–873 BC	1 Kings 15:9–24; 2 Chronicles 14:2–16:14
Jehoshaphat	873–849 BC	1 Kings 22:41–50; 2 Chronicles 17:1–21:1
Jehoram	849–842 BC	2 Kings 8:16–24; 2 Chronicles 21:2–20
Ahaziah	842 BC	2 Kings 8:25–9; 2 Chronicles 22:1–9
Queen Athaliah	842–837 BC	2 Kings 11; 2 Chronicles 22:10–21
Joash	837–800 BC	2 Kings 12; 2 Chronicles 24
Amaziah	800–783 BC	2 Kings 14:1–22; 2 Chronicles 25:1–26:2

Uzziah/Azariah	783–742 BC	2 Kings 15:1–7; 2 Chronicles 26:3–23
Jotham	742–735 BC	2 Kings 15:32–8; 2 Chronicles 27
Ahaz	735–715 BC	2 Kings 16; 2 Chronicles 28
Hezekiah	715–687/6 BC	2 Kings 18:1–20:21; 2 Chronicles 29–32
Manasseh	687/6–642 BC	2 Kings 21:1–18; 2 Chronicles 33:1–20
Amon	642–640 BC	2 Kings 21:19–26; 2 Chronicles 33:21–5
Josiah	640–609 BC	2 Kings 22:1–23:30; 2 Chronicles 34:1–36:1
Jehoahaz	609 BC	2 Kings 23:31–4; 2 Chronicles 36:2–4
Jehoiakim	609–598 BC	2 Kings 23:34–24:7; 2 Chronicles 36:5–8
Jehoiachin	598–597 BC	2 Kings 24:8–17; 25:27–30; 2 Chronicles 36:9–10
Zedekiah	597–587 BC	2 Kings 24:18–25:26; 2 Chronicles 36:11–20

Kings of Israel (northern kingdom)

Jeroboam I	922–901 BC	1 Kings 12:25–14:20
Nadab	901–900 BC	1 Kings 15:25–31
Baasha	900–877 BC	1 Kings 15:32–16:7
Elah	877–876 BC	1 Kings 16:8–14
Zimri	876 BC	1 Kings 16:15–20
Omri	876–869 BC	1 Kings 16:21–8
Ahab	869–850 BC	1 Kings 16:29–22:40
Ahaziah	850–849 BC	1 Kings 22:51–2 Kings 1:18
Joram	849–842 BC	2 Kings 3:1–8:15
Jehu	842–815 BC	2 Kings 9:1–10:36
Jehoahaz	815–801 BC	2 Kings 13:1–9
Jehoash	801–786 BC	2 Kings 13:10–25
Jeroboam II	786–746 BC	2 Kings 14:23–9
Zechariah	746–745 BC	2 Kings 15:8–12
Shallum	745 BC	2 Kings 15:13–15
Menahem	745–738 BC	2 Kings 15:16–22
Pekahiah	738–737 BC	2 Kings 15:23–6
Pekah	737–732 BC	2 Kings 15:27–31
Hoshea	732–722 BC	2 Kings 17:1–6

Kinnereth, Sea of see GALILEE, SEA OF.

Kiriath-Arba see HEBRON.

Kiriath-Jearim A border town between Judah and the Philistines, where the ark was kept before David brought it to Jerusalem (1 Samuel 6:21–7:1).

Kislev see CALENDAR, JEWISH.

kiss A common sign of greeting in the ancient world, including in the early church (Romans 16:16). It could also indicate homage (Psalm 2:12), though was used ironically by Judas as a means of betrayal.

knee, kneel Most often associated with respect or submission to higher authority (Philippians 2:10), or with lack of courage as in the phrase 'weak knees' (Hebrews 12:12).

knowledge The human ability to know is a gift from God, since God alone knows everything. The nature of knowing in the Bible, however, is less concerned with the modern idea of mastering a body of information and more concerned with understanding life. It is particularly concerned with people knowing and understanding one another and with an awareness of a good quality of life. Knowledge in the Bible therefore concentrates on experience rather than intellectual ability. The most important knowledge is about oneself and about God, and this can only be gained through what Jesus reveals (John 17:3).

Kohathites One of the three main divisions of Levites, who undertook various tasks in Israel's worship. Since Aaron was one of them, they included the priests (Numbers 3:27–32).

Korah 1. The leader of a rebellion against Moses and Aaron (Numbers 16).

2. A musician whose name appears in twelve Psalm headings.

L

Laban Rebekah's brother and Jacob's father-in-law. He was often in conflict with Jacob while the latter stayed with him for twenty years (Genesis 29–31).

Lachish An important city (modern Tell ed-Duweir) about 40 kilometres south-west of Jerusalem. Archaeological discoveries found in Nineveh include relief sculptures from Sennacherib's attack on Lachish (2 Kings 18:17) and letters confirming the city's desperate position before the Babylonians captured Jerusalem (Jeremiah 34:7).

lake Palestine's two main lakes are Lake Huleh and the 'Sea' of Galilee in the Jordan valley. The 'lake of fire' symbolizes God's final judgement (Revelation 19:20). See GALILEE, SEA OF.

lamb SEE PASSOVER; SHEEP AND GOATS.

Lamb of God A description of Jesus as a sacrificial lamb who died for the sins of others, either as a sin offering or as the Passover lamb (John 1:29, 36). He is also called simply 'the Lamb' (1 Peter 1:19; Revelation 5:12).

Lamech 1. A descendant of Cain who murdered for revenge (Genesis 4:23–4).
2. A son of Methuselah and father of Noah (Genesis 5:25–31).

lameness SEE DISEASES AND ILLNESSES.

lamentations, book of

Structure
    Meditation on the destruction of Jerusalem (1:1–2:22; 4:1–22)
    Individual prayer based on God's faithfulness (3:1–66)
    The people's prayer for restoration (5:1–22)

Famous passage
    'Great is your faithfulness' (3:21–4)

Five poems of lament, written in response to the Babylonian army's destruction of Jerusalem in 587 BC. Each poem has 22 verses, apart from chapter 3 which has 66 (= 3 × 22). The first four are all acrostics in Hebrew, i.e. each verse (or each triplet of verses in chapter 3) begins with successive letters of the Hebrew alphabet.

The poems have been traditionally attributed to Jeremiah, though firm evidence is lacking for this. Their prime concern is to understand Jerusalem's fall in the light of God's purposes. They emphasize God's righteous anger with his people's persistent sin, God's faithfulness as grounds for hope in dire circumstances (3:21–33), and God's continuing kingship over Israel (5:19).

lamp, lampstand Domestic lamps were made of pottery and burned olive oil or fat. Lampstands were used in wealthier homes, and several seven-branched candlesticks have been found, like that portrayed in Titus' arch in Rome which depicts the capture of Jerusalem in 70 AD. 'Lamp' is often used as a symbol, especially for the quality and length of life (Job 18:5–6). See also TABERNACLE; TEMPLE.

land see PROMISED LAND.

languages The Bible is written in Hebrew, Aramaic and Greek. Hebrew is the main language of the Old Testament, and was spoken in Israel for much of the Old Testament period. It was replaced in ordinary speech by Aramaic after the exile, and Aramaic was the common language in Palestine in New Testament times. Some chapters in Ezra and Daniel and a few scattered New Testament words such as *Abba* (= 'Father') are in Aramaic. New Testament Greek was the 'common' or *koine* language used by ordinary people in the Mediterranean world rather than the dialect of educated people.

Laodicea An important commercial city in Asia Minor (modern Turkey), whose church was probably founded by Christians from Ephesus. The New Testament mentions two letters to the church, which indicate a decline in the church's spiritual health (Colossians 4:16; Revelation 3:14–22).

last days A biblical term for the time when God will finally achieve his purposes. In the New Testament, it refers to the period between Christ's first coming and his second coming (Hebrews 1:1–2). It is a time when God is establishing his kingdom through Christ (Hebrews 9:26) and the Spirit (Acts 2:17–18), but is also marked by godlessness and persecution of Christians (2 Timothy 3:1–5).

Last Supper see LORD'S SUPPER.

last things One of the Bible's most important ideas, which is also known as eschatology, from the Greek word *eschatos* meaning 'last'.

Its central element is that history is moving towards a climax as a result of God's plan for the world. The idea begins with God's work in creation, which looks forward to a future completion (Genesis 1:28; 2:15–17) and is developed in many Old Testament promises. The clearest Old Testament picture is the prophets' descriptions of the 'last days', when all forms of evil and sin will be removed and God's original intentions for the human race restored. Isaiah even refers to 'new heavens and a new earth', i.e. a new creation (Isaiah 65:17; 66:22).

Jesus taught that this final plan, which he called the kingdom of God, had arrived (Mark 1:15). The evidence was to be seen in his miracles, his teaching, and especially his death and resurrection. However, Jesus also spoke about a future kingdom (Mark 13:26), illustrating one of the most important features of New Testament teaching, that the last days are already present as well as being expected in the future. The former aspect, which is sometimes called 'realized' or 'inaugurated eschatology', must be held in tension with future hope if one is to do full justice to the biblical idea.

God's kingdom will be completed at Jesus' second coming, when the present world will be destroyed and replaced (Revelation 21–2). Those who have opposed God, including the devil and his angels, will suffer final judgement and be excluded from God's presence for ever. The main task, however, will be to bring those with faith in Jesus into all the blessings of heaven. They will be transformed by resurrection and enabled to enjoy eternal life in the presence of Jesus (1 Corinthians 15). See also ETERNAL LIFE; HEAVEN; HELL; INTERMEDIATE STATE; MILLENNIUM.

laughter Usually associated with either enjoyment of life (Ecclesiastes 10:19) or God's action in people's lives (Psalm 126:1–3), but also a sign of unbelief (Genesis 17:17; 18:12–15). God's laughter mocks the arrogance of those who oppose him (Psalm 2:4).

law A term for the first five books of the Bible (also known as the Torah or the Pentateuch) and for the major concept found in those books. The Bible's idea of law is easily misunderstood, however, since it has little to do with the idea of publicly approved requirements concerning the way societies should behave. Law in the Old Testament is basically God's teaching or instruction, which is the meaning of the Hebrew word *Torah*. It was revealed at Mount Sinai and given to Israel so that they could enjoy freedom in the Promised Land. It was also intended to give expression to Israel's covenant relationship with God, enabling them to maintain their relationship with him through thick and thin. The law covered every area of life, including public worship and standards of personal and social behaviour as well as civil and criminal law. It was also as much concerned with people's inner motives as with outward actions, as in Jesus' summary of the law as being concerned primarily with love (Matthew 22:34–40).

Though the Old Testament has a very positive view of God's law (Deuteronomy 30:15–16; Psalm 1:2–3), by the time of Jesus some Jewish leaders had turned it into a great burden. They had added many further requirements and took a narrow view of its meaning, seeing it as a mark of national pride and a way of getting right with God. Jesus, however, fulfilled the law (Matthew 5:17) by his perfect obedience to God and dying as a perfect sacrifice. He also makes the benefits of his obedience available on the basis of faith rather than by the impossible goal of working for them, and by the gift of his Spirit he helps believers keep the law in a new way (Romans 8:1–4).

The law is therefore still important for Christians, though it does not all apply in the same way. Though Jesus' death has removed any further need for the ceremonial law, the moral law is strengthened by Jesus' new commandment of love (John 13:34). The Bible also recognizes the validity of natural law as a means of understanding God's will (Romans 2:14–15), but as with all law, it needs the work of Christ to make it effective.

lawlessness see EVIL.

laying on of hands A symbolic action concerning the provision of God's blessing, especially for healing (Luke 4:40), or setting a person apart for God's service (Acts 13:3). It could also symbolize the transfer of sins to a sacrificial animal (Leviticus 16:21), perhaps also indicating ownership of the animal (Leviticus 4:4). See also ORDINATION.

Lazarus 1. A poor man in one of Jesus' parables who went to heaven in contrast to his rich neighbour who suffered God's judgement (Luke 16:19–31).

2. Mary and Martha's brother whom Jesus raised from death (John 11).

laziness An attitude that is consistently discouraged. The Book of Proverbs especially contrasts the consequences of idleness and of hard work (Proverbs 6:6–11; 10:26), and Paul criticizes lazy behaviour as incompatible with Christianity (2 Thessalonians 3:6–15).

lead see METALS AND MINING.

leadership Leadership of God's people is based ideally on individuals called and appointed by God. The chief aim of biblical leadership is to enable the people of God to experience the purposes God has revealed in his covenants. Originally, people like Noah and Abraham received God's covenant promises and led others by their faith. Under the Sinai covenant, priests and prophets were Israel's spiritual guides, with kings providing political leadership. In the New Testament, Jesus appointed twelve apostles, and after his ascension gave prophets, evangelists, pastors and teachers as gifts to the church. These ministries were exercised locally by elders and deacons, though others like Paul and his colleagues travelled from place to place. The basic task of leaders was to teach God's word and to provide a good example to others. They were to be fundamentally different from secular leaders in adopting a servant model after the example of Jesus himself. See also APOSTLE; DEACONS; ELDERS; KINGS; PASTORS; PRIESTS; PROPHETS.

Leah Jacob's first wife. She was less favoured than her younger sister Rachel because she was not so attractive, but she bore him seven children (Genesis 29:16–30:21).

leaven see YEAST.

Lebanon A mountain range in ancient Syria and the name of the surrounding area which was divided from northern Galilee by the Litani river. Its main cities were Tyre and Sidon on the coast, and it was particularly famous for its cedar trees (Psalm 92:12). See map of OLD TESTAMENT ISRAEL; WORLD OF THE BIBLE.

Lebo Hamath A town on Israel's ideal northern border, probably modern Lebweh at the watershed of the Beqa valley (2 Kings 14:25).

legal system Israel's legal system was based on a mixture of covenant theology and traditional practices. Since God's revelation was the basis of civil law, crimes were regarded as offences against God as well as against people. Minor cases were tried at the city gate by local elders who acted as judges (Joshua 20:4). National responsibility for the conduct of law rested with the king. Little is known of legal procedure, though two witnesses were required as a minimum and the use of evidence was important. Under the Romans, the Jews were allowed to make their own decisions on religious matters, and despite the injustices of Jesus' death and of some of Paul's experiences, Roman law was sometimes helpful to Christians. The church, however, was encouraged to settle its own internal disputes without using the law courts (1 Corinthians 6:1–8). See also CRIME AND PUNISHMENT; WITNESS.

legion Technically a division of 6,000 Roman soldiers, but usually the numbers were smaller. Also a large number, used of angels (Matthew 26:53) and evil spirits (Mark 5:9).

lentils see FOOD AND DRINK.

leopard see ANIMALS.

leprosy Leprosy today, also known as Hansen's disease, is almost certainly different from the Bible's use of the term. The modern disease affects the extremities of the body, whereas the Bible describes symptoms relating to various skin diseases, and even includes buildings and textiles (Leviticus 13–14). These involved ritual impurity and were often curable only by God's miraculous intervention.

letter see WRITING.

Levi 1. Jacob's third son, who led an attack on Shechem in revenge for his sister's rape (Genesis 34). See also LEVITES.

2. One of the apostles, probably the same person as Matthew (Mark 2:14).

leviathan A sea creature, probably the crocodile (Job 41). The term also symbolizes nations opposed to God, and is probably a mythological term for a sea-snake borrowed from Canaanite literature.

levirate marriage see MARRIAGE.

Levites A tribe, descended from Levi, who were dedicated to God to be responsible for Israel's worship (Numbers 3). Some were priests, and the rest assisted them administratively, fulfilling the roles of musicians, treasurers and gatekeepers (1 Chronicles 23:28–32). They were neglected after the exile until they were restored to their position by Ezra and Nehemiah.

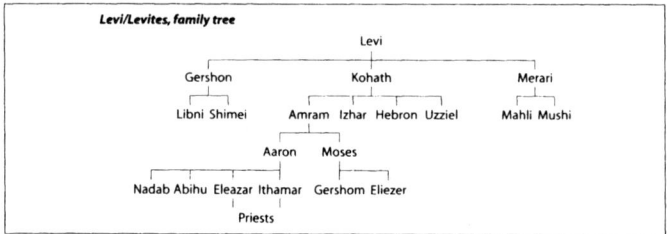

Levi/Levites, family tree

Levi

Gershon — Kohath — Merari

Libni Shimei — Amram Izhar Hebron Uzziel — Mahli Mushi

Aaron Moses

Nadab Abihu Eleazar Ithamar — Gershom Eliezer

Priests

Leviticus, book of

Structure
Sacrificial laws (1:1–7:38)
Institution of the priesthood (8:1–10:20)
Dealing with uncleanness and impurity (11:1–16:34)
Instructions for holy living (17:1–27:34)

Famous passages
The Day of Atonement or Yom Kippur (chapter 16)
The second greatest commandment (19:18)
The Jubilee year (25:8–55)

Leviticus is the only book in the Bible composed entirely of speeches by God. The speeches are addressed to Moses as instructions to be passed on to the Israelites. Moses' central position has given rise to a tradition that he was the book's author, but he is consistently portrayed as the recipient of God's words and his role cannot be clarified further. A contrasting but common view among scholars is to date the book to the sixth and fifth centuries BC. Linguistic and cultural factors, on the other hand, suggest that it may well come from a much earlier period in Israelite history. The name *Leviticus* comes from the central role played by the priests and their assistants from the tribe of Levi.

Leviticus is dominated by three themes, of which the most important is God's presence. God's presence was part of Israel's everyday life, though he also revealed his glory at special times and places (9:23–4). The phrase 'I am the LORD your God' (18:2; 19:3) reminded the Israelites that he was among them at all times. Secondly, Israel was to be holy, as indicated by the repeated phrase 'Be holy, because I am holy' (11:44–5; 19:2). This was important because individual Israelites were in danger of becoming unholy through certain kinds of behaviour or by contact with unclean things, which in extreme cases made them liable to banishment or even death (10:1–3). Thirdly, Leviticus is about God's provision of atonement, that is, the removal of sin and impurity. A comprehensive ritual dealing with the effects of moral and ritual sins took place on the annual Day of Atonement (16:16, 21–2), but other atoning rituals are also mentioned (4:1–7:10). The ideas in Leviticus are developed in Hebrews, where Jesus' sacrifice on the cross fulfils the Levitical sacrificial system.

liberty see FREEDOM.

Libnah An important town in the lowland hills of Judah, possibly modern Tell Burnat. It was captured by Joshua (Joshua 10:29–30) and besieged by Sennacherib of Assyria.

lie, lying Telling untruths and giving false witness is particularly condemned in the Bible, and is especially associated with the devil and the antichrist (John 8:44; 1 John 2:22). In contrast, it is totally foreign to God's nature (Titus 1:2). The only possible justification for lying under extreme persecution is the example of the Hebrew midwives in Egypt (Exodus 1:15–21), but it cannot be shown that they were not telling the truth.

life All forms of life are traced back to the God of the Bible, who is often called the 'living God'. He is alive for ever, and is the Creator of all other living things, which are by nature temporary and subject to death. God originally gave life to human beings by breathing into them, an action which conveyed his special gift to them of spiritual and physical life. Length or quantity of human life is closely bound up with its quality, since every person is accountable to God. Quality of life is measured in the Bible by a person's trust in God and obedience to him, though the idea is developed through two contrasting principles. On the one hand, long life is the reward of those who trust God, especially in Old Testament thought (Deuteronomy 4:40). On the other hand, a person's life before God is of higher value than their physical life, with the result that faith in God can lead to suffering and even loss of life. It is sometimes necessary to lose one's life for Jesus' sake in order to gain true life (Matthew 10:39).

Human life is full of contrasts. It is to be enjoyed to the full (Ecclesiastes 5:18–20) and is intended by God to be fruitful and prosperous (Genesis 1:28), but it is transitory and is full of trouble (Job 5:7; 7:7). Human beings have authority over all animal and plant life, but death treats them all the same way (Ecclesiastes 3:18–21). These contradictions are only resolved by Jesus, who is The Life (John 14:6). Through his own death and resurrection, he gives believers new abundant life (John 10:10), which he maintains through the gift of the Holy Spirit. This life is also eternal, so that when they die believers lose all their physical restrictions and are made fully immortal. See also DEATH; ETERNAL LIFE.

light All light comes from God, since he created it (Genesis 1:3). The sun, moon and stars belong to him, and light and darkness are equal before him, since even darkness is as light to him (Psalm 139:12).

God gives light to the world because he himself is Light. Jesus similarly is called 'the light of the world' (John 8:12). God is also the light of individual believers' lives (Psalm 27:1). He will provide them with all the blessings of life, including the benefits of guidance, peace, prosperity and continuing experiences of salvation. Believers are expected to 'walk in the light' (1 John 1:7), which means to live according to God's standards and expectations, especially those revealed in his word (Psalm 119:130). They will also 'see light' (Psalm 36:9), that is, experience the blessings of God's presence, often through the light of God's face shining upon them (Numbers 6:25).

Christians are called 'the light of the world' (Matthew 5:14) and 'children of light' (Ephesians 5:8). As such they are to provide a moral example to society, with different standards from a world in moral darkness. They are also a witness for God in the world, so that others will be drawn to God through them.

lightning In Israel is commonly experienced in thunderstorms, and sometimes described in Hebrew as fire (Exodus 9:23). It is also regarded as a sign of God's presence (Revelation 4:5), and is often associated with his appearance at Sinai (Exodus 19:16).

lily see PLANTS.

lime, limestone see METALS AND MINING.

linen A material made from flax, which was grown mainly in Egypt. Some priestly garments were made of linen, though a rougher version was probably worn for ordinary purposes (Mark 14:51). Linen was also used as a metaphor for the righteous deeds of believers (Revelation 19:8).

lion The Asiatic lion was well known throughout the ancient Near East, and only finally disappeared from the area in the early twentieth century. The Bible refers mainly to its strength and greed (Ezekiel 19:2–3).

lips see MOUTH.

liver and kidneys These animal parts were offered to God as a special sacrifice, though in ancient Near Eastern religion generally, the liver was often used in divination (Ezekiel 21:21). The kidneys also represented a person's innermost being, often being regarded as the seat of the emotions.

lizard see ANIMALS.

loaves see BREAD.

locust This insect was well known for two quite different reasons. It was good to eat as an important source of protein (Mark 1:6), but was more often feared for its destructive capabilities (Joel 1:2–2:11). See also INSECTS AND ARACHNIDS; PLAGUES OF EGYPT.

logos see JOHN, GOSPEL OF.

loneliness From the beginning, the Bible shows it is not good to be alone (Genesis 2:18). It usually describes loneliness as an unpleasant experience, associated with experiences such as disease, poverty, old age or social ostracism. It may also result from serving God faithfully (1 Kings 19:10), but believers are never really alone because of the promise of God's presence.

long-suffering see PATIENCE.

LORD, Lord see GOD, NAMES AND TITLES OF.

Lord of Hosts see GOD, NAMES AND TITLES OF.

Lord's Prayer, The The prayer which Jesus taught his disciples (Matthew 6:9–13; Luke 11:2–4). The first part asks God to make his rule in heaven evident on earth, and the second makes various requests for the physical and spiritual provision for believers. The whole prayer assumes a Father–child relationship, and summarizes what it means to be part of the kingdom of God. See also PRAYER.

Lord's Supper The Bible's term (1 Corinthians 11:20) for Holy Communion or the Eucharist. Holy Communion emphasizes the idea of a fellowship or communion meal (1 Corinthians 10:16), while Eucharist (which means 'thanksgiving') comes from the practice of giving thanks (1 Corinthians 11:24). The Lord's Supper is based on the meal which Jesus ate with his disciples the night before he died. Through his 'words of institution', however, Jesus transformed Old Testament practices into a celebration of the new covenant. The practice of taking bread and wine was originally part of a larger meal known as the 'breaking of bread' (Acts 2:42) or a special 'love feast' (Jude 12), but its significance is disputed by Christians. The bread and wine are mainly understood either as symbols of Jesus' death on the cross or in the Catholic idea of transubstantiation as changing into the substance of Jesus' body and blood. See also SACRAMENT.

lostness 1. The spiritual condition of those who do not acknowledge Jesus as Lord, and from which Jesus came to save them (Luke 19:10). **2.** The condition of those things, including life itself, which a person may voluntarily give up for the higher priority of serving God (Matthew 16:25).

Lot Abraham's nephew who lacked his uncle's faith. He and his family were rescued from Sodom only through Abraham's prayer, though Lot's wife became a pillar of salt. Lot became the ancestor of the Moabites and Ammonites in unsavoury circumstances (Genesis 19).

Lots, casting of A traditional Israelite method of making decisions, by which God communicated his will in matters that were his responsibility, such as the identification of a guilty person. It is used once in the New Testament in the context of prayer (Acts 1:21–6). See also URIM AND THUMMIM.

love Love is central to the message of the Bible, which is about the nature of God who is love (1 John 4:8). God expresses love within himself, as the three persons of the Trinity are united in love for one another (Mark 1:10–11). The Father's love for Jesus is the basis for God's love for human beings (John 17:23). Even in the Old Testament, love is God's most important characteristic, for he is 'the compassionate and gracious God, slow to anger, abounding in love and faithfulness, maintaining love to thousands and forgiving wickedness, rebellion and sin' (Exodus 34:6–7). The Old Testament shows that God is deeply affected by the lives of human beings. He refuses to deal with Israel's sin as they deserve because he loves them (Hosea 11:1–9).

God's love is fully revealed in the life and death of Jesus. Paul's definition of God's love is, 'While we were still sinners, Christ died for us' (Romans 5:8). John similarly speaks of God's action in sending Jesus to die for the world as the supreme example of love (John 3:16–17). This love is unique in its extent (it includes the world), its quality (it includes sinners to whom God is by nature opposed) and its effect (it forgives and transforms all who receive it).

Because love is central to what God has done in Jesus, it is also meant to be central to Christian experience. It is the most important characteristic of the Christian life, involving a Christian's relationship with God, with fellow believers and with the unbelieving world. Jesus made it the subject of his new commandment: 'Love one another. As I have loved you, so you must love one another' (John 13:34). He did not intend to replace the old commandments, which were also about love for God and for one's neighbour (Matthew 22:34–40), but to convey their inner meaning in the light of the cross. The qualities of Christian love are described in Paul's famous meditation in 1 Corinthians 13, which emphasizes its patience, its concern for others rather than self, and its eternal nature. Perhaps its most surprising feature, however, is that it is to be shown even to one's enemies (Matthew 5:44), though this is no more than a reflection of the love that believers have already received from God (Romans 5:10). See also COMPASSION.

loving-kindness see LOVE.

loyalty see FAITHFULNESS.

Luke A doctor who was a close friend of Paul and who travelled with him on some of his journeys (Colossians 4:14). He was the author of two New Testament books, Luke's Gospel and the Acts of the Apostles. See also ACTS OF THE APOSTLES; LUKE, GOSPEL OF.

Luke, Gospel of

Luke's Gospel is part of a two-part work including the Acts of the Apostles (cf. Luke 1:1–4 and Acts 1:1). Early Christian tradition that they were written by Luke the doctor is partly confirmed by the New Testament. The link with Acts suggests a date in the 60s, though the 70s is also a serious possibility. Luke's main sources are probably Mark's Gospel and a collection of Jesus' sayings known as Q, though Luke makes his own distinctive contribution.

At the centre of the Gospel is the person of Jesus. Only Luke tells the whole story of Jesus' earthly life from his birth to his ascension, showing what it means throughout for Jesus to be both Messiah and Lord. Jesus is also the one who fulfils the Old Testament, both as the royal son of David (1:31–3, 69) who finally ascends to God's right hand

---

Structure

Jesus is born and grows up (1:1–2:52)

Jesus prepares for his ministry (3:1–4:13)

Jesus' ministry in Galilee (4:14–9:50)

Jesus' journey to Jerusalem (9:51–19:27)

Jesus in Jerusalem (19:28–24:53)

Famous passages

Jesus is born (2:1–20)

Sermon on the plain (6:20–49)

The Good Samaritan (10:25–37)

The prodigal son (15:11–32)

The rich man and Lazarus (16:19–31)

Meeting the risen Jesus on the Emmaus road (24:13–35)

---

in heaven (22:69; 24:50–1) and as the one who must suffer and die in Jerusalem (23:26–56). The emphasis on the word 'today' suggests that God's plan has reached its climax in Jesus (2:11; 19:9), especially in relation to the manifesto of Isaiah 61 (4:16–21).

Jesus' work is that of salvation (19:9). Luke uses words for *salvation, to save* and *Saviour* more than any other Gospel writer. This salvation is for everybody, including the outcasts of society such as the poor, Samaritans, sinners and tax collectors (cf. 4:18). Women are particularly sensitive to Jesus' ministry (10:38–42; 24:1–11).

Luke gives particular attention to the community of disciples, perhaps having in mind the churches described in Acts. Jesus' ministry in the power of the Spirit is the pattern for Christian living (4:18; 24:46–9). A similar point is made in relation to praise and prayer. Luke includes more prayers of Jesus than any other Gospel, and these are often linked with encouragements to pray (11:1–13; 18:1–8; 22:40–6). Jesus teaches that the community's ethical standards must be different from the world (14:1–14; 22:24–7) and tells the church to take the gospel to the world (15:1–32; 24:47–9). Jesus' ministry to the lost, including Samaritans and Gentiles (10:25–37; 13:23–30), anticipates the church's mission to the Gentiles (Acts 13:46–8).

lust An insatiable desire for things and experiences, especially of a sexual nature. Jesus taught that lustful desire is equally as sinful as an act of adultery (Matthew 5:27–8), but lust can be resisted through the power of the Holy Spirit (Galatians 5:16–19).

Lydia A wealthy Jewish proselyte who was Paul's first convert in Europe at Philippi (Acts 16:14–15). Her home became an early house church (Acts 16:40).

lying see LIE, LYING.

lyre see MUSIC AND MUSICAL INSTRUMENTS.

Lystra A Roman colony in central Asia Minor (modern Turkey) where a church was founded in difficult circumstances (Acts 14:8–20). Timothy was a native of the town (Acts 16:1). See map of PAUL'S JOURNEYS.

m

Maacah 1. The name of several people, male and female, of whom the daughter of David's Aramean wife Talmai was the most important (2 Samuel 3:3).
2. A small Aramean state north of Israel which David conquered (2 Samuel 10:6–19).

Maccabees I see APOCRYPHA.

Maccabees II see APOCRYPHA.

Macedonia A Roman province in northern Greece in New Testament times. Paul's letters speak warmly about the Macedonian churches at Philippi and Thessalonica (2 Corinthians 8:1–5). See map of PAUL'S JOURNEYS; WORLD OF THE BIBLE.

Magdalene see MARY MAGDALENE.

magi A general term for priests in the ancient world, especially those who practised divination and astrology. The New Testament refers to non-Jewish astrologers who learned of the Messiah's birth from the stars (Matthew 2:1–12), but it does not mention how many there were, where they came from, and it does not describe them as kings. See also PERSIA.

magic see OCCULT.

Magnificat A traditional Latin name for Mary's song which she sang after hearing she would be the mother of the Messiah (Luke 1:46–55). See also BENEDICTUS; NUNC DIMITTIS.

Magog see GOG AND MAGOG.

Mahanaim A place east of the Jordan of unknown location. Jacob met angels there (Genesis 32:1–2), and later it was briefly the northern tribes' capital under Saul's son Ishbosheth (2 Samuel 2:8). See map of OLD TESTAMENT ISRAEL.

Malachi, book of

> **Structure**
>   Judah's unfaithful worship (1:1–2:16)
>   The coming of the LORD (2:17–4:6)
>
> **Famous passages**
>   Opening the windows of heaven (3:10)
>   The coming of Elijah (4:5–6)

The last but not the latest book in the Old Testament. It probably belongs to the early fifth century BC, since Ezra and Nehemiah dealt with many of the practices criticized by Malachi. Malachi's name means 'my messenger', and may be a kind of nickname based on the promise in 3:1 rather than an actual name. The book is arranged round a series of questions and answers (1:2, 6; 2:17; 3:7–8, etc.) which focus on Judah's half-hearted attitude to worship and to God. The prophet responds by calling for repentance but also promising future blessings in association with the coming day of the Lord.

Mamre A place near Hebron, probably modern Ramet el-Khalil, closely associated with Abraham (Genesis 13:18; 18:1).

man and woman Relationships between the sexes differed according to the nature of their relationship with God and their various roles in church and society. God created men and women to be complementary to each other (Genesis 1:26–7; 2:18), and conflict between them is mentioned only as part of God's punishment after they had disobeyed God (Genesis 3:16). This disharmony is reflected in the experiences of men and women throughout the Bible, though a distinction should be made between the general patriarchal nature of ancient society and specific instances of oppression. Even under these circumstances, however, many provisions of the Old Testament covenants treated men and women equally (Numbers 5:5–7; 6:1–4). Individual women in Israel also sometimes played a significant leadership role (Judges 4:4–22; 2 Kings 22:14–20), notably in the example of the ideal wife (Proverbs 31:10–31).

Jesus transformed male–female relationships. He challenged contemporary social expectations by treating women with full respect (John 4:7–27), and gave women an important place among his disciples (Luke 8:2–3; 10:38–42). The New Testament recognizes that males and females enjoy the same status in their relationship with God (Galatians 3:28), since faith in Christ is the basis for anyone to become a child of God. Within the church, men and women retain distinctive responsibilities (1 Corinthians 14:33–5; 1 Timothy 2:11–15), and are to relate to one another through mutual love and submission because of Christ (Ephesians 5:21). This is especially important in marriage, where the wife should submit to her husband because she is under Christ's authority and the husband must love his wife 'just as Christ loved the church and gave himself up for her' (Ephesians 5:25). See also HUMANITY.

Manasseh 1. Joseph's eldest son, whose privileges were given to his younger brother Ephraim by their grandfather Jacob (Genesis 48). **2.** A tribe descended from Joseph's son. Its people lived in central Palestine east and west of the Jordan. See map of OLD TESTAMENT ISRAEL.

Manasseh, King of Judah (c. 687–642 BC) Judah's longest reigning king but one of its most wicked rulers. He encouraged all kinds of pagan worship, persecuted the prophets, and was involved in violence. Though God announced that Judah would go into exile because of his behaviour, reference to his repentance and conversion shows that God listens to the prayers of the worst of sinners (2 Chronicles 33).

manger An animals' feeding-box, sometimes hollowed out of stone in a stable wall. The baby Jesus was placed in a manger after he was born (Luke 2:12).

mankind see HUMANITY.

manna Food miraculously provided for the Israelites in the wilderness. It looked like coriander seed and tasted like honey, but its name really means 'what is it?' (Exodus 16:15, 31) because it was different from any known substance. It became known as the 'bread from heaven' (John 6:31).

Manoah Samson's father. An angel told him his previously barren wife would have a son (Judges 13).

manslaughter see KILLING.

manuscripts Over 5,000 papyrus and parchment manuscripts of the Greek New Testament are currently in existence, more than for any other work of ancient literature. The earliest papyri date from the second century AD, while the earliest manuscripts of the whole Bible are the Codex Sinaiticus and Codex Vaticanus from the fourth century AD. The Old Testament is represented by Hebrew manuscripts from the third century BC to the twelfth century AD, though the most authoritative texts date from the tenth century AD. The Hebrew text of the Old Testament is often called the Massoretic text, after a group of Jewish scholars from c. 500–1000 AD called the Massoretes who carefully preserved the text in every detail. The Dead Sea Scrolls support the basic manuscript tradition of the

Old Testament. Early Bible translations also help to establish
the ancient text. The whole Bible is preserved in Latin (Vulgate)
and Syriac (Peshitta), and the Old Testament is additionally
preserved in Greek (Septuagint) and Aramaic (Targums). Though
the work of textual criticism is never finished, the reader can
be fully confident about the reliability of the existing text and
that manuscript variations concern only minor issues. See
also BIBLE.

marble see METALS AND STONE.

Marcheshvan see CALENDAR, JEWISH.

Mark, Gospel of

Structure
> Jesus begins his ministry (1:1–13)
> Jesus' ministry in Galilee (1:14–8:26)
> Jesus travels to Jerusalem (8:27–16:8)

Famous passages
> Jesus' parables (4:1–34)
> Signs of the end of the world (13:1–37)
> The shortest account of the resurrection (16:1–8)

Probably the earliest of the four Gospels, from the period c. 66–70 AD
just before the fall of Jerusalem. It has special significance as the first
attempt to put the story of Jesus in written form, and probably
formed the basis for Matthew and Luke and possibly also John.
Mark's description of his work as a Gospel (1:1) led to the use of this
term for all four New Testament accounts of Jesus. The actual author
is unknown, however, since the link with John Mark, a companion of
Peter and Paul, can be traced back only to an early second-century
Christian tradition.

Mark's Gospel tells the story of Jesus. It concentrates on
describing events in Jesus' life, and contains less of Jesus' teaching
than the other Gospels. For Mark, the gospel is summed up by Jesus'
proclamation of God's kingdom in word and action (1:14–15). Mark's
story is based on the relationship between Jesus and the people he
encounters, and is often expressed through irony. For example, Jesus
was opposed by those who would be expected to support him, such
as religious leaders, his family and neighbours, while evil spirits,
who were naturally against him, recognized his true identity. In
contrast, Jesus' followers often failed to understand who he really
was or what he was doing. Jesus himself is presented by Mark as the
expected Messiah and the Son of God (1:1; 14:61–2; 15:32, 39), though

the theme has some unexpected features. For most of the Gospel, the true nature of Jesus' Messiahship remains hidden, a feature sometimes known as the Messianic secret. It is only the cross, which is central to the whole of Mark's theology, that explains Jesus' Messiahship. As the Messiah Jesus had to suffer and die, and even Jesus' victory over death is expressed through discovery of the empty tomb rather than by explicit appearances of the risen Lord (16:1–8). Similarly, the disciples learn that their failures do not disqualify them but that true discipleship involves taking up one's own cross. The kingdom of God therefore takes seriously the weakness of the cross as well as the future power of God (9:1; 15:43). The mystery of the kingdom is revealed in Jesus, whose coming inaugurated God's rule on earth.

Mark, John A cousin of Barnabas and a companion of Paul and Barnabas on their first missionary journey, though his early return to Jerusalem caused severe disagreement (Acts 15:37–9). Mark then went to Cyprus with Barnabas, but was later reconciled with Paul (Colossians 4:10). See also MARK, GOSPEL OF.

market, market-place A popular meeting-place for all kinds of activities in the first century AD, giving Paul a natural opportunity to speak publicly about the gospel (Acts 17:17–18).

marriage The state, recognized by society, in which a man and a woman live together in the context of a sexual relationship. The Bible's concept of marriage is closely bound up with God's purposes, since marriage is viewed as a covenant parallel to the covenant relationship between God and his people. Marriage partners were to be chosen from among the community of believers, and husbands and wives were joined together by God (Matthew 19:6; 2 Corinthians 6:14). At certain periods, intermarriage between Israelites and foreigners was explicitly forbidden because of the potentially fatal consequences for the nation's spiritual well-being (1 Kings 11:1–8; Ezra 9–10). Polygamy was sometimes practised in Old Testament times, but it always provoked jealousy and dissension.

Jesus emphasized that marriage is an exclusive lifelong relationship, and that divorce is permissible only on the ground of adultery (Matthew 19:3–9). Remarriage after divorce was possible in certain limited circumstances (Deuteronomy 24:1–4). The practice of levirate marriage was a special arrangement in which a brother-in-law was responsible for marrying his dead brother's widow in order for his brother to have an heir (Deuteronomy 25:5–10). Though marriages were sometimes arranged, strong lasting relationships were established through mutual love and respect (Ephesians 5:21–33). Marriage was also intended to provide companionship as well as a secure family environment for raising children.

Betrothal was more important than the modern engagement, and was as binding as marriage itself. Gifts were usually exchanged, with the bride's family providing a dowry. The wedding ceremony could last for a week (Genesis 29:27), and was marked by special roles for the bride and groom and their attendants, and by the wedding banquet. Jesus' attendance at a wedding (John 2:1–11) showed his enjoyment of such occasions, and it is notable that the joys of heaven are symbolized by the happiness of a wedding feast (Revelation 19:9). See also DIVORCE AND REMARRIAGE; MAN AND WOMAN.

Martha Sister of Mary and brother of Lazarus. She acknowledged Jesus as the Messiah, but had to be reminded that faith in Jesus is more important than activity (Luke 10:38–42; John 11:27).

martyr A word, literally meaning 'witness', for a person who dies for their faith. Stephen was the first martyr of the Christian church (Acts 7:58–60), though the Bible mentions many other examples (1 Kings 19:10; Hebrews 11:35–8).

Mary 1. The wife of Clopas, the mother of James and 'the other Mary' probably all refer to a woman who saw Jesus' crucifixion and his resurrection (Matthew 27:56; 28:1).

2. The mother of John Mark (Acts 12:12).

Mary of Bethany Sister of Martha and brother of Lazarus. She anointed Jesus for burial in advance and is commended for her choice of priorities (Luke 10:42; John 11:2).

Mary Magdalene A woman whom Jesus delivered from evil spirits and who was one of the first to see the risen Lord (Luke 8:2; John 20:1–18).

Mary, mother of Jesus Though known mainly from the story of Jesus' birth, she also makes an important appearance at her son's crucifixion (John 19:25–7). She comes across as a woman of great faith and courage who supported Jesus throughout his ministry, despite much misunderstanding about the way he was conceived (Luke 1:38; John 8:41). See also MAGNIFICAT.

mason see OCCUPATIONS.

Massah see MERIBAH.

Massoretic text see MANUSCRIPTS.

Matthew One of the twelve apostles, also known as Levi. Originally a tax collector, he introduced others of the same occupation to Jesus (Luke 5:29–30). He may have written Matthew's Gospel, but certainty is not possible. See also MATTHEW, GOSPEL OF.

Matthew, Gospel of

Structure
Jesus is born and begins his ministry (1:1–4:11)
Jesus preaches in Galilee (4:12–11:1)
Jesus is rejected and accepted (11:2–20:34)
Jesus in Jerusalem (21:1–28:20)

Famous passages
Jesus is born (1:18–2:12)
The Sermon on the Mount (5:1–7:29)
Jesus' parables (13:1–52)
Peter acknowledges Jesus as the Messiah (16:13–20)
The sheep and the goats (25:31–46)
The great commission (28:16–20)

The first Gospel, though probably not the first to be written. Its most likely date is between 75 and 85 AD, and though it is associated with Matthew the apostle, it is not known for certain whether he was the author. Most scholars believe that the main sources are Mark's Gospel and a collection of the sayings of Jesus known today as Q, but this remains a hypothesis, and it is more helpful to consider the book's shape and purpose.

Matthew's Gospel is built round alternating sections of narrative and teaching, with five main blocks of teaching (chapters 5–7, 10, 13, 18, 23–5) woven into the story of Jesus' life. This arrangement indicates that Matthew's primary aim was to tell the story of Jesus, but with his own emphases. Four aspects of this teaching stand out. First, Matthew presents Jesus as Messiah and Son of God. As Messiah, Jesus fulfils the Old Testament (5:17) and all the promises of salvation and restoration come to fruition in him. This takes place because he is God's Son (3:17; 16:16) and God's obedient servant. Jesus especially fulfils the role of Isaiah's Suffering Servant (8:17; 12:17–21), being fully obedient to his heavenly Father both as a human being and as his Son. Jesus also makes known the kingdom of God, or as Matthew calls it, the kingdom of heaven. Second, Matthew sets the story of Jesus in the context of God's purposes throughout history. Jesus represents the climax of God's work in the Old Testament, especially in his death and resurrection, and continues his own ministry in the church. Jesus' continuing presence with his people is specially emphasized (1:23; 28:20). Third, Matthew understands Christian faith in terms of discipleship, emphasizing Jesus' final instruction to go and make disciples from every nation. No other

Gospel devotes as much space to Christian behaviour, which should be characterized by love and righteousness. Fourth, Matthew regularly quotes the Old Testament. This practice is partly explained if Matthew was writing for a mainly Jewish audience, but more importantly Jesus as the living Word of God is regarded as the personification of the Old Testament. According to Matthew, Jesus' person and work could not be understood without the Old Testament.

The relationship between the Old Testament and the New Testament

Dividing the Bible into two sections named the Old Testament and the New Testament immediately identifies a problem: what is the relationship between the 'Old' and the 'New'?

Calling one section 'old' already suggests some discontinuity with the 'new'. The first testament is set in the times of the nomadic patriarchs, the early tribal nation of Israel, and then later through the varying fortunes of the two kingdoms of Israel and Judah. In contrast, the New Testament breathes the air of Greek and Roman culture. Not only is the original language different, but there are also different cultural and philosophical ideas in the background. Many elements of the Old Testament, such as the priesthood and sacrificial system, appear to have no place in the New Testament, and it is sometimes claimed that even the picture presented of God is different, with the New Testament revealing God's love instead of his holiness and anger.

Some of these difficulties can be overcome by understanding the nature of progressive revelation. The story of the New Testament continues the story of the Old, but deals with God and his people at a later stage in history. Just as relationships develop over time as it becomes possible for each person to open up more to the other, so God could lead his people into a deeper understanding of himself, not because he had changed, but because through the events of Jesus' life, death and resurrection he could show more fully who he was. Close attention to the content of each testament shows that there is less of a difference between the portrayals of God's character than is sometimes thought. God remains a holy God, who loves his creation and seeks its salvation. That Jesus and the New Testament authors quote the Old Testament as the word of God shows that they saw no fundamental problem with its language about him.

An aspect of this understanding that both testaments reveal the same God in his interactions with creation is that there is continuity in their narrative. The broad storyline of the Bible stretches from Genesis to Revelation and narrates how God undertakes to deal with sin and brokenness in his world. Both testaments are tied together with the concept and language of God's covenant with his people, and his activity to deliver them and bring wholeness and salvation.

However, differences do remain. For instance, the New Testament does not view salvation in terms of either the national prosperity of Israel or the sacrificial worship of the temple in Jerusalem, as is often the case in the Old Testament. While New Testament authors see the Hebrew scriptures as the authoritative word of God, they are not afraid to reinterpret them in the light of the events and significance of Jesus.

The explanation for this ambiguous relationship between the two testaments lies in Jesus' own relationship with the Old Testament. He quoted it as the useful word of God, for instance when he was tempted by the devil in the wilderness (e.g. Matthew 4:4, 7, 10). He also saw his ministry as a fulfilment of the language and concepts of the Old Testament. The rich background of the history of Israel and the ministries of the prophets described effectively who Jesus was and what he was doing: for instance, he was the suffering servant of Isaiah 53, the host at the messianic banquet, or a prophet greater than Jonah (Luke 11:32).

However, Jesus did not only fulfil the Old Testament by being the One for whom the prophets had waited. He fulfilled some of it by bringing it to its completion. The temple and its sacrifices all pointed towards the work of Jesus, which, once completed, meant that the old ways of approaching God were no longer necessary. Similarly, Jesus brought an end to Jewish hopes for national prosperity by showing that salvation was to be for the whole of the world, not just the Jews. In this, he did not destroy what had gone before, but revealed it to be what God had truly intended, even though this could not have been anticipated by the Old Testament writers.

In the light of the climax of the New Testament, the Old Testament is 'old' because it can only point forward to Jesus as the coming way of salvation, whereas the New Testament points back to him and proclaims God's kingdom as reality. However, in another sense the Old Testament is not 'old'. It was the Bible of the first Christians and gives vital background for the understanding of Jesus and his work. Both the Old and New Testaments together are accepted by the church as the authoritative documents of the Christian faith.

Matthias The disciple who was chosen by lot to take Judas Iscariot's place among the apostles (Acts 1:23–6).

maturity The goal for which every believer should aim and for which Christ is the model (Ephesians 4:13–15). Christian maturity is based on a knowledge of God's word and is usually developed through testing. It is marked by a deeply rooted faith, an unshakeable love for God, a genuinely spiritual wisdom and behaviour that is increasingly Christlike (Ephesians 4:15–24). See also PERFECTION.

meals Food was usually fairly simple and the diet monotonous. For ordinary people, breakfast and lunch seem to have been light meals, often eaten at work, and perhaps comprising bread, cheese and fruit. The day's main meal was in the evening, and was probably prepared by the women. More varied menus were reserved for special occasions such as feast days or weddings and funerals (Jeremiah 16:5; Matthew 22:3–4). See also FOOD AND DRINK.

measures see WEIGHTS AMD MEASURES.

meat see FOOD AND DRINK.

Media, Medes Media was the north-west area of modern Iran. Its inhabitants the Medes were conquered by Cyrus of Persia, and were often associated in the Bible with the Persians (Daniel 8:20). See map of WORLD OF THE BIBLE.

mediator A person who intervenes between two parties in order to bring about a state of peace between them. Though the Bible mentions a few mediators between individuals (Genesis 41:9–13; Acts 9:26–7), the idea is used mainly of one who stands between human beings and God because they are estranged by human sin. Though prophets and priests undertook this role, Jesus is the one and only true mediator (1 Timothy 2:5) because he achieved permanent reconciliation through his death.

medicine see HEALTH AND HEALING.

meditation An important way for a person to deepen their relationship with God. Biblical meditation is based on God's written revelation of himself, though its immediate object may be any aspect of God's work or his creation (Psalm 1:1–3; 8:1–9).

medium see OCCULT.

meekness A personal quality that God often commends (Matthew 5:5), though it is frequently misunderstood today. It describes a person who humbly submits themselves to God and who is gentle in dealing with others. It can be combined with great strength of character, as with leaders like Moses and Jesus (Numbers 12:3; Matthew 11:29). See also HUMILITY.

Megiddo A city on the southern side of the Plain of Esdraelon, where it commands the most important pass to the Mediterranean coast. As the site of one of Israel's greatest victories (Judges 4–5), it gave its name in the New Testament to Armageddon (= 'mountain of Megiddo') as the place symbolizing God's final victory over his enemies (Revelation 16:16). See map of OLD TESTAMENT ISRAEL.

Melchizedek A king and priest from Salem (possibly Jerusalem) who blessed Abraham and to whom Abraham gave 10 per cent of the spoils of battle (Genesis 14:18–20). His superiority over Abraham gave Melchizedek a special status, enabling him to be compared with Christ (Hebrews 5:6–10; 6:20–7:28). Both share an eternal priesthood and combine the roles of king and priest.

melons see FOOD AND DRINK; FRUITS.

Memphis A leading city on the Nile, and the site of several pyramids. Some Jews were also exiled there (Jeremiah 44:1). See map of WORLD OF THE BIBLE.

Menahem, King of Israel (c. 745–738 BC) see KINGS AND QUEENS OF ISRAEL.

Mene, mene, tekel, parsin The mysterious writing on the wall which terrified king Belshazzar, and which announced God's judgement on him (Daniel 5:25–30).

menstruation During her monthly period, a woman was considered unclean and was forbidden to have sexual intercourse (Leviticus 15:19–23; 18:19).

Mephibosheth Son of Jonathan and grandson of Saul. David showed him great kindness because Mephibosheth was unable to walk (2 Samuel 9).

Merari, Merarites Levi's third son and founder of the Merarites, a leading Levitical family. They carried out various tasks at the tabernacle and the temple (Numbers 3:33–7). See also LEVI/LEVITES, FAMILY TREE.

merchant, merchandise see TRADE.

mercy A quality that is mainly associated with God. It is one of his most distinctive characteristics, and is closely linked with his love and compassion (James 5:11). God shows his mercy particularly towards those who turn from their sins. This is illustrated by David who, though under threat of severe punishment, preferred to fall into the hands of God rather than human hands because 'his mercy is great' (2 Samuel 24:14). People who are in any kind of need frequently call on God's mercy, even when they deserve judgement, because even in his wrath God will 'remember mercy' (Habakkuk 3:2).

Jesus perfectly demonstrates God's mercy by responding to those in need, and by forgiving those who had done great wrong (Luke 18:38–42; 23:34). However, the Bible also affirms that to those who persist in doing wrong, God will eventually show no mercy (Jeremiah 13:14). Believers are expected to be merciful in their dealings with other people, because they themselves have received mercy (Luke 6:36). See also COMPASSION; LOVE.

Meribah A name given to two separate places in the wilderness. It means 'argument, quarrelling', and recalls incidents when the Israelites quarrelled with God (Exodus 17:7; Numbers 20:13). The first of these places was also called Massah or 'Testing', referring to the Israelites' continuing failure to believe that God was with them.

Meshach SEE SHADRACH, MESHACH AND ABEDNEGO.

messenger Apart from those who speak on behalf of kings and prophets, the word is also used for prophets and angels in their role as God's messengers (Daniel 4:23; Haggai 1:13). The word 'angel' comes from the Greek word meaning 'messenger'. 'Apostle' and 'missionary' come from Greek and Latin words meaning 'sent'. See also ANGEL; APOSTLE.

Messiah A term based on a Hebrew word meaning 'an anointed person', and equivalent to the Greek word *christos*, i.e. Christ. It usually describes a long-awaited deliverer who would finally establish God's kingdom and destroy God's enemies. This sense of expectation is clearly evident in the New Testament (Luke 3:15). In the Old Testament, however, the word is rarely used, and refers to various anointed leaders such as kings or priests (Psalm 2:2; Daniel 9:25) rather than a future saviour.

Though Jesus' disciples eventually recognized him as the expected Messiah or Christ, Jesus generally avoided the title because most of his contemporaries were looking for a king descended from David who would remove the Roman oppression. Because Jesus saw his Messiahship in terms of suffering and death, based on Old Testament portraits like that of the Suffering Servant (Isaiah 52:13–53:12), many first-century AD Jews could not accept this kind of Messiah.

Belief in Jesus as Messiah was the result of God's revelation (Matthew 16:16–17). This conviction became the central feature of the church's gospel, which spoke of Jesus as the crucified and risen Messiah (Acts 2:36; 17:3).

messianic age A general description of the time when God will finally establish his kingdom by removing evil and fulfilling his promises. This will take place through the work of the Messiah, though many passages do not mention him explicitly. The Old Testament describes this period as the 'last days' or 'in those days' (Isaiah 2:2), but the New Testament divides it into two stages. The latter restricts the 'last days' to the time between Jesus' first and second coming (Hebrews 1:2), after which God will replace the present world by a new one and bring his purposes to their final completion (Revelation 21–2). See also LAST DAYS; LAST THINGS.

messianic banquet A picture of a heavenly meal symbolizing the supreme happiness of heaven and God's complete acceptance of all who believe in Jesus (Luke 14:15–24; Revelation 19:9).

metals and mining Israel had few metal deposits, though copper was mined in southern Palestine and limestone was also quarried in various areas of the country. Most metals were imported, especially in the period of David and Solomon, though some were also captured in war. Israel's unfamiliarity with iron is illustrated by Saul's wars against the Philistines (1 Samuel 13:19–22). A description of mining occurs in Job 28:1–11, and of smelting silver in Jeremiah 6:29–30. Precious metals were used in important buildings, particularly the temple in Jerusalem, and metals were also used for domestic and agricultural tools and for military purposes. Some metals, especially silver, were used as currency.

Metals and stone	
Bronze	1 Samuel 17:5–6
Copper	Deuteronomy 8:9
Gold	Daniel 2:32
Flint	Ezekiel 3:9
Iron	Job 28:2
Lead	Job 19:24
Marble	1 Chronicles 29:2
Silver	1 Kings 10:21
Stone	Joshua 7:5
Tin	Ezekiel 27:12

Methuselah The oldest man in the Bible at 969 years (Genesis 5:25–7). Despite his great age, the lifespans of the early patriarchs are very modest compared with those in Mesopotamian literature.

Micah 1. A man from Ephraim who set up his own shrine and priesthood during the judges period (Judges 17–18).

2. An eighth-century BC prophet from Judah and a younger contemporary of Isaiah. See also MICAH, BOOK OF.

Micah, book of

Structure

Judgement against Israel and Judah (1:1–3:12)

Salvation for God's people (4:1–5:15)

Further messages of judgement and salvation (6:1–7:20)

Famous passages

Bethlehem as the birthplace of the Messiah (5:2)

What God requires (6:6–8)

A God who pardons sin (7:18)

A collection of prophecies from the eighth century BC alternating between judgement and salvation. Although Micah prophesied impending disaster for Israel and Judah, his underlying message was about God's grace and pardoning love (7:18–20). He condemned the people for failing to keep the covenant, singling out the rich and powerful for criticism (2:1–5; 3:1–4), and emphasizing the priority of justice, mercy and humility (6:1–8). He also promised a complete reversal of God's judgement, when Jerusalem would again be central to God's purposes (4:1–5) and new leaders would replace those who had failed (5:5–6). The promise of a Messianic leader to be born in Bethlehem (5:2) was well known by the first century AD (Matthew 2:6).

Micaiah A ninth-century BC prophet who prophesied the death of King Ahab (1 Kings 22:8–28).

Michael The archangel, i.e. the most important angel. In the Bible, he fought to defend God's people (Daniel 12:1; Revelation 12:7), though he is better known in extrabiblical literature.

Michal David's first wife and Saul's daughter. Her turbulent marriage with David ended in bitterness and barrenness (1 Samuel 19:11–17; 2 Samuel 6:20–3).

Michmash A town (modern Mukhmas) 12 kilometres north of Jerusalem where Jonathan and his armour-bearer inspired a notable victory over the Philistines (1 Samuel 13:23–14:23).

Midian, Midianites A nomadic group who lived in the wilderness area south-east of Palestine. They are sometimes associated with groups such as the Amalekites or the Ishmaelites (Genesis 37:28; Judges 8:22–4). They were often hostile to Israel, though Moses' Midianite father-in-law (Exodus 3:1) is a sign of a more positive relationship.

midwife Two midwives disobeyed Pharaoh's order to kill Israelite male babies, effectively preserving Moses' life (Exodus 1:15–21).

milk An important part of the staple diet in Israel, usually taken from sheep and goats rather than cattle. In the phrase 'milk and honey' it symbolized prosperity (Exodus 3:8), but it also represented elementary things (Hebrews 5:12). See also FOOD AND DRINK.

millennium A period of 1,000 years, usually referring to the period before Satan's final overthrow in Revelation 20 when Satan is bound and believers are resurrected and reign with Christ. It has been understood in different ways: as a symbol of the present time between Christ's first and second comings (amillennialism), of a time when Christ will return and reign on earth before the final resurrection (premillennialism), and of a period of great success for the church and the gospel before Christ's second coming (postmillennialism). See also LAST THINGS.

millstone Corn was ground by upper and lower millstones, usually worked by women (Matthew 24:41). Since this activity was essential for providing daily bread, a millstone could not be given as a pledge (Deuteronomy 24:6).

mina SEE WEIGHTS AND MEASURES.

mind The seat of a person's thought, desires, and consciousness. The mind of God is perfect and is conveyed to human beings through his written word and through Jesus Christ. Though God's standards are absolute, God can change his mind in response to specific instances of human repentance and by recalling his own compassion (2 Kings 22:15–20; Hosea 11:8–9). Sometimes it is impossible to know what God's mind is in a particular situation, especially when he allows evil and suffering to persist. The Bible accepts that God is inscrutable, but also insists that God's intention is always merciful (Romans 11:32–4).

By itself, the human mind is permanently affected by a tendency towards sin, and cannot be relied upon (Jeremiah 17:9). Human beings can deduce from looking at the world that God exists, but they cannot establish a relationship with him through logic or other human thought processes (Romans 1:18–23). However, the mind can be renewed and lives transformed by faith and obedience towards God (Romans 12:1–2). A clear distinction is made between believers who have the mind of Christ revealed to them by the Holy Spirit and others who rely simply on human wisdom (1 Corinthians 2:6–16).

minerals SEE JEWELS AND PRECIOUS STONES; METALS AND MINING.

minister The term is mainly applied to Christian leaders in the general sense of one who serves Jesus Christ rather than to any particular task or status. It is used of apostles (Romans 15:16) and of other leaders, whether based in one church (1 Timothy 4:6) or travelling with Paul (Colossians 1:7; 4:7). See also LEADERSHIP.

ministry A term for the service of God. It tends to be associated in the Old Testament with the work of priests and Levites in the temple, though other forms of service such as prophecy are also mentioned (1 Chronicles 25:1, 6). The New Testament extends its use to all kinds of Christian service, with Christ himself as the model for Christian ministry (Matthew 20:26–8). Every believer is given a ministry to exercise (1 Corinthians 12:27–30), though the highest priority is given to the 'ministry of the word' (Acts 6:2–4), which may be carried out by apostles, prophets, evangelists, or pastors and teachers (Ephesians 4:11–12).

mint see HERBS AND SPICES.

miracles Miracles form an important part of the biblical record, though they usually occur in association with major events rather than at every stage of the biblical story. They are connected with critical periods such as the exodus from Egypt or the threat to Israel during the time of Elijah and Elisha, but they occur above all in the life of Jesus. The frequency and authority of Jesus' miracles and their integral relation to his ministry exceed all other instances of miracle-working in the Bible. The supreme miracle is Jesus' resurrection, which forms the climax of the gospel (Acts 2:22–36).

Miracles are never presented as proof of God's existence or his power. Jesus recognized that faith based on miracle-working is shallow and is distinct from saving faith (John 2:23–5). One reason for this is that miracle-working is not limited to those who believe in the God of the Bible (Exodus 7:10–13; Matthew 7:22). Rather, biblical miracles are signs pointing to the nature of God and of his purposes. Many of Jesus' miracles, for example, were signs of God's compassion for those who suffer or of the special nature of Jesus' mission.

Modern objections to miracles tend to assume that the laws of nature form a closed system in which supernatural intervention is impossible. This view may be countered, however, by noting that God is said to do amazing things in the context of natural laws as well as in unique events (Job 5:9–10). In fact, the continued occurrence of miracles in the early church after the time of Jesus suggests that they are more rather than less likely to continue in the church today (John 14:12; Hebrews 2:4). See also JESUS CHRIST, MIRACLES OF.

Miriam Moses' elder sister. She was probably the person who preserved his life when he was a baby (Exodus 2:4–8). She was a noted prophet, who also received healing from the effects of God's punishment (Exodus 15:20–1; Numbers 12).

mission see EVANGELISM.

missionary journeys see PAUL, LIFE OF.

Mizpah The name of several places, of which the best known was the capital of Judah during the exile (2 Kings 25:23–5). The site (modern Tell en-Nasbeh) is about 13 kilometres north of Jerusalem.

Moab, Moabites A nation east of the Jordan between Ammon and Edom that was often at war with Israel, especially during Israel's monarchy (2 Kings 3:4–27). The Moabite Stone, an important ninth-century BC inscription, describes how Mesha, king of Moab, rebelled against Omri's son Ahab. See map of OLD TESTAMENT ISRAEL.

Molech A deity known in the ancient world whose association with worshipping the dead and with child sacrifice is strongly condemned in the Bible (Jeremiah 32:35).

money Silver shekels were the commonest form of currency, though gold and copper were also used. Coinage was gradually introduced into Judah under Persian influence from the late sixth century BC, though Jewish coins were only minted from the second century BC. The widow's 'mite' (Mark 12:42) is the only Jewish coin mentioned in the Bible but several Roman coins are included, particularly the denarius (Matthew 20:1–16; 22:19) which was roughly equivalent to the Greek drachma (Luke 15:8–9). Money can be used to build God's kingdom (Philippians 4:15–19), but it can also ensnare people (1 Timothy 6:10), and Jesus taught that people cannot trust God and money at the same time (Matthew 6:24).

monotheism The belief that there is only one God was a revolutionary thought in a polytheistic age. Though the Bible contains clear monotheistic statements (Isaiah 45:18; 1 Corinthians 8:4–6), it is more concerned with God's qualities than simply whether he exists or not. The Old Testament in particular often emphasizes how far superior God is in comparison with others that are also called gods (Psalm 95:3).

months see CALENDAR, JEWISH; SEASONS; TIME.

moon The ancient world generally regarded the moon as a god (Job 31:26–7), but the Bible treats it as a created object (Genesis 1:16). Israel's lunar calendar involved observing the new moon at the start of each month as a holy day (Isaiah 1:13). See also CALENDAR, JEWISH; SUN.

morality Though the Bible demands the highest moral standards, observance of God's laws is not enough to achieve perfection. Moral standards are always to be set in the context of a person's love for God and for other people (Matthew 22:34–40). Jesus taught that believers had to do more than live upright lives according to the customs of the time (Matthew 5:20). As Jesus showed in the parable of the Good Samaritan and in his own experience, a life lived fully in accordance with God's laws involves giving oneself completely for those who might be regarded as one's enemies (Luke 10:25–37).

Mordecai The uncle of Queen Esther who helped her frustrate a plot to destroy the Jews in the Persian empire (Esther 4:1–14).

Moses The person who led Israel out of Egypt to the edge of the Promised Land. He also received the Ten Commandments and was the mediator of the Sinai covenant. He was effectively the founder of the Israelite nation, and for that reason still enjoys a unique status among the Jewish people. The Bible passes over most of the first part of his life, though his preservation from an Egyptian policy of infanticide and his subsequent adoption by an Egyptian princess are early signs of God's activity. Moses' name is an Egyptian word meaning 'child', and his Egyptian upbringing was an ideal preparation for his later role. However, an attempt to rescue a fellow Israelite from an Egyptian oppressor resulted in him fleeing to Midian, from where God called him at eighty years old to lead his people out of slavery (Exodus 3). Moses overcame many challenges in leading Israel to the Promised Land, including confrontations with Pharaoh, bringing about the plagues, crossing the Red Sea, meeting God at Mount Sinai, and crossing the Sinai wilderness. He did not succeed in bringing the Israelites into the Promised Land, however, since the people did not believe that God could make it possible. Moses himself was prevented from entering Canaan because he disobeyed God's command (Numbers 20:6–12).

Moses was an extraordinary man who filled a variety of roles. He was Israel's civil leader, he acted as prophet, priest and intercessor, and he was responsible for the system of justice. But he is chiefly known for his friendship with God (Exodus 33:11), and for his role as the mediator of the covenant and its laws. The latter led to his writing at least some of the Pentateuch. Because Moses is not referred to outside the Bible, some of his activities and occasionally even his existence have been questioned. However, the authenticity of the account of his life is supported by incidental features such as its Egyptian colouring, and reference to Moses' weaknesses is a sign of a realistic rather than an idealistic record. Despite his failings, his achievements are unparalleled, and the New Testament places him as second only to Jesus (John 1:17; Hebrews 3:1–6).

Most High see GOD, NAMES AND TITLES OF.

Most Holy Place see TABERNACLE; TEMPLE.

moth see INSECTS AND ARACHNIDS.

motherhood see FAMILY.

mountains Often regarded as the most permanent aspect of the created world and a symbol of great strength. The earth was thought to be based on their foundations, though God had only to touch them for them to quake and smoke (Psalm 104:5, 32). Mountains were closely associated with God's presence, especially Sinai and Zion where God revealed himself to Israel (Exodus 19; 1 Kings 8:10–13). Jesus was transfigured on a mountain (Matthew 17:1–8) (Mount Hermon?) and ascended from the Mount of Olives (Acts 1:9–12). The kingdom of God will be finally established on Mount Zion (Isaiah 2:1–4). See also CARMEL, MOUNT; HERMON, MOUNT; SINAI; TABOR, MOUNT; ZION. See map of NEW TESTAMENT ISRAEL; OLD TESTAMENT ISRAEL.

mourning see BURIAL AND MOURNING.

mouth Referred to mainly in connection with speaking, especially in the case of the words coming from God's mouth (Deuteronomy 8:3). God is said to enable people to speak for him by putting his words into their mouths (Jeremiah 1:9) or by touching their lips (Isaiah 6:7). Christians are warned to be very careful about the way they speak, since the mouth, and particularly the tongue, can be destructive as well as for praising God (James 3:2–12). Teeth occur mainly as symbols of power and anger, or, in the phrase 'gnashing of teeth', of anguish (Matthew 22:13).

mule Like the donkey, a beast of burden, sometimes used by members of the royal family (2 Samuel 18:9; 1 Kings 1:38).

murder see KILLING.

music and musical instruments Music was an important part of life in ancient Israel, both as part of general culture and in worship. It was used at times of great celebration and of great sadness, and musicians are known both in royal palaces and among the shepherds. Temple worship was organized around the Levitical musicians and singers, and the Psalms are full of references to music and musical instruments accompanying the praise of God (Psalms 95:2; 108:1). The music of the early church continued the same practices as in Israel. The New Testament encourages Christians to use music in their worship (Ephesians 5:19) and describes heavenly worship in a similar way to the music of the Old Testament (Revelation 18:22).

The three main types of musical instrument were stringed instruments, woodwind and brass, and percussion instruments.

Most musical instruments cannot now be identified precisely, nor is it possible to know what ancient Israelite music sounded like since their system of notation is unknown.

Musical instruments

Stringed instruments

Harp	Revelation 5:8
Lute	2 Chronicles 20:28
Lyre	1 Samuel 10:5
Ten-stringed lyre	Psalm 92:3
Zither	Daniel 3:5

Brass and woodwind

Flute	Matthew 9:23
Horn	Daniel 3:5
Pipe	Daniel 3:5
Ram's horn	Exodus 19:13
Trumpet	Joshua 6:4

Percussion

Cymbals	Psalm 150:5
Sistrum	2 Samuel 6:5
Tambourine	Exodus 15:20

---

mustard seed Jesus probably referred to black mustard in his illustration about faith (Matthew 13:31). A bush could grow 5 metres high, and it was cultivated for medicine and as a seasoning.

myrrh A yellowish-brown resin used as a cosmetic, in purification rites and for embalming. The wise men's gift to the baby Jesus was a sign of his death (Matthew 2:11).

mystery A mainly New Testament term for a secret whose meaning God will make known. Paul often uses it to refer to the gospel of Jesus Christ as the revelation of God's eternal purposes (Romans 16:25).

myths 1. Occasionally used in the New Testament for religious stories that are contrary to the gospel (1 Timothy 4:7).

2. A modern term used in a variety of senses, such as a pictorial story used to convey divine truth, a story of the origins of the world and of humanity, or an account which accompanies a religious ritual. The term is sometimes applied in one or other of these senses to various biblical stories, particularly in relation to Genesis 1–11. It should be noted, however, that the biblical material is quite different in outlook from comparable Mesopotamian texts dealing with similar subjects.

n

Naaman A Syrian general who was healed of a serious skin disease. The prophet Elisha and a young Israelite servant girl played key roles in his healing (2 Kings 5).

Nabal A rich Israelite landowner whose name means 'fool'. His sudden death was a punishment from God for belittling David's kindness towards him (1 Samuel 25).

Naboth A man whose family property was stolen by Ahab and Jezebel after they had murdered him (1 Kings 21).

Nadab and Abihu Aaron's two eldest sons. They were punished by death for failing to carry out God's requirements in their priestly duties of sacrifice (Leviticus 10:1–3).

Nadab, King of Israel (*c.* 901–900 BC) see KINGS AND QUEENS OF ISRAEL.

Nahor 1. Abraham's brother and ancestor of the Arameans (Genesis 22:20–4).

2. A city in northern Mesopotamia, known as Nahur in eighteenth-century BC texts (Genesis 24:10).

Nahum, book of

Structure

A God of power and judgement (1:1–15)

God's judgement on Nineveh (2:1–13)

Nineveh's complete defeat (3:1–19)

An Old Testament prophetic book about the end of the Assyrian empire, especially the fall of its capital, Nineveh. The prophecies relate to the period between the fall of Thebes in 663 BC (3:8–10) and the fall of Nineveh in 612 BC, and probably come from the latter part of that period. As the opening hymn indicates (1:2–8), the book is really about God's absolute sovereignty, and stresses that even when evil and cruelty abound he remains in control. Nineveh stands not just for the Assyrian empire but symbolizes all that is opposed to God, especially when it is characterized by oppression and false religion. In such a context, believers can still trust God as their refuge (1:7–8).

nakedness Though human beings were created in a state of innocence without the need to wear clothes, ever since the fall of Adam and Eve (Genesis 2:25; 3:7–11) public nakedness has been associated with shame, humiliation and sometimes poverty (Romans 8:35; Revelation 3:18). However, the Song of Songs celebrates the beauty of the human body in the context of ideal love between a man and a woman.

name A person's name may reflect special hopes associated with them, as when parents named their children after the circumstances of their birth (Genesis 29:31–30:24; 1 Samuel 1:20) or when Jesus changed Cephas' name to Peter to emphasize the church's foundation on a 'rock' (Matthew 16:18). On other occasions, a name indicated a person's special characteristics or the distinguishing features of their ministry, as in the link between Jesus' name and his work of salvation (Matthew 1:21).

Names were important in family and community life. Special customs enabled a family name to be continued to the next generation (Numbers 27:1–4; Deuteronomy 25:5–10), since people who died without heirs effectively removed their family from society's memory (Job 18:17–19). It was also important for the church that Christian leaders wherever possible should have a good reputation in society (1 Timothy 3:7).

God made himself known through names such as God Most High or the Eternal God which were a reminder of his distinctive qualities. The name of God was a special sign of his presence, and people were invited to call on his name as a basis for receiving salvation and to enable them to pray (Zechariah 13:9; Acts 2:21). God's own name Yahweh or the LORD referred especially to his activity for his people and his presence among them (Exodus 3:13–15), and in the New Testament, the name of Jesus was the only basis on which a relationship with God could exist (Acts 4:12). See also GOD, NAMES AND TITLES OF.

Naomi Ruth's mother-in-law. Though her name means 'lovely', she wanted to change her name to Mara, meaning 'bitter', because of tragedies that she suffered (Ruth 1:20–1).

Naphtali 1. The sixth son of Jacob (Genesis 30:7–8).

2. A tribe descended from Jacob's son that occupied fertile land in

eastern and central Galilee. Barak, Deborah's general, was its most famous member. See map of OLD TESTAMENT ISRAEL.

Nathan A prophet who challenged David about adultery but who also gave him God's promise that his dynasty would last for ever (2 Samuel 7:1–16; 12:1–14).

Nathanael A disciple mentioned in John's Gospel who is probably the same as Bartholomew who appears in the first three Gospels. He recognized Jesus as the Messiah, and Jesus described him as a person without guile (John 1:43–51).

nations see GENTILES.

nations, table of The list of seventy nations descended from Noah's sons (Genesis 10). The Japhethites are traditionally associated with Indo-European peoples, the Hamites with northern Africa and south-western Asia, and the Semites with Mesopotamia and the surrounding areas.

nature, human see HUMANITY.

Nazarene Originally a person from Nazareth, but applied in the Bible to Jesus and his followers (Matthew 2:23; Acts 24:5).

Nazareth A village in the Galilean hills where Jesus lived until he began his itinerant ministry (Luke 2:51). See map of NEW TESTAMENT ISRAEL.

Nazirite A person who was dedicated to the service of God. Nazirites took a vow, promising to avoid strong drink, not to touch a corpse, and not to cut their hair. Samson was a Nazirite (Judges 13:4–7), as also were probably Samuel and John the Baptist.

Nebuchadnezzar A Babylonian king, actually Nebuchadnezzar II (605–562 BC), who established the New Babylonian empire and built the Hanging Gardens of Babylon. His achievements included the destruction of Jerusalem and taking the people of Judah into exile in Babylonia (2 Kings 24:10–25:26).

Neco see PHARAOH.

necromancy see OCCULT.

Negev The largely wilderness area south of Gaza and Beersheba, occupied by the tribe of Judah, the Edomites and the Amalekites (1 Samuel 27:10). The Israelites lived at Kadesh-Barnea in the central Negev for most of their forty years in the wilderness. See map of OLD TESTAMENT ISRAEL.

Nehemiah A governor of the Jewish community in Judah in the fifth century BC. He was appointed by the Persian king Artaxerxes I, and served for two terms of office which began in 445 BC and 433 BC respectively. Nehemiah was a vigorous man who led by example, and who was known for his generosity (5:14–16), concern for the poor

(5:1–13), and prayerfulness (2:4; 6:9). He had a gift of discernment (6:1–14), and a special concern for the temple and its worship (13:1–14, 28–31). Together with Ezra 'the priest and scribe', he played a major role in restoring Judaism's viability after the exile. See also NEHEMIAH, BOOK OF.

Nehemiah, book of

Structure

Rebuilding the walls of Jerusalem (1:1–6:19)
List of returning exiles (7:1–73a)
Covenant renewal (7:73b–10:39)
Restoring Jerusalem (11:1–13:31)

Famous passages

Nehemiah inspects Jerusalem by night (2:11–16)
The wall completed in fifty-two days (6:15–16)
Ezra reads the Book of the Law (8:1–18)
Prayer of confession (9:5–37)

The book reports some of the achievements of Nehemiah, who was governor of Judah in the second half of the fifth century BC. It originally followed the book of Ezra, and should be read as the second part of a single work. Nehemiah continues the story of the restoration of the Jewish community under the Persians, though the task is only partially completed. The autobiographical style, notably a series of short prayers, suggests that part of the book is based on Nehemiah's own report, often called the Nehemiah Memoir (e.g. chapters 1–2, 4–6, 13).

The book concentrates on the remarkable rebuilding of the wall of Jerusalem in fifty-two days, which is achieved as everyone plays their part in the face of concerted opposition (chapters 1–6, 12). The central chapters describe Ezra's reading of the law (chapter 8) which becomes the basis of a renewal of the people's covenant with God (chapter 10). Here, as occasionally elsewhere, Ezra and Nehemiah are involved together (8:9; 12:36). The book concludes with various reforms, including the repopulation of Jerusalem, purifying temple worship, dealing with mixed marriages, and reinstating the Sabbath as a day of rest (chapters 11–13).

neighbour A person such as a friend or fellow Christian with whom one has a natural relationship and to whom one owes the obligation of love and support (Leviticus 19:18). Jesus revolutionized the concept by extending it to include not just outsiders in general but even one's enemies (Luke 10:25–37).

Nero see CAESAR.

nets see FISH; HUNTING.

new birth Jesus' teaching about the need for people to experience fundamental inner spiritual change. The idea is generally known as regeneration, and describes the Holy Spirit's action in making a person a child of God through the gift of spiritual life. It is a requirement for entering God's kingdom and involves a completely new start in life (John 3:5–8).

new covenant see COVENANT.

new moon see FEASTS AND FESTIVALS; MOON.

New Testament The second part of the Bible, comprising twenty-seven books. It contains the four Gospels which tell the story of Jesus, the story of the early church in the Acts of the Apostles, a number of letters mostly written by the apostle Paul, and the Book of Revelation. Its name comes from the new covenant which Jesus established with his people on the basis of his death and resurrection (Hebrews 9:15). See also BIBLE; OLD TESTAMENT.

New Year A special occasion in the Jewish calendar, sometimes known as the Feast of Trumpets. Because the New Year was probably originally observed in the autumn and later in the spring, the Bible sometimes describes it as occurring in the seventh month (Leviticus 23:23–5). See also FEASTS AND FESTIVALS.

Nicodemus A Jewish rabbi who learned about the new birth from Jesus. His support for Jesus in times of need, especially in providing him with a decent burial, suggests he was a secret disciple (John 3:1–21; 19:39–42).

night see TIME.

Nile, River Egypt's main river, on which the country depended then, as now, for its prosperity. The Israelites were well aware of its significance, especially the annual rising and flooding by which the land was irrigated (Amos 9:5). See map of WORLD OF THE BIBLE.

Nineveh The major city of Assyria, situated on the Tigris in northern Iraq. The Bible refers to it mainly as Sennacherib's capital and the place where Jonah prophesied so reluctantly (2 Kings 19:36; Jonah 1–4). It is also an extremely important archaeological site for understanding ancient Assyria. See map of WORLD OF THE BIBLE.

Nisan see CALENDAR, JEWISH.

Noah The hero of the flood. Because of his faith, he and his immediate family were preserved in a large boat called an ark (Genesis 6:8–8:22). The story is paralleled in other ancient literature, though the name of the chief character varies, and the details elsewhere are less realistic. God made a covenant with Noah (Genesis

9:8–17), and his descendants repopulated the earth after the flood.
See also ARK, NOAH'S; FLOOD.

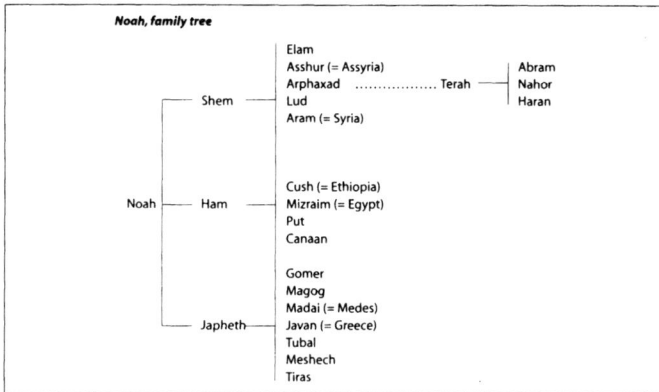

Noah, family tree

		Elam	
		Asshur (= Assyria)	Abram
	Shem	Arphaxad .... Terah	Nahor
		Lud	Haran
		Aram (= Syria)	
		Cush (= Ethiopia)	
Noah	Ham	Mizraim (= Egypt)	
		Put	
		Canaan	
		Gomer	
		Magog	
		Madai (= Medes)	
	Japheth	Javan (= Greece)	
		Tubal	
		Meshech	
		Tiras	

Nomads Israel's ancestors demonstrated different forms of
nomadism, though they did not engage in seasonal nomadism.
Abraham's family wandered from place to place, and the Israelites
travelled for forty years in the wilderness. Though a few Israelites
continued a nomadic form of existence (Jeremiah 35:6–10),
nomadism was mainly found in Israel's neighbours such as the
Amalekites and the Midianites to the east and south of Palestine.
The idea of a people without a settled home is sometimes used as a
picture of Christians in this world (1 Peter 2:11).

nose, nostrils Occurs mainly in a metaphorical sense as the seat of
anger (Psalm 18:15). It is also used to express contempt or to take
offence (Luke 16:14; 2 Samuel 16:21).

Numbers, book of

Structure
Israel at Sinai (1:1–10:10)
Israel travels from Sinai to Kadesh-Barnea (10:11–21:35)
Israel at the plains of Moab (22:1–36:13)

Famous passages
The Aaronic blessing (6:24–6)
The spies report on the Promised Land (13:1–14:45)
Moses not allowed to enter the Promised Land (20:6–13)
Balaam's donkey (22:21–35)

Numbers describes Israel's travels through the wilderness from
Mount Sinai to the edge of the Promised Land. Its goal is 'the land of

Canaan, which I am giving to the Israelites' (13:2; cf. 27:12), though Israel is actually stationary for much of the book, first at Sinai (1:1–10:10) and then at the plains of Moab (22:1–36:13). This is because Israel's relationship to the land is more important than their arrival, and Israel's preparation for the land is the key theme. The preparation takes place in three phases. The first phase is the organizing of Israel into a military force around the Tent or tabernacle (1:1–10: 10). The Tent symbolized God's presence among his people, whom God guided by a pillar of cloud and fire (9:15–23). The second phase is characterized by Israel's opposition to entering the land and rebellion against their leaders (10:11–21:35). Their negative views arose from a report by twelve spies who decided that occupying the land was too dangerous (chapters 13–14). As a result, God condemned the Israelites to wandering in the wilderness for forty years. Only Joshua and Caleb, who believed that the land could be possessed, were allowed to enter the land. This phase also includes Aaron's death, and the prohibition on Moses entering Canaan because he did not wholly obey God's instructions (chapter 20). The third phase is dominated by the blessings of Balaam (chapters 22–4). Although originally hired to curse Israel, he actually did the opposite under the influence of God's Spirit (24:2). The first major consequence of this is the occupation of Transjordan by two and a half tribes (chapter 32), and Israel's ultimate entry into the land is clearly dependent on God's blessing. It is also no coincidence that the best-known passage in Numbers is the Aaronic blessing still widely used in churches and synagogues today (6:24–6).

The arrangement of Numbers is unusual, in that story and instruction often appear alongside one another. The purpose of this is apparently to provide a basis for future behaviour in Canaan, with the legal sections often associated with an accompanying narrative. Little can be said about the origin of Numbers, except that as an alternative to the traditional view of Moses' authorship (and Balaam's for chapters 22–4), scholars usually treat the book as the product of three main sources, brought together in either the pre-exilic or early post-exilic era.

numbers, significance of Normally, numbers occur in their ordinary arithmetical sense, but certain numbers also have some additional special associations. Three is often significant (Matthew 12:39–40), and seven and sometimes ten are associated with perfection and completeness (Matthew 18:21–2). Twelve sometimes conveys the full number of God's people (Revelation 21:12). Ten thousand is the largest individual number in biblical thought, and larger numbers were counted in multiples of thousands. Approximate numbers were either ten or combinations of small numbers such as two or three. A distinctive custom is the use of an ascending pair of numbers, usually three and four, where the emphasis usually falls on the second figure (Proverbs 30:15–31).

Nunc Dimittis A Latin name for Simeon's song of praise when he took the baby Messiah in his arms (Luke 2:29–32). See also BENEDICTUS; MAGNIFICAT.

nurse Refers both to wet-nurses, who breast-feed babies on behalf of the mother (Exodus 2:7–9), and to those with the responsibility of caring for children (2 Samuel 4:4).

O

oak SEE TREES AND BUSHES.

oath May be in various forms such as a solemn promise or to enforce a command. Oaths were usually considered binding (Numbers 30:2), though they were occasionally revoked (1 Samuel 14:45). Jesus taught that oaths were unnecessary for those who spoke honestly (Matthew 5:33–7), but God sometimes underlined his commitment to his promises by confirming them with an oath (Hebrews 6:13–18).

Obadiah A common name meaning 'servant or worshipper of the Lord'. **1.** One of Ahab's leading officials who risked his life to help prophets under persecution (1 Kings 18:3–16).

2. The prophet who gave his name to the book of Obadiah. See also OBADIAH, BOOK OF.

Obadiah, book of

Structure
Judgement on Edom (1–14)
The Day of the Lord (15–21)

The shortest book in the Old Testament, usually dated to soon after the exile began in 587 BC. It is a prophecy mainly concerned with God's judgement on Judah's southern neighbour Edom, because Edom gloated over Judah and occupied her land during the exile. The book also speaks of the Day of the Lord as a time of salvation as well as judgement for all nations. The book's main theme is that God will establish his kingdom (21) over all forms of human sin, especially pride.

Obed-Edom A Philistine whom God blessed because the ark of the covenant was in his house (2 Samuel 6:10–12), and perhaps the same person as the founder of a family of gatekeepers at the temple.

obedience and disobedience The requirement of obedience is central to the relationship between human beings and God. This requirement is based on the idea that God is Lord of all and has ultimate power to command and to make his will known through his word, especially his laws. However, after Adam and Eve first disobeyed his command, no one was able to obey him perfectly, even among the covenant people of Israel (Genesis 3:1–7; 1 Kings 8:46). Only the perfect obedience of Jesus achieved acceptance with God and enabled others to become acceptable to him (Romans 5:15–19). Believers must also obey God, but are to express their commitment to his will through faith and love. True obedience involves motives as well as actions, and is in sharp contrast with merely complying with a legal and ethical code. Disobedience to God's word is extremely serious, and those who disobey the gospel of Jesus will be subject to God's punishment (2 Thessalonians 1:8).

God also requires obedience to the basic institutions of human society, including civil and family authority (1 Peter 2:13–15). Only when the state makes demands that confiict directly with God's will are Christians permitted to obey God rather than human authority (Acts 5:29).

occult The occult world was a major feature of the cultures of biblical times. The practices mentioned most frequently are: (i) divination, by which people attempted to tell the future; (ii) astrology, involving the worship of sun, moon and stars; (iii) necromancy, by which people consulted spirits of the dead through mediums; and (iv) magic rituals for infiuencing unseen spiritual powers (Deuteronomy 18:9–13; Daniel 2:1–11), sometimes including sorcery and witchcraft. Involvement with the spirit world without reference to God, however, was strongly forbidden. It was dangerous to those who practised such things, and was in direct opposition to the worship of God. People who came from such backgrounds to Christ had to abandon their occult ways completely (Acts 8:9–24; 19:19).

occupations In a largely agricultural society like ancient Israel, most people had to develop a variety of skills just to survive. The majority of the population were involved in some way in working the land, including arable and animal farming. Others were occcupied in related trades such as blacksmithing or were connected with basic activities such as food production or the building trade. However, a number of more specialist activities are mentioned, which could be as varied as working in metals or precious stones, serving as priests and Levites in the temple, or working as tax collectors or other officials of the state.

Occupations

Artisan	2 Kings 24:14
Baker	Genesis 40:1–22
Blacksmith	Isaiah 44:12
Builder	2 Kings 12:11
Carpenter	Matthew 13:55
Civil servant	1 Kings 9:22–3
Cook	1 Samuel 9:23–4
Cupbearer	Nehemiah 1:11
Doctor	Mark 5:26
Embroiderer	Exodus 38:23
Farmer	Matthew 13:3
Fishers	Mark 1:16
Gardener	John 20:15
Goldsmith	Isaiah 40:19
Governor	Nehemiah 5:14
Launderer	Malachi 3:2
Lawyer	Acts 24:1
Linen worker	1 Chronicles 4:21
Mason	Ezra 3:7
Merchant	Genesis 37:28
Metalworker	2 Timothy 4:14
Midwife	Exodus 1:15–21
Musician	2 Chronicles 5:12
Perfumer	1 Samuel 8:13
Potter	Jeremiah 18:1–4
Priest	Luke 1:5–9
Sailor	Acts 27:27
Secretary	2 Kings 22:3–12
Shepherd	Ezekiel 34:1–16
Silversmith	Acts 19:24
Soldier	Luke 7:8
Steward	2 Samuel 19:17
Tanner	Acts 9:43
Tax collector	Matthew 9:9–11
Tentmaker	Acts 18:3
Treasurer	John 13:29
Watchman	Psalm 127:1
Weaver	Exodus 39:22

offerings SEE SACRIFICE AND OFFERING.

oil Usually refers to olive oil. It was widely used domestically, in food preparation, as fuel for oil lamps, as a soothing medicine, and for the comfort of guests. Oil is also referred to symbolically, especially in anointing ceremonies. It was poured on the head of a new priest or king as a picture of God's gift of his Spirit (1 Samuel 16:13), and was used in the church in association with prayer for healing (James 5:14). See also ANOINTING, ANOINTED.

old age Is generally associated with God's blessing, though the weaknesses of old age were also familiar (Deuteronomy 5:33; Ecclesiastes 12:1–7). The elderly were generally treated with respect and were looked up to for their wisdom (Job 12:12). Normal life expectation was around seventy years (Psalm 90:10), though the long life of people before Moses' time might be explained by a healthier environment (Genesis 5:1–32; 25:7–8). See also YOUTH.

Old Testament The first part of the Christian Bible, and the Bible of the Jews. Its thirty-nine books describe the period before Christ, from the creation of the world to the beginning of the intertestamental period. The Old Testament contains God's words to Israel in a rich variety of literature, including laws and prophecies, narratives and beautiful poems. Despite its great variety, the Old Testament exhibits an underlying unity which focuses on God's purposes for all people as well as for Israel. The many prophecies towards the end of the Old Testament leave a sense of incompleteness and look forward to its future fulfilment through Christ. See also BIBLE; NEW TESTAMENT.

olive One of the commonest trees in ancient Palestine, with olive groves frequently found in the valleys (Deuteronomy 6:11). Individual trees grow to about 6 metres high, and mainly provided oil extracted from the berries, though the wood was also used for furniture. The tree often symbolized splendour and prosperity (Jeremiah 11:16).

Olives, Mount of A range of small hills east of Jerusalem originally covered in olive trees. The name comes from the fact that the hills were thickly wooded with olive trees in the first century AD. The area was important to Jesus, since he visited it several times in the week before his crucifixion (Luke 22:39) and it was the place of his ascension (Act 1:12). It was also associated with the final coming of God's kingdom (Zechariah 14:4–5).

Omri, King of Israel (c. 876–869 BC) see KINGS AND QUEENS OF ISRAEL.

Onesimus A slave who became a Christian through contact with Paul in prison. Paul's letter to Onesimus' former master Philemon contains a moving appeal for Onesimus' restoration (Philemon 8–21).

onyx see JEWELS AND PRECIOUS STONES.

Ophel see JERUSALEM.

Ophir A place from which Solomon imported exotic goods such as gold, ivory and apes (1 Kings 10:11, 22). It has been located in southern Arabia, Somaliland or India.

opposition Faith in God normally results in some form of conflict. Jesus was frequently opposed by various groups, leading eventually to his death, and promised his followers they could not expect any different treatment (John 15:18–25). Believers are expected to oppose sin and evil in their lives by changing their behaviour (Galatians 5:16–18), but should learn to suffer for what is right when they are persecuted or otherwise unfairly treated (1 Peter 3:9–17). See also PERSECUTION.

ordination The recognition and setting apart of individuals for public ministry. A formal ordination ceremony is clearer to identify for the Old Testament priesthood (Leviticus 8:1–36) than for the ministries of the early church. The New Testament places greater emphasis on gifts for ministry than on particular ceremonies, though church leaders were often recognized through the laying on of hands (2 Timothy 1:6).

origins see CREATION.

Orion see STARS.

ornaments The use of decoration was widely practised in the ancient world, and included personal jewellery, artistic objects such as painted pottery, and decorated buildings. The Bible encourages the appreciation of beauty, but condemns mere ostentation (Isaiah 3:18–23; 1 Peter 3:3–4).

orphans The need for special care for those whose parents had died is a distinctive biblical concept, based on God's loving concern for the underprivileged (Psalm 68:5). God's people are to show the same concern (Deuteronomy 24:17–21; James 1:27), and exploitation of orphans is a sign of wickedness (Isaiah 1:23).

ostrich see BIRDS.

Othniel The first of the judges, who defeated Aramean (Syrian) invaders and ruled the Israelite tribes for forty years (Judges 3:7–11). He was probably Caleb's nephew and married Caleb's daughter as a reward for capturing Debir, a Canaanite town.

outsider see ALIEN; FOREIGNER.

oven see COOKING.

overseer see BISHOP; ELDER.

owl see BIRDS.

oxen see ANIMALS; CATTLE.

p

Paddan Aram An area, also known as Aram Naharaim (Genesis 24:10), around ancient Haran on the Syria-Turkey border where Abraham and his descendants lived before moving to Palestine (Genesis 25:20).

pain SEE SUFFERING.

palace The usual description for the administrative centre of an area, normally incorporating the living quarters of the king or governor, several temples or sanctuaries, and administrative, legal and military buildings. Complexes of this kind existed in several Israelite cities, including Jerusalem and Samaria (1 Kings 7:1–8).

palm-tree SEE TREES AND BUSHES.

Pamphylia An area on the south-western coast of Asia Minor visited by Paul on his first missionary journey (Acts 13:13; 14:24). See map of PAUL'S JOURNEYS.

papyrus SEE WRITING.

parable A short descriptive story told to convey a message about God and his will. As a traditional form of Israelite teaching, parables were used by prophets and others in the Old Testament (Judges 9:7–20; 2 Samuel 12:1–10), but they were particularly important in Jesus' teaching in his message about the kingdom of God. Parables are often distinguished from allegory because they emphasize only one point, but the several points made in the parable of the sower show the impossibility of making any sharp distinction of this kind (Matthew 13:1–23). Parables were so central to Jesus' ministry that he regarded people's responses to them as an indicator of whether they accepted his message or not. See also JESUS, PARABLES OF.

Paradise An Iranian loan-word for a walled garden used in the New Testament as a picture of the delights of heaven (Luke 23:43; Revelation 2:7).

Paran A rocky, desolate wilderness north-west of the Gulf of Aqabah.

Mount Paran, which was loosely associated with Mount Sinai, was probably a peak in the area (Habakkuk 3:3).

parchment see WRITING.

pardon see FORGIVENESS.

parents see FAMILY.

parsin see MENE, MENE, TEKEL, PARSIN.

partiality see FAVOURITISM.

participation see FELLOWSHIP.

partridge see BIRDS.

Passover An important annual Jewish festival still widely celebrated today. It was closely associated with the idea of redemption, both in connection with the exodus from Egypt and with Jesus' death. The highlight of the original Passover was the eating of a lamb symbolizing each family's escape from oppression in Egypt (Exodus 12:1–13, 21–30). Similar symbolism was later applied to Jesus who as a human Passover lamb (1 Corinthians 5:7) brought freedom from the bondage of sin.

Passover retained a strong family emphasis, even when it became centralized in Jerusalem. It was combined with the Festival of Unleavened Bread, which was observed during the following week. Though the two festivals may have originally been separate, the Bible always links them together (Leviticus 23:4–8). See also FEASTS AND FESTIVALS.

Pastoral Letters A term commonly used for the New Testament letters 1 and 2 Timothy and Titus, which are addressed to pastoral leaders and for the most part deal with pastoral issues in local church life. Their distinctive outlook shows a concern for 'godliness' and 'sound doctrine' in the context of dealing with false teachers. Since these letters assume a greater degree of organization in the church than Paul's other letters, they are often thought to have been written by a person who made use of Paul's teachings, though others still hold to the strong early church tradition that they are the work of Paul. See also TIMOTHY, LETTERS TO; TITUS, LETTER TO.

pastors A term occurring only once where it refers to a group of church leaders called 'pastors and teachers' (Ephesians 4:11). Its connection with the common biblical term 'shepherd' indicates the importance of care for one's people in the biblical concept of leadership (1 Peter 5:1–4). See also LEADERSHIP.

patience A special quality of God, frequently described by the distinctive phrase 'slow to anger' (Exodus 34:6). God is patient towards sinners, either reducing their punishment or being willing to forgive those who repent, and even delaying Christ's return

(Romans 2:4; 2 Peter 3:15). god also gives patience to believers, enabling them to cope with opposition and suffering (James 5:7–11).

Patriarchs A term for Abraham and his main descendants, viz. Isaac, Jacob and Joseph. For this reason, Genesis 12–50 is often known as the Patriarchal narratives. See also ABRAHAM; ISAAC; JACOB; JOSEPH, SON OF JACOB.

Paul, life of The outstanding leader in the early church, and a person of many gifts. He was the leading missionary/evangelist and teacher/theologian of the early church, and through his letters, the most prolific contributor to the writings of the New Testament.

Born in Tarsus in Cilicia (south-eastern Turkey), he was a Jewish Pharisee and a Roman citizen. His Jewish name was Saul, his Roman name Paul. As a Pharisee, he vigorously persecuted the church and supported the killing of Christians, though it is unclear whether he was directly involved in their deaths (Acts 26:10). He became a Christian in c. 34 AD in dramatic circumstances. While travelling to Damascus to continue his persecution, he was temporarily blinded as a result of seeing the risen Christ, but almost immediately, God commissioned him through a prophetic message to be a witness of the living Christ, especially to the Gentiles.

After a long period of preparing for this ministry, Paul was sent out from the church at Antioch in c. 47 AD on the first of three missionary journeys. Antioch remained his base throughout his travels, which took him through Asia Minor and Greece. On his last journey he was arrested at Jerusalem, but, knowing he would not receive a fair trial from the Jews, he appealed to Caesar. This led to his journey to Rome, where he spent two years preaching the gospel while under house arrest. The New Testament implies that he was then released for a few years before being rearrested and executed as part of Nero's persecution c. 65 AD.

Paul's experience of the risen Jesus qualified him to be an apostle (1 Corinthians 15:1–11). As the early church's leading teacher and church planter, he exercised apostolic authority in churches throughout the Roman Empire. Though this authority was challenged, especially at Corinth, it was also recognized in churches like Rome that he had never personally visited.

As far as we know, Paul never married, but he enjoyed excellent personal relationships, and his letters reveal a warmhearted interest in many individuals. He was also extremely concerned not to burden the churches with the cost of his ministry. He continued to support himself through his trade as a tentmaker, and for about a decade organized a collection to help alleviate the poverty of the church at Jerusalem. See map of PAUL'S JOURNEYS.

Paul, teaching of Though much of Paul's teaching is in the form of a response to issues raised by the churches to whom he wrote rather than a systematic presentation, it can still be understood as a coherent pattern of thought. Its basis is the person and work of Christ. Both in his speeches in Acts and in his letters, Paul presents Jesus Christ as the one who was shown to be Son of God by his death and resurrection (Romans 1:2–4). As creator and sustainer of the universe (Colossians 1:15–20), Christ holds absolute supremacy over all things seen and unseen (Philippians 2:9–11), but he is especially the Saviour of all who put their faith in him (Colossians 1:12–14, 20–3).

Paul's understanding of the gospel is best understood in terms of redemption and reconciliation. God reconciled the world to himself through Christ's atoning death on the cross, providing forgiveness of sins for a world where everyone is under the power and guilt of sin. By this free gift of God's grace, sinners are put right with God through their faith in Christ rather than having to justify themselves by trying to keep God's law. As a result, they become spiritually identified with Christ or 'in Christ', and receive the gifts of eternal life and of the Holy Spirit. Paul's letters are also concerned with right living. Christians live by faith in Christ and by the power of the Spirit who gives them the ability to live as God requires.

In Paul's view, the work of Christ is the decisive achievement by which the kingdom of God is established, though this work is said to be both already complete and yet still awaiting completion. This is because sin and evil still exist in the world even though the new creation has arrived in Christ. In this context the church as the body of Christ plays a vital role in reflecting the light of Christ to a dark world. The church must also think constantly in terms of mission to unbelievers, just as Paul himself was compelled by Christ's love to proclaim the good news about Christ. Everything in Paul's teaching is to be understood in terms of this desire to make the gospel of Christ as clear and accessible as possible.

peace The Hebrew word *shalom* is a comprehensive term which includes all the positive aspects of good relationships rather than just the absence of hostility. Peace in the Bible usually has a spiritual dimension, since true peace is a gift from God. Perfect peace will only be established through the promised Prince of Peace (Isaiah 9:6–7), but in the meantime human beings can have peace with God because Christ's death has dealt with the power and consequences of human sin (Romans 5:1–2). God gives believers the inner peace of a clear conscience and the ability to establish new relationships with people who may previously have been their enemies (Ephesians 2:14–18; Philippians 4:7). Believers are also to work and pray for peace in the world (Matthew 5:9; 1 Timothy 2:1–2), though they will sometimes be obstructed by people's hatred of God's ways and desire to have their own way (John 15:18–25; James 4:1–2).

peace offering see FELLOWSHIP OFFERING.

pearl see JEWELS AND PRECIOUS STONES.

Pekah, King of Israel (*c.* 737–732 BC) see KINGS AND QUEENS OF ISRAEL.

Pekahiah, King of Israel (*c.* 738–737 BC) see KINGS AND QUEENS OF ISRAEL.

Pelethites see KERETHITES AND PELETHITES.

Peniel, Penuel An Israelite city by the Jabbok east of the Jordan where Jacob wrestled with an angel (Genesis 32:30; 1 Kings 12:25).

Pentateuch A term, meaning 'five scrolls', which refers to the first five books of the Old Testament. It is also known, especially by Jews, as the Torah or the Law (as in the phrase 'Law and Prophets'). The five books contain a continuous story from the creation of the world to the point where Israel was about to enter the Promised Land. God's original plan to bless the world was frustrated by human sin and resulted in the judgement of the flood, but it was partially restored through the fulfilment of God's promises to Abraham and the establishing of his covenant with Israel. Moses is the dominant character of the Pentateuch, and has traditionally been regarded as its author, though scholars for a long time attributed its origins to a Documentary Hypothesis which assumed the existence of four sources labelled J, E, D and P coming from a much later period than Moses. In recent years, however, this theory has been amended or even replaced, and while still acknowledging the existence of different sources, scholars have tended to focus more on the final form of the Pentateuchal text as a more productive approach to its interpretation. See also DEUTERONOMY; EXODUS; GENESIS; LAW; LEVITICUS; NUMBERS.

Pentecost One of the three major Jewish festivals, which was celebrated fifty days after the beginning of the barley harvest (Leviticus 23:15–22). It was also known as the Feast of Weeks in Bible times and is usually known today as Whitsun. Pentecost is mainly associated with the offering of firstfruits, though by the time of Jesus, Jews regarded it as the anniversary of the law-giving at Sinai. The Holy Spirit was first poured out on the church at Pentecost, probably to symbolize the firstfruits of Christ's resurrection (Acts 2:1).

Penuel see PENIEL.

perfection Though only God is naturally without fault, human beings may also achieve perfection. It is a status given to all who believe in Christ (Colossians 1:28; 2:10) because their sins have been completely forgiven (Hebrews 10:14), and it is a process which will be completed only in heaven. Though Christians cannot avoid sin in this life (1 John 1:8), they must aim at perfection in the sense of wholehearted commitment to God's will (Matthew 5:48). They must seek to become spiritually mature (Philippians 3:15). Christ's perfection, which he has by nature and by experience, qualifies him to serve as a high priest on behalf of believers (Hebrews 2:10–18). See also MATURITY.

perfume see COSMETICS AND PERFUMERY; HERBS AND SPICES.

persecution Christians often experienced persecution for their faith (2 Timothy 3:12), just as Jesus warned would happen (John 15:18–25). Persecution might come from any source, whether friends and family or hostile foreign armies, and actual experiences might vary from deception and ridicule to violence and even death. Whatever form persecution took, however, God could use it to bless his people and mature their faith (Matthew 5:10–12; 1 Peter 4:12–19). See also ENEMIES.

Persia, Persians Located south-east of the Persian Gulf, from the mid-sixth century BC to the late third century BC Persia was the centre of the largest empire the world had yet seen. The Persians were helpful to the Jews, allowing the exiles to return home and rebuild their temple (Ezra 1:1–4) and appointing Ezra and Nehemiah to restore Jewish life. The priestly Magi probably also came from Persia (Matthew 2:1). See map of WORLD OF THE BIBLE.

Peter A fisherman who was one of Jesus' three closest disciples. Originally called Simon, Jesus gave him the name or nickname Peter (or Cephas in Aramaic), meaning 'rock'. The new name refers to Peter's acknowledgement of Jesus as the Messiah (Matthew 16:16–18), though it is debated whether 'rock' refers to Peter himself or to his statement as the foundation of Christian teaching. Peter was a natural leader, but had to learn to overcome an innate impulsiveness, especially through his denial of Jesus (Mark 14:29–31, 66–72) and subsequent restoration (John 21:15–19). He became a leader of the church in Jerusalem, and was one of the first to take the gospel to Gentiles. He suffered for his faith, and seems eventually to have been martyred at Rome during Nero's persecution. See also PETER, 1 AND 2.

Peter, 1 and 2

Structure

1 Peter
> The foundations of the Christian life (1:1–2:10)
> Living as Christians in society (2:11–4:11)
> Living in hope as Christians (4:12–5:14)

2 Peter
> The Christian message is reliable (1:1–15)
> Attacks on false teachers (1:16–3:13)
> Encouragement to grow in God's grace (3:14–18)

Famous passages
> 'Be holy because I am holy' (1 Peter 1:16)
> The church as a chosen people (1 Peter 2:9–10)

Though there is no strong reason to date 1 Peter later than the last years of Peter's life in the 60s AD, many scholars believe on grounds of style and content that 2 Peter was written by a later author, based on Peter's original teaching, about the end of the first century.

1 Peter was written to persecuted Christians in northern Asia Minor (northern Turkey), with part of it perhaps containing instruction for a baptismal service (1:3–4:11). Attention is centred on Christ's suffering, as the basis of Christians' salvation and an example of how to live in a hostile environment. Emphasis is placed on the importance of true Christian behaviour as a witness to a pagan society, and on the believers' status as a new people and family of God.

2 Peter also reflects a situation of conflict, in this case arising from false teachers. Through extensive use of the Old Testament, the letter shows that false teaching has always been and will be a problem for God's people. It can be resisted, however, through reliance on the grace of God and the Scriptures, and by living in expectation of Christ's imminent return.

petition SEE PRAYER.

Pharaoh An Egyptian word meaning 'great house', used for the kings of Egypt. Several Pharaohs are mentioned, though, like the Pharaohs of the exodus, not always by name (Exodus 2:23; 3:10). The best known are Shishak (= Sheshonq I) who attacked Jerusalem in Rehoboam's reign (1 Kings 14:25), and Neco who killed Josiah (2 Kings 23:29). See also EGYPT.

Pharisees A Jewish party which emerged in the second century BC. Despite their original emphasis on God's law or Torah, their insistence on equal prominence for oral law and their emphasis on human behaviour rather than God's work brought them into conflict with Jesus. Jesus accused some Pharisees of being hypocrites, because their teaching was inconsistent with their actions (Matthew 23:1–36). They, however, saw Jesus as a blasphemer and a law-breaker (Luke 5:17–21; 6:1–2), though some did become believers (Acts 15:5). See also SCRIBE.

Philemon, letter to

Structure
Paul's thanks for Philemon (1–7)
Paul's request to Philemon (8–25)

The shortest and most personal of Paul's letters. It was written about the same time as Colossians to Philemon, a leader in the Colossian church, about Philemon's slave Onesimus. Onesimus was probably a runaway slave but had become a Christian after meeting Paul in prison, and Paul appeals to Philemon on the basis of Christian love to welcome him back as a brother rather than as a slave (16). It is a cameo of the revolutionary way in which, even in the first century AD, the Christian gospel undermined slavery.

Philip 1. One of the apostles, often mentioned alongside Andrew. His introduction of Greeks to Jesus was the start of events leading to the crucifixion (Matthew 10:3; John 12:20–3).
2. An evangelist who brought Samaritans and the Ethiopian eunuch to faith in Christ (Acts 8:5–13; 26–38). See also HEROD ANTIPAS.

Philippi A major city in Macedonia in northern Greece. It was the site of the first church in Europe (Acts 16:11–40), and references in the New Testament allude to the fact that its citizens enjoyed special privileges from Rome (Philippians 3:20). See map of PAUL'S JOURNEYS.

Philippians, letter to the

Structure
Thanks for the Philippian church (1:1–11)
Appeal to follow Christ's pattern of life (1:12–2:30)
Appeal to follow Paul's example (3:1–4:1)
Unity, joy and generosity in the church (4:2–23)

Famous passages
'For me, to live is Christ and to die is gain' (1:21)
Jesus as a servant and exalted (2:5–11)
Counting everything as loss for Christ (3:4–11)
'Rejoice in the Lord always' (4:4)

As with Ephesians, Colossians and Philemon, Paul wrote Philippians from prison, probably from Rome in the early 60s AD or possibly Ephesus in the mid 50s. The letter illustrates the warm personal relationship between Paul and the Philippian church which Paul describes as a 'partnership in the gospel' (1:5). Paul expresses gratitude for their support in his difficulties and their repeated personal gifts (4:14–18).

There were, however, still problems at Philippi. People were obstructing the work of the gospel because of their insistence on Jewish practices (3:2, 18–19), and Paul also notes a tendency to perfectionism within the church (3:12–16). His response is to encourage them to press on towards their God-given goal, assuring them that God will complete what he has begun (1:6; 3:12–21). In a magnificent passage often called the 'Christ-hymn' (2:5–11), Paul tells them to focus their lives on the pattern set by Christ. Paul quotes his own experience to show that serving Jesus is worth giving up everything else for (3:4–11), and that even death is 'gain' (1:21).

Philistines A group who came from the Aegean to south-west Palestine as part of a movement of Sea Peoples in the twelfth century BC. They became one of Israel's most hostile enemies, and were finally defeated by David (1 Samuel 17; 2 Samuel 5:17–25). Evidence suggests the Philistines in Genesis may have been a smaller group from the same place of origin (Genesis 21:32–4). Palestine receives its name from the Philistines. See map of OLD TESTAMENT ISRAEL.

Phinehas see HOPHNI AND PHINEHAS.

Phoenicia, Phoenicians The coastal area of Syria and Lebanon, often identified by its major cities, Tyre and Sidon. Their inhabitants provided Israel with an architect and materials for the temple, and ships and sailors for overseas trade (2 Chronicles 2:3–16; 1 Kings 9:27). See also TYRE AND SIDON.

pig An animal which the Israelites were not allowed to eat because it was regarded as unclean. This was probably because of associations with its eating habits rather than for hygienic reasons, but it led to pigs being treated with great disgust (Luke 15:15).

pigeons see BIRDS.

Pilate, Pontius The Roman prefect, later procurator, in charge of the province of Judea from 26 to 36/37 AD. Ancient sources show he regularly offended the Jews, and his weak actions over Jesus' crucifixion were probably based on concern about his reputation with the emperor Tiberius (Matthew 27:24–6).

pine see TREES AND BUSHES.

pint see WEIGHTS AND MEASURES.

pipes see MUSIC AND MUSICAL INSTRUMENTS.

Pisgah The edge of the Moabite plateau in Transjordan, and the ridge on Mount Nebo in the same area from which Moses saw the Promised Land (Deuteronomy 34:1–4).

pity see COMPASSION.

plagues of Egypt Ten disasters by which God punished the Egyptians for persistently oppressing their Israelite slaves and failing to acknowledge God's power. Though some plagues may have been the result of natural causes, this does not convincingly explain the suddenness of the events described or the final plague which brought death to the firstborn in Egyptian households but not to the Israelites.

Plagues of Egypt		
First plague	Water turned to blood	Exodus 7:14–24
Second plague	Frogs	Exodus 7:25–8:15
Third plague	Gnats	Exodus 8:16–19
Fourth plague	Flies	Exodus 8:20–32
Fifth plague	Against livestock	Exodus 9:1–7
Sixth plague	Boils	Exodus 9:8–12
Seventh plague	Hail	Exodus 9:13–35
Eighth plague	Locusts	Exodus 10:1–20
Ninth plague	Darkness	Exodus 10:21–9
Tenth plague	Death of the firstborn	Exodus 11:1–12:30

plain, cities of the The five cities of Sodom, Gomorrah, Admah, Zeboiim and Bela or Zoar, located at the southern end of the Dead Sea. Abraham twice rescued Lot from disaster in these cities, including when God finally destroyed them because of their complete moral breakdown (Genesis 14:1–24; 19:24–9). See also SODOM AND GOMORRAH; ZOAR.

plants Identification of plants is complicated by the rarity of some biblical names and the difficulty of comparing ancient and modern terms. Plants were part of God's creation. As well as bringing beauty and variety to the environment, they were also intended as food (Genesis 1:29–30). They were often used as an example of the temporary nature of life (Matthew 6:30).

Plants

Aloes	Psalm 45:8
Calamus	Jeremiah 6:20
Carob	Luke 15:16
Castor-oil plant	Jonah 4:6
Crocus	Isaiah 35:1–2
Gourd	1 Kings 6:18
Hyssop	John 19:29
Lily	Luke 12:27
Lotus	Job 40:21
Mandrake	Genesis 30:14–16
Mustard	Matthew 13:31–2
Myrtle	Zechariah 1:8–10
Nettles	Isaiah 34:13
Reed	Exodus 2:3
Rose of Sharon	Song of Songs 2:1
Rush	Isaiah 19:6
Thistles	Genesis 3:18
Thorns	Matthew 13:7
Tumbleweed	Psalm 83:13
Vine of Sodom	Deuteronomy 32:32
Weeds	Matthew 13:25

Pleiades see STARS.

plough see AGRICULTURE; TOOLS.

poetry Though no sharp distinction can be made between poetry and elevated and rhythmic prose, poetry is widespread in the Old Testament, occurring frequently in the prophetic literature as well as major poetic books such as Psalms, Proverbs and Job. It is much rarer in the New Testament, though several hymns and psalms and quotations from biblical and other sources are poetic in form (Luke 1:46–55; Titus 1:12). The main characteristics of Hebrew poetry are the line in two parallel parts and the compactness of language. However, these simple features are capable of endless variation, and the Hebrew poets showed real creativity in producing imaginative literature of high quality, as for example in the Book of Job or Isaiah 40–55.

polygamy see MARRIAGE.

pomegranate see FOOD AND DRINK; FRUITS.

poor see POVERTY.

poplar see TREES AND BUSHES.

possessions see WEALTH.

potsherd see WRITING.

potter, pottery Common household objects in the ancient world such as jars, cups and lamps were usually made of pottery. Because they have been preserved in such large quantities, archaeologists have used them for dating purposes by comparing different styles and techniques.

Potters and their work are referred to several times. They illustrate God's sovereign ability to create or remove his people (Jeremiah 18:1–12), and God himself is sometimes described as a potter (Isaiah 45:9–10). However, by using the metaphor of an ordinary clay pot for the believer, God shows he is also able to use ordinary people for his own glorious purposes (2 Corinthians 4:7).

pounds see WEIGHTS AND MEASURES.

poverty Though Jesus taught that poverty was an inevitable feature of human society, he urged the importance of providing for poor people (Matthew 26:11; Mark 9:41) since God was specially concerned for them (Psalm 35:10). The early church continued the well-established Old Testament tradition of practical care for the poor in various ways (Deuteronomy 14:28–9; James 1:27), such as Paul's collection in his churches for poor Christians in Jerusalem (Acts 24:17).

Spiritual poverty also frequently occurs, in relation to those who suffer for their faith and those who are conscious of their sin (Psalm 40:17; Matthew 5:3). Jesus experienced great spiritual poverty by becoming a human being, though he was also materially poor (2 Corinthians 8:9). However, the gospel was good news for the poor (Luke 4:18), enabling people to experience the spiritual riches of God's kingdom (James 2:5). See also WEALTH.

power Absolute power is God's alone, and since all other forms of power are dependent on his authority (John 19:10–11), even kings and emperors have limits set for them (Daniel 2:21). In fact, God will ultimately destroy all powers that oppose him, including that of Satan and evil, and replace them with the kingdom of God. God shows his power in his mighty acts such as the creation and the exodus, and in all the work of Jesus Christ and the Holy Spirit. However, its supreme demonstration is seen in Jesus' cross and resurrection (1 Corinthians 1:18; Ephesians 1:19–20), and in the gospel's ability to bring salvation to people's lives (Romans 1:16).

praise A vital aspect of worship, involving giving God the honour due to his name as the creator of all things and the saviour of his people. Praise is sometimes commanded as a duty, since God is worthy of people's praise irrespective of their attitude or feelings towards him (Psalm 96:1–3; 1 Peter 2:9). More often, however, it is a natural expression of thanksgiving for what God has done or a response to a fresh realization of his character (Psalm 126:1–3; Acts 3:8–9). Praise was often accompanied by music, and could sometimes take the form of spontaneous dance (Exodus 15:20–1). See also HYMN.

prayer At its heart, prayer enables a person to enjoy a genuine sense of fellowship with God. This is clearly illustrated by Jesus, who often took time to pray to his Father, especially before important events such as choosing his disciples or in the Garden of Gethsemane before his death (Luke 6:12–16; Matthew 26:36–44). His most extensive prayer, often called his high priestly prayer (John 17), shows his concern that all believers as well as himself would be faithful to God and bring glory to him. Jesus' teaching on prayer emphasized the importance of a right attitude of heart involving faith, humility, and persistence. He encouraged believers to pray directly to their heavenly Father but warned them to pray privately rather than draw attention to themselves (Matthew 6:5–15).

The nature of prayer as expressing a relationship with God is shown by Abraham's and Moses' description as friends of God. Moses had a special sense of God's presence and even experienced his face shining as he talked with God (Exodus 33:7–11; 34:29–35). Prayer also brings believers a fresh awareness of their status as children of God (Romans 8:15–16). Many prayers are based on the conviction of God's covenant love for his people, and are offered in the name of the Lord. God always promises to respond to any such prayer (1 Kings 8:31–53), whether a person is experiencing deep distress (Psalm 88) or great joy (Psalm 100).

The Bible contains many kinds of prayers, though the main elements are confession, praise, adoration and intercession. Confession is a necessary prelude to all other forms of prayer, though those who pray in repentance can always be sure of God's forgiveness (1 John 1:9). Praise includes the acknowledgement of God's character as well as specific thanksgiving for what he has done, often through answered prayer (Psalm 145; Ephesians 1:3–16). Adoration, which often includes meditation, allows believers to express the depth of their love for God. This aspect of prayer often emphasizes the delight of being in God's presence (Psalm 27). Intercession is concerned with bringing the needs of others or of oneself before God (Hebrews 4:16). Its purpose is that God's will may be done in people's lives, not to fulfil their selfish desires (John 14:13–14; James 4:2–3). See also LORD'S PRAYER, THE.

Prayer of Manesseh, The see APOCRYPHA.

preaching The act of making God's word publicly known, especially the good news about Jesus Christ. Though this activity was undertaken by Old Testament priests and prophets, it received a new priority in relation to the gospel of Christ's death and resurrection. The task of proclaiming the gospel was carried out by ordinary believers as well as by those whom God appointed especially to the task (Acts 8:4–5; 26:16–20). It often included teaching, whether in the form of short parables or long addresses, and could be addressed both to unbelievers and to the church. It was also sometimes accompanied by special signs of God's power (Matthew 4:23; Acts 19:8–20). See also EVANGELISM.

precepts see LAW.

precious stones see JEWELS AND PRECIOUS STONES.

predestination The belief that God knows in advance what will take place and that he will carry out his purposes for human history and for the salvation of his people (Romans 8:28–30; Ephesians 1:4–14). However, the emphasis on God's personal involvement rules out any concept of rigid determinism. The concept emphasizes God's sovereign control and loving protection for his people, and makes room for God to respond to all who turn to him in repentance. See also FOREKNOWLEDGE.

predictions see PROPHECY AND PROPHETS.

Preparation, Day of A term for the day before the weekly sabbath (Mark 15:42) and before the annual Passover (John 19:14).

pride Though not actually described in the Bible as one of the seven deadly sins, pride is consistently regarded as one of the most serious offences against God. It is based on an attitude which acts independently of God, and therefore strikes at the root of the relationship of faith and trust which God expects from all human beings. It is also given as the reason for Satan's punishment (1 Timothy 3:6). God always opposes the proud, and humbles even the most powerful rulers (Daniel 4:29–33). Pride based on any form of human achievement is therefore contrary to the gospel (Ephesians 2:8–9).

priest A person who enjoyed direct access into God's presence. A priest had a two-way function, as a representative of others who offered sacrifices and prayers to God and as a mediator of God's will to those he represented. The Bible mentions several different kinds of priests: (i) the early patriarchs who worshipped God on behalf of their households (Genesis 35:7, 14–15); (ii) the descendants of Aaron who were responsible for Israel's system of sacrifices and for teaching the law (1 Chronicles 6:49; Jeremiah 18:18); (iii) the royal line of David who had a more limited role in leading Israel's worship and blessing the people (2 Samuel 6:12–18); (iv) the nation of Israel who seem to have represented other nations before God (Exodus 19:6); (v) Jesus as God's great high priest (Hebrews 2:17–18); (vi) the church whose members collectively and individually enjoyed the privilege of worshipping God directly and declaring his praises to the world (1 Peter 2:9); and (vii) various Israelite and pagan priests who either established their own pattern of sacrifice or worshipped other deities (Judges 17:5–6; 2 Kings 23:5).

Aaron's descendants were Israel's main family of priests, representing the rest of the nation to God. The chief (or high) priest had the special responsibility of making atonement once a year (Leviticus 16:32–4). Some of the priest's distinctive clothes had a symbolic function, such as the breastplate with the names of every tribe written on it which the priest bore into God's presence. Other special clothes included an ephod or smocklike garment, a special turban, and a robe with tassels to which bells were attached so that the priest could be heard by the people while he was unseen inside the temple (Exodus 28). A distinction is made, however, between all human priests who needed to offer sacrifices for themselves as sinners as well as for others, even when they carefully observed God's holy laws, and the perfect sinless self-offering of Jesus (Hebrews 7:23–8). In contrast to all other priests, Jesus offered one sacrifice that was effective for all time and therefore became the ultimate high priest (Hebrews 2:17). In this role, he now sits on God's throne and prays constantly to his Father for his people (Hebrews 7:25; 8:1–2). He also enables believers to exercise their own priestly ministry, especially in the form of sacrifices of praise and of Christian service (Hebrews 13:15–16).

Priscilla see AQUILA AND PRISCILLA.

prison, prisoner People could be confined in dungeons, fortresses, or even cisterns. Their offences might include being out of favour with the authorities, being in debt, being captives of war, or holding unpopular views about God (Jeremiah 38:6; Matthew 18:30; Acts 12:4–7; 16:23–40). Conditions were, however, sometimes better in cases of house arrest (Acts 28:16).

prize A New Testament description of what every believer will receive in heaven (Philippians 3:14).

proconsul A provincial governor in the Roman Empire who did not need a standing army (Acts 13:7; 18:12).

prodigal son see JESUS, PARABLES OF.

Promised Land A reference to the land of Canaan or Palestine which God promised to Abraham and his descendants (Genesis 12:1). Though it extended theoretically from the Euphrates to the border of Egypt, Israel controlled such a large area only briefly (Genesis 15:18; 1 Kings 4:21). The description 'land flowing with milk and honey' sums up its attractiveness and fertility (Exodus 33:3).

promises The promises of God are an important feature of biblical thought. The Old Testament in particular contains a series of promises confirmed through various covenants, centring on God's purpose to bless the world through his people and eventually create a new world without evil and suffering (Genesis 12:1–3; Isaiah 11:1–9). These promises are fulfilled in Jesus (2 Corinthians 1:20), some through his death and resurrection and others at his second coming. See also COVENANT.

prophecy and prophets A prophet was a person, male or female, who spoke God's word. Prophecy began with Abraham (Genesis 20:7), but it did not become established until first the Mosaic period and then the time of Samuel in the eleventh century BC. It flourished particularly from the ninth to the fifth centuries BC, when major prophets such as Isaiah, Jeremiah and Ezekiel were active. Malachi was probably the last Old Testament prophet, though John the Baptist continued in the same tradition (Matthew 11:13–14).

Jesus was the supreme prophet, since he not only fully spoke God's word but was himself God's incarnate word (John 1:14; 4:19). The church experienced an increase in prophetic activity as a result of the coming of the Holy Spirit (Acts 2:17–18) and prophets played an important role in the early church (Acts 11:27–8; 1 Corinthians 14). However, it remains true that prophecy is associated more with the Old than the New Testament.

Prophets were often called by God to speak his word in times of crisis or at other critical moments in the life of God's people. Especially between the ninth and the sixth centuries BC, they continually drew attention to Israel's desperate state before God, though they also showed how Israel would be restored after the disaster of the exile.

The prophets' task was basically to explain to their contemporaries the meaning of God's covenant, its demands as well as its promises. They emphasized that God was concerned about the whole of life, including family matters, social issues and politics, faith and worship. This often meant they brought words of judgement, and though their intention was to stir the people to repentance, persecution was a common experience (2 Chronicles 36:16). However, they also spoke about God's long-term plans to fulfil his covenant purposes by recreating a new and perfect world (Isaiah 65:17–19).

Prophets were usually aware of some specific form of divine inspiration (Micah 3:8), though they received their messages through such varied means as visions or mini-dramas. Some of their methods seem strange today, but the most important feature of their ministry was the message they brought. Despite their unpopularity and the many challenges to their authority and authenticity (Deuteronomy 18:18–22; Jeremiah 23:16–22), the significance of their words has stood the test of time.

propitiation The turning aside of God's anger against sin. This was achieved through Jesus' self-offering on the cross, and resulted in the cancellation of all penalties for sin (Romans 3:21–6; 1 John 2:2). See also ATONEMENT.

proselyte Someone who was a Gentile by birth but became a Jew by choice (Matthew 23:15). In New Testament times, such people were more common outside than inside Palestine (Acts 13:43).

prosperity SEE WEALTH.

prostitution Apart from a few individual prostitutes who are held up as examples of faith (Matthew 21:31–2; James 2:25), the practice is always regarded as unacceptable for God's people (Revelation 21:8). The presence in Israel of religious prostitution involving both men and women, as in much of the ancient world, illustrated how far they had turned away from God (Ezekiel 23:35–7).

Proverbs, book of

Structure
True wisdom (1:1–9:18)
The main collection of proverbs, associated with Solomon
(10:1–22:16)
Thirty sayings of the wise (22:17–24:22)
Further sayings of the wise (24:23–34)
A collection of proverbs associated with Solomon and Hezekiah
(25:1–29:27)
Sayings of Agur (30:1–33)
Sayings of King Lemuel (31:1–9)
The ideal wife (31:10–31)

Famous passages
The fear of the LORD is the beginning of wisdom (1:7; 9:10)
Wisdom and the creation of the world (8:22–31)
The ideal wife (31:10–31)

The Book of Proverbs contains several collections of proverbial sayings. These collections are of two types. One consists of short individual sayings covering a wide variety of subjects, such as home and family, business, politics, ethics, wealth and poverty. The second type is the extended poem, found especially in chapters 1–9. Important examples are the poems about God's use of wisdom in creation (8:22–31) and the ideal wife who personifies true wisdom (31:10–31).

Wisdom in Proverbs is a basic principle of life by which people can find success and blessing. Though this has sometimes been criticized for being too materialistic, the emphasis on faith and morality shows its deeper qualities (3:5–6). Such wisdom has nothing to do with mere academic attainment or worldly wisdom, but is practical wisdom concerned with how people should live.

Proverbs is sometimes thought to reflect the training of young men for Solomon's administration, though the frequent references to parental instruction makes the setting of the extended family equally plausible. The traditional association with Solomon probably arose from his role as a collector of educational material (cf. 1 Kings 4:29–34), though the book was not completed until the eighth century BC at the earliest and possibly not until after the exile. See also WISDOM.

providence An important idea that includes God's loving provision of the good things of life for everyone, alongside his often unseen working in human events to fulfil his purposes. A belief in providence assumes that God is active throughout the world as well as the church, and that he is constantly engaged in looking after people's physical and spiritual needs (Matthew 5:45; James 1:17). Many examples are given of God providing for individuals as well as communities, as an encouragement to trust in God in difficult circumstances (Genesis 45:5–11; 1 Kings 17:1–9). The idea of providence takes human freedom fully into account, showing that God works through suffering rather than removing it. Despite such temporary difficulties, however, it also underlines that God will ultimately achieve his intention to establish his kingdom (Revelation 11:15).

prudence see WISDOM.

Psalms, book of

Famous passages

The LORD is my shepherd (Psalm 23)
A psalm of confession (Psalm 51)
Entering the gates with praise (Psalm 100)
The shortest chapter in the Bible (Psalm 117)
The longest chapter in the Bible (Psalm 119)

The longest book in the Bible, containing 150 chapters. The word psalm comes from *psalmos*, which is found in the Greek title of the Book of Psalms and means a song accompanied by a *psalterion*, a type of stringed instrument. A better clue to the contents of the book comes from the Hebrew title *tehillim*, 'praises', which indicates that it contains songs sung in praise of God. The basic concept underlying these songs of praise should not be narrowly understood, however, since the Psalms contain a wide variety of material. The commonest type of psalm is in fact the lament or prayer for help, which may be offered on behalf of the nation of Israel or by individuals. Other common types of psalm include the hymn, praising God for his nature and his work, the thanksgiving which draws attention to specific acts of God, and the royal psalms which celebrate God's choice of the line of Davidic kings.

Psalms were widely used in Israel's public worship, though a number also reflect more personal concerns. They share a conviction that any Israelite could approach God on the basis of the covenant that existed between God and his people. Psalms were composed by people in all kinds of circumstances, including being depressed (e.g. Psalm 88), suffering guilt because of sin (e.g. Psalm 51), being confused about the meaning of life and death (e.g. Psalm 49), happily anticipating worship in the temple (e.g. Psalm 24), or celebrating God's creation of life (e.g. Psalm 8). The wide variety of human experience reflected in the Psalms, together with the often unspecific nature of their language, makes them applicable to many modern situations and so contributes to their continuing popularity.

Psalms were used during and after the Old Testament period. Though the Psalms have traditionally been associated with David, the Bible says little about who actually wrote them down, and the majority probably arose during the period between David's reign and the exile. Discoveries of further psalms among the Dead Sea Scrolls testify to their continuing value in Judaism, while the frequent quotation of psalms in the New Testament (Luke 4:10–11) and the development of psalm-like hymns in the Book of Revelation (4:11; 7:15–17) show their important influence on the worship of the early church.

Poetry and Wisdom Books

The poetry and wisdom literature of the Old Testament connects the faith of the Israelites with the experiences and emotions of their lives. This material was used not only in religious contexts and at special occasions, but also as a means of expressing faith throughout the mundane realities of life.

Poetry can be found everywhere in the Old Testament. Most of the prophetic writings are in poetic form, while poems and songs break out at significant moments in the historical writings (e.g. Exodus 15:1–18; 1 Samuel 2:1–10). Hebrew poetry relies not so much on rhyme as on rhythm and the accumulating effect of word images. Its most notable characteristic is parallelism, where the first line is repeated, expanded, or contrasted by the second line.

Wisdom language can also be found in many places in the narratives, psalms and prophetic writings (e.g. Judges 9:7–15; Psalm 1; Hosea 14:9). Wisdom is not about intellectual ability, but rather about looking at and reflecting on the world from within the framework of faith. It does not explicitly mention God all the time, but it does focus on the implications of life lived in the 'fear of the Lord' (Job 28:28; Proverbs 9:10).

While poetry and wisdom can be found throughout the Old Testament, there are six books which specifically fall into this category and form part of the 'Writings' section of the Hebrew scriptures. These are Job, Psalms, Proverbs, Ecclesiastes, Song of Songs and Lamentations. Of these, three (Job, Proverbs and Ecclesiastes) have the special designation of 'Wisdom Literature'.

The Book of Psalms is a collection of 150 poems written over a period spanning from the early days of the monarchy to the end of the exile (c.1000–586 BC). Some were written by David, others by worship leaders at the temple, but many remain anonymous. They were probably brought together for use in the worship at the temple in Jerusalem, but the collection contains more than just communal hymns of praise, thanksgiving, and petition. Many refer to individual struggles, joys, temptations, times of repentance and experiences of forgiveness, drawing upon contemporary culture and language for their imagery. Numerous attempts have been made to categorise the psalms, but there is no neat arrangement. The psalms reflect the rich spectrum of human emotions and show how the whole of life can be brought into the presence of God through prayers and songs.

The Song of Songs is a good example of the expression of human emotion in poetry. The book is a series of poems celebrating the romantic relationship between a young woman and her lover. Though its colourful descriptions of sexual attration and human love have caused embarrassed readers to interpret it as a picture of God's love for his people, or Christ's love for the church, the inclusion of the Song of Songs as a love poem in the Hebrew scriptures is a reminder that even the most intense of human passions has a place within God's world.

Lamenatations is traditionally attributed to the prophet Jeremiah. It is a compilation of five poems lamenting the destruction of Jerusalem, which happened in 587 BC at the hands of the Babylonians. Beyond the grief of having lost the city of Jerusalem, with all it stood for, Lamentations is aware that judgment had come upon God's people because of their sin.

Turning to the wisdom books, each reflects on a different aspect of reality from within the framework of the Israelite religion. Job is an extended reflection on suffering, but does not give guidance so much in terms of why people suffer as how they should live under suffering. It focuses on the story of Job and his sufferings, from around the time of the patriarchs, and recounts in poetic form the conversations he had first with his friends, and then with God. The book deals with Job's feelings of abandonment, and shows that wisdom is trusting God himself, who is larger than human categories of doctrine.

Proverbs draws together wise sayings and poems from around the time of Solomon. The royal court in Jerusalem would have included courtiers from other nations, so it is no surprise that some of the wisdom has parallels in Egyptian literature, for instance. Proverbs, however, is not a random collection of witty sayings, but an instruction book to train its readers in practical wisdom for life. It deals with ordinary decisions and experiences, and has much that today would be labelled 'common sense'. The 'wisdom' of Proverbs is that life lived in God's world has a certain discernible order.

Ecclesiastes acknowledges that this order is not always visible, and is often contradicted. The author, known as *Qohelet*, laments that all is 'absurd' (1:2, 2:15, etc.), because what he knows to be true within the framework of his faith (e.g. that the righteous are rewarded and the wicked punished) does not measure up to the experiences of his life. *Qohelet* points out the real contradictions of life lived with God in a broken world, but the 'wisdom' of Ecclesiastes is that these contradictions do not ultimately undermine faith, but are held in tension with it.

punishment SEE CRIME AND PUNISHMENT.

Purim, Feast of A Jewish festival established to celebrate the Jews' deliverance from the threat of a widespread massacre in the Persian period (Esther 9:20–8). The name comes from the word *pur*, meaning 'lot', since the festival's date in the twelfth month was originally selected by lot. See also FEASTS AND FESTIVALS.

purity The standard of life which God requires and which is characteristic of God himself (1 John 3:3). True purity can only come from within a person, but this is only possible through the work of Christ and through faith (Hebrews 9:14; Titus 1:15) since the human heart is not pure by nature (Mark 7:20–3). The Old Testament's extensive requirements for ritual purity illustrated the need for inner purity in all contact with God. However, they sometimes became an end in themselves and Jesus had to remind people of the need and privileges of being pure in heart (Matthew 5:8; 15:1–20).

purple see COLOURS.

put A term for Libyan soldiers occurring in seventh-century BC prophets, possibly meaning 'archers' (Ezekiel 27:10).

q

quail see BIRDS.

quarry see METALS AND MINING.

Queen Athaliah was the only Israelite queen who ruled alone. Though Bathsheba and Jezebel played vital roles as the respective wives of David and Ahab, the more important position in Israel belonged to the queen mother (1 Kings 15:2,10,13). Other importan queens were Esther, a wife of the Persian emperor Xerxes, and the queens of Sheba and Ethiopia (1 Kings 10:1; Acts 8:27).

Queen of Heaven A goddess to whom Israelite women made offerings, probably Ashtoreth, the Babylonian Ishtar (Jeremiah 7:1; 44:17–25).

Qumran A place north-west of the Dead Sea where many importar biblical and other scrolls were found from 1947 onwards. The site was the home of a Jewish community, probably the Essenes, from second century BC to the first century AD. See also DEAD SEA SCROI MANUSCRIPTS. See map of NEW TESTAMENT ISRAEL.

r

Rabbah The capital city of the Ammonites (modern Amman), and also one of the cities of the Decapolis (Amos 1:14; Mark 5:20). See map of OLD TESTAMENT ISRAEL.

Rabbi, Rabboni Jewish titles for a teacher, used as a mark of respect as well as officially. They were often used of Jesus (John 3:2; 20:16).

race see GAMES AND SPORT.

Rachel Jacob's second wife, and Leah's younger sister. Jacob waited fourteen years to marry her because he loved her so much, but her life was tinged with sadness (Genesis 29:16–31:35). She died giving birth to her second son, Benjamin. See also JACOB.

Rahab 1. A prostitute in Jericho whose faith in God led her to assist the Israelite destruction of her city (Joshua 2; James 2:25).
2. The name of an ancient chaos monster, symbolizing Egypt and the Red Sea (Psalm 87:4; 89:9–10).

rain see WEATHER.

rainbow A symbol of God's covenant promise to Noah that he would never again destroy the world through a flood (Genesis 9:12–17).

raisins see FOOD AND DRINK.

ram see SHEEP AND GOATS.

Ramah The name of several places, of which the most important was Samuel's home town (modern er-Ram), between Jerusalem and Bethel (1 Samuel 7:17).

Rameses 1. An Egyptian city which the Israelite slaves helped to build (Exodus 1:11).
2. Rameses II (*c.* 1290–1224 BC), probably one of the Pharaohs of the exodus (Exodus 3:10).

Ramoth Gilead A walled city east of the Jordan, possibly modern Tell er-Ramith, often disputed by Israel and the Arameans (1 Kings 22:3–38). See map of OLD TESTAMENT ISRAEL.

ransom see REDEMPTION.

raven see BIRDS.

reaping see AGRICULTURE.

reason God's ways with his people and the good news about Christ are reasonable and can be discussed by rational argument (1 Peter 3:15). However, reason must be combined with faith, since human reason alone is liable to lead people away from God (1 Corinthians 1:18–31).

Rebekah Isaac's wife and the mother of Jacob and Esau. Though she trusted God's guidance in travelling hundreds of miles to marry Isaac, she was primarily responsible for Jacob's deception of her husband and her son over Esau's birthright (Genesis 24:57–67; 27:5–17). See also ISAAC.

rebellion Sin is often described as rebellion against God (Leviticus 16:16; Isaiah 30:1), since people prefer their own way to God's. Even Israel rebelled regularly against God, and forfeited much blessing as a result (Hebrews 3:7–15). Though rebellion against human authorities is often mentioned, Christians were encouraged to submit rather than rebel out of respect for God's authority (1 Peter 2:13–17). See also SIN.

rebirth see NEW BIRTH.

rebuke see DISCIPLINE.

reconciliation A concept which expresses the heart of the gospel, focusing on the peace with God which Christ's death achieved. Reconciliation involves the complete restoration of a relationship previously damaged or broken. Human beings are by nature God's enemies since they do not want to do his will (Romans 5:10), but by removing sin which was the root cause of the problem, Christ's death on the cross made it possible for God to renew full fellowship with human beings. Though Jesus established a basis for this reconciliation, however, it had to be received through faith in order to be made effective in individual lives. For the apostles therefore, the gospel involved telling people that God had reconciled the world to himself but that they needed to be reconciled to God (2 Corinthians 5:17–21). The apostles also taught that those who had been reconciled with God must be reconciled with one another. Christ's death is therefore the motivation for ending disputes in the church and encouraging harmonious relationships between believers (Ephesians 2:14–22). See also ATONEMENT; PEACE.

red see COLOURS.

Red Sea The Israelites crossed from Egypt to Sinai through the (Hebrew) *yam suph*, literally 'sea of reeds' (Exodus 13:18). Though ancient tradition identifies this as the Red Sea, it may refer to one of the large lakes between Suez and the Mediterranean such as the Bitter Lakes area. See also EXODUS, THE. See map of WORLD OF THE BIBLE.

Redeemer see REDEMPTION.

redemption The buying back or deliverance of someone or something from some form of bondage or imprisonment. It often involved the payment of a ransom, as when releasing a person from the death penalty (Exodus 21:30) or, as commonly in the Graeco-Roman world, from slavery.

The concept was applied in different ways to God and Christ as the Redeemer above all others. Christ's death redeemed people from sin through the payment of a ransom (1 Peter 1:18–19) and delivered them from its power when they were enslaved by it (Romans 6:15–18). Jesus spoke of giving his life as a ransom in exchange for those who were in bondage to sin and death (Mark 10:45), while in many contexts redemption was also closely related to sacrifice (Exodus 13:15; Hebrews 9:15).

The Old Testament contains other distinctive uses of this concept, especially the demonstration of God's great power in redeeming Israel (Exodus 6:6). Also, the practice in Israelite law by which a close relative rescued another member of the family in deep trouble was applied to God (Leviticus 25:25; Isaiah 43:14).

Redemption therefore is a picture of salvation which focuses on liberation from sin and its effects. It provides encouragement for believers to live as free people rather than go back to their old sinful ways (Romans 6:19–23). See also SALVATION.

reed see PLANTS.

refining Impurities in crude metals, especially gold and silver, were removed in a furnace, though this was not always successful (Jeremiah 6:29–30). This process often illustrates the way in which God refines his people, often through suffering (Malachi 3:2–4; 1 Peter 1:6–7). See also METALS AND MINING.

refuge see CITIES OF REFUGE.

regeneration see NEW BIRTH.

Rehoboam, King of Judah (c. 922–915 BC) Solomon's son, in whose reign Israel separated into the southern kingdom of Judah and the northern kingdom of Israel. Though Rehoboam could have averted this division, his harsh attitude only accelerated the disaster (1 Kings 12:1–24).

rejection It was not uncommon for believers to experience rejection (Jeremiah 15:10; 2 Timothy 3:12). God was also frequently rejected, while Jesus on the cross felt that even God had rejected him (Matthew 27:46). God, however, promises never to abandon his people (Romans 8:35–9). See also PERSECUTION; SUFFERING.

rejoicing see JOY.

religion A set of beliefs and practices associated with belief in a particular God or group of gods. The Bible distinguishes outward forms of religion, whether pagan or Christian (James 1:26–7), from inner faith and repentance (Mark 7:1–13). Though appropriate forms of worship and behaviour are essential to biblical religion, as far as God is concerned the attitude of a person's heart always has the greater priority (1 Samuel 16:7).

remember, remembrance Though the activity of remembering is emphasized throughout the Bible, it is particularly associated with the Lord's Supper (1 Corinthians 11:24–5). Believers are encouraged to remember what they know about God as a means of strengthening their faith (Revelation 3:3). Though even believers can sometimes forget God, he always remembers his promises to his people and acts accordingly (Isaiah 49:14–16).

remnant An expression describing the minority of Israelites who continued to show genuine faith in God, in contrast to the majority whose interests were taken up with the outward forms of their religion. The idea was particularly common in times of persecution or of divine judgement, when despite Israel's difficulties, God promised to preserve the remnant of true believers (Isaiah 10:20–2; Romans 9:27).

renewal God's intention was to bring about the spiritual transformation or renewal of God's people and of the natural world. It was based on the new covenant (Jeremiah 31:31–4) through which individual believers experienced the gift of a new heart and continuing personal renewal (Ezekiel 36:26; Romans 12:2). It will culminate in the creation of a new heaven and a new earth (Revelation 21:1–5). See also REVIVAL.

repentance Alongside faith in Christ, repentance towards God was an essential requirement for people who wanted to know God for themselves (Mark 1:15; Acts 20:21). Repentance included two main elements. The first was a complete change of direction in life (Luke 15:17–20) and involved a turning away from a life of sin and a turning towards God (Acts 3:19). The second was a genuine sense of sorrow and remorse for sin (Luke 18:13).

Repentance is both a human activity and a gift of God. When it is associated with faith the former is emphasized, but the latter comes to the fore in the context of God's gift of forgiveness (Acts 5:31). The need for Christians to continue to repent of sin in their lives is also often mentioned (2 Corinthians 7:9–10; Revelation 2:5).

Apart from a few extreme cases (Hebrews 6:4–6), God was always ready to respond favourably to people who repented (Isaiah 55:6–7). This helps to explain the striking idea that God himself sometimes repents, which has nothing to do with moral failure on his part. God repents of sending judgement, and the fact that he delights to do so underlines the positive nature of this attribute (Exodus 32:14; Psalm 106:44–5). See also FAITH; FORGIVENESS.

Rephaim A valley south-west of Jerusalem, near Bethlehem, where David twice defeated the Philistines (2 Samuel 5:17–25). See also REPHAITES.

Rephaites One of the pre-Israelite groups in Palestine, who were noted for their great size (Deuteronomy 2:20–1; 2 Samuel 21:15–22).

representation see SUBSTITUTION AND REPRESENTATION.

respect An attitude of deference to God and to others which should characterize God's people. The 'fear of the Lord' is a typical expression involving trust in God as well as submission to him (Psalm 31:19). Respect for others was to be shown not only to those in authority such as parents, elders, masters and rulers (1 Peter 2:17), but to everyone, including women, the elderly and outsiders, since all are made in God's image (Genesis 9:5–6; Leviticus 19:32–4; 1 Peter 3:7).

responsibility The duty of all human beings to be accountable for their actions. Ultimately, they are responsible to God for the way they look after his world, including their attitude to other people and the natural world (Genesis 1:26). Everyone must give account to him at the final judgement (Hebrews 9:27), and special emphasis is placed on a person taking responsibility for their own sins and not those of others (Ezekiel 18:1–32).

rest A spiritual concept of rest is often mentioned alongside normal physical rest. It is characterized by peace with God and is therefore superior to the common human desire for tranquillity. It is available to all who trust in Christ (Matthew 11:28–30). One aspect of this is the concept of heaven as a place of eternal rest (Hebrews 4:9–10; Revelation 14:13). See also PEACE; SABBATH.

restitution see CRIME AND PUNISHMENT.

restoration see RENEWAL.

resurrection A concept that forms the centrepiece and climax of the biblical gospel. Jesus' resurrection (Luke 24:1–12; John 20:1–9) is understood as the turning-point of history which brought about the transformation of God's work on earth and established the kingdom of God with power.

The authenticity of the biblical account of the resurrection as an event in time and space has often been challenged. Despite this, the evidence for Jesus' resurrection appearances remains strong, especially the unexpected transformation in the disciples, the appearance to 500 people at once, the evidence of the grave clothes, and the failure of the authorities to produce a corpse. Also, the written testimony of five separate witnesses (the four Gospels and Paul) makes Jesus' resurrection one of the better attested events in ancient history.

The idea of resurrection is present in the Old Testament, as both an actual event and a future hope (1 Kings 17:17–24; Daniel 12:2). However, apart from isolated instances where a person was translated to heaven without dying (Genesis 5:24; 2 Kings 2:1–12), all resurrections before Christ, and those performed by Christ (John 11:38–44), were temporary resuscitations after which the person concerned died again.

Christ's resurrection, however, was fundamentally different from previous resurrections. As a vindication of Christ's sacrifice for sin (Romans 1:4), it was an eternal resurrection and resulted in the transformation of the human body. The resurrection of Christ also became the promise and the pattern for the bodily resurrection of believers, though the latter occurs in two stages. Believers have already been spiritually raised 'with Christ' (Ephesians 2:6) and share in Christ's risen life, but they will experience the full resurrection only at the last day (John 6:44). Unbelievers too will experience resurrection, but only for judgement (John 5:29). See also INTERMEDIATE STATE; LAST THINGS.

return from exile The Jews returned from exile in Babylon as a result of an edict of the Persian emperor Cyrus in 539 BC (Ezra 1:1–4). The return lasted over a century, however, and included Ezra's and Nehemiah's reforms in the second half of the fifth century BC.

Reuben Jacob's eldest son. He experienced mixed fortunes, defending his youngest brother Benjamin against the other brothers, but losing his special inheritance for sleeping with his father's concubine (Genesis 37:21–2; 49:3–4). See also REUBENITES.

Reubenites Apart from occasional acts of conquest (1 Chronicles 5:1–10), little is known of this tribe who lived east of the Dead Sea. See map of OLD TESTAMENT ISRAEL.

Reuel see JETHRO.

revelation An essential element of biblical faith is that human beings can know God only because he has made himself known to them and not because they can discover him by themselves. Though this is made clear throughout the Bible, it receives special emphasis in relation to the revelation of God in Jesus (John 1:14–18).

God's revelation of himself is usually divided into general and special revelation. General revelation deals with the ways in which everyone can know something about God. This includes the natural world, the human conscience, and people's general religious awareness (Romans 1:19–21; 2:14–15). Special revelation, however, makes people aware of God's particular nature and his particular plan of salvation.

God reveals himself in many ways, but especially through his self-revelation as a person, through his word, through his mighty deeds, and through the pattern of worship he established. As the agent of this revelation, the Holy Spirit points people to Christ as God in human form, to their own condition as sinners, and to Christ as Saviour (John 16:12–15). The Bible also reveals what will take place in the future, when God's plan of salvation will be completed by the renewal of all things under Christ's lordship (Revelation 4:1; 11:15).

Revelation, book of

Structure
    Prologue (1:1–20)
    Letters to seven churches (2:1–3:22)
    A vision of heaven (4:1–5:14)
    Seven seals (6:1–8:5)
    Seven trumpets (8:6–11:19)
    Conflict between the church and evil powers (12:1–14:20)
    Seven bowls (15:1–16:21)
    God's triumph (17:1–20:15)
    A new heaven and a new earth (21:1–22:5)
    Epilogue (22:6–21)

Famous passages
    Vision of Jesus risen from the dead (1:12–20)
    Letters to seven churches (2:1–3:22)
    'Worthy is the Lamb' (5:1–14)
    144,000 in heaven (7:1–8; 14:1–5)
    The fall of Babylon (18:1–24)
    Satan is bound for 1,000 years (20:1–10)
    A new heaven and a new earth (21:1–22:5)

A most extraordinary book which is difficult to categorize. It is probably best described as an apocalypse, which is a special type of literature dealing with the last things, but it has the form of a letter and also exhibits several features of prophecy. It has been understood in various ways, as a message for the first-century AD churches, as a description of events immediately preceding a millennium (cf. 20:2–7), as a prediction of what will happen at the end of the world, or as symbolizing how Christians can survive under persecution.

It was written to persecuted Christians in Asia Minor, probably during the period 90–5 AD when the Roman emperor Domitian demanded to be worshipped. The book's author was suffering in exile (1:9), and though he is called John, he cannot be certainly identified with the apostle John, because of differences with John's Gospel and Letters and the lack of any direct connection with the apostle or with Jesus' earthly life. The book's message depends on making a connection between the suffering of the early church and the attacks on Jesus and his church in every age. It encourages struggling believers that Jesus the Lamb of God now sits triumphantly on God's throne (chapter 5) and that Satan's final fall is certain (chapter 20).

One of the extraordinary features of Revelation is its breadth of vision and purpose. By making use of visions and symbolic language and by its extensive reference to the Old Testament, it brings together the seen world with the unseen and the beginning of God's work with its end. In particular, its portrayal of God's work of creation in Genesis being completed in the final vision of heaven (chapters 21–2) shows how the totality of human history finds its fulfilment in the kingdom of God.

Apocalyptic writings

Apocalyptic writings are a distinctive genre of literature that was common in Jewish writing from around 200 BC to AD 200. This was one of the most difficult periods in the nation's history, for although the people had returned from exile, the promises of the prophets had not been fulfilled and instead, the Jews were subject to occupation and religious persecution. Apocalyptic writings were written during these times of crisis to encourage readers to look beyond present hardships to God's kingdom, which would fulfil all their hopes.

Apocalyptic takes its name from the Greek word for 'revelation', and books written in this style were thought to reveal secrets the authors had received in visions from God. There are several common characteristics of apocalyptic writing. The authors

normally wrote under pseudonyms; that is, they claimed to be
writing as one of the great figures in Israel's history (Noah, Adam,
Moses, etc.). By claiming to be a figure from the past, they were
able to 'predict' events that were actually happening at the time of
writing. Apocalyptic writings tended to stress a dualism between
the world of human experience, which was perceived as evil, and
the spiritual world, where God was at work. There was an
emphasis on dreams and visions, in which it was common for
angels to act as messengers and guides. Apocalyptic writings often
picked up language from the Old Testament prophets using
symbolism and strange imagery. The coded language and the
identity of mythological beasts were probably well understood by
the first readers.

A recurring theme of apocalyptic writing was the cataclysmic
coming of God's kingdom, which would wipe away the present evil
world order. However, apocalyptic writings were not necessarily
predicting an agenda for the end of the world; rather, it could be
seen as offering a 'revelation' of what was really going on behind
the scenes of present events. Apocalyptic writings lifted the
curtain on that particular stage of world history to let readers see
what God was doing. In Jewish apocalyptic writings, the message
was the triumph of good over evil: despite appearances, God
remains in control.

Jewish apocalyptic literature is found mainly in the writings of
the inter-testamental period, the time between the close of the
Old Testament and the ministry of John the Baptist, and into the
first centuries AD. For example, chapters 3–14 of 2 Esdras, which
can be found in the Apocrypha, are written as the visions of Ezra
as he laments the destruction of Jerusalem during the exile.
1 Enoch was a very influential apocalyptic work, which is even
quoted in Jude 14–15 in the New Testament. The general theme
of both is the judgment of the wicked and the salvation of the
righteous.

In the Old Testament itself there are a number of passages in
the prophets that match the apocalyptic genre and may well have
been the inspiration for later apocalyptic works. Isaiah 24–27,
Ezekiel 38–39 and Zechariah 14 all deal with events related to the
destruction of wicked nations and the coming of God's reign,
pictured in symbolic and cataclysmic language. Daniel 7–12,
though, is the best example of apocalyptic literature in the Old
Testament. It records the visions of Daniel, in which he sees the
rise and fall of human kingdoms and, through hardship and

persecution, the ultimate deliverance of the faithful people of God and the establishment of God's universal kingdom.

Apocalyptic writing can also be found in the New Testament. The style is in use in passages such as Mark 13, where Jesus describes events that will precede and accompany the 'coming of the Son of Man'. Paul too made use of the language in his discussions about eschatological (ultimate or final) events in 1 Thessalonians 4:13–18, 2 Thessalonians 1:5–2:12 and 1 Corininthians 15:51–57. Our best example of apocalyptic writing in the NT is the Book of Revelation.

Revelation is traditionally understood to have been written by the apostle John while he was in exile on the island of Patmos. This makes it unlike other apocalyptic literature in that it is not pseudonymous. It was written as a letter to seven churches in Asia Minor (modern-day western Turkey) which were going through a period of persecution. Its purpose was to encourage them that behind the recurring cycle of evil, God was at work, bringing the world to his triumphant climax when all that stands against him and his people will be put away as he reigns forever. Despite attempts to interpret Revelation literally, the book does not follow a strict chronological order, and is more interested in revealing the often unseen realities of God's sovereignty in the world and Christ's lordship over the world than in dictating a programme of events for the end times.

Apocalyptic literature must be interpreted in the light of the context of the communities of faith in and for which it was written. Through persecution and hardship, God's people experienced a radical tension between their own life and history and what they understood life and history were supposed to be like in God's plan. The apocalyptic writings included in the Bible, just like the prophets, pointed to God's future action in the world as a guarantee that he is in control. Unlike the prophets, though, there is a strong interest in the language of mystery and a generally negative attitude towards the present world order, which is seen as evil, and which will be completely overturned and replaced by the coming universal kingdom. For these reasons, the apocalyptic must be set alongside other biblical emphases, such as the goodness of the created order and the open revelation of salvation in Christ.

revenge Believers are encouraged by Christ's example to practise non-retaliation and not engage in personal revenge (1 Peter 2:23).

They should leave issues of justice to the proper authorities, and trust God to punish all who do evil (Romans 12:19).

reverence see FEAR.

revival A period of special evidence of God's activity. Signs of revival include unusually large numbers of people turning to Christ, dramatic answers to prayer, miraculous healings, and renewed commitment to do God's will (John 4:29; Acts 4:31; 19:11–20). See also RENEWAL.

reward God's nature as one who is just and generous leads to two related but distinct understandings of reward. While God justly punishes the wicked and rewards those who obey him, he will also reward all believers with all the blessings of heaven (Colossians 3:23–5; 1 Peter 5:4).

Riblah Nebuchadnezzar's military base (modern Ribleh) on the River Orontes in Syria, from where he organized the capture of Jerusalem (2 Kings 25:6).

riches see WEALTH.

ridicule see SCORN.

righteousness This important biblical concept does not correspond precisely with any individual idea in modern Western thought, but brings together several different aspects of God's relationship with human beings. The Bible distinguishes between the righteousness of which God approves and those forms of righteousness of which he does not approve. The latter includes both self-righteousness and righteousness based on some form of merit or badge of identity (Judges 21:25; Romans 3:10).

Righteousness usually combines two main emphases, that of being faithful to an established relationship and of conforming to a recognized standard of law. In the context of God's covenant relationship with human beings, righteousness means that God and his people are to be faithful to each other according to the standard which God has revealed in his laws. On this basis, of course, only God can be righteous, and the Bible recognizes this as well as its corollary that that no human being is righteous (Romans 3:10). However, Christ makes available the gift of his righteousness to sinners, which anyone may receive by faith (Philippians 3:9).

God's righteousness is very similar to his salvation, since he always acts to deliver his people, and the two ideas are often combined (Isaiah 45:21). It also overlaps with the ideas of justification and sanctification, since the righteousness which believers receive gives them a new status of being in the right with God and leads them to live right lives in accordance with God's will. However, believers will only become fully righteous in heaven when they become like Christ (1 John 3:2). See also JUSTIFICATION; SALVATION; SANCTIFICATION.

ritual The formal aspects of Israelite worship, by which God's people learned how to have fellowship with a holy God. The Old Testment rituals, which involved such things as washings, blood sacrifices, special places, people and times, pointed to Christ but were also abolished by him (Hebrews 8:6).

Rivers

Rivers	
Abana (Damascus)	2 Kings 5:12
Euphrates (Mesopotamia)	Joshua 1:4
Gihon (Eden)	Genesis 2:13
Habor (Syria)	2 Kings 17:6
Jabbok (Transjordan)	Genesis 32:22
Jordan (Israel)	Matthew 3:6
Kebar (Babylon)	Ezekiel 1:1
Kishon (Northern Israel)	Judges 5:21
Nile (Egypt)	Exodus 7:18
Pharpar (Damascus)	2 Kings 5:12
River of the water of life	Revelation 22:1
Shihor (Egyptian border)	Joshua 13:3
Tigris (Mesopotamia)	Daniel 10:4

See MAP OF NEW TESTAMENT ISRAEL; OLD TESTAMENT ISRAEL; WORLD OF THE BIBLE.

roads see TRAVEL.

robbery see STEALING.

robe see CLOTHING.

rock Used for a variety of purposes, especially in building and in relation to burial places (Matthew 7:24–5; 27:59–60). More often, however, the word symbolizes strength, stability and shelter, especially when it occurs as a name for God (Psalm 18:2). See also GOD, NAMES OF.

rod Often occurs as a symbol of military power or of proper authority (Psalm 23:4; Isaiah 9:4).

Roman Empire The New Testament is set against the background of the Roman Empire, which had a direct bearing on the life of Jesus and the church. However, while the Roman peace encouraged the expansion of the gospel (Romans 15:19), Christians suffered increasingly at Roman hands (Revelation 1:9). See also CAESAR.

Romans, letter to the

> **Structure**
>
> The gospel is the power of God for salvation (1:1–17)
> The gospel involves receiving God's righteousness by faith (1:18–8:39)
> The gospel and Israel (9:1–11:36)
> Living the gospel (12:1–15:13)
> Paul's future plans and personal greetings (15:14–16:27)
>
> **Famous passages**
>
> God's wrath against human wickedness (1:18–32)
> Abraham justified by faith (4:1–25)
> Nothing can separate us from the love of God (8:28–39)
> God's plan for Israel (9:1–11:36)

The most important of Paul's letters, not only because of its length, but because it summarizes the essential teachings of the Christian gospel. The letter was written c. 55–7 AD to a church which Paul had never visited. Paul was concerned in his own life and theirs about total commitment to God (chapters 12–16). For the church in Rome, this meant offering themselves to God as living sacrifices (12:1–2), while Paul's aim was to preach the gospel wherever possible, especially where Christ was not known (15:14–29). Since within a few years both Paul and many Christians in Rome died in Nero's persecution, this teaching has a certain poignancy.

The heart of the letter is a carefully constructed argument about God's saving purposes for the human race (chapters 1–11). This gospel, which Paul describes as the power of God, is demonstrated in Christ's resurrection and in believers' lives (1:2–4, 16–17). Paul then develops his major theme about God's righteousness and the gospel (chapters 4–8). Although human beings without exception are under the threat of God's judgement, God puts them in a right relationship with himself through the righteous sacrifice of Jesus' death (3:21–6). God's righteousness works in several ways. It condemns all forms of sin, it keeps God's Old Testament promises, it characterizes Jesus' death, and it is a gift to all who believe in Jesus. To make the point that this is not a new idea, Paul uses Abraham as his chief example (chapter 4).

This righteousness can only be received by faith in Christ, not through human achievement, and shows itself in believers' lives as they oppose sin with the help of God's Spirit (chapters 4–8). God is also concerned to include Gentiles as well as Jews in his purposes, which raises the question of the role of Old Testament law (chapter 7). Paul attacks Israel's pride in the law, either because it encouraged legalism or because it had become a badge of Jewish privilege. Since the law is not a sufficient basis for knowing God, despite its continuing role for Christians, people can trust only the grace of God. The availability of this grace to everyone is ultimately a mystery, and the basic reason why God should be praised (chapters 9–11).

Romans has been extremely influential in Christian history, especially through the teaching of Augustine and Luther. The latter's emphasis on justification by faith was especially crucial in the fundamental changes which took place in the church during the Reformation.

New Testament Letters

As Christianity spread throughout the ancient world, one of the most pressing issues concerned the growth and development of the faith of young churches and their leaders. Missionaries such as Paul stayed in cities for short periods of time, gathering small groups of new believers together, before moving on to other areas. In the cultural, religious and philosophical melting-pot of society, the fledgling communities of disciples could easily be led astray. Paul and his companions were not the only people travelling around, and many of the new churches found themselves confronted with teachers who brought a different message. Other young churches were already encountering persecution for their faith. Where it was impossible for the missionary to return personally to deal with the issues, a letter was written, often by an amanuensis or scribe, and was sent to the church by a messenger who could report back. These letters followed the letter-writing conventions of the day, and generally had a similar structure: an opening section identifying both sender and recipient and giving greetings; a section of thanksgiving; the main body of the letter; and closing greetings. The content, though, was specifically determined by the message of the Christian faith and the circumstances of the churches to whom the letters were sent.

Considering the amount of travelling Paul did, it is not surprising that 13 of the 21 letters in the New Testament are attributed to him. The letters are difficult to date, not least because the chronology of Paul's own ministry is not fully recoverable from available evidence. However, they can be arranged into three roughly chronological groups: the 'travel letters' (1 and 2 Thessalonians, Galatians, 1 and 2 Corinthians, Romans), the 'prison letters' (Ephesians, Colossians, Philippians, Philemon), and the 'pastoral letters', written shortly before Paul's death (1 and 2 Timothy, Titus). Of these, Paul's authorship of Ephesians, Colossians and the pastoral letters is often disputed, though it is not conclusive that he did not write them. There are some recurring themes in Paul's letters, such as the 'in Christ' motif, reconciliation, and faith, hope and love as the basics of the Christian life, but in each letter Paul applies his mind to a different situation and so reveals the breadth of his thinking about the message of salvation.

Paul wrote 1 and 2 Thessalonians around AD 50 to the church he had founded in Thessalonica. These letters show Paul's pastoral concern for the faith and lifestyle of the new Christians, dealing particularly with misunderstandings regarding the return of Christ. In the letter to the Galatians, Paul is disturbed by the arrival of Jewish Christian teachers who tell the Galatians that they must follow the Jewish law as well as Christ. Paul responds by saying that freedom is achieved by the gospel. However, these false teachers proved to be a continuing problem for the early church. The issue in the church in Corinth, though, was not so much false teaching as internal division. 1 Corinthians tackles this issue and gives guidance on how the church as a whole should conduct its communal life. In his second letter to Corinth, Paul must answer accusations that had been made against him, doing so in a way that shows his intense concern for the Corinthians as well as his profound understanding of the gospel ministry. The final letter in this group, perhaps written around AD 57, was addressed to the church in Rome, which Paul had not yet visited. There are no obvious pastoral problems dealt with in this letter; rather, Paul intended to go to Rome in order to extend his missionary journeys further west, so he outlined the big picture of the gospel message – the faithfulness of God which is able to bring righteousness to both Jews and Gentiles.

The next group of letters was written while Paul was in prison in the early 60s, possibly in Rome, because of his missionary work. Ephesians, which may be a circular letter, is concerned to show that in the gospel, all people and things are reconciled to God and to each other, and that the church is the living illustration of this. Similar material is found in Colossians, though this letter is more personal and deals with false teaching in the church. Paul's letter to the Philippians is full of joy, as he reminds them of the privilege of belonging to Christ, even with the threat of persecution and false teaching on the horizon. Philemon is a personal letter from Paul which reveals his concern for Onesimus, a runaway slave who had become a believer.

Paul's final letters are again addressed to individuals, this time Timothy and Titus, who had leadership roles in the churches in Ephesus and Crete respectively. Paul writes in the mid- to late-60s, knowing that he soon may be executed for his faith. They are Paul's final warnings, encouragements and instructions to the churches he loved so much.

The remaining eight letters in the New Testament are known as 'General' or 'Catholic' letters. On the whole, they appear to reflect the issues of churches from a more Jewish than Gentile background. The anonymous work of Hebrews compares the Christian faith with the Jewish faith and shows how the person and work of Christ supersede the ideals of Judaism. James reads like Jewish wisdom literature, and contains much practical teaching. The apostle Peter writes firstly to encourage a church suffering for their faith (1 Peter), and then to warn against false teachers (2 Peter). The three short letters of John, which may have been written by the apostle in his old age, highlight the type of love which marks out true Christians. Jude deals again with the issue of false teaching in the church, a reminder that the first decades of the Christian faith were by no means easy.

Rome Christianity reached the capital of the Roman Empire before Paul's arrival (Acts 28:17–31), though it is not known how or when this happened. The church was probably large and organized around households (Romans 16:1–23). Paul was imprisoned and probably executed in the city. Rome under the symbol of Babylon persecuted the church, and much celebration greeted its ultimate downfall (Revelation 17:1–19:10). See also ROMANS, LETTER TO THE. See map of PAUL'S JOURNEYS; WORLD OF THE BIBLE.

roof see HOME.

room see HOME.

rope Often used symbolically, either of bondage to suffering and death (Psalm 18:4–5) or to the ties of love (Hosea 11:4).

Rose of Sharon see PLANTS.

ruby see JEWELS AND PRECIOUS STONES.

rue see HERBS AND SPICES.

ruler Refers to various kinds of officials, including religious leaders such as synagogue rulers (Mark 5:36) and political leaders such as city rulers and rulers of countries (1 Kings 1:35; 22:26). God is the ultimate ruler (1 Timothy 6:15) who has absolute authority over all human rulers (Isaiah 40:23).

rush, rushes see PLANTS.

Ruth A young Moabite widow who was one of the ancestors of David and Jesus (Ruth 4:17; Matthew 1:5). Ruth is an outstanding example of a non-Israelite who commits herself to the Lord and to Israel (Ruth 1:16). Her great kindness to her Israelite mother-in-law and respect for the Israelite law of levirate marriage illustrate the depth of her faith. See also RUTH, BOOK OF.

Ruth, book of

Structure

Naomi and Ruth return to Bethlehem (1:1–22)
Ruth and Boaz in the harvest-field (2:1–23)
Ruth and Boaz at the threshing-floor (3:1–18)
Ruth's marriage and son (4:1–17)
Genealogy of Perez (4:18–22)

A short story about a young Moabite widow, who came to Bethlehem with her widowed Israelite mother-in-law. Its overall theme shows how God works behind the scenes of human life, and reverses the bitter effects of his people's experiences. The book's purpose may be to illustrate God's providence in David's family history, to emphasize the importance of a welcoming attitude to outsiders, or simply to tell a story about divine and human love. Any or all of these would be sufficient motivation for including this unique literary gem in the Bible. Though the book is set in the judges period, its author and date remain unknown.

S

sabaoth see GOD, NAMES AND TITLES OF.

Sabbath A Hebrew word meaning 'rest'. The Old Testament laws required rest from ordinary work every seventh day and allowing the fields to lie fallow every seventh or sabbatical year (Exodus 23:10–12). By the first century AD, observing the Sabbath had become an important mark of being a Jew, though the original concept of enjoyment and restoration was submerged in tradition (Matthew 12:1–14). The Sabbath was less significant for the early church, which celebrated the first day of the week as the day of Jesus' resurrection rather than the Jewish Sabbath (Acts 20:7). See also REST.

sabbatical year see SABBATH.

sackcloth A coarse garment, often made from goats' hair, worn as a sign of mourning or repentance (Genesis 37:34; Matthew 11:21).

sacrament The word is not found in the Bible, but usually refers to the visible signs which Jesus commanded the church to observe, namely baptism and the Lord's Supper (Matthew 28:19; 1 Corinthians 11:23–6). These sacraments enabled believers to receive the spiritual blessings of God's covenant and to express their initial and continuing commitment to God's church. See also BAPTISM; LORD'S SUPPER.

sacrifice and offering The biblical pattern of worship required the offering of gifts to God on an altar. According to the laws of the covenant, various kinds of sacrifices were to be offered at a special place on set occasions by priests specially appointed for the task. This system of Old Testament sacrifices, however, was incomplete in itself, and its true significance was only fulfilled by Christ's death on the cross. Jesus' self-offering as the supreme, perfect sacrifice in effect made it obsolete (Hebrews 8:1–10:18). Jesus' death also changed the nature of worship for ever, since all believers now gained access to God's heavenly presence on the basis of what Jesus had done (Hebrews 10:19–25).

Sacrifice fulfilled the three main functions of praise, fellowship and atonement. These were all reflected in the Israelite system, but were completely transformed as a result of the cross. Jesus' achievement of permanent atonement and permanent fellowship with God meant that sacrifices need be offered no longer for these purposes. On the other hand, Jesus enabled all believers to offer their own sacrifices of praise (Hebrews 13:15–16). He also brought a new prominence to worship from the heart and established a new pattern of worship based on the offering of one's whole life to God (Romans 12:1–2). Each of these emphases was found already in the Old Testament, where the old sacrificial system was never intended to be a purely formal matter (Isaiah 1:10–17; Hosea 6:6). The supreme Old Testament sacrifice was the death of the Suffering Servant (Isaiah 52:13–53:12), and it was Jesus' fulfilment of this prophecy rather than any fundamentally new emphasis that brought about the transformation of sacrifice in the New Testament. See also BURNT OFFERING; GRAIN OFFERING; GUILT OFFERING; SIN OFFERING; WORSHIP.

Sadducees A Jewish party of the intertestamental and New Testament periods. They were a conservative group whose membership was drawn from priestly and well-to-do families. They accepted the authority only of the written Pentateuchal law, they rejected the ideas of the resurrection, angels and demons, and believed that people's experiences were the result of their own choices (Acts 5:17; 23:6–8). See also PHARISEES; ZEALOT.

sadness see SUFFERING.

saints A term meaning 'holy people' used in reference to the people of God. In the New Testament it is a synonym for 'Christians' (Romans 1:7).

Salem see JERUSALEM.

salt Found on the shores of the Dead Sea. Its use as a preservative made it a natural symbol for things that were permanent (Numbers 18:19; Matthew 5:13).

Salt Sea see DEAD SEA.

salvation The major theme of the Bible. It is presented in the form of a story that describes the outworking of God's eternal plan to deal with the problem of human sin. The story is set against the background of the history of God's people and reaches its climax in the person and work of Christ. The Old Testament part of the story shows that people are sinners by nature, and describes a series of covenants by which God sets people free and makes promises to them. His plan includes the promise of blessing for all nations through Abraham and the redemption of Israel from every form of bondage. God showed his saving power throughout Israel's history, but he also spoke about a Messianic figure who would save all people from the power, guilt, and penalty of sin. This role was fulfilled by Jesus, who will ultimately destroy all the devil's work, including suffering, pain, and death (1 John 3:8). Jesus will finally replace the present evil world with a new heaven and new earth over which he will reign for ever.

Alongside this grand story is an emphasis on the need for individual salvation. According to the New Testament, this salvation is a gift from God which anyone may receive by exercising faith in Christ and repentance for their sin (Acts 20:21). Through this salvation, people become part of a new creation in Christ (2 Corinthians 5:17), their sins are forgiven, they receive eternal life and become children of God. They also receive the Holy Spirit, who enables them to live a new life based on God's requirements and to spread the gospel to others (Acts 1:8; 2:38).

The basis of salvation is the person and work of Jesus. Though this is described in many ways, it centres on his roles as the Messiah or Christ who fulfilled the Old Testament and as the Lamb of God who died to take away the sin of the world (John 1:29). Jesus' resurrection vindicates his death and his victory is confirmed by his exaltation to God's throne. For this reason, the New Testament portrays Jesus as the only Saviour of human beings (Acts 4:12), and the early church regarded his salvation as a message for everyone, Gentiles as well as Jews (Acts 13:47).

Samaria The capital of the northern kingdom of Israel from the ninth century until its end in 722 BC, and the general name given to the surrounding area (Acts 8:5). Archaeology supports the Old Testament's testimony to the city's wealth (Amos 6:1–7). See map of NEW TESTAMENT ISRAEL; OLD TESTAMENT ISRAEL.

Samaritans A group who in the late Old Testament period separated from mainstream Judaism, with whom they maintained a relationship of mutual antagonism (John 4:9). The Samaritans had their own temple on Mount Gerizim near Shechem, and accepted only the first five books of the Bible. Some of them became Christians (Acts 8:25).

Samson One of the judges, who led Israel for twenty years (Judges 13–16). He often fought single-handedly against the Philistines, and destroyed 3,000 occupants of a Philistine temple at his death. Though he was dedicated to God as a Nazirite and received great strength from God, he seems to have accepted rather than challenged the low spiritual and moral standards of his day. See also DELILAH; NAZIRITE.

Samuel An important Old Testament prophet and the last of the judges. His chief role was to choose and anoint Israel's first two kings, Saul and David, though as one who brought God's word to Israel, he found himself in opposition to Saul as the latter increasingly acted independently of God. His early life was remarkable for two reasons. His mother Hannah prayed for a son after being barren for many years (1 Samuel 1:1–2:11), and he received his first prophecy while still a child (1 Samuel 3). See also SAMUEL, 1 AND 2.

Samuel, 1 and 2

Structure

Samuel's early years (1 Samuel 1:1–7:17)
Samuel and Saul (1 Samuel 8:1–15:35)
Saul and David (1 Samuel 16:1–31:13)
David becomes king over Israel (2 Samuel 1:1–8:18)
David's family troubles (2 Samuel 9:1–20:26)
Epilogue (2 Samuel 21:1–24:25)

Famous passages

The boy Samuel in the temple (1 Samuel 3:1–4:1)
Samuel anoints David as the future king (1 Samuel 16:1–13)
David and Goliath (1 Samuel 17:1–58)
Saul consults a medium (1 Samuel 28:3–25)
God's covenant with David (2 Samuel 7:1–17)
David and Bathsheba (2 Samuel 11:1–12:25)
The rape of Tamar (2 Samuel 13:1–22)
Absalom's rebellion (2 Samuel 15:1–37)

During the period covered by 1 and 2 Samuel, Israel was transformed from a scattered collection of tribes into an established monarchy. The key figures were Samuel himself and Israel's first two kings, Saul and David. Samuel reversed the chaotic situation of the judges period by giving a new importance to prophecy and by anointing Saul and David as kings (1 Samuel 1–16). Though Saul initially submitted to God's will, he showed little respect for the words of either God or Samuel. God therefore rejected him as king, and replaced him with 'a man after his [i.e. God's] own heart' (1 Samuel 13:14). The account of Saul's subsequent jealous persecution of David is often called 'The story of David's rise' (1 Samuel 16–31). David's reign occupies the whole of 2 Samuel, and reaches its climax in a covenant in which God promised that David's dynasty would last for ever (2 Samuel 7). The story of David's final years in the so-called 'Succession narrative' (2 Samuel 9–20, 1 Kings 1–2), however, is marked by rape, rebellion, and revenge. This is understood as God's punishment for David's adultery with Bathsheba and murder of her husband Uriah.

Kingship forms the main theme of the books, but there is an intricate interplay between God's kingship and the attitudes of Saul, David and the people towards Israel's monarchy. Although God chose Saul and David and confirmed the position of David's family, neither Saul nor David emerge with great credit. The crucial difference between them, however, was that while Saul stayed unrepentant, David repented of his sins (2 Samuel 12:13; 24:10), though it was God's unseen providence that really kept Israel's hope alive (2 Samuel 21:17).

The two books form an important historical source for early Israel and are an outstanding example of early narrative literature. They are especially notable for their candid criticisms of Israel's leaders. They have been incorporated into the Deuteronomic History, whose distinctive style is particularly evident in various speeches and prayers (e.g. 1 Samuel 12; 2 Samuel 7). The books are probably best described as prophetic history, since they are less concerned with recording mere events than with indicating what God had to say through prophets such as Samuel, Nathan and Gad.

Sanballat, Tobiah and Geshem Three officials who opposed Nehemiah in his attempt to rebuild Jerusalem's wall (Nehemiah 2:19). Sanballat was governor in Samaria, though the exact status of the other two is less certain. See also NEHEMIAH.

sanctification The setting apart of somebody or something to God. It has two main emphases among its various meanings in the New Testament, referring either to believers' status of being made fit for God's holy presence (1 Corinthians 6:9–11), or to the process by which believers' lives are morally and spiritually transformed through the Holy Spirit (1 Peter 1:2). It can also be used for setting someone or something apart for God's service (Matthew 23:17; John 17:17, 19), or for having a godly influence on someone (1 Corinthians 7:14). See also HOLINESS.

sanctuary see TABERNACLE; TEMPLE.

sandal see CLOTHING.

Sanhedrin The ruling council of the Jews in the New Testament period, before whom Jesus and some members of the early church were tried (Matthew 26:57–68; Acts 22:30–23:10). It enjoyed wide political and religious powers, though these were subject to Roman authority.

Sapphira see ANANIAS AND SAPPHIRA.

sapphire see JEWELS AND PRECIOUS STONES.

Sarah Abraham's wife and his half-sister, and the mother of Isaac. Her name, meaning 'princess', was changed from Sarai to emphasize her importance as the mother of God's promised child (Genesis 17:15–22). However, she (naturally!) found it incredible that she would bear a child at ninety years old (Genesis 18:10–15). See also ABRAHAM.

sardonyx see JEWELS AND PRECIOUS STONES.

Satan The name of the devil, though the word is actually a Hebrew term meaning 'the enemy' or 'the accuser' (Job 1:6). Most information about him occurs in the New Testament, and it is significant that it is the coming of Jesus that brings him out of the shadows. His various names, such as 'the ruler of the kingdom of the air' (Ephesians 2:2) or 'the prince of this world' (John 12:31), reveal him as a personal spirit who led unseen opposition to God in the spiritual and the earthly realms. His overall aim was to undermine the kingdom of God, whether by tempting people to disobey God's will or through occult activities (Matthew 12:22–8; 16:23). His freedom, however, was always subject to God's authority, and he was permitted to cause trouble only within strict limits. Jesus' death on the cross was the decisive moment of his defeat (John 12:31). As a result, the gospel had the power to turn people from Satan to God, and believers could successfully resist Satan's temptations (Acts 26:18; James 4:7). His defeat will be confirmed when Jesus returns, when Satan will be punished for ever and his work destroyed (Revelation 20:10).

satrap A Persian word for the governor of a province of the Persian empire (Esther 3:12; Daniel 6:1).

Saul, King (c. 1000 BC) The first king of Israel. He was a complex character who was initially chosen by God in response to the people's request for a king, but his reign increasingly fell apart. Because Saul preferred to pursue his own interests rather than trust God, God rejected him as his king while allowing him to remain in power (1 Samuel 15). He was publicly overshadowed by his son-in-law David, privately tormented by depression, and was finally killed in battle by the very Philistines God had chosen him to defeat. Saul's is one of the saddest stories in the Bible, illustrating the consequences of rejecting God's word.

Saviour see SALVATION.

saw see TOOLS.

scapegoat A live goat which symbolically carried away Israel's sins and impurities into the wilderness in the annual Day of Atonement ceremonies (Leviticus 16:20–2).

scarlet see COLOURS.

sceptre see ROD.

scorn An attitude commonly shown towards God and his servants (Numbers 14:11; Psalm 69:7). Jesus particularly experienced ridicule and scorn during his trial and on the cross, and his failure to retaliate is an example to believers (Matthew 27:27–31; 1 Peter 2:20–3).

scorpion see INSECTS AND ARACHNIDS.

Scribe A scholar of the Jewish law, sometimes called 'teacher of the law'. The scribes preserved and taught the law, especially in synagogues and the Sanhedrin (Mark 15:1). Jesus criticized them because they did not distinguish sufficiently between God's written word and oral tradition (Mark 7:5–13). See also PHARISEES.

Scripture, Scriptures 'Scripture' literally means 'a writing', but it refers in the Bible to God's authoritative written word, as in the common phrase 'it is written' (Matthew 4:4). The collection of the sixty-six books of the Bible is also sometimes known as the canon, though this latter term which means 'rule' was only used from the fourth century AD onwards. 'Scripture' or 'The Scriptures' usually means the Jewish Bible, that is the Christian Old Testament (2 Timothy 3:15–16), though by including Paul's letters among the Scriptures, the early church recognized that the latter had the same authority as the existing books of the Bible (2 Peter 3:16). See also BIBLE.

scroll see WRITING.

sea 1. In addition to the geographical seas listed in the accompanying chart, the sea is sometimes used symbolically, either representing the nations of the world (Daniel 7:2–3) or as a sea of glass referring to the radiant majesty surrounding God's throne (Revelation 4:6). 2. The Sea in the temple was a large bronze water tank used for washing (1 Kings 7:23). See MAP OF NEW TESTAMENT ISRAEL; OLD TESTAMENT ISRAEL; WORLD OF THE BIBLE.

Seas	
Adriatic Sea	Acts 27:27
Sea of the Arabah (= Dead Sea)	Deuteronomy 3:17
Eastern Sea (= Dead Sea)	Joel 2:20
Egyptian Sea (= Red Sea)	Isaiah 11:15
Sea of Galilee	Mark 1:16
Great Sea (= Mediterranean Sea)	Joshua 23:4

Sea of Jazer	Jeremiah 48:32
Sea of Kinnereth (= Sea of Galilee)	Numbers 34:11
Sea of the Philistines (= Mediterranean Sea)	Exodus 23:31
Red Sea	Exodus 15:22
Salt Sea (= Dead Sea)	Numbers 34:3
Sea of Tiberias (= Sea of Galilee)	John 21:1
Western Sea (= Mediterranean Sea)	Deuteronomy 11:24

seah see WEIGHTS AND MEASURES.

seal, sealing Cylinder-seals, stamp-seals and signet rings were widely used in the ancient world as a way of indicating a person's authenticity and ownership, especially in witnessing legal documents (Jeremiah 32:11–14). They were also used by people in authority as a mark of their official status (Esther 8:8). The New Testament mentions the sealing of people, whether by God or by Satan (2 Corinthians 1:21–2; Revelation 13:16–17). This is usually understood as a mark of ownership, but can also refer to the gift of the Holy Spirit as a guarantee of the fulfilment of all God's promises to believers (Ephesians 1:13–14).

seasons The main seasons in Palestine are the hot drought of summer from mid-June to mid-September and the rainy season from roughly late October to early April. Autumn and spring are more transitional. The seasons were closely associated with the agricultural year, with harvest taking place towards the end of summer (Proverbs 10:5), autumn being the time for ploughing and sowing and spring as the time of growth in the gentle spring rains (Song of Songs 2:11–13).

seed 1. Apart from the normal agricultural use of seeds, Jesus often mentioned seeds in his parables to illustrate patterns of growth in the kingdom of God (Mark 4:1–20, 30–2).
2. A term with Messianic associations, indicating a special descendant of Abraham and of David (Galatians 3:16–19).

seeking To seek God usually means to follow his will and worship him, especially in repentance or in looking for specific guidance (Jeremiah 29:13; Matthew 6:33). It refers less frequently to a person searching for God when they do not know him (Isaiah 55:6–9; Matthew 7:7–8).

Seer A prophet, especially one who receives messages from God through visions (1 Samuel 9:9). See also PROPHECY AND PROPHETS.

Seir The name of a mountain and the surrounding country, sometimes used as a synonym for Edom and the Edomites (Genesis 32:3). See also EDOM.

Selah A musical term of uncertain meaning, possibly indicating either a division in a song or a specific instruction to worshippers (Psalm 46:3, 7, 11).

self-control The ability to do God's will by controlling one's selfish desires and living a disciplined life. It is a distinctive feature of Christian character produced by the work of the Holy Spirit (Galatians 5:23). Through the Spirit, a person is able to resist temptation and overcome sin, and so enjoy God's blessing in every situation (Philippians 4:12–13).

self-denial A willingness to put one's own interests and ambitions aside for the sake of following Christ. Jesus required his disciples to follow the same pattern as himself so that they might gain true life (Matthew 16:24–6; Hebrews 12:3).

self-righteousness see RIGHTEOUSNESS.

Sennacherib A king of Assyria (705–681 BC) whose siege of Jerusalem in 701 BC was unsuccessful because God miraculously answered the prayer of King Hezekiah (2 Kings 18:13–19:37). Several basic details of the Bible's account are paralleled in Sennacherib's own version of the event.

Septuagint see MANUSCRIPTS.

Sermon on the Mount A collection of Jesus' teachings in Matthew 5–7 set in the context of a crowd gathered on a Galilean mountainside. It contains many essential elements of Jesus' teaching, especially about the way Christians ought to live. It includes the Beatitudes, a famous series of blessings for people who live according to the principles of the kingdom of God.

servant The expression 'servant of the Lord' is used particularly for someone who carries out God's will, especially the prophets (2 Kings 9:7). Isaiah refers both to Israel as God's servant (Isaiah 42:18–22) and to a Suffering Servant who would obey God's will perfectly and give his life as a sacrifice for sinners (Isaiah 52:13–53:12). Jesus' willingness to undertake this role is the supreme example of Christian service and a model for all believers (Philippians 2:1–11).

Seth Adam and Eve's third son. He was born after Abel's murder and was an ancestor of Noah (Genesis 5:3).

seven see NUMBERS, SIGNIFICANCE OF.

seven churches The churches in Asia Minor to whom the ascended Jesus sent seven letters via John, the author of Revelation (Revelation 1:19–3:22). See also REVELATION, BOOK OF.

sexuality God created human beings in his image as male and female. This meant that people's sexuality was a vital aspect of their relationship with God and with one another, and that it was a God-given aspect of what it meant to be a human person. Men and women were made to be complementary to each other, and marriage was for companionship as well as procreation (Genesis 2:18–25). A sexual relationship within the context of faithful love was something in which to delight (Song of Songs 4:1–15), though it was to be confined to marriage for the sake of everyone's happiness. Sexual activity outside marriage is strongly condemned, whether between people of the opposite sex or the same sex, especially when it was carried out for religious purposes (Amos 2:7). Faithfulness in sexual matters, however, was a mark of one's commitment to holy living (1 Corinthians 6:12–20). See also HOMOSEXUALITY; MAN AND WOMAN; SINGLENESS.

Shadrach, Meshach and Abednego Daniel's three friends who rose to high office in the Babylonian empire. God miraculously preserved them in a blazing furnace after they had refused to worship a golden statue (Daniel 2:49–3:30). See also DANIEL.

Shallum, King of Israel (c. 745 BC) See KINGS AND QUEENS OF ISRAEL.

shame May refer to feelings of guilt and humiliation after having done or thought something wrong (Romans 6:20–1), to the effects of misfortune or disaster, or to punishment that results from a sinful action, usually against God (Jeremiah 23:40). It is in this last sense that Jesus accepted the shame of crucifixion (Hebrews 12:2). Though feelings of shame can sometimes lead to repentance (Ezekiel 43:10), the consequences of being without shame are very serious (Jeremiah 6:15).

Shaphan Secretary of Judah under Josiah, who with his children, respected God's word (2 Kings 22:8–14; Jeremiah 36:10–25). His grandson, Gedaliah, was the first governor of Judah under the Babylonians (Jeremiah 40:11–12).

Sharon A coastal plain in northern Palestine, stretching for 80 kilometres north of Joppa. Its fertile soil was largely covered with forests in ancient times. The 'rose of Sharon' (Song of Songs 2:1) was distinctive to the region, but its identification remains uncertain. See map of OLD TESTAMENT ISRAEL.

Sheba An area in south-west Arabia, whose people, the Sabeans, traded spices and jewels. Its queen visited Solomon, perhaps on a trading mission (1 Kings 10:1–10).

Shebat see CALENDAR, JEWISH.

Shechem An important town in the hills of central Palestine, which later became the home of the Samaritans. It had close associations with Abraham and Jacob, and was also a significant centre for worship and covenant-making (Joshua 24; 1 Kings 12:1–19). See also SAMARITANS. See map of OLD TESTAMENT ISRAEL.

sheep and goats Flocks of sheep and goats were common, and since both animals were usually herded together, it was difficult to distinguish them at a distance (Matthew 25:32–3). They were kept for their meat and their wool, and were often used in sacrifice. Gideon used a sheep's fleece to discover God's guidance (Judges 6:36–40). Metaphorical uses are also frequent, and both Israel and the church are described as God's flock (Psalm 100:3; John 10:14–16).

shekel SEE MONEY; WEIGHTS AND MEASURES.

Shem, Ham and Japheth Noah's three sons who survived the flood with him and from whom the world was repopulated (Genesis 6:10; 9:18–19).

Sheol The Hebrew word for the world of the dead, though a minority view is that it refers only to the grave. All the dead went to Sheol where they lived a shadowy existence in darkness and silence. Some of the dead suffered judgement there (Ezekiel 32:21, 27), but God ruled in Sheol and was able to bring the dead back to life (Psalms 16:10; 139:8). See also HADES.

shepherd A hard and demanding occupation that often had a low social status. The shepherd was also a common model for leadership, though God was the only shepherd who truly cared for his flock (Psalm 23:1; John 10:11).

shewbread SEE BREAD.

shibboleth A word meaning 'a stream in flood'. Different pronunciations of the initial sound as 'sh' or 's' enabled Israelites west of the Jordan to identify and put to death those from the east who were trying to escape after a battle (Judges 12:5–6).

shield SEE ARMOUR AND WEAPONS.

Shihor, River SEE RIVERS.

Shiloh A place in the central hills of Palestine (modern Seilun) where the tabernacle was kept for most of the judges period (Judges 18:31). See map of OLD TESTAMENT ISRAEL.

Shimei A supporter of Saul's family to whom David showed mercy even though Shimei had supported Absalom's rebellion against David (2 Samuel 16:5–14; 19:18–23).

ships SEE BOATS AND SHIPS.

shovels SEE TABERNACLE.

shrines Places of worship, perhaps located in a house, by the roadside, or at a sanctuary. Shrines were associated with idol worship, sometimes involving ritual prostitution (2 Kings 23:7; Ezekiel 8:12).

Shunem, Shunammite A place (modern Sulam) near Jezreel, associated with two Shunnamite women who gave different kinds of assistance to David and Elisha (1 Kings 1:3; 2 Kings 4:8–37).

sickle see AGRICULTURE; TOOLS.

sickness see DISEASES AND ILLNESSES.

Sidon see TYRE AND SIDON.

siege see WAR.

sign Though a sign can refer to a specific feature which God fulfils (Isaiah 38:7–8), it is used most frequently in the phrase 'signs and wonders'. These were special acts of God, associated especially with the exodus, with the healing ministry of Jesus and the early church, and with the Second Coming. John's Gospel especially refers to Jesus' miracles as 'signs' (John 2:11), though Jesus also warned of the danger of trusting in signs as distinct from the God to whom they pointed (Matthew 16:1–4).

signet see SEAL, SEALING.

Sihon An Amorite king in Transjordan whom the Israelites defeated on their journey to the Promised Land (Numbers 21:21–31).

Silas Also known as Silvanus, Paul's colleague on some of his missionary journeys who was involved in sending some of Paul's letters (Acts 15:40–1; 1 Thessalonians 1:1; 1 Peter 5:12).

silver The most important metal next to gold, and frequently used as a currency. It was used for expensive transactions, such as buying land or providing a dowry (Genesis 23:15–16; 24:53). Though Solomon made silver plentiful, it was not mined in Palestine (1 Kings 10:27). See also GOLD.

Simeon 1. Jacob's second son, who attacked Shechem in revenge for his sister's rape and who was taken as a hostage for Benjamin in Egypt (Genesis 34; 42:24). See also SIMEONITES.
2. A devout old man who gave two prophecies about the baby Jesus, one of which is known as the Nunc Dimittis (Luke 2:29–35). See also NUNC DIMITTIS.

Simeonites A tribe in the far south of Palestine. They were partly absorbed into Judah, but maintained a separate identity during the monarchy (1 Chronicles 4:41–3; 12:24–5). See map of OLD TESTAMENT ISRAEL.

Simon Peter see PETER.

Simon the Zealot One of the twelve apostles (Matthew 10:4; Luke 6:15). The term Zealot probably indicates his previous Jewish nationalist tendencies. See also ZEALOT.

sin Any action, word or thought that is against God's will. Sin also describes the state of each human being before God, and is the biblical explanation of the basic flaw in human nature (Jeremiah 17:9).

Sin can be described in several ways, but it is basically about disobeying God's word. Though sin is often called injustice or lawlessness, it is more than just falling short of God's standards or failing to keep the Ten Commandments (Romans 3:23). It is rebellion against God himself, since human beings often deliberately reject God's word, especially by not believing the gospel of Jesus Christ. Sin therefore damages or destroys a person's relationship with God (John 3:18–19).

Though human beings were originally created without sin, it has become an inevitable and incurable element in human nature ever since the first disobedience in Eden (Genesis 3:1–7). It also results in the inevitable consequences of guilt and punishment. Guilt is the legal status of each individual before God, and is often accompanied by feelings of shame and by attempts to avoid or cover up the full significance of sin. The basic punishment for sin is death, though because of God's mercy and his desire for people to repent he rarely imposes this punishment immediately (Romans 6:23).

Since human beings cannot solve the problem of sin by themselves, the only solution lies in Jesus' death on behalf of all sinners (Isaiah 53:5–6). Jesus removes the power as well as the penalty of sin, giving to all believers a new nature as children of God and a new status of being right with God (Romans 8:1–4). The Holy Spirit also helps them overcome temptations to sin (Romans 8:9–14), though complete transformation of life must wait for heaven. See also FALL, THE; GUILT; REBELLION; SALVATION.

sin offering One of the offerings in the Israelite sacrificial system, also known as the purification offering. It cleansed people from unknowing sin and ritual impurity and, on the annual Day of Atonement, removed the effects of all sin from Israel (Leviticus 16:15–22). The purpose of the sin offering was fulfilled once and for all by Jesus' death (Hebrews 10:11–18).

Sinai 1. The mountain at which God made a covenant with Israel and gave them their laws through Moses (Exodus 24:16–18). The traditional site at Jebel Musa (Arabic for 'Moses' mountain') in the south of the Sinai peninsula is probably in the right area.

2. The Sinai peninsula, where the Israelites lived in the wilderness for forty years (Numbers 26:64). See map of WORLD OF THE BIBLE.

sincerity An important quality of the Christian life, since God expects a person's actions and words to come from the heart. It should be demonstrated in people's attitudes to God and in their love for one another (Romans 12:9; Hebrews 10:22).

singing see MUSIC AND MUSICAL INSTRUMENTS.

singleness Neither singleness or marriage is intrinsically better than the other, but some people are encouraged to stay single so that they can serve God better (Matthew 19:12; 1 Corinthians 7:7–8). Unmarried women and widows were normally supported within their extended family (1 Timothy 5:4).

Sisera A Canaanite general who was defeated by Deborah and Barak and killed by Jael, despite his superior military strength (Judges 4).

Sivan see CALENDAR, JEWISH.

skill The ability to carry out any task and to do it well is God's gift, though any skill can be improved by training (1 Chronicles 25:7). God also gives special skills for carrying out his purposes (Exodus 31:1–6; Romans 12:6–8).

Skull, Place of a see GOLGOTHA.

slander see MOUTH.

slave, slavery Slavery was a common feature of ancient society, but the Bible is more concerned with stimulating good attitudes in individuals than with undermining the system. The New Testament in particular encourages Christian masters and slaves to treat one another as brothers, since Christ makes no distinction between the slave and the free person (Galatians 3:28; Philemon 16).

sleep God's gift for the purposes of rest and avoiding anxiety (Psalm 127:2), though God sometimes sends a particularly deep sleep to carry out his will in individual lives (Genesis 2:21; Daniel 8:18). Sleep also occurs as a metaphor for death (1 Thessalonians 4:13) and for spiritual apathy (Romans 13:11).

sling see ARMOUR AND WEAPONS.

smelling Pleasing aromas are associated mainly with expressions of love (Song of Songs 4:16–5:1) and with sacrifices that are acceptable to God (Genesis 8:21; Ephesians 5:2). In contrast, the idea of displeasing someone can be expressed as giving off a bad smell (Exodus 5:21).

snake The only snakes that can be identified with any confidence are the adder (Job 20:16), cobra (Isaiah 11:8) and viper (Acts 28:3). Moses' model of a bronze snake on a pole through which the Israelites were healed from a plague is used to illustrate the positive healing effects of Jesus' cross (John 3:14–15). Snakes are also used symbolically, especially of Satan (Revelation 12:9).

snares see HUNTING.

snow see WEATHER.

Sodom and Gomorrah Two cities which are now probably buried under the southern part of the Dead Sea (Genesis 18:16–19:29). God destroyed them because of their extreme wickedness, violence and sexual perversion though some generations of Israelites did not behave any better (Isaiah 1:9–10; Matthew 10:14–15). See also PLAIN, CITIES OF THE.

soldier see ARMY.

Solomon, King (c. 961–922 BC) David's successor as king, during whose reign Israel enjoyed unparalleled prosperity and peace. His wealth was based largely on trade, and included the use of ocean-going ships, but his greatest achievement was his building activity. This took place in various cities, but was concentrated in Jerusalem with the temple as its centrepiece (1 Kings 5:1–9:28). However, Solomon changed Israel's character for ever by replacing the tribal system with a centralized civil service.

His taxation and conscription policies were unpopular, however, and he was also criticized for the pagan influence of his extensive harem. God therefore announced that Solomon's kingdom would be divided, an event which duly took place within months of his death (1 Kings 11:29–12:24).

Solomon's Porch see TEMPLE.

son see FAMILY.

Son of God A title for Jesus, conveying different aspects of the close relationship between Jesus and his Father. It particularly expresses Jesus' eternal fellowship with the Father (Mark 9:7), the association between Jesus' resurrection and his sonship (Romans 1:3), and the divinity of the human Jesus. Other aspects of Jesus' sonship include his conception by the Holy Spirit (Luke 1:35), his union with the Father (John 5:19–23), and the Father's giving of his Son to suffer and die (Romans 8:32). Accepting Jesus as Son of God and Messiah is a vital element of the biblical gospel (Matthew 16:16–17).

The plural form is used for angels (Job 1:6) and for believers who enjoy the privileges of being God's adopted children (Galatians 4:4–7).

Son of Man Jesus' preferred title for himself (Mark 2:10). The fact that it rarely appears outside the Gospels suggests it came primarily from Jesus rather than the early church. Jesus' adaptation of 'one like a son of man' (Daniel 7:13–14) shows the connection between the title and the ruler of the future kingdom of God, but it is primarily associated with Jesus' humiliation and humanity. Jesus preferred this title to Messiah to emphasize that he would establish God's kingdom through suffering and death. The Old Testament echoes of the phrase also suggest that Jesus was the ideal human being and represented the true Israel (Psalm 8:4).

Song of Deborah see DEBORAH.

Song of Songs

Structure

The Song is made up of speeches by a male and a female lover, interspersed with contributions by one or more choruses

Famous passages

Love in the banqueting house (2:3–13)

'Many waters cannot quench love' (8:6–7)

The title of this unique book means the best song, though it is really a collection of love poems. They express the joy of romantic love through an extensive use of metaphor and symbolic language, exploring the full range of human senses. It is possible to trace a plot which reaches its climax in the conviction that love is greater even than death (8:6–7). Jewish and Christian tradition have understood the poems as an allegory of God's love for his people and Christ's love for his church (cf. Ephesians 5:25–33), but a complementary approach celebrating both physical and spiritual love is equally valid. It is usually placed in the post-exilic period on linguistic grounds.

Song of the Three Holy Children, The see APOCRYPHA.

sonship see ADOPTION.

sorcery see OCCULT.

sorrow see SUFFERING.

soul The Bible understands the soul as the psychological, emotional and intellectual areas of a person's life rather than the Greek concept of something separate from the body. It also underlines a person's dependence on God. Though the soul is sometimes distinguished from the spirit (Hebrews 4:12), it is sometimes equated with a person's whole inner being (Psalm 103:2) or their existence after death (Revelation 6:9).

sovereignty of God see GOD, NATURE OF.

sowing see AGRICULTURE.

span see WEIGHTS AND MEASURES.

sparrow see BIRDS.

spear see ARMOUR AND WEAPONS.

speech see MOUTH.

spices see HERBS AND SPICES.

spider see INSECTS AND ARACHNIDS.

spinning and weaving Both were common domestic activities, though there are indications that weaving was also a specialist skill (Exodus 39:22; Isaiah 19:9). Spinning was usually women's work, though weaving was undertaken by people of either sex. Weavers' rods were also used as weapons (1 Samuel 17:7).

spirit The concept of spirit is closely associated with God, angelic beings and human beings, and may refer to their nature, the form in which they exist, or the kind of person they are. First, God (John 4:24) and angelic beings are by nature entirely spiritual, in contrast to human beings who have both a spiritual and a physical nature. God is Spirit, and his activity in the world is often called the work of the Holy Spirit or the Spirit of God. Angelic beings are divided into good and bad spirits. The former are normally called angels but are also known as ministering spirits (Hebrews 1:14), and the latter are known as evil or unclean spirits or demons. Human beings are partly spiritual because God breathed his Spirit into them (Genesis 2:7; Romans 8:2). The spirit of a person is sometimes distinguished from the body and the soul (1 Thessalonians 5:23), though more often it is thought of as fully integrated with the person's physical nature. The fact that human beings have a spirit and are spiritual by nature emphasizes that they may have a spiritual relationship with God.

Second, whereas both God and angelic beings normally take the form of spirit, human beings are distinct because they normally exist in physical form. However, only the angelic beings remain unchanged, with the one exception that evil spirits and demons will be destroyed at the last judgement. Human beings invariably change from a physical to a spiritual form of existence when they die (Hebrews 12:23), though this does not prevent believers having a new spiritual body at the resurrection (1 Corinthians 15:44). God, on the other hand, has not remained a purely spiritual being, but took on a human body in the incarnation of Jesus Christ (Philippians 2:6–7). As the Holy Spirit, he is also active in the created world and lives in believers' lives.

Third, reference to a person's spirit is often an indication of the quality of their life, especially their characteristics and attitudes (Numbers 14:24; Hosea 4:12). An individual's character or spirit is not predetermined, however, but may be developed through continued dependence on the Holy Spirit, whose purpose is to produce his own spiritual fruit in human lives (Galatians 5:22–3). See also ANGELS; HOLY SPIRIT; SOUL; SPIRITUALITY.

spiritual gifts see GIFTS, SPIRITUAL.

spiritual warfare see WAR.

spirituality The spiritual quality of life that believers enjoy in their relationship with God. A biblical approach to spirituality involves the whole person, but is based on an individual's spiritual relationship with God, especially through the activity of the Holy Spirit (Galatians 5:25). Sin constantly threatens this relationship, though believers sometimes have a deep longing to know God (Psalm 27:8). Biblical spirituality emphasizes prayer, meditation on God's word, love and service to others, holiness of life, the testing of faith and obedience to God's will, and results in greater spiritual maturity (Ephesians 4:14–19).

sport see GAMES AND SPORT.

spring see SEASONS.

springs see WELLS.

sprinkling An action symbolizing purification or cleansing through blood or water in sacrificial rituals (Leviticus 4:6). On the same pattern, believers are spiritually cleansed from sin by the sprinkled blood of Christ (Hebrews 10:22).

sprinkling bowls see TABERNACLE.

staff see ROD.

stars The ancient Israelites regarded the stars as God's creation, though most of their contemporaries either worshipped them or communicated with the unseen world through astrology. A scientific explanation of the star of Bethlehem remains elusive, but it could have been a comet, a supernova, or a planetary conjunction (Matthew 2:2). The only stars specifically named are the Bear, Orion and Pleiades (Job 9:9; 38:31–2; Amos 5:8).

state, responsibility to Though the nations of the world were generally opposed to God, Christians were encouraged to submit to the civil authorities as God's means of maintaining law and order. It was part of Christian witness to obey them, even when it was painful to do so (Romans 13:1–7; 1 Peter 2:13–17). The only exception involved preaching the gospel (Acts 4:18–20), but even then the early church was concerned with its own evangelism and not with political opposition to the authorities.

stealing Though this activity is consistently condemned, thieves could become Christians if they changed their ways (1 Corinthians 6:9–11). Some compensated their former victims, even when their former wrongdoing had official sanction (Luke 19:8).

Stephen A leading administrator in the Jerusalem church who became the first Christian martyr. His death was an important influence in Paul's conversion, and the persecution which followed his death led to the spread of the gospel throughout Palestine (Acts 6:8–8:4).

steward see OCCUPATIONS.

stewardship Material possessions and individual skills are gifts from God, for which people are accountable to God. Even the gospel is regarded in this way (1 Corinthians 4:1–2), and authentic Christian fellowship involves sharing one's possessions for God's sake (Acts 4:32–7).

stomach see BODY, HUMAN.

stone see METALS AND STONE.

stoning The usual method of capital punishment in ancient Israel. Executions usually took place outside a city, and the first stone was thrown by the prosecution witnesses (Acts 7:57–8). See also DEATH PENALTY.

stork see BIRDS.

storm see WEATHER.

stranger see FOREIGNER.

stubbornness An attitude, also described as being hard-hearted or stiff-necked, that characterized the Israelites in the wilderness and before the exile (Psalm 78:8; Jeremiah 5:23). God consistently punishes those who adopt such deep-seated resistance to doing his will (Romans 2:5).

stumbling-block An obstacle that is usually related to some aspect of unbelief. It may refer to an idol (Ezekiel 14:3–4), to the effect that Jesus has on unbelievers (1 Corinthians 1:23), and to ways in which believers can hinder others from doing God's will (Matthew 16:23).

submission The attitude that God expects of people in response to his loving authority. Jesus' willing submission to the Father provides the pattern for everyone else. God also expects believers to be submissive to one another (Ephesians 5:21), both within the context of loving family relationships and to those in authority such as the state or the owners of slaves (Colossians 3:18–22).

substitution and representation Two closely related terms which seek to explain the meaning of sacrifices offered to God on behalf of sinners, especially in relation to Jesus' death. If emphasis is placed on Jesus dying as a representative, his work on the cross is understood as being for sinners who then receive all the benefits of his death and resurrection (2 Corinthians 5:14–15). The idea of substitution, however, focuses more narrowly on passages which speak of Christ dying in the place of others. This is expressed through Christ giving himself as a ransom to set sinners free (Mark 10:45) and as a sinless servant who took on himself the punishment due to others (Isaiah 53:4–6). See also ATONEMENT.

success While some believers did achieve traditional forms of success such as prosperity and power, especially in the Old

Testament, these were not guaranteed since they were no more than by-products of faith (Job 1:3). Faithfulness to God, whatever the circumstances, was a higher priority. This always brought God's blessing, which was of greater worth than other more temporary achievements (Ephesians 1:3–10).

Succoth 1. The first place the Israelites reached on their journey out of Egypt (Exodus 12:37).

2. A site east of the Jordan, probably modern Tell Deir-Allah, visited by Jacob (Genesis 33:17).

suffering Like everyone else, God's people experienced their full share of suffering. Though this often belonged to the common experiences of life, the Bible emphasizes that suffering did not occur outside God's authority and was ultimately the consequence of human disobedience (Genesis 3:16–19). The book of Job as well as the teaching of Jesus demonstrate that there is no inevitable connection between people's suffering and their sins. Indeed, God's servants regularly suffered opposition and persecution for their faith though their suffering was always regarded as a temporary rather than a permanent experience (Revelation 7:13–17). God was directly involved in human suffering. People's sins brought him pain and grief (Genesis 6:6), and he participated fully in the cost of Jesus' redeeming work at the cross (Acts 2:23–6).

suffering servant see SERVANT.

sulphur Traditionally translated 'brimstone', Middle English for 'burn(ing)-stone', it occurred in volcanic regions. It was usually a symbol for God's anger (Genesis 19:24).

summer see SEASONS.

sun Its great light made it an object either for admiring God's creative power (Psalm 19:4–6) or for worship (Ezekiel 8:16–17). It was a natural symbol for justice and righteousness, sometimes representing God himself (Malachi 4:2), though God's light was greater and more enduring (Revelation 22:5). See also MOON.

superstition see OCCULT.

supper see LORD'S SUPPER; MEALS.

Susa The winter residence of the Persian kings and the chief city of ancient Elam, now south-west Iran (Nehemiah 1:1; Esther 1:2). See map of WORLD OF THE BIBLE.

Susanna, History of see APOCRYPHA.

swallow see BIRDS.

swearing see OATH.

swine see PIGS.

sword see ARMOUR AND WEAPONS.

sycomore-fig see FIG; TREES AND BUSHES.

symbols Symbolism is very common in the Bible, as an ordinary property of language and to represent God's person and activity. Special symbols of God's presence included the Tabernacle and Temple and the Lord's Supper (Ezekiel 43:1–7; Matthew 26:26–9), while symbolic actions such as healing miracles represented and demonstrated God's power. Establishing a covenant with God also involved rich symbolism, through sacrifice, circumcision and baptism (Genesis 17:10–14; Romans 6:3–4).

synagogue A word that means 'assembly, gathering together', usually referring to local meeting-places of the Jews. The synagogue developed some time after the destruction of the Temple (587 BC) as a means of maintaining Jewish life. Its main activities were worship, studying the biblical law and administration. Christian faith also began in the synagogue, but the church soon found itself in sharp conflict with the synagogue authorities and often had to distance itself from this particular expression of Judaism (Luke 4:16–30; Acts 13:14–15, 42–8).

Syria, Syrians The geographical area north of Palestine. It appears in the New Testament as the name of a Roman province (Luke 2:2), but is referred to more often in the Bible as the land of the Arameans (1 Kings 22:1). See also ARAM. See map of PAUL'S JOURNEYS.

t

Tabernacle The portable tent in which God was worshipped from Moses' time until Solomon's (Exodus 25–7). It was also called the Tent of Meeting or the Tent of the Testimony. Originally made for use in the wilderness as the Israelites travelled from place to place, it also served as Israel's main place of worship in the Promised Land. Even there, it seems to have moved from one site to another, and was used finally at Gibeon before the temple in Jerusalem replaced it (2 Chronicles 1:5).

The Tabernacle's layout reflected its role as God's dwelling-place on earth (Exodus 25:8). It was surrounded by a courtyard where the people gathered, and the tent was divided into two parts by a curtain. The main section was called the Holy Place, and the innermost area was the Most Holy Place (the Holy of Holies). The latter was where God would appear annually in a cloud of glory on the Day of Atonement and where the high priest was allowed to enter only on that day.

The Tabernacle furniture included the washing basin and the bronze altar of burnt offering in the courtyard, the golden incense altar, the golden lampstand and the table for the bread of God's presence in the Holy Place, and the ark of the covenant and the cherubim in the Most Holy Place. Each of these represented different aspects of God's presence and of the covenant he had made with Israel. The Tabernacle was also equipped with various items for offering the sacrifices and sprinkling the blood of the sacrificial animals, such as sprinkling bowls, dishes, forks and shovels. Censers were also used for offering incense or carrying burning coals.

The New Testament calls the Tabernacle a 'copy and shadow' of things in heaven, that is, it foreshadowed the pattern of worship which was fulfilled by Christ (Hebrews 8:5; 9:1–10). Through the sacrifice of himself on the cross, Christ entered God's presence in the Most Holy Place in heaven (Hebrews 8:1–2; 9:11–12) and established a new covenant with every believer in Christ. See also ARK OF THE COVENANT; CHERUB; TEMPLE.

Tabernacles, Feast of The Jews' harvest festival, and possibly also a New Year festival before the exile. It was usually known as Tabernacles or Booths after the temporary shelters which were erected for the week (Leviticus 23:33–44), but was also called Ingathering (Exodus 23:16). Jesus alluded to a practice of pouring water at this feast in his promise about the Spirit (John 7:37–9).

tablets see WRITING.

Tabor, Mount A mountain in the Plain of Esdraelon in northern Israel. It was near the site of the battle of Megiddo (Judges 4–5), and is the traditional mountain of Jesus' transfiguration (Matthew 17:1). See map of NEW TESTAMENT ISRAEL; OLD TESTAMENT ISRAEL.

talent see WEIGHTS AND MEASURES.

Tamar 1. The mother of the twins Perez and Zerah by her father-in-law Judah (Genesis 38) and an ancestor of David and Jesus (Matthew 1:3). 2. David's daughter who was raped by her half-brother Amnon (2 Samuel 13:1–22).

tamarisk see TREES AND BUSHES.

tambourine see MUSIC AND MUSICAL INSTRUMENTS.

Tammuz see CALENDAR, JEWISH.

tanner see OCCUPATIONS.

Tarshish Usually identified with Tartessus in Spain, but could have been in East Africa or Turkey. To most Israelites, it was simply a far-off place reached by 'ships of Tarshish', that is ocean-going ships (Ezekiel 27:25).

Tarsus Paul's home city near the southern coast of ancient Cilicia (modern Turkey). It was an important commercial centre which enjoyed certain privileges under the Romans (Acts 21:39). See also PAUL, LIFE OF.

tassel see PRIEST.

tax collector A person employed to collect taxes from the local population on behalf of the Romans. They were extremely unpopular with Jews, partly because of the tendency to corruption and partly because they had to work closely with the Romans (Luke 19:1–8). They were often associated with sinners (Matthew 9:10–11). See also MATTHEW; ZACCHAEUS.

taxes In addition to the tax and tithes required for the upkeep of the temple (Nehemiah 10:32, 37), all civil authorities imposed taxes. They were introduced in Israel by the monarchy, though exemptions were common for both religious and personal reasons (1 Samuel 17:25;

Ezra 7:24). The Persians and the Romans were well known for their taxation systems. The Jews were sharply divided about paying taxes to the Romans, but the New Testament clearly indicates that payment of taxes is a Christian duty (Matthew 22:17–21; Romans 13:6–7). See also TITHE; TRIBUTE.

teacher see EDUCATION; RABBI.

teacher of the law see SCRIBE.

teaching see EDUCATION; FALSE PROPHETS/TEACHERS; PREACHING.

Tebeth see CALENDAR, JEWISH.

teeth see MOUTH.

Tekoa A village 10 kilometres south of Bethlehem. It defended the main part of Judah, and was also Amos' home town (2 Chronicles 11:6; Amos 1:1). See map of OLD TESTAMENT ISRAEL.

Teman A major Edomite city, possibly modern Tawilan, and the home of Job's friend Eliphaz (Amos 1:12; Job 2:11).

temperance see SELF-CONTROL.

tempest see WEATHER.

temple Three successive temples were built in Jerusalem for worshipping the Lord. Solomon built the first one, but it had to be replaced after being destroyed by the Babylonians in 587 BC. The temple of the New Testament period was built by Herod the Great but not completed until 64 AD, just before the Romans destroyed it in 70 AD. Temples also existed in Israel for the worship of other deities such as Baal (2 Kings 10:23), and archaeologists have discovered temples of uncertain use at places such as Arad or Hazor.

The Jerusalem temple was built on the same pattern as its predecessor the Tabernacle, though the temple was larger and grander in style. It continued the Tabernacle's role as the special place of God's presence on earth, though the temple was directly associated with God's covenant promises to David (1 Kings 8:14–21). It housed the ark of the covenant until the latter was destroyed, probably by the Babylonians, as well as the bread of God's presence and the golden lampstand symbolizing God's light. A distinctive feature of the temple were the two free-standing pillars Jakin and Boaz at the front, though they had no obvious religious significance (2 Chronicles 3:17).

Jesus taught that the temple's true purpose had become obscured, and as a result the New Testament speaks of a transformation of the whole understanding of the temple. Though Jesus worshipped and taught in the Jerusalem temple, he predicted its destruction, because it had become 'a den of robbers' rather than 'a house of prayer'

(Matthew 21:12–13). The death of Jesus, symbolized by the tearing of the temple veil, led directly to the new understanding of the temple (Matthew 27:51). From now on it would exist in two forms, one on earth and the other in heaven. The earthly temple took the form of a living body, which was variously understood as Jesus' resurrection body (John 2:19–21), the church as the body of Christ (1 Corinthians 3:16) and believers' physical bodies (1 Corinthians 6:19). The heavenly temple was the reality of which the Tabernacle and temple were merely copies (Hebrews 9:24). The existence of temples on earth and in heaven meant that God could live freely among his people instead of being restricted to a building and that his people could have direct access to him. In the new Jerusalem, identifying the heavenly temple with God and his Son indicated that all restrictions to God's presence among his people would ultimately be removed (Revelation 21:22). See also TABERNACLE.

temptation Any suggestion that a person should not obey God's will. The experience was common to every human being, but was something of which Christians became particularly aware. Temptation could come from a person's own internal desires or from the external influence of the devil, and was the beginning of a process that could lead to sin (James 1:14–15). A sharp distinction must be made between temptation and sin, however, since Jesus never gave in to sin even though he was frequently tempted (Hebrews 4:15). Temptation can be successfully resisted by trusting God's word and by submitting to God (Matthew 4:1–11; 1 Peter 5:8–9). See also TESTING.

Ten Commandments A series of ten instructions which God inscribed on two stone tablets at Mount Sinai. They are usually called in the Bible the Ten Words, that is, the Decalogue. The first four commandments deal with God's relationship with his people and the last six with relationships between human beings (Exodus 20:1–17; Deuteronomy 5:6–21). They sum up Old Testament law, but Jesus emphasized in the Sermon on the Mount that keeping the Ten Commandments was a matter of motive as well as action (Matthew 5:21–30). See also LAW.

Tent of Meeting A common alternative name for the Tabernacle, though the phrase also referred to a small tent outside the Israelite camp in the wilderness where Moses used to meet with God (Exodus 33:7–11). As a description of the Tabernacle, it emphasized its role as the place where God met with his people (Exodus 29:44–6). See also TABERNACLE.

tentmaker see OCCUPATIONS.

Terah Abraham's father, who travelled with his son from Ur in Mesopotamia to the Promised Land but died in Haran (Genesis 11:24–32).

Teraphim Idols that were usually in the form of small household gods (Genesis 31:34), though they could be the size of a human being (1 Samuel 19:13–16). They were known throughout the Old Testament period, and were especially associated with divination and occult practices (2 Kings 23:24; Ezekiel 21:21). See also GODS; IDOLATRY.

terebinth see TREES AND BUSHES.

testament see COVENANT.

Testimony, Tent of the see TABERNACLE.

testing Refers either to God's testing of his people or to the testing of God. God tests his people in order to strengthen their faith (Genesis 22:1–14). This is to be distinguished from temptation, where the intention is to draw a person away from God. When people test God, they may do so either to discover his will (Judges 6:36–40) or as an alternative to trusting his promises (Exodus 17:1–7).

tetrarch A regional ruler in the Roman Empire. It refers in the New Testament mainly to two of Herod the Great's sons, Herod Antipas and Philip, who ruled parts of northern Palestine (Luke 3:1, 19).

text and versions see MANUSCRIPTS.

Thaddaeus One of the twelve apostles (Matthew 10:3), probably the same as Judas son of James (Luke 6:16).

thank-offering An important type of sacrificial offering. It could be freely offered to God by individuals or communities in response for a particular act of God or answer to prayer (Psalms 50:23; 107:22).

thanksgiving Since biblical worship was a response to God's loving actions, it took on the nature of thanksgiving. The practice of giving thanks to God therefore commonly occurs in both Old and New Testament worship. It was often expressed through music and prayer (Psalm 100:4; Philippians 1:3), and was sometimes accompanied by a specific thank-offering (2 Chronicles 29:31).

theft see STEALING.

theocracy A form of government in which God is recognized as having ultimate authority. Though the term is sometimes restricted to the organization of ancient Israel before the monarchy (Exodus 19:5–6), it is applicable to various patterns of government in Israel and the church in which the leaders express their conscious dependence on God (1 Kings 3:9; Acts 15:28).

theophany A direct revelation of God, often accompanied by specific recognized signs of God's presence such as fire, lightning, smoke and a cloud of glory. The awe-inspiring theophany at Mount Sinai was often recalled as having special significance (Exodus 19:16–19; Habakkuk 3:3–6), but God also made himself known to individuals (Isaiah 6:1–7) and in human form (Joshua 5:13–15).

Thessalonians, 1 and 2

Structure

1 Thessalonians
Thanks for the Thessalonian church (1:1–10)
Paul's relationship with the Thessalonian church (2:1–3:13)
Instructions for Christian living (4:1–5:28)

2 Thessalonians
Teaching on Christ's Second Coming (1:1–2:12)
Living by Christian teaching (2:13–3:18)

Famous passages
The coming of the day of the Lord (1 Thessalonians 4:13–5:11)
The man of lawlessness (2 Thessalonians 2:1–12)

With the possible exception of Galatians, 1 Thessalonians is probably Paul's earliest letter. It was written from either Athens or Corinth in about 51 AD on the missionary journey when the church in Thessalonica was founded. 2 Thessalonians was probably written soon afterwards, though the chronological order of the two letters is not absolutely certain and Paul's authorship of 2 Thessalonians is sometimes questioned.

Both letters deal with similar issues. Paul's thanks to God for the Thessalonians' faith and love exudes a sense of excitement about what God had done in a few short years (1 Thessalonians 1:1–10; 2:13; 2 Thessalonians 1:3–4). They were a model church (1 Thessalonians 1:7), though in need of further teaching. A special problem clearly existed about their understanding of Christ's Second Coming, so Paul instructs them at length about what will happen to believers (1 Thessalonians 4:13–5:5) and to unbelievers (2 Thessalonians 1:6–10). Those church members who had actually given up working are advised to adopt a more mature and constructive attitude. Overall, Paul shows a pastoral concern to disciple the young believers, encouraging them to keep to the teaching he had already given them (2 Thessalonians 2:15; 3:6).

Thessalonica An important port and the chief city of Macedonia in northern Greece, located on the Egnatian Way linking Asia Minor with Italy. Paul founded the church, which included Jews as well as many Greeks who had turned to Christ from idol-worship (Acts 17:4;

1 Thessalonians 1:9). Paul and his co-workers enjoyed good relationships with the Christians there (1 Thessalonians 2:17–20; Acts 20:4). See also THESSALONIANS, 1 AND 2. See map of PAUL'S JOURNEYS.

Thirty, the A special group of David's most trusted soldiers similar to the Three, though their number was not fixed literally at thirty (2 Samuel 23:24–39).

thistles see THORNS.

Thomas One of the twelve apostles, known as Didymus or 'the twin'. Despite Thomas' pessimistic tendencies (John 11:16; 20:24–5), Jesus responded positively to his doubts about the resurrection. Thomas' subsequent declaration that Jesus was Lord and God is one of the most succinct New Testament statements concerning Jesus' identity.

thorns Despite frequent references to the various thorn bushes and thistles that grew in the dry Palestinian soil, it is difficult to identify specific species, including the plant from which Jesus' crown of thorns was made (Matthew 27:29). Thorns and thistles also often have a symbolic meaning, especially in relation to fruitless activity and to God's judgement (Genesis 3:18; Isaiah 5:6).

thousand years see MILLENNIUM.

three see NUMBERS, SIGNIFICANCE OF.

Three Holy Children, Song of the see APOCRYPHA.

threshing-floor see AGRICULTURE.

throne A throne represented a monarch's authority to rule and to exercise judgement (Matthew 25:31). God's throne was both in heaven, where Jesus sits with his Father after his ascension (Revelation 22:1), and on earth, where it was represented by the temple (Ezekiel 43:7) and by the reigning king (1 Chronicles 29:23). Jesus Christ gives his people the privilege of sitting with him on his throne in heaven (Revelation 3:21).

Thummim see URIM AND THUMMIM.

thunder see WEATHER.

Thyatira A city in western Asia Minor, modern Akhisar in western Turkey. It was the site of a church (Revelation 2:18–28) and the home of Lydia (Acts 16:14).

Tiberias, Sea of see GALILEE, SEA OF.

Tiberius see CAESAR.

Tigris see RIVERS.

time Two aspects of time are emphasized in the Bible. One is its regularity, which was measured by the sun and the moon and was divided into day and night, weeks, months and years. The beginning of all these periods of time was marked by specific occasions of worship (2 Chronicles 8:13). Time was usually measured in hours

from sunrise (Matthew 20:3). The other emphasis is that of appointed
or significant time, especially in relation to God's activities
(Galatians 4:4; Titus 1:3). Since the time for responding to God is
brief, people are encouraged to make the most of whatever
opportunity God gives them (Isaiah 55:6; Ephesians 5:15–16).

timidity see FEAR.

Timothy A younger colleague of Paul, to whom Timothy was both a
son (Philippians 2:22) and a brother (1 Thessalonians 3:2). Timothy
entered Christian ministry as a result of a prophecy, and became
Paul's representative as well as his assistant (Romans 16:21;
Philippians 2:19–23). Despite a rather self-effacing personality,
Timothy led the church at Ephesus (1 Timothy 1:3). He was also
imprisoned for his faith (Hebrews 13:23), and eventually succeeded
Paul. See also TIMOTHY, LETTERS TO.

Timothy, letters to

Structure

1 Timothy
 Warning against false teachers (1:1–20)
 Instruction about church worship and leadership (2:1–3:16)
 Instructions to Timothy as church leader (4:1–6:21)

2 Timothy
 Paul's personal word to Timothy (1:1–2:13)
 God's word and false teaching (2:14–4:5)
 Paul's personal circumstances (4:6–22)

Famous passages
 Paul as the worst of sinners (1 Timothy 1:15)
 Role of women in the church (1 Timothy 2:9–15)
 'The love of money is a root of all kinds of evil' (1 Timothy 6:10)
 'I have fought the good fight' (2 Timothy 4:7)

Personal letters written to Timothy, whom Paul had left in charge of
the church at Ephesus (1 Timothy 1:3). 1 Timothy is mainly concerned
with guidance about church life, especially Christian leadership. It
emphasizes the personal qualities rather than the roles of church
leaders who are called overseers or bishops and deacons, though these
terms probably mean something rather different from their modern
associations. Both letters deal with problems caused by certain false
teachers who taught a mixture of Jewish and early gnostic ideas.
Timothy is advised not to get too involved in their controversies but
to rely on Scripture as the authority for Christian life and learning.

In contrast, church issues hardly figure in 2 Timothy, which is almost entirely concerned with Paul's anticipation of his own death. Paul remains confident in God and is more concerned that Timothy is not discouraged, though Paul does ask for some personal comforts and the presence of Christian friends such as Mark and Luke. These personal touches lend support to the traditional view that these letters were written between Paul's two imprisonments in Rome in the mid-6os, rather than there being a second-century development of Pauline thought.

tin SEE METALS AND MINING.

Tirzah The first capital of the northern kingdom of Israel (1 Kings 16:6). The site of Tell el-Far'ah on the west side of the Jordan valley shows continuous occupation from before 3000 to about 700 BC. See map of OLD TESTAMENT ISRAEL.

Tishri SEE CALENDAR, JEWISH.

tithes, tithing A tithe is a 10 per cent tax or levy on crops and herds, required from every Israelite family for the ministry of the Levites and priests and for the upkeep of the central sanctuary (Numbers 18:21–32). The New Testament shows it is possible to concentrate on the details of tithing and neglect more important issues, but suggests that the underlying principle remained relevant for Christians (Matthew 23:23).

Titus A 'partner and fellow-worker' of Paul (2 Corinthians 8:23). He probably travelled with Paul on several of his journeys, but is best known as Paul's representative to Corinth (2 Corinthians 7:14–15; 8:16–23) and as the leader of the churches in Crete (Titus 1:5). See also TITUS, LETTER TO.

Titus, letter to

Structure

Titus as church leader and teacher (1:1–2:15)

Encouraging Christians to do what is good (3:1–15)

A letter to Paul's colleague Titus, whom Paul had left in charge of the churches in Crete. It was probably written about the same time as 1 Timothy, before Paul's final imprisonment. Titus was instructed to complete the church planting work that Paul had recently started in Crete, though this is not mentioned in Acts. Titus was to appoint leaders in the churches in each town and to teach various groups in the church about their responsibilities. Paul also encouraged the believers to do whatever is good as the guiding principle of Christian living in a hostile society (3:1, 8).

Tobiah see SANBALLAT, TOBIAH AND GESHEM.

Tobit see APOCRYPHA.

tomb see BURIAL AND MOURNING.

tongue see MOUTH.

tongues Normally used in the sense of foreign languages, especially in relation to the Holy Spirit's gift of 'speaking in tongues' (Acts 2:4–11). This gift could also include speaking languages unknown to other human beings such as angelic languages (1 Corinthians 13:1). Paul encouraged the practice, but gave instruction that the separate gift of 'interpretation of tongues' should be exercised when a person spoke 'in tongues' in church (1 Corinthians 14:4–5). See also GIFTS, SPIRITUAL.

tools A wide variety of tools made from wood, metal or stone were in use, though the Israelites were hampered by their early lack of skill in working with iron (1 Samuel 13:19–21). Ploughshares, hoes and mattocks, forks for winnowing, sickles for harvesting corn and goads for driving oxen (Acts 26:14) were among common agricultural implements. Tools used mainly for building purposes included axes, saws, chisels, knives, hammers and nails, though they were also employed for making idols (Jeremiah 10:3–4).

topaz see JEWELS AND PRECIOUS STONES.

Topheth A place outside Jerusalem where children were sacrificed. It was characterized by a fire pit (Isaiah 30:33; Jeremiah 7:31–2).

Torah, the see LAW.

tower see FORTIFICATION.

town see CITY.

trade Solomon and Jehoshaphat were rare examples among Israel's leaders who took advantage of Palestine's position on the main north–south trade routes. Solomon in particular gained most of his wealth from engaging in imports and exports and imposing taxes. He brought in exotic goods such as spices and precious stones from the travelling caravans from Arabia (1 Kings 10:10–12,22), and exported agricultural products such as olive oil, wine and wool and metals such as iron. Otherwise, it is mainly foreign merchants who are referred to (Ezekiel 27:12–36), though their materialism is sometimes sharply criticized (Revelation 18:11–24).

tradition A belief or a practice handed down from earlier generations. Human traditions such as those accumulated by the Pharisees are sharply distinguished from the faith-centred traditions of the Scriptures (Mark 7:1–13). In the New Testament, the latter included the basic aspects of Jesus' life (1 Corinthians 15:1–7), the apostolic teaching and the Christian way of life (2 Thessalonians 3:6–7).

Transfiguration The significant moment when Jesus, accompanied by Moses and Elijah, shone with the glory of God. It emphasized the close link between Christ's ministry and Old Testament revelation and anticipated what Jesus would achieve through his death and resurrection. God's voice identifying Jesus as the Son of God confirmed Peter's earlier acknowledgement of Jesus' Messiahship (Matthew 16:13–17; 17:1–8).

transgression see SIN.

travel Until the Roman system of roads was constructed, land travel in the ancient Near East was difficult though by no means impossible. Significant movements of people often took place, both for migration and trade. International routes were well established, and two major roads ran north–south through Palestine, the Way of the Sea along the coast and the King's Highway east of the Jordan valley. Coastal and river transport was always available, and Paul took advantage of these as well as Roman roads on his missionary journeys. The donkey was the main beast of burden, but trading caravans sometimes used camels. Chariots and horses were used mainly for military purposes. Travellers had to rest at whatever resting-place was available, but did not always find what they hoped for (Genesis 28:10–11; Luke 2:7). Many lodging-places had poor reputations, which explains the importance of providing hospitality for visiting Christian preachers (3 John 5–8). See also BOATS AND SHIPS.

treasure Jesus taught the importance of distinguishing between treasure as spiritual riches and the accumulation of material wealth, since only the former was of lasting worth. The true indication of which of these an individual valued most lay in the heart (Matthew 6:19–21). See also WEALTH.

treaties Formal agreements between individuals or nations (1 Kings 20:34). Similarities exist in form and wording between international vassal treaties and God's covenants with Israel. These analogies have strengthened arguments for the antiquity and authenticity of Old Testament covenants, and have sometimes led to the interpretation of Deuteronomy as a covenant document. See also DEUTERONOMY, BOOK OF.

trees and bushes Much of the hill country of ancient Palestine was covered by forest and woodland, especially on west and north facing slopes, but it was often associated with scrub woodland and thickets. The most impressive trees were undoubtedly the cedars in Lebanon, though Bashan in northern Transjordan was another important source of timber (Isaiah 2:13; Ezekiel 31:3–9).

Trees and bushes	
Acacia	Exodus 25:10
Almond	Jeremiah 1:11
Apple	Song of Songs 2:3
Balsam	2 Samuel 5:23–4
Cedar	1 Kings 10:27
Cypress	Isaiah 41:19
Fig	Luke 21:29
Fir	Isaiah 60:13
Myrtle	Zechariah 1:8–10
Nut	Song of Songs 6:11
Oak	2 Samuel 18:9–10
Olive	Zechariah 4:3
Palm	Exodus 15:27
Pine	Psalm 104:17
Plane	Genesis 30:37
Pomegranate	Haggai 2:19
Poplar	Isaiah 44:4
Sycamore-fig	Amos 7:14
Tan.arisk	Genesis 21:33
Terebinth	Hosea 4:13
Thornbush	Judges 9:14–15
Vine	Micah 4:4
Willow	Ezekiel 17:5

tribe Israel had a strong family structure, at the heart of which were twelve tribes descended from Jacob's twelve sons. Because the Levites were treated separately from the other tribes, being set apart for God's service, the twelve tribes sometimes included the two sons of Joseph, Ephraim and Manasseh. The tribal structure remained an important element of Jewish identity through the exile and into the New Testament (1 Chronicles 1:1–9:1; Revelation 7:4–8). See also ASHER; BENJAMIN; DAN; EPHRAIM; GAD; ISSACHAR; JUDAH; LEVI; MANASSEH; NAPHTALI; REUBEN; SIMEON; ZEBULUN.

tribute Annual payments by one country to another as a sign of submission. They were required for example by David and the Assyrians (2 Samuel 8:2, 6; 2 Kings 17:3–4). Jehu is probably represented on the Black Obelisk paying tribute to Shalmaneser III of Assyria.

Trinity, the see GOD.

Troas An important seaport on the north-western coast of Asia Minor (modern Turkey). Paul visited it twice and was greatly encouraged by

the reception given to the gospel. A church was soon founded there
(Acts 16:8–11; 20:5–12; 2 Corinthians 2:12). See map of PAUL'S
JOURNEYS.

troops see ARMY.

trumpet see MUSIC AND MUSICAL INSTRUMENTS.

trust An aspect of faith which emphasizes that a person's belief in
God is part of a personal relationship with him and involves the
whole person. God provides for those who put wholehearted trust in
him, especially in difficult circumstances (Isaiah 26:3–4; Proverbs
3:5–6). Trust in God leads also to loving trust of other people
(1 Corinthians 13:7). See also FAITH.

truth The biblical approach to truth is broader than the usual idea of
that which is factually correct or objectively verifiable. This
intellectual concept of truth as a property of statements is certainly
present in the Bible, and is especially important in legal contexts
(Deuteronomy 13:4; John 19:35). However, the New Testament also
emphasizes the idea of truth as reality, in contrast both to what is
false and to what is a mere shadow (Ephesians 4:25; Hebrews 8:5).
Equally important, however, are the personal and moral dimensions
of truth, since truth is not simply a matter of philosophy and the
intellect. Ultimate truth is an attribute of God which is fully revealed
in the person of Jesus Christ (Isaiah 65:16; John 14:6), and is
communicated in the world primarily through God's word (John
17:17). Special emphasis is also placed on truth as that which is
reliable and trustworthy, and it is interesting that its opposites are
lies and deception, not just error (2 Corinthians 7:14; Titus 1:2).
Believers must therefore live by and in the truth, since it sets them
free from the slavery of sin (John 8:32–6; 1 John 1:6).

tunic see CLOTHING; PRIEST.

turban see CLOTHING; PRIEST.

Twelve, the A common expression for the twelve apostles or disciples
who accompanied Jesus during his ministry (Mark 3:14–19). See also
APOSTLE; DISCIPLE.

twins Only two pairs of twins are mentioned, Isaac's sons Jacob and
Esau and the sons of Judah (Genesis 25:24; 38:27).

Tychicus Paul's companion on his journey to Jerusalem and his
representative to the churches in Colossae and Ephesus (Ephesians
6:21–2; Colossians 4:7).

Tyre and Sidon The two major Phoenician ports, whose people were
known for their seafaring and trading achievements. Hiram, King of
Tyre, provided the architect and supplies for Solomon's temple, but
the marriage of Jezebel, daughter of Ethbaal, King of Tyre and Sidon,

to Ahab had less positive results (1 Kings 5:1–12; 16:31). Jesus found
the region more receptive to the gospel than Israel (Matthew 11:21–2).
See also PHOENICIA, PHOENICIANS. See map of NEW TESTAMENT
ISRAEL; OLD TESTAMENT ISRAEL; PAUL'S JOURNEYS; WORLD OF THE
BIBLE.

u

unbelief A failure to trust God. Unbelief is located in the human heart and can take many forms. It includes ignoring one's conscience, disobeying God's laws including the basic moral principles of justice and truth, and rejecting Jesus, his words and his actions (Hebrews 3:12). Believers often mature in their faith by overcoming specific instances of unbelief (Mark 9:24), but the ultimate consequence of unbelief is God's condemnation (John 3:18–19).

unclean see CLEAN AND UNCLEAN.

ungodliness Attitudes and behaviour involving rejection of God's laws or a conviction that he does not intervene in human lives (Psalm 73:8–11). This way of life was sometimes combined with a veneer of faith, but is always subject to God's judgement (Jude 14–15).

union with Christ The idea that believers are mysteriously and spiritually joined with Christ, so that he lives in them and they in him. It is a particularly important element in Paul, especially in the phrase 'in Christ' (Ephesians 1:13). Paul emphasizes that believers share in Jesus' circumcision, death, resurrection and ascension (Colossians 2:11–12; 3:1–4). Christ's living in the believer makes it possible to live by faith (Galatians 2:20).

unity Ultimately, the bringing together of all things under the lordship of Christ (Ephesians 1:9–10). This is God's purpose for the created world, but it will only take place when Christ's former opponents are forced to acknowledge his supreme authority at his final exaltation (Philippians 2:9–11). In the meantime, the gospel of Christ has the power to break down all divisions between human beings. It gives all believers an equal status as God's children (Galatians 3:26–8) and enables them to accept one another through Christ's new commandment to love one another (John 13:34–5). Despite this and Jesus' prayer that all believers might share the unity that exists between the Father and the Son (John 17:20–1), continuing disputes and disagreements clearly took place in the early church (1 Corinthians 1:10–13; Philippians 1:15). The New Testament's response was to encourage the early Christians to be committed to unity in the gospel, remembering the work of Christ and the Spirit among them and looking to Christ's example of being a servant (Philippians 1:27–2:8). See also CHURCH; FELLOWSHIP.

universe Often described as 'the heavens and the earth', the universe includes the world of unseen powers as well as visible things. It was created by Christ and is sustained and controlled by him (Colossians 1:15–17). It will ultimately be replaced by a new universe without evil and suffering where Christ will reign among his people (Revelation 21:1–22:6).

Unleavened Bread, Feast of A week-long festival which followed the Passover, in which yeast was not to be used in any form. It reminded the Jews of when they left Egypt in a hurry and had to eat bread made without yeast (Exodus 12:8, 14–20; 1 Corinthians 5:8).

upper room see HOME.

Ur of the Chaldeans The place in southern Iraq (modern Tell el-Muqayyar) where Abraham's family lived before travelling to Palestine (Genesis 11:31). It was an important city in the third millennium BC. See map of WORLD OF THE BIBLE.

Uriah the Hittite The husband of Bathsheba. David arranged his death to cover up his affair with Bathsheba while Uriah was fighting on Israel's front line, but God sent the prophet Nathan to confront David with what he had done (2 Samuel 11:6–25; 12:1–10).

Urim and Thummim Two objects belonging to the high priest by which God communicated decisions (Exodus 28:30). Exactly what they were or how they worked remains unclear, but the most likely possibility is that they were two stones or dice which produced a clear answer when they agreed and no reply when they disagreed. See also GUIDANCE; LOTS, CASTING OF.

usury see DEBT; INTEREST.

utensils Most containers used in the home were made of either earthenware or terracotta, and only the more expensive types were decorated and painted. A wide variety of bowls, dishes, cups, jugs and jars were used, though those discovered by archaeology cannot be certainly identified with the names used in the Bible. Distinctive examples that have been discovered from the biblical period in Palestine include graceful 'dipper juglets' for ladling liquids from large jars or water-pots, decanters with narrow necks, and the so-called 'pilgrim flask', a round two-handled vessel which was probably hung over the shoulder (Genesis 24:14–18; Jeremiah 19:1, 10).

Uzzah A man who was struck dead after touching the ark of the covenant while it was being transported on an ox-cart (2 Samuel 6:3–8).

Uzziah, King of Judah see AZARIAH, KING OF JUDAH.

ν

Valleys Apart from the great Jordan Rift Valley and a few other river valleys such as the Yarmuk and the Jabbok, most valleys are wadis which are wet only in the rainy season. Jerusalem's two main valleys, the Valley of Ben Hinnom to the south and west and the Kidron Valley to the east, had special associations. The former was a place of pagan sacrifices, including child sacrifice (Jeremiah 19:1–6), and the latter was crossed by David and Jesus at significant moments in their lives (2 Samuel 15:23; John 18:1). Other valleys were also sometimes named after specific people or events.

Valleys	
Achor (= Trouble)	Joshua 7:24
Aijalon	Joshua 10:12
Arabah (= Dead Sea)	Amos 6:14
Aven (= Wickedness)	Amos 1:5
Baca (= Weeping)	Psalm 84:6
Ben Hinnom	Jeremiah 7:31
Beracah (= Blessing)	2 Chronicles 20:26
Craftsmen	Nehemiah 11:35
Elah	1 Samuel 17:2
Eshcol (= Cluster)	Numbers 13:23
Gerar	Genesis 26:17
Gibeon	Isaiah 28:21
Hamon Gog (= Hordes of Gog)	Ezekiel 39:11
Hebron	Genesis 37:14
Iphtah El	Joshua 19:14
Jehoshaphat (= the Lord judges)	Joel 3:2
Jericho	Deuteronomy 34:3
Jezreel	Hosea 1:5
Kidron	John 18:1

Kishon	1 Kings 18:40
Lebanon	Joshua 11:17
Mizpah	Joshua 11:8
Rephaim	2 Samuel 5:18
Salt	2 Samuel 8:13
Shaveh (or King's Valley)	Genesis 14:17
Siddim	Genesis 14:8
Sorek	Judges 16:4
Succoth	Psalm 60:6
Zeboim	1 Samuel 13:18
Zephathah	2 Chronicles 14:10
Zered	Numbers 21:12

Vashti A Queen of Persia who displeased King Xerxes and was replaced by Esther (Esther 1:9). Vashti may be another name for Amestris, mentioned in classical sources.

vegetables see FOOD AND DRINK.

veil see CLOTHING; TEMPLE.

vengeance Taking personal revenge is always forbidden, and individuals were encouraged to respond positively to insult and provocation (Matthew 5:38–45). Righting of wrongs was the responsibility of the public authorities and ultimately of God, who ensured that any wrong done to any of his people would be noted and punished appropriately (Romans 12:19). The avenger of blood in Old Testament times also had to respect the proper processes of law, and special provision was made in cases where the avenger of blood might take matters into his own hands (Numbers 35:9–28). A number of examples occur in the Psalms of people pleading with God to exact vengeance on their persecutors (e.g. Psalm 139:19–22).

victory God's decisive victory against those who oppose him was achieved when Jesus defeated the devil and all forms of evil through his death and resurrection (1 John 3:8). God also gives his people victories, though usually in the context of physical conflict or of struggles with temptation, sin and suffering, rather than by avoiding such experiences completely (Romans 8:31–9). Though Jesus' final victory is not yet complete, it is certain (Hebrews 2:8). Victory is a prominent theme in Revelation. Jesus conquers through his suffering, and believers also conquer through faithful witness and acceptance of suffering (Revelation 5:5; 2:11). See also SALVATION.

village Small unwalled settlements which were often dependent on a local town (Leviticus 25:31). The example of Bethlehem shows that a distinction between town and village was not always maintained (Luke 2:4; John 7:42).

vine, vineyard The widespread reference to vines and vineyards is due to the importance of vines in Palestinian agriculture, and to the idea that Israel was God's vineyard (Isaiah 5:7). Vineyards were planted mainly on terraced hillsides. The ground had to be carefully prepared and the vineyard was often protected by watchtowers (Isaiah 5:1–2). Vines were grown mainly for wine, though grapes and raisins were also important as food. Jesus used vineyard imagery to show that he was the source of all spiritual life as God's true vine, even though Israel rejected him as the one in charge of God's vineyard (Matthew 21:28–46; John 15:1–8).

vinegar A fermented acidic drink made from wine, often drunk by ordinary people such as farm-workers or soldiers (Ruth 2:14; Matthew 27:48).

violence A characteristic of human society, and the main reason why God sent the judgement of the flood (Genesis 6:11–13). Christians, however, are to follow Jesus' example and avoid violence for the sake of the gospel (Isaiah 53:9; Ephesians 4:31). They are also to give assistance to victims of violence (Luke 10:30–7).

viper see SNAKE.

virgin An important custom in Israelite marriage required a bride to be able to provide proof of her virginity (Deuteronomy 22:13–21). She also had to keep herself pure during the period of betrothal, which explains Joseph's horror at the news of Mary's pregnancy. Mary's virginal conception, however, was the work of the Holy Spirit, and also fulfilled Old Testament prophecy (Matthew 1:18–23).

visions A common method by which God communicated messages to his prophets. The coming of the Spirit at Pentecost also widened the potential for visions in the church (Acts 2:17). Visions enabled people to see heavenly scenes, spiritual objects, or fresh interpretations of ordinary objects (Zechariah 1:7–6:8; Revelation 4:1–22:6). A vision's validity derived not from the experience itself but from whether what was seen was part of God's purposes. See also DREAMS.

vow A promise made to God to be fulfilled at a later time. The promise was often fulfilled by making an offering, known as a votive offering, to God. Vows might be made to dedicate a person to God or in anticipation that God would deliver a person from trouble (Judges 13:2–5; Jonah 2:9). Though vows were voluntary, they were normally binding. A person could only be released from a careless vow because of a greater benefit (1 Samuel 14:24–45). See also NAZIRITE.

Vulgate see MANUSCRIPTS.

vulture see BIRDS.

W

wages Employers were instructed to pay fair wages, though work[ ]
were also required to do a fair day's work (Deuteronomy 24:15; J[ ]
5:4; 2 Thessalonians 3:10–12). Christian ministers were included
among those who should be paid for their labours (1 Timothy
5:17–18). Sin brought its own wages of God's judgement, in cont[ ]
to the free gift of the gospel (Romans 6:23).

wailing see BURIAL AND MOURNING.

walls see ARCHITECTURE.

wanderings see WILDERNESS.

war War was an accepted reality of human life, whose origin is
explained as envy and hatred in the human heart (James 4:1–2).
Despite this, God is often portrayed as being actively involved i[ ]
wars. He fought on behalf of his own people, though because he[ ]
concerned with his own purposes, he sometimes had to punish
people for their wicked behaviour by bringing foreign invaders
against them (Exodus 14:14; Jeremiah 21:3–7). He also dissociate[ ]
himself from some of the cruel and violent behaviour of war, ev[ ]
when a victorious army was carrying out his purposes (Habakk[ ]
2:4–8).

Armies generally went on campaigns in the spring and summ[ ]
because of the difficulties of winter travel. Reconnaissance and
diplomacy played an important part in an army's tactics, and a v[ ]
variety of battle strategies were employed. These included amb[ ]
sieges, guerrilla warfare and pitched battles, as well as the single
combat in which David and Goliath were involved.

Although Jesus ruled out violence as a means of spreading th[ ]
gospel, the church was involved in spiritual warfare against sin
unseen spiritual forces (Ephesians 6:10–18). The outcome of thi[ ]
spiritual conflict was not in doubt, since the decisive victory ag[ ]
the devil was achieved at the cross. Jesus' final battle with the fo[ ]

of evil will take place at Armageddon, after which war will be abolished for ever (Micah 4:3; Revelation 19:11–21). See also ARMOUR AND WEAPONS; ARMY; BATTLES.

washing Clothes were washed by either treading or rubbing them. The main cleansing agents for washing people's bodies and for laundry were soap and washing soda (Job 9:30), though the rich might use milk as a beauty treatment (Song of Songs 5:12). Ceremonial washing was a sign of purification or of innocence (Matthew 27:24).

watchman, watchtowers Watchmen guarded towns, lands or animals, and were also the first to see messengers arriving from a distance (2 Samuel 18:24–7). Watchtowers were often built into city walls, but they were also found in vineyards or out in the fields (Isaiah 5:2).

water The presence or absence of water was an important element of daily life in a climate where it does not rain for six months from May to October. Water supplies from the rivers, many of which were seasonal, were supplemented by the many springs and wells dotted across the land (Deuteronomy 8:7). Underground cisterns were also an important means of storing water.

Water is often used symbolically. Abundance of water was a sign of blessing and refreshment, and God as 'the fountain of living waters' was the ultimate source of spiritual and physical vitality (Jeremiah 2:13; John 7:38). However, the waters of the flood were a sober reminder of God's judgement. See also RIVERS; WEATHER.

water-pots see UTENSILS.

wave offering Usually the breast and right thigh of a sacrificial animal given to the priests as part of a fellowship offering, though other types of sacrifice were also presented in this way. It was either waved horizontally before God or was simply a special contribution to him (Leviticus 7:30–2). See also SACRIFICE AND OFFERING.

Way, the The earliest name for the Christian church, probably based on Jesus' claim as the Way to God (John 14:6; Acts 9:2).

wealth Material wealth is God's gift, but is not to be treated as an end in itself. Pursuing and collecting riches for their own sake is foolish (Luke 12:20), since they are unreliable and belong only to this life (1 Timothy 6:6–10, 17–19). Material riches were sometimes a sign of God's blessing, especially in the Old Testament, but most members of the early church possessed few of this world's goods. The gospel reveals God's intention to make his people spiritually rich through Christ's poverty (2 Corinthians 8:9). See also POVERTY; TREASURE.

weapons see ARMOUR AND WEAPONS.

weather Palestine's climate and weather is basically the same today as in biblical times. It is dominated by the hot, dry summer from May to September and the rainy season from roughly mid-October to mid-April. Average summer temperatures are 24°C in Jerusalem and 38°C in Jericho, and in winter are 8°C in Jerusalem and 19°C in Jericho. Rainfall varies from less than 20 centimetres per year in the far south to 75 centimetres on the mountains, though the dew is also an important source of moisture in summer. Longing for the autumn rains is intense, and though the clouds can be deceptive (Jude 12), cyclones and heavy thunderstorms always bring the winter rains (Matthew 7:27). Snow is rare except on the highest parts of the hills, though hail is commoner on the coastal plain (Psalm 147:16–17). Biblical references to whirlwinds include the sirocco which brings dry hot winds from the eastern desert across the land, especially in autumn and spring (Ezekiel 17:10), and the dust and sand storms of the summer (Isaiah 21:1).

weaving see SPINNING AND WEAVING.

wedding see MARRIAGE.

weeds see PLANTS.

weeks, feast of see PENTECOST.

weights and measures It is impossible to provide precise modern equivalents for ancient weights and measures, since despite attempts to impose a common system, standards varied from one city to another (2 Samuel 14:26). The actual weights were carved stones, often inscribed with their weight and the standard on which they were based. Linear measures were often based on bodily distances, such as the cubit which was the distance between elbow and finger tip or the span which was the width of an outstretched hand. Dry and liquid measures were based on the size of individual receptacles.

The figures in the table below are calculated on the basis of a shekel equalling 11.5 grams, a cubit equalling 18 inches and an ephah equalling 22 litres. It is based upon the best available information, but it is not intended to be mathematically precise; it merely gives approximate amounts and distances. Weights and measures differed somewhat at various times and places in the ancient world. There is uncertainty particularly about the ephah and the bath; further discoveries may give more light on these units of capacity.

Weights and measures

	Biblical unit	Approximate imperial equivalent	Approximate metric equivalent
Weights			
Talent	60 minas	75 pounds	34 kilograms
Mina	50 shekels	$1^1/_4$ pounds	0.6 kilogram
Shekel	2 bekas	$^2/_5$ ounce	11.5 grams
Pim	$^2/_3$ shekel	$^1/_4$ ounce	7.7 grams
Beka	10 gerahs	$^1/_5$ ounce	5.8 grams
Gerah		$^1/_{50}$ ounce	0.6 gram
Length			
Cubit		18 inches	0.5 metre
Span		9 inches	23 centimetres
Handbreadth		3 inches	8 centimetres
Capacity: dry measure			
Cor [homer]	10 ephahs	6 bushels	220 litres
Lethek	5 ephahs	3 bushels	110 litres
Ephah	10 omers	$^3/_5$ bushel	22 litres
Seah	$^1/_3$ ephah	13 pints	7.3 litres
Omer	$^1/_{10}$ ephah	4 pints	2 litres
Cab	$^1/_{18}$ ephah	2 pints	1 litre
Capacity: liquid measure			
Bath	1 ephah	5 gallons	22 litres
Hin	$^1/_6$ bath	7 pints	4 litres
Log	$^1/_{72}$ bath	$^1/_2$ pint	0.3 litre

wells As well as being important sources of water, wells and springs were significant as landmarks and meeting places (Genesis 24:11–27; John 4:6–26). They were also the subject of several disagreements (Genesis 26:18–22).

wheat see CEREALS.

whirlwind see WEATHER.

white see COLOURS.

wholeheartedness An attitude of service that God desires, whether in relation to a person's devotion to God or to human work (1 Chronicles 28:9; Ephesians 6:7). It especially characterized the faith of the two Israelite spies who entered the Promised Land (Numbers 32:11–12).

wicked, the Those whose way of life shows that they either ignore or disobey God's will. Though the term emphasizes wrong actions, wickedness is also an act of will which has its origin in the human heart (Proverbs 15:26; Jeremiah 17:9). In the Old Testament, the wicked are often contrasted with God's people (Psalm 1).

widow Special provision was made for widows who could not be looked after by their own family, reflecting God's special concern for them (Psalm 68:5). The same principle applied in the church, who were only to support older widows who had no family of their own and who showed evidence of practical Christian faith (1 Timothy 5:3–16).

wife see FAMILY; MARRIAGE.

wilderness The southern and eastern areas of Palestine where it is not possible for a settled population to farm the land. It includes steppe and pasture lands suitable for grazing as well as desert. The Israelites spent forty years in the wilderness on their way to the Promised Land, where they were kept alive only by God's miraculous provision (Deuteronomy 8:2–4).

will of God The purpose of God, both generally and in relation to individuals. Its broader meaning is especially associated with the law of the Old Testament and with the gospel of Jesus Christ (Ephesians 1:9). God's will for individuals is that they obey his particular intention for their lives, as Jesus demonstrated perfectly in Gethsemane (Matthew 26:39; Romans 12:2).

wind see WEATHER.

wine and beer Wine was the usual alcoholic drink in Palestine, and though beer was certainly drunk it was more popular in Mesopotamia. 'New wine' was made from grape juice before the winepress was trodden. Wine was freely available, and could either gladden a person's heart or distort their mind (Psalm 104:15; Proverbs 23:29–35). Some whose lives were dedicated to God abstained from strong drink, but this was not a general rule (Numbers 6:3; Luke 1:15).

winnow see AGRICULTURE.

winter see SEASONS.

wisdom An important biblical concept with several interrelated meanings. It is first a type of biblical literature found in books such as Proverbs, Job, Ecclesiastes and James, dealing with the practical realities of faith. The main concerns are how to live in accordance with the basic moral and spiritual principles of life, and how to face perplexing issues like suffering and death. Second, wisdom is a theological term for the way God carries out his will in the world. This wisdom is different in kind from the more limited intellectual emphasis of human wisdom, and is demonstrated supremely in the cross of Christ (1 Corinthians 1:18–2:16). It is also personified by God and Christ (Proverbs 8:22–31; 1 Corinthians 1:30). Third, wisdom defines the various skills and abilities by which people may enjoy success. This kind of wisdom is especially necessary for leadership, but is relevant to skills as varied as craftsmanship and navigation (Exodus 31:1–11; Psalm 107:23–30). It is also a special ability given by the Holy Spirit by which a believer receives special spiritual insight into God's will (1 Corinthians 12:8). Fourth, it incorporates the teaching of the wise men (Jeremiah 9:23), who used various techniques such as parables, riddles, proverbs and short stories to put their message across.

Biblical wisdom involves experiences that are common to all human beings. However, the basic principle of wisdom that 'the fear of the Lord is the beginning of wisdom' (Proverbs 9:10) shows that true wisdom comes through trust in God. Wisdom is also something that all believers need and should seek for. Both the ignorant and the mature need it for practical Christian living, and God gives wisdom generously to all who ask for it in faith (James 1:5–8).

Wisdom of Solomon, The see APOCRYPHA.

wise men see MAGI.

witchcraft see OCCULT.

witness In a court of law, two or three witnesses were required for someone to be convicted of a crime. Anyone found guilty of being a false witness was liable to suffer the punishment of the person being accused (Deuteronomy 19:15–21). A witness was also someone who bore testimony to what God had done through Jesus and the Spirit (Acts 2:32; 10:39), especially Jesus' sufferings and resurrection (Luke 24:48; 1 Peter 5:1). The spreading of the gospel by the early church was understood as bearing witness in this way (Acts 1:8). See also LEGAL SYSTEM.

wolf see ANIMALS.

woman see MAN AND WOMAN.

wonder see SIGN.

wool see SHEEP AND GOATS.

Word of God The idea that the Bible is God's word is based on occasions when God actually spoke to his people. Notable examples include God's giving of the law at Mount Sinai, his speaking directly to the prophets (Deuteronomy 4:10–14; Jeremiah 1:4–6), and especially his communication with people through Jesus as God's living Word (John 1:1,14). As well as God's explicit words, the Bible contains many instances of God speaking indirectly through others and of human words addressed to God. These were all gradually written down and collected together to form the Bible, which was recognized as God's authoritative written word on which people could base their daily lives (Deuteronomy 8:3).

In the New Testament 'the word' often means 'the message of Jesus' or 'the good news about Jesus' (Mark 2:2; Acts 8:4). See also BIBLE; SCRIPTURE.

work, works God gave people purpose and happiness by giving them the task of caring for his world. This brought a sense of fulfilment to life and dignity to human labour, but the effects of sin also produced a sense of pain and frustration (Genesis 3:17–19; Ecclesiastes 3:11–13). Jesus showed that work was truly fulfilling when it was concerned with obeying the Father's will (John 5:36). Though it was impossible to please God simply through working, work done through faith was acceptable to God (Colossians 1:10). The New Testament confirms that work is a necessary part of Christian life and should be properly rewarded (Luke 10:7; 2 Thessalonians 3:6–13).

world God created and sustains the natural world through Christ. Though God's original good purposes have been spoiled by cruelty, disease and death, the natural world still declares God's glory and provides evidence of his existence (Psalm 19:1–2; Romans 1:20).

More often, however, the world is the place that human beings inhabit or even simply the people in the world. This world is dominated by sin and evil and is temporarily under the control of 'the prince of this world', that is the devil (John 12:30). But God also loves this world and sent his Son as its Saviour to die for all its sins (1 John 2:2).

Believers in Christ live as part of two worlds, being in this world but not of it (John 17:14–16). They are often in conflict with the world, which is basically hostile to God and his church. Believers must continually guard against worldliness, that is, the attitudes of the unbelieving world, though this is just as likely to be found in the believer's heart as in contemporary society. However, believers can overcome the world by resisting temptation and by taking the message of Christ's love throughout the world (Acts 1:8; 1 John 5:4–5). Finally, because the present world has been corrupted by sin, it will be entirely replaced by God's new creation (Romans 8:19–21).

worldliness see WORLD.

worm see ANIMALS.

worry see ANXIETY.

worship Public worship in Israel was based on sacrifices and offerings which were offered on a daily, weekly, monthly and annual basis, first at the Tabernacle and then the Temple. After the exile Jewish worship increasingly took place in synagogues, a practice which the early Christians continued alongside Temple worship. Following the split with Judaism, however, Christians met for worship in houses. The New Testament shows more interest in the spirit than the form of Christian worship, but it is clear that the church met on the first day of the week rather than the Sabbath, and regularly engaged in prayer, praise, teaching and the Lord's Supper (Acts 2:42). Emphasis was placed on the inspiration and gifts of the Spirit and on participation by all members of the church (John 4:23–4; 1 Corinthians 14:26).

Whether the worship of God took place in private or public, it was always intended to be a wholehearted response to the covenants God had made with his people, and concentrated on giving honour to God through sacrifice and loving service. The Old Testament sacrifices were fulfilled and replaced by a new attitude of self-sacrifice (Romans 12:1–2), through which believers expressed their service to God and to one another in acts of love (1 John 4:19–21; Hebrews 13:15–16). See also BAPTISM; LORD'S SUPPER; PRAISE; PRAYER; SACRIFICE AND OFFERING.

wrath see ANGER.

wrestling see GAMES AND SPORT.

writing Writing developed in order to communicate with a wider audience, especially later generations (Isaiah 30:8). Scribes or secretaries, who were largely restricted to the Levites and to legal and administrative officials, were probably responsible for actually writing down most biblical books (Jeremiah 36:2; Romans 16:22) as well as other documents such as letters and records (1 Chronicles 29:29). The commonest form of writing material was probably the scroll made of papyrus or parchment, and it was written on both sides. Notes were often scribbled with ink on pieces of broken pottery known as potsherds. Less common were writing-boards and stone inscriptions. The stone tablets on which the Ten Commandments were inscribed may have been similar to those used for official documents.

X

Xerxes A Persian king (486–465 BC) whom the Bible calls Ahasuerus (Esther 1:1). He is also known in classical sources for his wars against Greece. See also ESTHER.

y

Yahweh see GOD, NAMES AND TITLES OF.

year see CALENDAR, JEWISH; TIME.

Year of Jubilee see JUBILEE.

yeast Was excluded from Old Testament sacrifices and from all food during the Feast of Unleavened Bread, mainly to remind the Israelites that they did not have time to make bread with yeast when they left Egypt (Exodus 12:39; 13:6–7). In the New Testament, yeast was usually a symbol of evil, except in Jesus' parable about the kingdom (Matthew 13:33).

yoke A wooden frame linking two animals, usually oxen, together. Being yoked with someone was a symbol of partnership, sometimes marriage, and being under a yoke was a symbol of submission. Jesus' yoke was much lighter than those required by the teachers of the law (Matthew 11:29–30; 23:4).

youth Despite the common association of youth with vigour, inexperience and particular vulnerability to temptation, young people were capable of outstanding faith (Jeremiah 1:4–8; 1 Timothy 4:12). Trust in God and respect for parents and other older people are important in one's youth (Exodus 20:12; Ecclesiastes 12:1).

Z

Zacchaeus A Jewish tax collector whom Jesus described as one of the lost he came to save. He is also noted for his determination to see Jesus, despite being short (Luke 19:1–10).

Zadok A priest who was loyal to David. He became high priest towards the end of David's reign and anointed Solomon as king (1 Kings 1:7–8, 32–40). After the exile, only his family were allowed to act as priests because they were faithful to God (Ezekiel 44:15–16).

Zarephath A small Phoenician town (modern Sarafand) south of Sidon where Elijah was fed during a famine and where he raised a widow's son from the dead (1 Kings 17:9–24; Luke 4:26). See map of NEW TESTAMENT ISRAEL.

zeal A single-minded commitment, which may be good or bad. God's zeal guarantees he will do what he says (Isaiah 9:7). Though closely related to his special concern for his people (Isaiah 26:11), it is no automatic privilege, since God is zealous against all forms of sin (Deuteronomy 29:19–21). Human zeal for God may be a sign of total commitment to him (John 2:17) or a serious failure to understand his will (Romans 10:1–3). See also JEALOUSY.

zealot A term used in the first century AD for those with Jewish nationalist sympathies. The Zealot party as such was active in the revolt against the Romans from 66 AD. See also SIMON THE ZEALOT.

Zebulun 1. The tenth son of Jacob.
2. The tribe descended from Zebulun, which lived in a fertile area of southern Galilee and made its most significant contribution in the judges period (Judges 5:18; 6:35), but was overrun by the Assyrians in the eighth century BC (Isaiah 9:1). Nazareth, where Jesus grew up, was in its traditional area. See map of OLD TESTAMENT ISRAEL.

Zechariah, book of

> **Structure**
> Zechariah's visions (1:1–6:15)
> Fasting and feasting (7:1–8:23)
> The day of the LORD (9:1–14:21)
>
> **Famous passages**
> 'Not by might, not by power, but by my Spirit' (4:6)
> A king riding on a donkey (9:9)
> Thirty pieces of silver (11:12–13)

An Old Testament prophetic book from the post-exilic period. The first part (chapters 1–8) consists of eight visions accompanied by several prophecies in which the main concern is that the temple should be rebuilt after the exile. It belongs in the period between October-November 520 BC and the dedication of the temple in March 515 BC. Zechariah has a particular message for Israel's two leaders, Zerubbabel and Joshua, that God will enable them to complete the rebuilding, reminding them that God has control of the whole world, including unseen spiritual forces. It is a time for blessing and feasting instead of fasting (chapters 7–8). The second part of the book (chapters 9–14) looks to a more distant future, and reaches a climax in the prophecies in apocalyptic style about the day of the LORD in chapter 14. Two themes stand out, both continuing ideas in the earlier part of the book. One is about future leadership, which will be increasingly characterized by humility and suffering (9:9; 12:10). The other is the kingship of God, which will be established over all nations, though only after a final assault by God's enemies (chapter 14).

Zechariah, father of John the Baptist A priest who was struck dumb when an angel told him his barren wife would have a son. He only began to speak again when he called the child John (the Baptist) (Luke 1:5–25, 57–66). Zechariah's song is sometimes called the Benedictus (Luke 1:67–79). See also BENEDICTUS.

Zechariah, King of Israel (c. 746–745 BC) See KINGS AND QUEENS OF ISRAEL.

Zechariah the prophet A late sixth-century BC prophet who motivated the Jews to rebuild the temple (Ezra 5:1–2; Zechariah 3:6–7; 4:8–9). See also ZECHARIAH, BOOK OF.

Zechariah, son of Jehoiada A priest who was murdered by order of Joash, King of Judah, because he gave an unpopular prophecy. Matthew 23:35 probably refers to the incident, which occurs in

the last book in the Hebrew version of the Old Testament
(2 Chronicles 24:20–2).

Zedekiah, King of Judah (597–587 BC) The last king of Judah, who was
really a puppet king of the Babylonians after the first deportation of
Jews to Babylon in 597 BC (2 Kings 24:18–25:26). Though he showed
some sympathy for the prophet Jeremiah, he was a weak character
who finally rebelled against the Babylonians. His sons were executed
in front of him before he was blinded and taken to Babylon.

Zelophehad A man from the tribe of Manasseh whose family
circumstances led to a change in Israel's inheritance laws. Because
he had no sons, it was agreed that daughters could inherit property
provided they married within their tribe (Numbers 27:1–11; 36:1–12).

Zephaniah, book of

Structure
  The day of the LORD (1:1–2:3)
  A day of judgement for all nations (2:4–3:8)
  A day of restoration (3:9–20)

Famous passage
  The day of wrath (1:14–18)

A prophetic book from the end of the seventh century BC. Its main
theme is the day of the LORD, which, as in other prophets, is a time
both of God's action against sin and of his restoration of blessing.
Zephaniah's description of the day as one of God's anger in 1:14–18 is
one of the most dramatic in the Bible, when all nations, and not just
Judah, will be affected. Though no explicit connection is made with
Josiah's reforms in 622 BC, Zephaniah probably describes the post-
reformation period. He is particularly critical of the worship of
other gods and of social exploitation by the rich. However, God also
promises to restore the blessings of his kingship (3:9–20). Evildoers
will be replaced by those who humbly trust in God. The prophet
even paints an idyllic picture of God quietly singing them songs of
love. See also DAY OF THE LORD.

Zerah 1. One of Judah's twin sons (Genesis 38:29–30), and the
ancestor of an important clan in Judah of whom Achan was the
most infamous member (Joshua 7:1–26; 1 Chronicles 2:6–7).
2. A Cushite general, from either Sudan or south-western Palestine,
whose attack on Judah was successfully rebuffed by Asa (2 Chronicles
14:9–15; 16:8).

Zerubbabel A descendant of David's line who became governor of
Judah under the Persians in the first generation who returned from

exile. He was involved in starting the rebuilding work (Ezra 3:1–13), but had to be encouraged by Haggai and Zechariah nearly twenty years later to complete it. Prophecies given to Zerubbabel formed part of the Messianic hope (Haggai 2:7, 20; Zechariah 4:14).

Ziba A servant of Saul and his grandson Mephibosheth. In Absalom's rebellion, he betrayed Mephibosheth to David but was forgiven (2 Samuel 16:1–4; 19:24–30).

Ziklag A small town in southern Judah given to David by the Philistines (1 Samuel 27:5–7). After he recaptured it from the Amalekites (1 Samuel 30), it remained permanently in Judah's hands. See map of OLD TESTAMENT ISRAEL.

Zilpah Leah's female servant whom she gave to her husband Jacob and by whom he had two sons, Gad and Asher (Genesis 29:24; 30:9–13).

Zimri, King of Israel, c. 876 BC An army official who became king for a week, but who was quickly overthrown and killed by Omri, Israel's army commander (1 Kings 16:9–20).

Zin A wilderness area in the northern part of the Negev, between Kadesh-Barnea to the south and Judah to the north (Numbers 34:3–4).

Zion Originally the name of either the south-eastern hill of Jerusalem or the Jebusite fortress which stood on it. It became synonymous with the 'City of David', since David captured the site, and with it the whole city of Jerusalem. The temple was also known as Mount Zion. However, the Bible mainly uses Zion symbolically, both of Israel and the church, especially as the object of God's love and blessing. The prophets saw it as the focus of God's future restoration of his people and a place to which all nations would come (Isaiah 2:2–4; Jeremiah 30:17–22). The name was finally used of heaven itself (Hebrews 12:22). See also JERUSALEM.

Ziph A town near Hebron in the Judean hills and the associated wilderness area (1 Samuel 23:14–24). The town was an administrative centre in Hezekiah's time.

Zipporah Daughter of Jethro and Moses' first wife, who bore him Gershom and Eliezer (Exodus 2:21–2).

zither See MUSIC AND MUSICAL INSTRUMENTS.

Ziv See CALENDAR, JEWISH.

Zoan An important city in the north-east Delta area of Egypt, also known by its Greek name Tanis (Isaiah 19:11; Ezekiel 30:14).

Zoar A town near Sodom and Gomorrah whose name means 'small'. It survived the destruction of its neighbours because of Lot's prayer (Genesis 19:20–2), but was eventually destroyed by the Babylonians (Jeremiah 48:34). See also PLAINS, CITIES OF THE; SODOM AND GOMORRAH.

Zobah An Aramean kingdom north of Damascus which fought against Saul, David and Solomon and was defeated by the latter two (2 Samuel 8:3–12).

zophar see ELIPHAZ, BILDAD AND ZOPHAR.